Majoring in Psychology

About the Authors

Jeffrey L. Helms

Dr. Helms is a Professor of Psychology at Kennesaw State University where he joined the faculty in 2003. Prior academic appointments included teaching not only at the undergraduate level but also at the master's, specialist, and doctoral levels. His research interests are predominantly in the areas of the scholarship of teaching and attitudes toward individuals who identify as bisexual. Currently, he holds licensure as a psychologist in Georgia and Hawaii and maintains a small private consulting practice. His clinical experience includes work in the community mental health arena, inpatient psychiatric facilities, and multiple forensic environments. He has previously practiced and taught in California and Kentucky. Dr. Helms is a member of the American Psychological Association.

Daniel T. Rogers

Dr. Rogers is an Associate Professor of Psychology at Kennesaw State University where he joined the faculty in 2005. His research interests are in the areas of assessment and scale development pertaining to interpersonal functioning, student–teacher alliance, and teaching styles. Currently, he holds licensure as a psychologist in Georgia. He previously practiced and taught in Michigan. His clinical experience includes work across the age spectrum and across levels of impairment, with emphasis on psychological assessment and psychodynamic interventions. Dr. Rogers is a member of the American Psychological Association; the Division for Quantitative and Qualitative Methods; and the Society for Personality Assessment.

Majoring in Psychology

Achieving Your Educational and Career Goals

Second Edition

Jeffrey L. Helms
Daniel T. Rogers

WILEY Blackwell

Library of Congress Cataloging-in-Publication Data

Helms, Jeffrey L.
Majoring in psychology : achieving your educational and career goals / Jeffrey L. Helms
and Daniel T. Rogers. – Second Edition.
      pages cm
  Includes bibliographical references and index.
  ISBN 978-1-118-74102-3 (cloth) – ISBN 978-1-118-74103-0 (pbk.)
1. Psychology–Vocational guidance.   2. Psychology–Study and teaching.   I. Rogers, Daniel T.   II. Title.
  BF76.H45 2015
  150.71′1–dc23
                                                2014044022
A catalogue record for this book is available from the British Library.

Cover image: © Gregor Schuster / Getty Images

Set in 10/13pt Sabon by SPi Publisher Services, Pondicherry, India

3   2017

Brief Table of Contents

Contents

List of Boxes

List of Tables

Preface

This book grew out of our experience teaching and working with psychology students on issues related to academic and career success. Whether in the classroom of our Careers in Psychology course, which addresses these topics, or in the midst of advising a student, we have developed a deep appreciation for how simultaneously exciting and overwhelming the process of pursuing academic and career goals can be. Students are passionate about discovering the options available to them and identifying their unique goals. Instructors relish the opportunity to guide students through this process and watch them succeed. However, students and instructors alike can at times feel lost given the range of complex issues involved in academic and career development. In fact, some of the most helpful information, strategies, and resources for meeting these goals go unused simply because students or their instructors are unaware of their existence. Our appreciation for this mixed experience from both the students' and instructors' perspectives led us to write this book.

This book provides to students interested in psychology, and the instructors who work with them, information that is vital to academic and career success in the field. As such, the book is an ideal text for courses that address aspects of majoring in psychology (e.g., academic strategies, career and graduate school preparation) and/or aspects of career planning (e.g., learning about the careers of psychologists in various subfields and their education and training). Even outside of the context of a college course, students of psychology who are seeking to clarify academic and career goals and develop knowledge and skills to support achieving these goals will find the book helpful.

There are other texts available that concentrate on one or two of the areas covered in this book, such as selecting a career, navigating your academic path, or preparing for graduate school. Many of these texts are excellent resources, and we encourage students and instructors to examine them according to interest and need. However, our goal was to bring these and other related topics together in one place. In doing so, we compile sound, research-based information and strategies on succeeding as a psychology major in college and beyond. We strive to communicate this information in an interesting and compelling way. We hope that the book answers questions about the major and its career paths while supporting the pursuit of academic and career goals.

This book is divided into two sections. Part I concentrates on student success in achieving general educational and career goals. In this section we examine such issues as the utility of a psychology degree, strategies for academic success, career decision making, and employment and graduate school preparation. In addition to content, the chapters offer suggested exercises, readings, and resources to enhance understanding of the issues at hand. Part II of the book concentrates on student success in achieving specific educational and career goals. In this section we examine the various career options within psychology and issues related to these careers. Each chapter addresses a major area within psychology and provides valuable information about the focus, training, and work of individuals with careers in these areas. The chapters also include information about relevant career options at both the graduate *and* bachelor's levels. In addition to suggested exercises, readings, and resources, each chapter offers a glimpse into the careers and perspectives of two (inter)nationally recognized psychologists working in their respective subfield.

It is our belief that success as a psychology major cannot simply be defined as earning good grades, securing a job after graduation, or gaining acceptance into graduate school. Instead, success involves becoming a strong student who is well informed not only about the field but also about her or his relationship to it. As such, we hope that this book serves as a reliable and trustworthy guide for students curious about the field, and their place within it, and for instructors who are assisting them in their pursuits.

Acknowledgments

As with any undertaking of this size, many people contributed to its realization. Among these are the individuals at John Wiley & Sons Publishers and the reviewers of the manuscript at various points. The feedback provided throughout the process was invaluable. We thank Daniel Segrist for authoring the ancillaries, which make the book even better. We also thank the contributors to the Professional Spotlights and short topical articles included throughout the book. Their contributions bring the book to life. These individuals are:

Marie Balaban, Eastern Oregon University
Chris Carr, St. Vincent Sports Performance Center
John Chan, QBE Insurance Group Limited
Christine Dunkel Schetter, University of California, Los Angeles
Regan A. R. Gurung, University of Wisconsin, Green Bay
Kate F. Hays, The Performing Edge
Matthew T. Huss, Creighton University
Russell E. Johnson, Michigan State University
Kimberlyn Leary, Cambridge Health Alliance and Harvard Univesity
Rebecca S. Martinez, Indiana University
Laura L. Mayhew, University of South Florida
Robert McGrath, Fairleigh Dickinson University
William Pfohl, Western Kentucky University
Cynthia L. Pickett, University of California, Davis
Antonio E. Puente, University of North Carolina, Wilmington
Maria Teresa Schultheis, Drexel University
Randolph A. Smith, Moravian College
Gina M. Vincent, University of Massachusetts Medical School
Janie H. Wilson, Georgia Southern University

Lastly, we thank our students for their enthusiasm and curiosity about this wonderful field of study. In short, thank you all.

JLH: I would like to thank my coauthor for accepting my offer to work on the first edition to the book. Little did we know at the time that there would be a second edition. I could not have chosen a better collaborator. On a more personal note, I thank my family for their support throughout my education, career, and life. It is to them that I dedicate this work. Thank you for everything.

DTR: To my coauthor, thank you for planting the seeds for this project and inviting me to help bring it to fruition the first time and again for this revision. To my family, April and Noah, thank you for your tremendous support throughout this ongoing project, the ones before, and those yet to come.

About the Website

This book is accompanied by a companion website for instructors:

www.wiley.com\go\helms\majoringinpsychology

The website includes:

- multiple-choice questions and answers (~50 for each chapter);
- short answer and essay questions (~10 for each chapter); and
- PowerPoint slides for each chapter.

Please note that the resources are password protected and can only be accessed by instructors who register with the site.

Part I
Majoring in Psychology

Chapter One
Why Major in Psychology?

Introduction

Psychology is a fascinating and diverse field of study. It attracts students with varied backgrounds, interests, and abilities, all of whom are hoping that psychology will be a good fit for them. In addition to simply pursuing topics that they find compelling, these students stand to benefit from devoting themselves to the study of such a broad field. Psychology's breadth is what makes it possible for students to acquire a wide range of knowledge and skills that are applicable to a variety of careers. In other words, psychology offers many different things to many different types of individuals. Although this is a strength of the field, it also can make it difficult to determine if psychology is the *best* fit for you. Consider for a moment three students, all undergraduates who have come to think that majoring in psychology is what is best for them.

Valerie

Valerie is 19 years old and always knew she would go to college. Since middle school she had planned to become a teacher, so she first chose education as her major. After taking several introductory courses and talking with faculty members in the education department, Valerie decided that teaching was not for her. She next considered majoring in nursing, but the admission standards for local nursing programs are highly competitive. Valerie feared that the grades she earned in several courses required by nursing programs

Majoring in Psychology: Achieving Your Educational and Career Goals, Second Edition.
Jeffrey L. Helms and Daniel T. Rogers.
© 2015 John Wiley & Sons, Ltd. Published 2015 by John Wiley & Sons, Ltd.

would make her acceptance unlikely. One day last semester, Valerie's roommate described an interesting demonstration her psychology professor had presented in class. This reminded Valerie of her interest in psychology in high school, and she decided to take a course to see what psychology was like at the college level. Valerie enjoyed the course and performed well. As a result, she decided to change her major to psychology. When she recently mentioned the change to her parents, they were not especially positive. They asked probing questions about what she could do with a psychology degree and how her career options would compare to those of education or nursing majors. Valerie was unsure how to answer their questions. She had not thought much about what she can or will do with her degree. But, she figures that if so many other people major in psychology, there must be employment options out there.

Ajay

Ajay is 37 years old and has attended college at several points in the past at two different institutions. Most recently he stopped attending after his first child was born. Between working full-time and raising children, he was unsure if he would ever return to school to complete his degree. Now that Ajay's children are older and his financial status is more secure, he has decided to return to college part-time in order to get back into the academic routine. Ever since he was young, Ajay has had a desire to become a clinical psychologist. He was involved in family therapy as a child and individual therapy as an adolescent. He has fond memories of the psychologists he interacted with and the benefits of these treatments. His interests have prompted him to read psychological theory and some of the latest research in the field. Now that he is returning to school again, Ajay has committed himself to taking his education seriously and staying focused on his career goal. He knows meeting this goal will require completing a doctoral degree. Although Ajay is excited to begin moving forward along this path, he is also concerned that the road ahead seems long.

Katrina

Katrina is 25 years old. She began college 2 years ago after working for several years in her family's business. Katrina's first major was computer science, an area of interest for her since high school. Her teachers, family, and friends encouraged her to pursue this major given her talents and technological skills. She enjoyed the courses at first but later realized that she did not feel passionate about the topics or the prospects of future careers in the field. Due to her growing apathy, and her working 30–40 hours a week, Katrina's grades suffered. Then she took a psychology course and started a dialogue about her interests with the professor. As a result, Katrina decided to switch majors to psychology. Since that time she has invested herself in her coursework and excelled academically. After serving as a research assistant in one of her professor's labs over the past year, Katrina is now planning to pursue a research career in cognitive psychology. She intends to merge her computer science skills with her developing interest in human memory. Although changing majors extended her graduation date for another year, Katrina now knows exactly what it is she wants to do in her career and has worked diligently to learn about the field, improve her academic skills, and gain valuable experience.

> Valerie, Ajay, and Katrina represent typical undergraduate psychology majors. Many of you will identify with one or more aspects of their histories and experiences. Some of you may not see parts of yourself in these particular students, but there are still several things you all have in common. Each of you has decided to major in psychology, or is seriously considering it, as a result of intertwining experiences and life circumstances. Each of you has found something intrinsically interesting within the field. And each of you is hoping that this major will be the one that satisfies your interests and allows you to accomplish your goals. In essence, each of you hopes that you have found a home in psychology.

As professors of psychology, we have taught, advised, supervised, and mentored thousands of undergraduate students in all areas of their academic and career pursuits. Among them have been students like Valerie, Ajay, and Katrina. Although every student's context is somewhat unique, chances are we have also worked with students who have a lot in common with you. Our focus is on helping these students succeed in the ways that best match their goals, and we find this work to be incredibly rewarding. Perhaps the least satisfying aspect of this work is encountering students who could have benefited significantly from having key questions answered and guidance provided when they were first navigating the psychology major. Instead, these students find themselves playing catch-up, and they often feel confused and frustrated about their education and potential careers. Our focus on student success, coupled with our awareness of students' needs for information and guidance, prompted us to write this book. It is our hope that you find elements of it informative and instructive in pursuing your academic and career goals.

In this opening chapter, we first offer some brief suggestions on how to use the book effectively. The remainder of the chapter considers a question that may be looming large in many of your minds – why psychology?

Regardless of whether you have already firmly committed to the major or are still trying to make a decision, this section will help all students formulate and explore their specific interests in the field.

How to Use this Book

This book seeks to cover a range of issues relevant to psychology majors in a comprehensive manner. As a result, some chapters will likely appeal to you immediately because they address your current situation or pressing concerns (e.g., deciding if psychology is the right major, preparing a résumé, obtaining research experience). However, we want to encourage you not to neglect chapters that seem less relevant at this particular moment in your education. The information contained in such chapters will be helpful to you in the near future, and it may challenge your current thinking about how you are approaching your education or weighing the career options available to you. For example, those of you who are first- or second-year students may feel like the chapters on preparing for employment and graduate school address concerns that you will tackle in the distant future. You are partly correct in that the point at which you submit résumés and applications may be a few years away. But most of the steps and strategies that will allow you to succeed in these endeavors must be put into place right now. Many students applying to jobs and graduate schools wish they had prepared better, including taking important steps in their first and second years of college. Also, those of you who feel certain of your career interests should keep in mind that careers are selected for many reasons. But choosing not to pursue a certain area in the field simply because you know little about it might ultimately cheat you out of a rewarding career. By the same token, writing off graduate school because of a misconception you have about it, or abandoning psychology as a major because you believe you cannot work in your area of interest with a bachelor's degree, would be mistakes that are preventable only if you are well informed.

Why Major in Psychology?

Majoring in Psychology for What Psychology Is

One of the primary goals of this book is to have students who are majoring in psychology do so with a clearer sense of their specific interests in the discipline and how these interests will translate into career goals and plans. This would involve students majoring in psychology for reasons that have to do with the discipline itself and how a program of study in this field will support their future endeavors. To facilitate this process, it is vital to first consider what psychology is.

Psychology is the scientific study of behavior and mental processes in both human and nonhuman animals. The field focuses on outward, easily observable behavior as well as more covert experiences and processes such as memory, attitudes, and emotions. Psychologists study typical and atypical behavior and mental processes at both the individual and group levels. Given this focus, psychologists often engage in both generating new research and applying research findings to real-world problems and situations. Some have careers that concentrate exclusively on either research or applied endeavors, but many psychologists are involved in both activities.

The field's scientific foundation leads many psychologists to gather new knowledge about behavior and mental processes. This knowledge is generated in systematic ways, typically building on previous knowledge in a steady march toward greater understanding. Psychologists generate questions about aspects of behavior, propose possible explanations, and design methods of collecting data to test their hypotheses and help answer their questions. This process leads to new questions and additional research.

The field's applied foundation means that many psychologists work to address problems in the functioning of behavior and mental processes. This work involves developing new techniques and tools for addressing problems, putting these interventions into practice, and evaluating their effectiveness. The applied endeavors of psychologists serve the needs of human and nonhuman animals while simultaneously generating new ideas and opportunities for research.

The mixture of research and applied endeavors is evidence that psychology is an incredibly diverse field. This diversity in part results from the field's focus on the broad topic of behavior and mental processes. In fact, psychologists who may appear to have little in common in terms of their day-to-day work still understand and operate within the basic foundations of the discipline. For example, consider the following three psychologists:

- Dr. Rivera is an industrial–organizational psychologist. She works for a large consulting firm that contracts with major, international businesses to provide services related to their workforce and the workplace. Dr. Rivera's specialty is employee selection and leadership. She travels extensively when training new clients on the implementation of her firm's techniques and software.
- Dr. Neal is an experimental psychologist who studies stress reactions, often by using nonhuman animals as a model for human behavior. She is a faculty member at a large state university where she teaches

undergraduate and graduate courses, supervises graduate students' research, and operates a research lab. Dr. Neal recently secured grant funding to conduct a new study on stress and caffeine tolerance.

- Dr. Janowitz is a school psychologist who works for two school districts in a rural county. He is assigned to two high schools, three middle schools, and four elementary schools. He works directly with students by conducting psychological evaluations, creating educational plans, coordinating mental health and academic services, and facilitating prevention programs on substance abuse.

The daily activities of these psychologists appear so diverse that you might believe they were trained in different fields of study. But closer examination reveals that each is engaged in the study of behavior and mental processes. It is also evident that the research and applied areas of the field are relevant to all three. Although only Dr. Neal appears to be actively conducting research, Dr. Rivera's and Dr. Janowitz's work is closely tied to the scientific aspects of the field. Both use assessment tools and techniques that are products of extensive research. In addition, both utilize research and statistical methods to gather and analyze data on the effectiveness of their work. Although Dr. Rivera and Dr. Janowitz are clearly involved in applied activities, Dr. Neal's research on stress has potential applications that she considers when writing about her work and attempting to secure funding. In addition, her involvement in the teaching and supervision of students is an applied endeavor. As these psychologists illustrate, the breadth of the psychology discipline provides room for people with diverse interests and talents to make contributions to the field.

Despite the commonalities among all psychologists, there are some stark differences in the specific focus of their work. Most psychologists specialize in a particular subfield of the discipline. They acquire this expertise in graduate school where training is focused on a narrow range of the field. In contrast to this specificity of training at the graduate level, training in psychology at the undergraduate level is broad in its attempt to provide students with a basic foundation. In fact, the objectives for student learning are similar across programs, as reflected in the guidelines for undergraduate majors provided by the American Psychological Association (APA; 2013). These guidelines emphasize knowledge of and capacity to effectively use:

- the major concepts, theories, themes, empirical findings, and applications in the field;
- scientific reasoning, psychological sources, research methods, and statistical analyses;

- ethical standards and socially responsible behavior;
- written, oral, and interpersonal communication; and
- applications of psychological content and skills (e.g., project management, teamwork, self-regulation) toward career development.

Undergraduate programs in psychology emphasize this core set of learning objectives in order to prepare students for the next phase of their careers. Students who graduate with this knowledge and skill set are prepared to move into a variety of careers or enter graduate school for specialized training.

Popularity of the Degree

For decades psychology has been among the most popular majors on college and university campuses. According to a report from the US Department of Education's National Center for Educational Statistics (2013), students earned 108,896 bachelor's degrees in psychology in the United States during the 2011–2012 academic year. The only major with more graduates was business administration (138,910). There are more students earning bachelor's degrees in psychology than in education (105,785), nursing (92,029), engineering (81,382), and communication (88,752). Clearly students are gravitating to the psychology major in large numbers. Odds are on your campus a substantial proportion of your peers are pursuing the psychology major. This popularity has some general advantages for you.

First, consider that when departments have large numbers of majors, institutions must provide adequate resources to facilitate the education of these students. As a psychology major, you may have access to resources (e.g., technology lab, advising center, tutoring) that students in smaller, less popular departments do not. Second, because psychology has attracted large numbers of undergraduate majors over time, the field has established a rich tradition of developing and researching effective ways to teach. In fact, psychology is often viewed as a leader among disciplines in teaching and providing a quality undergraduate education. This means that many of your psychology professors will be devoted to helping students succeed both within and outside of the classroom. Third, although the popularity of a major does not always closely follow the job market for its graduates, if a large portion of the 100,000+ yearly graduates were struggling to find employment, the popularity of psychology over time would likely decrease. Therefore, these graduates must be having reasonable success securing employment.

A Multipurpose Degree

Part of the popularity of psychology, and other similarly structured degrees, is that it can serve two basic purposes. Some psychology majors will use their degree to seek employment and perhaps begin their careers. These students are often described as pursuing a bachelor's degree that is liberal arts in nature. Others will use their degree to enter graduate school and complete additional training prior to beginning their careers. These students are often described as pursuing a bachelor's degree that is preprofessional in nature. Which of these two paths you choose is largely based on your career objectives and plans. Although students pursuing either liberal arts or preprofessional degrees typically fulfill the same curriculum requirements for graduation, they are on different trajectories. As a result, they should each be focused on gathering the types of knowledge, skills, and experiences that will be most beneficial to their particular path.

The preprofessional degree path is discussed in greater detail in later chapters, but for now it is important to understand that all careers as psychologists require extensive graduate education and training. The bachelor's degree alone does not prepare you to work as a psychologist. Instead it can prepare you to seek certain types of graduate education, many of which are covered in detail in the chapters on the various careers in the field. The liberal arts degree path is also discussed in depth in a subsequent chapter. In the meantime, keep in mind that if you plan on pursuing employment or beginning your career after earning your bachelor's degree in psychology, this degree will not equip you with a specialized set of skills in the same way that a degree in nursing, engineering, education, accounting, or computer science would. As a liberal arts degree, your degree in psychology will provide you with general knowledge about the field as well as skills necessary to engage in lifelong learning (e.g., critical thinking, information gathering, and analysis).

Majoring in Psychology for Reasons Unrelated to Psychology

The diversity and flexibility of psychology as a field of study helps explain part of its enormous popularity as an undergraduate major. But if you talk to your peers about their reasons for majoring in psychology, you will likely hear a wide array of experiences and explanations. Some of these reasons will pertain to the nature of the psychology discipline and what it has to offer students. However, many of your peers, and perhaps even you, will give reasons that are unrelated to psychology as a field of study. In our experience, students repeatedly cite three such reasons as motivating factors in their interest in psychology.

The "path of least resistance" reason.   Students sometimes choose to major in psychology because they believe it provides a more favorable route to earning a bachelor's degree compared to other majors. For example, some students acknowledge that a factor in their selection of the major was that the psychology curriculum at their institution does not require a course they wanted to avoid (e.g., foreign language, higher-level math, natural science). Other students assert that they simply need to finish a bachelor's degree in something in order to obtain a job or advance in their current position. They have determined that the focus of their degree will not impact their career plans and that they simply need a degree in something. Still other students openly acknowledge that they selected psychology because they perceived it to be an easier or more popular path compared to majors they have already unsuccessfully attempted.

Some of you may have originally come to psychology because it seemed like the path of least resistance. Our purpose here is not to make you feel ashamed. Instead, we want you to aggressively pursue the notion that your major can be something far more than the quickest or easiest path. Whatever your ultimate career plans, major in psychology with clear objectives and understand how the major will help you accomplish your goals.

The "one course and I was sold" reason.   Students often choose to major in psychology because they had a positive experience in their first psychology course (Rajecki, Williams, Appleby, Jeschke, & Johnson, 2005). Many claim that the material was so interesting that they simply felt this was the major for them. Others assert that the concepts in their first course came so easily to them that psychology just seemed like common sense. Still others note that they tried alternative majors first, but upon taking one psychology course they knew what they wanted to do. Typically these students are referring to courses such as Introductory Psychology or perhaps Advanced Placement Psychology in high school. These courses provide a broad overview of the field as a whole. In highlighting major points and themes, they often address the most interesting and compelling topics and research. The fact that students have positive learning experiences in these courses is great news, but it is quite a common experience. Their enjoyment of this experience can be the result of many factors such as having excellent teachers, being motivated to study, earning a good grade, and being interested in the subject matter. None of these factors alone, especially in the context of a single, brief course, should be a deciding factor in determining one's major and future career. Consider for a moment what would have happened had these same students taken a different section of the course with a less engaging teacher or perhaps enrolled in an equally compelling introductory course in another major? Could the entire fate of their college and professional lives have been altered by this slightly different experience? If they based the selection of their major and career on a single course, then the answer is yes.

As concerning as this sounds, do not be alarmed if you are currently a psychology major in large part because of a positive experience in an introductory course. The fact that you are excited about some aspect of psychology is great, and it will be important to preserve this passion and follow your interests. But you still need to determine whether the major is right for you and whether your career objectives are in line with what the degree offers.

The "I'm destined to be a helper" reason. A large proportion of students chose psychology as their major because they "want to help people" or have "always been fascinated by human behavior." This is a significant factor identified by first-year and senior psychology majors alike (Stewart, Hill, Stewart, Bimler, & Kirkland, 2005). By claiming they want to help others, these students are often referring to career goals that have to do with providing mental health services to patients. When pressed for additional details, many of these students assert that they have always had a talent for listening to or "reading" people and helping them with their problems. For example, some students state that they are the one in their family or circle of friends who is the most compassionate and supportive when others are in need, and that the people around them routinely seek out their advice and comfort. These are certainly worthy goals and important personal experiences. But the truth is most people have a strong curiosity about human behavior, and many of us possess high levels of empathy and good listening skills as part of our makeup. In addition, many people desire to have careers in which they can positively impact the lives of others. Were we to ask, we would find these same interests and desires among teachers, civil servants, attorneys, researchers, business owners, politicians, physicians, and artists, to name a few. Many of them chose their career paths in part because they saw an opportunity to use their talents and pursue their interests in ways that would help others or contribute to society.

If you are searching for a career in which you can positively impact the lives of others, our goal is not to dissuade you from this admirable pursuit. Instead, we want you to understand that a desire to help others, and even some possible inherent skill at doing so, is not a sound reason on its own to major in psychology. Those of you who possess this interest must work to learn about whether psychology is the right vehicle for you to accomplish your specific career goals.

Determining if Psychology is for You

Determining whether psychology is the best major for you can be difficult. The decision can in part be made easier by answering three questions in relation to the major. First, *do you understand and appreciate psychology as a scientific discipline?* Answering yes to this question means that regardless of your career interests in the field, you understand the purpose and value of having your undergraduate education be rooted in both the research and applied foundations of the field. Second, *are you and psychology a good fit?* An affirmative answer to this question means that what psychology offers at the undergraduate level matches your interests, skills, abilities, values, and ways of thinking about the world. Third, *is psychology the right vehicle to help you accomplish your career goals, even if they are not well defined at the moment?* In answering yes to this question, be sure that majoring in psychology will at least not impede your goals and will at most give you the best foundation for achieving them.

Determining whether psychology is right for you is going to require effort on your part. You will need to examine thoroughly the field and what it has to offer. This means learning about the field in general and investigating the specifics of the major as it is offered at your institution. The remainder of this book will provide extensive information to guide you in this process. We encourage you to engage the information with an open and critical mind, thinking carefully about your choices in your academic and career pursuits. Regardless of whether you decide psychology is right for you or determine that your interests and career goals are best served in another discipline, the process of exploring the field and yourself will have been well worth the effort.

Suggested Exercises

1. If you are still undecided about your major, talk with at least one faculty member in each of the areas you are considering in order to gain their perspectives on the advantages and limitations of the major at your institution. Also talk with individuals in the community who are working with degrees in the areas you are considering in order to gain their perspectives.
2. Talk with junior- and senior-level psychology majors about their experiences and any suggestions they have for students in your position. If you do not know any advanced students, contact a psychology student organization at your school (e.g., Psi Chi) to ask for names of students who would be willing to talk to you. The officers of these groups are often an excellent resource.
3. Talk with peers in your classes about why they are pursuing psychology. Listen for reasons that you think match yours as well as any different or novel reasons you may not have considered. Notice which of your peers seem to have given this more or less thought than you.

4. Ask the department of psychology at your institution if they can provide you with contact information for some recent alumni. Many departments maintain alumni databases, and many alumni are willing to take the time to talk with current students. If your department makes such information available, contact a few recent graduates to ask about their experiences as a student and see if they have any advice for you.

Suggested Readings by Topic Area

Introduction to Psychology

King, L. A. (2014). *The science of psychology: An appreciative view* (3rd ed.). Boston, MA: McGraw-Hill.

Myers, D. G. (2013). *Psychology* (10th ed.). New York, NY: Worth Publishers.

Weiten, W. (2013). *Psychology: Themes and variations* (9th ed.). Belmont, CA: Wadsworth.

Selecting a Major

Fogg, N. P., Harrington, P. E., Harrington, T. F., & Shatkin, L. (2012). *College majors handbook with real career paths and payoffs: The actual jobs, earnings, and trends for graduates of 50 college majors* (3rd ed.). St. Paul, MN: Jist Publishing.

Shatkin, L. (2011). *Panicked student's guide to choosing a college major: How to confidently pick your ideal path*. Indianapolis, IN: Jist Publishing.

The College Board. (2013). *Book of majors 2014*. New York, NY: Author.

References

American Psychological Association. (2013). *APA guidelines for the undergraduate psychology major: Version 2.0*. Washington, DC: Author. Retrieved from http://www.apa.org/ed/precollege/about/psymajor-guidelines.pdf

Rajecki, D. W., Williams, C. C., Appleby, D. C., Jeschke, M. P., & Johnson, K. E. (2005). Sources of students' interest in the psychology major: Refining the Rajecki–Metzner Model. *Individual Differences Research, 3,* 128–135.

Stewart, R., Hill, K., Stewart, J., Bimler, D., & Kirkland, J. (2005). Why I am a psychology major: An empirical analysis of student motivations. *Quality & Quantity, 39,* 687–709. doi:10.1007/s11135-005-4484-9

US Department of Education, National Center for Education Statistics. (2013). *Table 318.30: Bachelor's, master's, and doctor's degrees conferred by postsecondary institutions, by sex of student, and discipline division: 2011–12.* Retrieved from http://nces.ed.gov/programs/digest/d13/tables/dt13_318.30.asp

Chapter Two
Succeeding in College
Transitions, Strategies, and Resources

Introduction

How did you decide to attend college? Some students struggle with the choice over time, weighing the pros and cons of continuing their education beyond high school. But in recent years, more students are simply assuming that attending college will be a part of their life. Why might this be? A major contributing force in this trend has been the shifting job market. Data from the US Department of Education's National Center for Education Statistics (US NCES) helps shed some light on these changes. In 2012, individuals between the ages of 25 and 34 who had earned a bachelor's degree or higher had an employment rate of 82%; those with only a high school diploma had an employment rate of 67% (US NCES, 2013e). Salary data indicate that among workers in this same age range, those with a bachelor's degree earn an average of $46,900; this salary is over $11,000 more than those with associate's degrees and almost $17,000 more than those with high school diplomas (US NCES, 2014c). Completing a bachelor's degree clearly puts an individual in a better position to secure employment and earn a higher salary.

The allure of job opportunities and higher salary is impacting college enrollment. Enrollment in post-secondary institutions in 2010 was just over 21 million students, which is a 74% increase from 30 years earlier (US NCES, 2014b). This rise in college attendance comes from multiple sources. For example, although just under half of all high school graduates in 1980 immediately enrolled in some type of postsecondary education, the number

Majoring in Psychology: Achieving Your Educational and Career Goals, Second Edition.
Jeffrey L. Helms and Daniel T. Rogers.
© 2015 John Wiley & Sons, Ltd. Published 2015 by John Wiley & Sons, Ltd.

increased to 68% in 2010 (US NCES, 2014a). During the same time period, the percentage of college students who were over the age of 35 also increased, rising from 13.0% to 18.3% (US NCES, 2013a).

Clearly greater numbers of students are seeking a college education, but are they succeeding? There are many ways to define college success. Two factors that postsecondary institutions often consider are retention (i.e., whether or not students stay in school) and graduation. Recent data indicate that among first-time undergraduate students, 28% of those who attend full-time and 58% of those who attend part-time did not return to their institution for their second year (US NCES, 2013d). Among first-time full-time bachelor's degree-seeking students, 38% complete their degree in four years and 58% complete their degree by the 6-year mark; the rest take longer or do not complete their degree (US NCES, 2013c). The reasons students fail to return to college or take longer to complete their degree are varied, but lack of adequate preparation is one likely factor. As more students view college as a necessity and attend based on this pressure, many are not ready to handle college-level work. In fact, only about one third of all public high school students are adequately prepared to enter a 4-year college (Greene & Forster, 2003). Approximately 20% of undergraduate students complete at least one remedial course in their first year (US NCES, 2013b).

Despite the value of a college education, and its apparent desirability, these data suggest that a sizeable portion of students choosing to attend college may not experience the success they had originally expected. In addition to being underprepared academically, students who start college without a clear sense of focus and motivation for being there are at a significant disadvantage. At some point in their undergraduate education, many of these students discover their career interests and goals, but others struggle to do so. When focus, motivation, and a clear sense of purpose are lacking, academic difficulties can emerge and may carry serious consequences (e.g., loss of scholarships, academic probation, damaged GPA). Fortunately, a large portion of these academic difficulties can be prevented.

This chapter explores several important steps students can take to help ensure success in college. Although none of these are quick fixes for serious academic problems, they are relatively simple to integrate into your educational life. The first section describes some common elements of students' experiences in adjusting to college. Understanding how college differs from high school and the workplace, and how these changes can impact your academic performance, is an important first step in taking control over your education. The second section explores strategies for academic success and suggests ways for incorporating them into your academic efforts. The final section describes resources that are available to most college students at their institutions and how these resources can enhance the academic experience. You likely will discover that you already are aware of some aspects of these steps. However, few students are aware of them all, and even fewer routinely implement them in their academic life. Therefore, this chapter should be beneficial whether you are successful, struggling, or just getting started in your college experience.

The Experience of Adjusting to College

What was your experience like coming to college? This will be a fresh memory for those of you who are first-time students in your first or second semester. Others of you may have to reflect back on the years or perhaps decades that have passed since you first stepped onto a college campus. Regardless, what was that transition to college like, and how has your progression since that time affected your views of college? Box 2.1 provides questions to help you reflect for a moment on some of the key aspects of your transition experience.

College can be one of the most exciting and formative periods of your life. But adjusting to college can be difficult because of the scope of changes involved. One of the biggest adjustments that must be made is to the academic environment. Compared to most students' high school experiences, the information learned in college, and the degree to which it is learned, is largely dependent upon their own initiative. This section of the chapter

---

Box 2.1   *Reflecting on the Transition to College*

- What messages did you receive from others (e.g., friends, siblings, parents, teachers) about going to college?
- How did you make your decision to apply?
- What were you most excited about?
- What were you most fearful of?
- What was your very first college class like?
- How did the environment and work differ from high school or your employment setting?
- What aspects of the academic work did you struggle the most with?
- What, if anything, would you do differently if you could start over?
- What advice would you give to a first-year student?

provides an overview of several academic changes that occur in the transition from high school to college. Regardless of whether or not you entered college directly after high school, these academic changes are common experiences. Each is directly related to the active role students must adopt in their learning at the college level. The section concludes by examining common problems students experience as a result of these changes. Having a clear understanding of these changes is an important part of ensuring that you have realistic expectations for your college experience and are prepared to handle the inevitable difficulties by taking an active role in your education.

Appleby (2005) conducted a study in which he polled freshmen about their perceptions of the differences between academic life in high school and college. Certainly any one student's perceptions are unique to them, but Appleby distilled several themes from the responses that likely resonate with most students' experiences. Many of these themes have also been echoed in previous research, and they are summarized here into four characteristics of the college academic environment: the academic work, students' responsibility for their learning, the structure of courses, and interactions with others. We then conclude this section by considering one framework for how students might think about transition problems.

The Academic Work

The fact that the difficulty of academic work increases significantly in college is unlikely to come as a surprise to you. However, many students are caught off guard by the ways in which the work becomes harder. Often they assume that the increased difficulty will be comparable to the changes that occurred when advancing a grade in high school. But college academic work is different in quantity and quality. The amount of material that is assigned in readings, covered in lectures, and expected to be learned, can be extensive. If you are taking four or five courses per term, the workload can be all consuming. Changes in the quality of the academic work are the direct result of professors assigning and expecting work to be completed at an advanced level. Many college courses overlap with subjects you have already completed in high school, but taking the course at the college level requires understanding the material in greater depth as concepts and topics are explored in more detail. You will also be expected to demonstrate purposeful and reflective thinking about the material in addition to the memorization of facts and mastery of skills.

With the shifts in the quality and quantity of the academic work, students must increase the amount of time they devote to assignments. Simultaneously, many report a decrease in the amount of time they are given by professors to complete this work. The assignments are more labor intensive because they often have multiple steps or components. In high school these steps are often broken into discrete assignments. But professors in college tend to assign larger projects as a whole, even if they provide feedback at intermediate stages. Writing assignments also tend to be broader in scope, requiring more extensive reviews of existing literature and greater integration of material. With students enrolling in multiple courses, completing them in only a few months, and already experiencing an increased workload in terms of the material assigned, these more involved assignments contribute to the dramatic increase in time that must be invested in academic work.

Students' Responsibility for their Learning

High school teachers bear much of the responsibility for their students' learning. In college, professors are less involved in ensuring that you learn the course material. Instead, college students must take on a substantial portion of the responsibility for their learning. Professors carry some of this responsibility, but they fulfill this duty by organizing and facilitating the course and promoting student engagement. The actual engagement in the learning process is up to you to initiate and sustain. One indication that the responsibility for learning shifts can be seen in the amount of time that students spend in class. High school students are physically at school for 6–8 hours each weekday. In contrast, many full-time college students have classes on 2–3 days, often for no more than 12–16 hours total of direct instruction each week. These hours are even lower for students enrolled in hybrid or online courses. And, because the student carries the burden of coming to class and investing in the learning process, attendance in college courses is typically not monitored as closely as in high school, if at all.

If the academic work in college is more difficult in terms of quantity, quality, and the time pressures involved, and students are spending limited time in class, then where and when is the academic work taking place? It primarily takes place outside of class and during your free time. Many students feel prepared and are excited to accept this increased responsibility for their learning. Along with this responsibility comes greater freedom and flexibility in decision making. Some anticipate that assuming a more active role in their learning will be a straightforward task because they will have much more time on their hands as a result of spending fewer hours in the classroom. Indeed this experience can be liberating for students who wisely choose where to allocate their time and resources. But others fail to anticipate the multitude of nonacademic responsibilities and interests that will compete for this time. In high school these other obligations and distracters often had to wait, but in college the increased free time is there for the taking.

Structure of Courses

In addition to the shortened time frame and reduced meeting times, college courses also have a different structure compared to those in high school. Part of this structure is evident in college professors' reliance on a syllabus as the primary organizing element of the course. Regardless of how detailed or open-ended professors make a syllabus, the course structure it outlines is typically kept intact and serves as a guide throughout the term. You can use the syllabus at the beginning of a term to determine whether the course will meet your learning needs and whether, given your other commitments, you can sufficiently engage in the course with a positive outcome.

College courses have fewer restrictions on student behavior. Although the syllabus may contain guidelines for student conduct, most courses have few rules about behavior in the class. Some professors will establish classroom rules, but they are likely to be more in the spirit of promoting open dialogue than trying to regulate problematic behaviors. Despite there being fewer behavioral rules, most college students will notice that the transition from high school brings many more rules for their academic work. In fact, the strictest aspect of most course structures is the schedule according to which the academic work must be completed. Professors vary in their flexibility, but most establish specific deadlines for the material to be covered and assignments to be completed. As a result, some students report feeling there was much more leeway in high school to complete assignments.

Interactions with Others

The academic and social environment of college differs from that of high school in terms of the interactions you have with your peers and professors. Student populations are often quite diverse in college. One result of this is the increased emphasis placed on openness to and tolerance of different backgrounds and points of view, particularly within the classroom. Another implication is that students often have personal schedules and priorities that do not necessarily align with their peers. As a result, relationships with fellow students can be less likely to form and harder to sustain than in high school. Relationships with peers in college are more likely to form when you are frequently present on campus and the campus environment is conducive to student interactions outside of class (Kulm & Cramer, 2006; Lundberg, 2004).

Interactions with college professors are quite different from those with high school teachers. With the decreased time spent in the classroom, professors are typically less accessible. You may also sometimes experience your professors as being less personable than your high school teachers because your interactions often exclusively focus on academic issues. However, professors do form strong mentoring relationships with outstanding students who are interested in working with them on their research or teaching. These students often get to know professors much better than they ever did their high school teachers.

Thinking about One's Transition Problems

The scope of the changes that occur in the academic environment when transitioning to college contributes to some academic difficulty for many students. For instance, most students discover at some point that a particular subject or academic task does not come as easily as it once did, especially when these demands are numerous. Box 2.2 presents several scenarios in which students are encountering common problems in adjusting to the academic environment of college. Consider whether any of these students' difficulties correspond to your experience.

Many students encounter difficulties when making the college transition. Struggling at times is not a sign that you do not belong or that you will not succeed. It is also important to remember that each student's experience is somewhat unique. However, research suggests that students tend to understand or interpret their difficulties in learned, patterned ways. These explanatory styles are based on your beliefs about the causes of positive and negative events in your life and the degree to which you think you have control over them (Rotter, 1966). In one type of explanatory style, students perceive their academic difficulties as having a direct relationship to their abilities and actions. This response, called an internal locus of control, leads them to believe they have influence over their academic performance and are responsible for both good and bad outcomes. In the second type of explanatory style, known as an external locus of control, students perceive their academic difficulties as having little to no relationship to their abilities and actions. Instead, they believe their academic performance is largely outside of their direct control and is instead influenced by chance, societal factors, or the will of others (e.g., professors).

It is important to be aware of how you typically explain your academic experiences, both positive and negative, because adopting an internal or external locus of control may have consequences. For example, college students with an internal locus of control tend to achieve at a higher level

Box 2.2 *Examples of Common Academic Problems in Adjusting to College*

- Throughout high school and even her first semester of college, Elaina had always earned excellent grades. However, the first paper assignment in her history course this term was just returned. She earned a "D," and her professor suggested that given the number of problems in her paper that Elaina get assistance with her writing. Elaina was shocked. She had never received anything below a "B" on a paper, and no previous teacher had suggested that she might not be a strong writer. She feels overwhelmed by the experience and is concerned what this means for her overall grade in the course.
- Alex studied extensively for his final exam in economics. He felt as though he put more time and effort into preparing for this exam than he did for the entire class up until this point. Yet when he sat down to take the exam, he found question after question that he had no idea how to answer. For a fleeting moment he wondered if he had been given the wrong exam. Alex completed as many items as he could then left the classroom feeling disoriented and confused.
- Sana returned home from work late on a Saturday evening and sat and stared at the mound of schoolwork on her desk. She had two papers and a quiz the coming week in courses that are critical to her major. On top of that, she was behind in her reading in every course. She had always been skilled at managing her time and completing her academic work. Now she feels that she has dug a hole she might not be able to climb out of.

academically (Kalechstein & Nowicki, 1997) and adjust better in the transition to college (Ogden & Trice, 1986). This is particularly true for first-generation college students (Aspelmeier, Love, McGill, Elliott, & Pierce, 2012). Students with an external locus of control tend to experience higher levels of stress (Gadzella, 1994), more frequent illness (Roddenberry & Renk, 2010), and higher rates of substance use (Segal, 1974). In addition to these correlates, a major problem with both explanatory styles is that a struggling student can become resigned to their academic difficulties. Those with an internal locus of control may become convinced that they lack the ability to succeed. Those with an external locus of control may become convinced that forces outside of themselves will always thwart their success. Both types of students may accept that they are unable to achieve and subsequently reduce their efforts or quit school altogether. Research suggests that rather than one explanatory style being uniformly favorable over the other, students who are flexible in their approach to coping fare better than those who are unable to adapt based on the particulars of the challenge at hand (Gan, Shang, & Zhang, 2007). Regardless of whether the academic difficulties actually stem from personal shortcomings or external factors, there are effective academic strategies that can increase all students' academic success.

Academic Strategies

Academic success in college is largely based on your ability to learn new information and master new skills. Research in cognitive psychology and related disciplines has taught us much about how humans learn. Three elements are critical. New information must be: (1) actively processed, (2) reduced to meaningful and manageable units, and (3) rehearsed and reviewed repeatedly over time. Strategies that facilitate one or more of these processes in your academic efforts will enhance your learning. This section explores six areas in which specific strategies can bolster academic success.

Manage Time Wisely

Time management involves being selective when choosing activities in order to maximize accomplishments within a limited amount of time. The concept receives tremendous attention in business and educational settings as a desirable skill, but it has not been shown to have a consistent impact on grades (Claessens, van Eerde, Rutte, & Roe, 2007). This finding may stem from the fact that time management has an indirect effect on academic performance. In other words, although effective time management may not always translate into academic success, poor time management seems likely to interfere with positive academic results. Effective time management creates the opportunity to engage in other beneficial strategies. For example, setting personal goals appears to play an important role in working efficiently. Students who set such goals work in a more structured manner and are less distracted (Strickland & Galimba, 2001). Some students incorporate this strategy by creating "to do lists" for their academic work that are personal, or tailored to their experience, rather than simply listing the tasks that have been assigned.

Almost every college student at some point procrastinates, and over half of them engage in systematic procrastination that leads to academic problems

(Day, Mensink, & O'Sullivan, 2000). Students tend to procrastinate on tasks that they perceive to be difficult, boring, imposed on them, or requiring skills that they lack (Milgram, Sroloff, & Rosenbaum, 1988; Steel, 2007). Because these perceptions are based in how one interprets and thinks about both the task and one's ability to complete it, they can be altered. When you find yourself procrastinating on an important academic task, carefully examine your thinking about the assignment. Work to change any negative perceptions (e.g., it's too difficult, not fair, beyond my abilities, not that important) that may be leading you to engage in delay and distraction. Pushing yourself to begin engaging in the work ahead of any deadlines will also help support a positive outlook on the benefits of the task.

In addition to avoiding procrastination, students who segment large academic tasks into smaller units often perform better on these tasks. Wagner, Schober, and Spiel (2008) discovered that students who worked in series of 30-minute intervals on a variety of tasks had the best academic performance. They surpassed the achievements of students who worked in fewer, larger blocks of time focusing on fewer tasks. You could incorporate this strategy by resisting the tendency to complete large amounts of academic work in one sitting. Spacing out the tasks in smaller units will be a more efficient use of the time and will likely enhance learning.

Reading Course Material for Comprehension

The amount of material students are assigned to read in their courses dramatically increases in college. Some feel overwhelmed by the sheer volume of material they must consume to keep pace. Reading effectively requires processing new information, developing understanding, and retaining this new knowledge. Reading in this manner may be the most important academic skill you master.

Students often believe that when a professor assigns readings that the task is to simply read the corresponding pages. But your professors' objective is for you to comprehend the information and concepts contained in those pages; reading is merely a vehicle to accomplish this. Consider whether you have ever heard fellow students complain about a low exam grade by saying, "I actually read the chapters this time!" These students' exam grades are evidence that they are struggling with comprehension of the material. Comprehension cannot occur through passively reading words on a page. It requires engaging the information in order to process ideas in an active and deliberate manner.

Numerous reading strategies have been designed to help students comprehend written material. But adopting a specific strategy is unlikely to be uniformly helpful to all students. Instead, you should model the reading tactics of effective readers: (1) read the material thoroughly, (2) actively think about or process the material, and (3) examine this processing and whether it is successful in promoting learning (Yang, 2006). These steps ensure an active construction of meaning from the text. Several strategies that can facilitate these steps are provided in Box 2.3.

Being Engaged in the Classroom

Compared to high school students, college students spend far less time in the classroom. The way you make use of this limited time can significantly impact your academic performance. Professors view classroom time as precious and often use it to expose students to vital or complex information rather than giving general overviews or summaries. This might involve lectures on new material, further explanations and extensions of previously covered material, or activities to enhance understanding of the material.

Box 2.3 *Techniques for Boosting Reading Comprehension*

- Examine major topics/concepts to be covered prior to starting reading.
- Generate a list of questions about the topics/concepts that you want answered.
- Think about the topics/concepts before, during, and after reading.
- Skim material that you know is unimportant to comprehending the main topics/concepts.
- When you complete a section, think about the meaning of it and its implications.
- Make notes as you read to capture your questions, insights, and understanding.
- Link the topics/concepts and their meaning to knowledge you already possess.
- As you read, skip forwards and backwards as necessary in order to link key topics/concepts.
- When you finish reading, quiz yourself about the major topics/concepts.
- Have a positive self-concept as a reader – be confident in your ability and encourage yourself.

Consequently, improving your ability to learn within this setting should be a priority.

Research indicates there is a modest correlation between class attendance and grades (e.g., Brocato, 1989; van Blerkom, 1992). Of course this correlation does not resolve whether attendance is causing the grade (e.g., students who attend more learn more), the grade is causing the attendance (e.g., students who learn more attend more), or grades and attendance are being influenced by a third factor (e.g., students attend more and learn more when they find the material interesting). But being present in class certainly provides exposure to course information and the opportunity for you to engage with the material. Engaging in class can be uncomfortable for some students, perhaps even anxiety provoking. It can be difficult to answer a professor's question or ask one of your own when none of your classmates are doing so. The fear of being wrong can be strong, but learning is not about always being right. Given the importance of class interaction for your learning, encourage yourself to be bold and resist the temptation to passively occupy your seat. Speak up, ask for clarification, and volunteer. You may be surprised at how many of your peers follow your lead.

There is a body of research showing that taking and reviewing notes in class is related to improved performance (e.g., Kiewra et al., 1991). Note taking is a difficult skill that requires multiple cognitive tasks such as holding information in memory, deciphering its meaning, and transcribing it quickly. Research suggests that two components of this process are the most important to taking good lecture notes. Students who are able to copy or transcribe efficiently construct better notes and perform better on assessments (Peverly et al., 2007). Students who add additional information to the notes they transcribe are better able to apply the concepts (Stefanou, Hoffman, & Vielee, 2008). Although some sources for academic strategies recommend that you not write everything down in your notes, enhancing your transcription skills does appear to be an important step. You should then work to add additional information to your notes that captures your understanding of the concepts.

Performing Well on Assignments

Academic performance in college is synonymous with grades. A course grade reflects the degree to which the student has met the learning objectives. Assignments within a course are designed to both facilitate and assess learning. For example, taking an exam prompts you to study the material and provides an indication of how successful you have been. As a result, the surest way to succeed is to learn the material. But as you well know, understanding the material is only one part of doing well on an assignment. You must have a host of other skills that allow you to demonstrate your learning.

Assignments in college often require you to write. These take many forms, but there are several strategies that are helpful in all writing endeavors. First, start early. Good writing requires time. Assignments completed at the last minute appear that way – hurried, disorganized, incoherent, and error-filled. Second, work in stages. Most assignments have several components that can be developed independently until tied together in the later stages. Third, compose a draft and revise it repeatedly. Students are frequently surprised at the errors they committed in a paper after it is graded and returned. This is a clear sign of either not having a draft or failing to revise. If you have difficulty editing your writing, many professors will allow you to ask others for feedback to help detect problems related to spelling, grammar, clarity, and organization.

College courses often use exams to assess student learning. Several strategies for completing traditional exams can have a positive effect on performance. First, always look over the exam before starting in order to develop a plan for working through the items. Second, plan your response to short-answer and essay items before starting to write. Students are often surprised that they failed to include a key concept in their response or answer a part of the question. Last, despite what many of you have been taught, there are numerous research studies demonstrating that when students change their answers on a multiple-choice item, on average they improve their score (e.g., Benjamin, Cavell, & Shallenberger, 1984; Prinsell, Ramsey, & Ramsey, 1994). This is particularly true if you change answers because you have new information or a new insight that is guiding your decision.

Any discussion of test-taking strategies would be remiss not to mention test-wiseness. Test-wise students are able to use features of a test in conjunction with their test-taking experience to improve their score. For example, because the items on exams often pertain to overlapping concepts, some students who struggle with a particular item will glean information from other items to help them determine the answer. Although test-wise strategies vary and their utility on any given test is never certain, students who are taught these strategies tend to perform better (for a review, see Rogers & Yang, 1996). When this occurs on an exam, it highlights two concerns. First, the grades on such an exam do not solely reflect student learning. Second, students who are not test-wise are at a disadvantage. Consequently, solutions to test-wiseness involve either making exams less susceptible to test-wise

Box 2.4 *Sample Test-Wise Strategies*

- If only correct answers are counted (i.e., there is no guessing penalty), answer every item.
- For items where partial credit is offered, provide as much information as you know.
- Answer items as the test constructor intended (i.e., keep the author of the test in mind).
- Read all instructions and items carefully, being alert for key words (e.g., except, not, all, but).
- Underline the most important terms in an item, letting these guide your answer.
- Eliminate options you know are incorrect by physically removing them from consideration.
- Mark items you are unsure about and return to them once you have completed the other items.
- Use content from other test items to identify correct answers.
- If it is allowed, ask your professor for clarification when needed.
- Check to see if the grammatical structure of items provides a clue to the answer.
- Recognize patterns/tendencies on a professor's test (e.g., "none of the above" is never correct).
- Check your work to be sure your final answer is the one you intended.

strategies or educating all students to be test-wise. Students who have not been exposed to these strategies may be well served to learn them in order not to be at a disadvantage in comparison to peers on exams that are susceptible to test-wise strategies. A sampling of common test-wise strategies is listed in Box 2.4. It is important to remember that test-wise strategies should only be applied when your knowledge and logic have failed to identify the correct answer.

Studying Effectively

Students often consider studying to be the most important factor determining their academic performance. Unfortunately many students, even those who performed well in high school, never learned effective study strategies or prepared to be independent learners, capable of modifying their study strategies to the task at hand. Developing a strong but flexible approach to studying that becomes a routine is essential to your sustained academic success. Students who study in a thoughtful and reflective manner perform better (Zimmerman, 1998). This type of studying is facilitated by creating a study plan based on the demands of each course. Study plans provide you with a clear sense of what is required and help you manage the allocation of your resources to meet these demands (Biggs, 1985). The plan will work best if it is consistent with the type of material you are learning and the ways in which your learning will be evaluated (Zimmerman, Bandura, & Martinez-Pons, 1992).

Virtually every college student has had the experience of cramming the night before an exam or while sitting in class before a quiz. The research literature on memory provides a clear verdict on the effectiveness of this strategy (Glenberg, 1977; Melton, 1970). The most effective way to learn information is to space studying out over time. Spaced practice or rehearsal is the exact opposite of cramming. It involves studying small segments of the material in a repeated, systematic way. This spacing of the learning process increases comprehension and recall of information, which is required to perform well on exams. Many students also believe that the longer they study the better their grades will be. Yet a systematic investigation into this issue found little to no direct correlation between hours spent studying and grades earned (Schuman, Walsh, Olson, & Etheridge, 1985). Subsequent research has found that there is a significant relationship between investment in studying and grades, but investment is not synonymous with the amount of time spent studying. Rather than counting the hours spent studying, you would be better served by adopting a methodical, disciplined approach in which you are committed to academic effort over other competing activities (Rau & Durand, 2000).

Caring for Yourself

For some students, the transition to college involves taking on a new level of responsibility for their physical and mental health. For other students who have already had to tackle this responsibility, some fail to appreciate that their health and well-being are important components of their academic success. Just as time management makes reading for comprehension possible, and attendance makes engaging in class possible, taking care of yourself will allow you to function at your best. There is an array of things you can do to ensure self-care, and of course there are many things you can do that have a deleterious effect on your health. Two factors that are known to impact academic performance, and which you have some control over, are sleep and stress.

Most college students experience at least occasional sleep difficulties, but nearly 75% report not getting enough sleep and over 20% experience poor sleep quality (Buboltz et al., 2009). Insufficient sleep places students at risk to experience problems with concentration, negative emotions, and low mood, all of which adversely impact academic performance (Angus, Heslegrave, & Myles, 1985; Taub & Berger, 1973). Research also indicates that students who are sleeping less are not aware of the decline in their functioning (Pilcher & Walters, 1997). They are unlikely to be aware of their decreased performance in a way that motivates them to alter their behavior. Taken together, this research suggests that you should make your sleep routine a priority. In addition, if you conclude that your poor sleep habits are not impacting your academic performance, recognize that your lack of sleep is likely affecting your ability to accurately make such a judgment.

College students typically identify grades as the biggest contributing factor to their stress level (Furr, Westefeld, McConnell, & Jenkins, 2001), and stress has been shown to have a negative impact on academic performance (Felsten & Wilcox, 1992). Research has revealed that stress also has a substantial negative effect on the body's immune responses (for a review, see Segerstrom & Miller, 2004), and illnesses can significantly hinder students' academic performance. It is important to note that much of the research defines stress as a perception that one's resources are inadequate to deal with demands (Lazarus & Folkman, 1984). The positive news in this is that perceptions of stress can be modified. Numerous techniques for coping with stress exist (e.g., progressive muscle relaxation, exercise, breathing, meditation, etc.), and you would be well served to explore these and determine which stress coping strategies work best for you.

Campus Resources

Regardless of whether or not you are currently experiencing academic difficulties, you can benefit from being aware of strategies for improving academic performance. In addition, most institutions have resources available to you that will support your academic efforts. Some students actively choose whether or not to make use of these resources, but a large portion of students are not even aware that they exist. This section of the chapter provides a brief overview of six resources that are commonly available to college students.

Academic Advising

The role that academic advising plays in the lives of students differs across institutions. Some require students to attend advising each semester before they are allowed to register for courses. Others have no requirement that students ever attend advising. Regardless, all institutions offer academic advising to their students because they believe it to be a valuable resource. But students often report that helpful contacts with an academic advisor are few and far between compared to those with friends and family (Smith & Zhang, 2009). Thus, students must be proactive about seeking advising when needed and taking steps to ensure that the contact is helpful. Academic advising provides an opportunity for you to meet with an advisor, often a professor in your major department, who has expertise in guiding students in academic matters. Advisors can assist you in selecting courses that will best fit your needs and interests. They can also provide suggestions and guidance regarding your academic performance. Lastly, advisement may be a time when you consider future career plans. Getting the most out of academic advising requires that you come prepared by bringing specific questions about your academic progress to help structure the meeting.

Writing Centers

Many institutions have writing centers or labs on campus. These centers assist students with all types of writing that are a part of their academic work. Typically these centers are located within English departments and may be staffed by professors or graduate students. You can seek help for either a specific writing assignment or repeated difficulties you are having with your writing. In either case, you must provide samples or drafts of your writing to the staff for them to review. Students who find the writing center experience helpful often return throughout their education for help with various assignments.

Tutoring

Tutoring services are commonly offered in a variety of areas on college campuses. Some students have access to tutoring as a result of their status (e.g., athletes, international students, adult learners). Others can access tutoring through academic departments if they are a major in that department or enrolled in certain courses (e.g., the math department may provide tutoring to all students enrolled in certain courses). These types of tutoring services are typically free to students who meet the eligibility requirements.

Of course, additional tutoring is also available in a variety of formats in the private sector for a fee. Advanced undergraduate and graduate students pursuing degrees in an area often provide affordable tutoring services and advertise around campus.

Disability Support Services

Services provided through disability support programs assist students who have disabilities that impact their academic performance. These programs work with the students to ensure that they have the resources necessary to allow them to perform at their best. Students typically seek these services for physical/medical, learning, and psychological disabilities by registering with the disability support program. This usually requires providing documentation of their disability from a licensed professional. Registered students can then benefit from a variety of services including educational programs, tutoring, and accommodations for completing their academic work (e.g., extended time on exams).

Career Development Services

Career development programs are designed to provide students with the education and assistance they need to identify and achieve their career goals. These programs provide extensive resources to help you learn about career fields and jobs that may be of interest to you. They also maintain educational resources for learning about your interests, skills, and abilities. These programs provide direct assistance to students who are seeking to gain experience and those who are striving to meet a career goal. For example, some career development programs coordinate opportunities for internship experiences and organize career or graduate school fairs. Others provide services such as résumé and interview preparation. Increasingly these centers are assisting students with using technology to conduct job searches and submit application materials.

Physical and Mental Health

Institutions with sizeable student populations often provide some level of medical and mental health services. The nature and extent of these services vary, but most student health centers are able to provide low-cost services that students would typically obtain from their primary care or family physician. Counseling centers usually are able to assist students with vocational, academic, and personal matters that are causing distress or disrupting their functioning. Many counseling centers provide services to students at low or no cost because they are supported by fees collected in conjunction with tuition. Students sometimes are unaware that their fees help make these services available on their campus. If these types of centers are not the best setting to address your situation, the staff will assist you in getting connected with a professional in the community who can provide the services you need.

Conclusion

We began this chapter by asking you to consider how you decided to attend college and how the experience has shaped you. In focusing on the adjustment to college, potential problems were identified and strategies were highlighted for ensuring academic success. The chapter concluded by considering resources available to you to help you succeed. It is important to remember that college students are diverse with varied backgrounds, abilities, and interests. Not all strategies or resources will be a good fit for everyone's experiences and problems. But being aware of these issues, and knowing how to take action in response to them, will give you a significant advantage in pursuing your educational and career goals.

Suggested Exercises

1. Keep a time log for a few days, noting the activities you engaged in and the amount of time you spent on each (e.g., reading, sleeping, browsing the internet, exercising, eating, studying, texting, working). Think of this like a register for a bank account where you record each transaction. At the end of the week, calculate the percentage of time you spent engaged in each activity. Compare major categories of activities to see where your time was used. You may want to use these data to create a budget in order to gain better control over where you spend your time.
2. Using the campus resources section of this chapter, identify and become familiar with each of these resources at your institution. They may be listed on your institution's website, often under the title of "student services" or "academic services." Many of these resources maintain their own websites that provide students with information about their services.
3. Attend an academic advising meeting with a professor in your major department in addition to that which may be normally required of you. Rather than focusing on course selection or career issues, use this time to talk in detail about your academic performance. Be honest about your strengths and weaknesses. Let this advisor know that you are interested in honest feedback.

4. Pick one course that you will take next semester and plan an academic makeover for yourself. In the course you select, experiment with some of the academic strategies described in this chapter to alter your typical approach to reading, studying, completing assignments, and engaging in class. Monitor your progress early to be sure that the changes are not adversely affecting your performance. Take notice of what does and does not work for you, and consider which of your new strategies you could incorporate into your other courses.

Suggested Readings

Gardner, J. N., & Barefott, B. O. (2012). *Step by step to college and career success* (5th ed.). Boston, MA: Bedford/St. Martin's.

Feaver, P., Wasiolek, S., & Crossman, A. (2008). *Getting the best out of college: Insider advice for success from a professor, a dean, and a recent grad*. New York, NY: Crown Publishing Group.

Newport, C. (2005). *How to win at college: Surprising secrets for success from the country's top students*. New York, NY: Broadway Books.

References

Angus, R. G., Heslegrave, R. J., & Myles, W. S. (1985). Effects of prolonged sleep deprivation, with and without chronic physical exercise, on mood and performance. *Psychophysiology, 22*, 276–282. doi:10.1111/1469-8986.ep11027385

Appleby, D. C. (2005, March). *How do college freshmen view the academic differences between high school and college?* Paper presented at the annual meeting of the Midwest Institute for Students and Teachers of Psychology, Glen Ellyn, IL.

Aspelmeier, J. E., Love, M. M., McGill, L. A., Elliott, A. N., & Pierce, T. W. (2012). Self-esteem, locus of control, college adjustment, and GPA among first- and continuing-generation students: A moderator model of generational status. *Research in Higher Education, 53*, 755–781. doi:10.1007/s11162-011-9252-1

Benjamin, L. T., Jr., Cavell, T. A., & Shallenberger, W. R. (1984). Staying with initial answers on objective tests: Is it a myth? *Teaching of Psychology, 11*, 133–141.

Biggs, J. B. (1985). The role of metalearning in study processes. *British Journal of Educational Psychology, 55*, 185–212. doi:10.1111/j.2044-8279.1985. tb02625.x

Brocato, J. (1989). How much does coming to class matter? Some evidence of class attendance and grade performance. *Educational Research Quarterly, 13*(3), 2–6.

Buboltz, W. C., Jr., Jenkins, S. M., Soper, B., Woller, K., Johnson, P., & Faes, T. (2009). Sleep habits and patterns of college students: An expanded study. *Journal of College Counseling, 12*, 113–124.

Claessens, B. J. C., van Eerde, W., Rutte, C. G., & Roe, R. A. (2007). A review of the time management literature. *Personnel Review, 36*, 255–276. doi:10.1108/00483480710726136

Day, V., Mensink, D., & O'Sullivan, M. (2000). Patterns of academic procrastination. *Journal of College Reading and Learning, 30*, 120–134.

Felsten, G., & Wilcox, K. (1992). Influences of stress and situation-specific mastery beliefs and satisfaction with social support on well-being and academic performance. *Psychological Reports, 70*, 291–303. doi:10.2466/pr0.1992.70.1.291

Furr, S. R., Westefeld, J. S., McConnell, G. N., & Jenkins, J. M. (2001) Suicide and depression among college students: A decade later. *Professional Psychology: Research and Practice, 32*, 97–100. doi:10.1037//0735-7028.32.1.97

Gadzella, B. M. (1994). Locus of control differences among stress groups. *Perceptual and Motor Skills, 79*, 1619–1624. doi:10.2466/pms.1994.79.3f.1619

Glenberg, A. M. (1977). Influences of retrieval processes on the spacing effect in free recall. *Journal of Experimental Psychology: Human Learning and Memory, 3*, 282–294. doi:10.1037/0278-7393.3.3.282

Gan, Y., Shang, J., & Zhang, Y. (2007). Coping flexibility and locus of control as predictors of burnout among Chinese college students. *Social Behavior and Personality, 35*, 1087–1098. doi:10.2224/sbp.2007.35.8.1087

Greene, J. P., & Forster, G. (2003). *Public high school graduation and college readiness rates in the United States* (Education Working Paper No. 3). Retrieved from Center for Civic Innovation website: http://www.manhattan-institute.org/html/ewp_03.htm

Kalechstein, A. D., & Nowicki, S., Jr. (1997). A meta-analytic examination of the relationship between control expectancies and academic achievement: An 11-yr follow-up to Findley and Cooper. *Genetic, Social, and General Psychology Monographs, 123*, 27–56.

Kiewra, K. A., DuBois, N. F., Christian, D., McShane, A., Meyerhoffer, M., & Roskelley, D. (1991). Note-taking functions and techniques. *Journal of Educational Psychology, 83*, 240–245.

Kulm, T. L., & Cramer, S. (2006). The relationship of student employment to student role, family relationships, social interactions and persistence. *College Student Journal, 40*, 927–938.

Lazarus R. S., & Folkman S. (1984). *Stress, appraisal, and coping*. New York, NY: Springer.

Lundberg, C. A. (2004). Working and learning: The role of involvement for employed students. *NASPA Journal, 41*, 201–215.

Melton, A. W. (1970). The situation with respect to the spacing of repetitions and memory. *Journal of Verbal Learning and Verbal Behavior, 9*, 596–606. doi:10.1016/S0022-5371(70)80107-4

Milgram, N. A., Sroloff, B., & Rosenbaum, M. (1988). The procrastination of everyday life. *Journal of Research in Personality, 22*, 197–212. doi:10.1016/0092-65 66(88)90015-3

Ogden, E. P., & Trice, A. D. (1986). The predictive validity of the Academic Locus of Control scale for college students: Freshman outcomes. *Journal of Social Behavior and Personality, 1*, 649–652.

Peverly, S. T., Ramaswamy, V., Brown, C., Sumowski, J. Alidoost, M., & Garner, J. (2007). What predicts skill in lecture note taking? *Journal of Educational Psychology, 99*, 167–180.

Pilcher, J. J., & Walters, A. S. (1997). How sleep deprivation affects psychological variables related to college students' cognitive performance. *Journal of American College Health, 46*, 121–126. doi:10.1080/07448489709595597

Prinsell, C. P., Ramsey, P. H., & Ramsey, P. P. (1994). Score gains, attitudes, and behavior changes due to answer-changing instruction. *Journal of Educational Measurement, 31,* 327–337. doi:10.1111/j.1745-3984.1994.tb00450.x

Rau, W., & Durand, A. (2000). The academic ethic and college grades: Does hard work help students to "make the grade"? *Sociology of Education, 73,* 19–38.

Roddenberry, A., & Renk, K. (2010). Locus of control and self-efficacy: Potential mediators of stress, illness, and utilization of health services in college students. *Child Psychiatry and Human Development, 41,* 353–370.

Rogers, W. T., & Yang, P. (1996). Test-wiseness: Its nature and application. *European Journal of Psychological Assessment, 12,* 247–259. doi:10.1027/1015-5759.12.3.247

Rotter, J. B. (1966). Generalized expectancies for internal versus external control of reinforcement. *Psychological Monographs: General and Applied, 80*(1), 1–28. doi:10.1027/1015-5759.12.3.247

Schuman, H., Walsh, E., Olson, C., & Etheridge, B. (1985). Effort and reward: The assumption that college grades are affected by quantity of study. *Social Forces, 63,* 945–966. doi:10.2307/2578600

Segal, B. (1974). Locus of control and drug and alcohol use in college students. *Journal of Alcohol and Drug Education, 19*(3), 1–5.

Segerstrom, S. C., & Miller, G. E. (2004). Psychological stress and the human immune system: A meta-analytic study of 30 years of inquiry. *Psychological Bulletin, 130,* 601–630.

Smith, W. L., & Zhang, P. (2009). Students' perceptions and experiences with key factors during the transition from high school to college. *College Student Journal, 43,* 643–657.

Steel, P. (2007). The nature of procrastination: A meta-analytic and theoretical review of quintessential self-regulatory failure. *Psychological Bulletin, 133,* 65–94. doi:10.1037/0033-2909.133.1.65

Stefanou, C., Hoffman, L., & Vielee, N. (2008). Note-taking in the college classroom as evidence of generative learning. *Learning Environments Research, 11,* 1–17.

Strickland, O. J., & Galimba, M. (2001). Managing time: The effects of personal goal setting on resource allocation strategy and task performance. *Journal of Psychology: Interdisciplinary and Applied, 135,* 357–367. doi:10.1080/00223980109603704

Taub, J. M., & Berger, R. J. (1973) Performance and mood following variations in the length and timing of sleep. *Psychophysiology, 10,* 559–570. doi:10.1111/j.1469-8986.1973.tb00805.x

US Department of Education, National Center for Education Statistics. (2013a). *Table 224: Total fall enrollment in degree-granting institutions, by attendance status, sex, and age: Selected years, 1970 through 2021.* Retrieved from http://nces.ed.gov/programs/digest/d12/tables/dt12_224.asp

US Department of Education, National Center for Education Statistics. (2013b). *Table 270: Percentage of first-year undergraduate students who took remedial education courses, by selected student and institution characteristics: 2003–04 and 2007–08.* Retrieved from https://nces.ed.gov/programs/digest/d12/tables/dt12_270.asp

US Department of Education, National Center for Education Statistics. (2013c). *Table 376: Percentage of first-time full-time bachelor's degree-seeking students at 4-year institutions who completed a bachelor's degree, by race/ethnicity, time* to completion, sex, and control of institution: Selected cohort entry years, 1996 through 2005. Retrieved from http://nces.ed.gov/programs/digest/d12/tables/dt12_376.asp

US Department of Education, National Center for Education Statistics. (2013d). *Table 378: Retention of first-time degree-seeking undergraduates at degree-granting institutions, by attendance status, level and control of institution, and percentage of applications accepted: 2006 to 2011.* Retrieved from http://nces.ed.gov/programs/digest/d12/tables/dt12_378.asp

US Department of Education, National Center for Education Statistics. (2013e). *Table 431: Employment to population ratios of persons 16 to 64 years old, by age group and educational attainment: Selected years, 1975 through 2012.* Retrieved from https://nces.ed.gov/programs/digest/d12/tables/dt12_431.asp

US Department of Education, National Center for Education Statistics. (2014a). *Table 302.10: Recent high school completers and their enrollment in 2-year and 4-year colleges, by sex: 1960 through 2012.* Retrieved from http://nces.ed.gov/programs/digest/d13/tables/dt13_302.10.asp

US Department of Education, National Center for Education Statistics. (2014b). *Table 303.10: Total fall enrollment in degree-granting postsecondary institutions, by attendance status, sex of student, and control of institution: Selected years, 1947 through 2012.* Retrieved from http://nces.ed.gov/programs/digest/d13/tables/dt13_303.10.asp

US Department of Education, National Center for Education Statistics. (2014c). *Table 502.30: Median annual earnings of full-time year-round workers 25 to 34 years old and full-time year-round workers as a percentage of the labor force, by sex, race/ethnicity, and educational attainment: Selected years, 1995 through 2012.* Retrieved from https://nces.ed.gov/programs/digest/d13/tables/dt13_502.30.asp

van Blerkom, M. L. (1992). Class attendance in undergraduate courses. *Journal of Psychology: Interdisciplinary and Applied, 126,* 487–494. doi:10.1080/00223980.1992.10543382

Wagner, P., Schober, B., & Spiel, C. (2008). Time investment and time management: An analysis of time students spend working at home for school. *Educational Research and Evaluation, 14,* 139–153.

Yang, Y. (2006). Reading strategies or comprehension monitoring strategies? *Reading Psychology, 27,* 313–343.

Zimmerman, B. J. (1998). Developing self-fulfilling cycles of academic regulation: An analysis of exemplary instructional models. In D. H. Schunk & B. J. Zimmerman (Eds.), *Self regulated learning: From teaching to self-reflective practice* (pp. 1–19). New York, NY: Guilford.

Zimmerman, B. J., Bandura, A., & Martinez-Pons, M. (1992). Self-motivation for academic attainment: The role of self-efficacy beliefs and personal goal setting. *American Educational Research Journal, 29,* 663–676.

Chapter Three
Succeeding in the Psychology Major
Adjustments, Common Difficulties, and Strategies

Introduction

What do you think will be the most challenging aspect of your academic work as a psychology major? If you have completed several psychology courses, you may be able to generate answers to this question. If you have had limited experience in the major, you may feel unsure of what challenges could lie ahead. Regardless of your progress toward completing your degree, being prepared to address challenges when they arise will go a long way toward ensuring your success as a psychology major.

Your fellow students have likely shaped your impression of what the academic experience as a psychology major will be like. In fact, many students utilize the input and advice of their peers as their primary source of information about their major. Often conversations among classmates focus on the topics of courses, assignments, and professors. Box 3.1 presents several examples of such advice as might be phrased by one psychology major speaking to another. This kind of information can be incredibly useful when it offers accurate insight or helpful strategies. But students sometimes share such information in ways that dramatize and exaggerate reality. In addition, what one student views as an obstacle or difficulty may be seen by another student as an essential part of their learning experience. Note how the validity and

Majoring in Psychology: Achieving Your Educational and Career Goals, Second Edition.
Jeffrey L. Helms and Daniel T. Rogers.
© 2015 John Wiley & Sons, Ltd. Published 2015 by John Wiley & Sons, Ltd.

Box 3.1 *Examples of Advice Shared Among Fellow Psychology Majors*

- "You only need to study your notes to make an A in that course. Don't buy the book."
- "Dr. Nguyen is the best professor – you'll learn so much in her classes."
- "You can't count that course toward your degree requirements, so taking it is a waste of time."
- "You should definitely join Psi Chi because it helps you get into grad school."
- "Attendance in that course is not necessary in order to get a good grade."
- "You should wait to take that course until your junior year so that you have more experience."
- "Papers in that course feel impossible. They have to be at least 30 pages long."
- "You learn almost nothing in Professor Hamilton's courses – avoid him at all cost."
- "Be sure to get internship or research experience – grad schools care most about those kinds of things."
- "Dr. Torres only lets students conduct research with her if they have a 4.0 GPA."

utility of the examples in Box 3.1, as well as their accuracy for any one particular student, cannot be determined without additional information.

Relying on the advice of peers or on trial and error is problematic. As an alternative, this chapter provides information that will enhance your chance for academic success in the psychology major. In Chapter 2, we provided an overview of common difficulties all students encounter in college as well as strategies and resources for overcoming them, but there are additional challenges that occur for students within the psychology discipline. These challenges often surprise students who initially think that psychology is based on common sense or intuition. Students who gravitate to psychology believing it to be a relatively easy route to a bachelor's degree are also often caught off guard by the academic rigor of the major. Understanding these discipline-specific challenges and how to overcome them is an essential step in your progression as a student of psychology. To assist you in this process, the first section of this chapter examines the nature of academic work within psychology. The second section identifies common difficulties that students experience in completing this academic work and examines ways to prepare for addressing these challenges. The final section describes strategies for succeeding in the psychology major, with emphasis given to utilizing available resources. You may find that you are already aware of some of this information, but remember that effectively implementing this knowledge into your academic work is the goal. Simply knowing about it is insufficient. Be sure to read the chapter carefully, regardless of your academic success and degree progress to date.

The Nature of Academic Work in the Psychology Major

Academic disciplines are unique not only in their areas of focus but also in the work required of students. Once students select a major and begin taking courses, they must adjust to the specific structure, content, and skills emphasized in that particular discipline. Some students select their major in part because they believe the academic work within that discipline is a good fit for their abilities. But even these students will need to modify their academic work to be in line with the unique demands and expectations of their chosen area of study.

Adjusting to the demands and expectations for academic work within the psychology major can lead to difficulties. But remember that it is these challenges, and your ability to successfully overcome them, that make your academic work worthy of a degree in the field. Students respond to these challenges in various ways. Some leave psychology for other majors and seek a degree path that offers less resistance. Others pursue psychology while trying to avoid these difficulties by selecting courses and professors that will minimize the academic demands placed on them. Many others put forth the effort required to adjust successfully to the academic demands and, in doing so, acquire the knowledge and skills that are the foundation of the psychology degree. It is our hope that you will aspire to be among this last group. In helping you meet this goal, this section of the chapter is designed to prepare you for potential difficulties by making you aware of the nature of academic work in psychology. Such preparation will allow you to respond to academic difficulties by working to overcome these challenges rather than letting them dictate your academic efforts.

What is Psychology?

Remember that psychology is the scientific study of human and nonhuman animal behavior and mental processes. The field also focuses on the implications and utilization of knowledge discovered through scientific study. In other words, psychologists both generate new research and apply research findings to real-world situations. Based on the content of the field and scope of its influence, psychology is considered to be one of the few hub sciences (Cacioppo, 2013). Its findings have clear, structured links to numerous related disciplines such as nursing, education, neurology, public health, psychiatry, statistics, gerontology, and neuroscience (Boyack, Klavans, & Börner, 2005). This status reflects psychology's historical breadth as well as its likely future as a highly interdisciplinary field well positioned to contribute to our understanding of the interface of biological, societal, and psychological factors on behavior. Undergraduate degree programs in psychology strive to cover this broad scope of the field by teaching students: (1) how psychological science is conducted, (2) what knowledge psychological science has yielded thus far, and (3) how such knowledge can be applied toward conducting additional research and assisting with behavioral and functional problems.

In pursuing its focus on behavior and mental processes, psychology as a field strives to adhere to rigorous ethical standards. These ethics permeate the research and applied work of psychologists. As a result, they play an important role in the education of students within the field. Published by the American Psychological Association (APA, 2010a), the current ethics code seeks to accomplish several goals: (1) create and maintain integrity in the profession, (2) create and maintain public trust in the profession, (3) guide the practice of psychologists, and (4) establish enforceable standards that are to be followed by psychologists (Fisher, 2003). The enforceable standards in the ethics code cover the diverse range of psychologists' professional behavior. Given the importance of the code to the identity of psychology as a discipline, it is readily available to the public through APA's website (http://www.apa.org/ethics/code/index.aspx).

What Students Expect to Learn

Research has indicated that students' expectations for their education in psychology are often incongruent with what psychology degree programs emphasize. McGovern and Hawks (1986) asked undergraduate students and faculty within a psychology program to rate the importance of 19 expectations for what a psychology major should learn. The faculty and students agreed on the relative importance of many of the expectations. For example, learning about lifespan development, career options, and scientific principles of behavior were all viewed as important, and learning about animal laboratory work was viewed as less important. The greatest disagreement between student and faculty views involved the two expectations students rated as the most important: gaining applied experience and learning how to help others.

Out of the 19 expectations considered, the faculty rated these expectations as the 14th and 16th most important, respectively. Nearly 20 years later, Gaither and Butler (2005) asked a similar question of undergraduate psychology majors regarding their expectations for learning. Consistent with previous research, students expected to learn the science of psychology and skills relevant to research activities. However, they had equivalent expectations to acquire applied skills that are used to address behavioral and functional problems in human populations. In fact, of the 10 skills that students ranked as most likely to be emphasized in the major, seven were clinical skills that are traditionally taught and honed at the graduate level (e.g., therapy and counseling techniques, interpretation of psychological tests). The research suggests that despite considerable overlap between psychology majors' expectations for their learning and the nature of undergraduate psychology programs, differences are pronounced in expectations for gaining applied experience and skills. Interestingly, student expectations for these learning goals have persisted over time despite the fact that faculty in psychology programs do not see these goals as a core part of the undergraduate psychology degree.

The Nature of the Academic Work

In order to fully appreciate the nature of academic work within the psychology major, it is best to examine the specific areas that the degree program emphasizes and values. Psychologists have given considerable attention to this topic in recent years. One key component of this work has been the development and revision of guidelines for the undergraduate major by the APA (2013). The guidelines were briefly described in the first chapter, but a more detailed description is presented in Box 3.2. Although undergraduate programs in psychology are free to determine their own learning objectives, the APA guidelines provide an excellent summary of the areas psychology majors can expect will be emphasized in their academic work.

Each undergraduate program in psychology selects requirements for the degree based on the learning objectives they have for their students. As a result, the specific courses and academic work within the major possess certain characteristics that reflect these objectives. Four such characteristics are prominent within most undergraduate psychology programs. First, the academic work emphasizes a broad base of knowledge. Undergraduate programs provide students with a breadth of knowledge and skills across the numerous subfields rather than a specific expertise in any one. Second, given the breadth of knowledge and skills taught, the academic work is rigorous. The amount of content students must master is substantial, and the topics are diverse. Third, learning is often demonstrated through writing. In fact, many

---

Box 3.2 *APA Guidelines for the Undergraduate Psychology Major*

1. *Knowledge Base in Psychology*: Develop knowledge and understanding of the core elements of the field, including major concepts, theories, trends, and empirical findings, as well as how such elements can be applied to understand and/or address behavior.

2. *Scientific Inquiry and Critical Thinking*: Develop and hone the abilities to solve problems and reason scientifically, specifically through research methods, including the use of psychological sources, study design, data collection, and statistical analysis.

3. *Ethical and Social Responsibility in a Diverse World*: Develop an understanding of and ability to apply ethical standards and socially responsible behavior in both personal and professional arenas.

4. *Communication*: Develop and hone written, oral, and interpersonal communication skills that allow for the clear, effective presentation of ideas.

5. *Professional Development*: Apply psychological content and skills toward academic and career goals. Develop and hone skills that promote academic and career success, including career planning, teamwork, project management, and self-regulation.

---

undergraduate psychology programs can be described as writing intensive. Students write frequently and do so in ways that promote their mastery of content and ability to synthesize disparate pieces of information. Given the prominence of writing within the major, the academic work also emphasizes the development of writing skills. Fourth, knowledge is acquired in an active manner that involves consistent use of critical thinking skills. Academic tasks frequently require students not only to master information but also to analyze and synthesize it. As a result, students are asked not only to learn specific content but also to carefully evaluate the validity of this information.

Common Challenges for Psychology Majors

Adjusting to the specific nature of academic work within psychology can be difficult. An important first step is squaring your expectations for what you will learn with the actual learning objectives of your program. It is also helpful to develop an awareness of some of the common challenges that psychology majors encounter. Whether these particular problems will occur for you during your pursuit of the degree is not certain, but being knowledgeable about these trouble spots and prepared to address them if they arise will offer good insurance against academic difficulties.

Understanding the Scientific Basis of the Field

Many students experience difficulties in understanding the scientific basis of psychology. Some struggle with this concept because they continue to view the discipline solely as a practice-oriented or applied field. For example, some claim that scientific knowledge and skills are irrelevant to their interests in mental health careers. These same students are often frustrated at the lack of applied skills being taught in their psychology courses. Other students struggle in a more direct manner with aspects of academic work that relate to the scientific basis of the field, such as understanding concepts in research methodology, experimental design, and statistical analyses. Many of these struggles occur among students who fail to see the relevance of the research process to their learning and future careers. Still others have difficulty with these aspects of their academic work because they lack the proficiency in math and writing skills that would allow them to approach new concepts and ideas with confidence.

Your success in adjusting to academic coursework that emphasizes the scientific basis of the field can be greatly facilitated by taking several steps. First, examine your expectations for the psychology major and compare them to the information shared in this chapter about the nature of academic work in the discipline. Understand that the focus of the field is the *scientific* study of behavior and mental processes and consider what types of learning objectives, courses, and academic work would be supportive of this focus. Second, recognize that the research and applied areas of the field are intertwined. Arbitrarily separating the two is misguided, and carrying out applied endeavors devoid of a grounding in scientific research is unlikely to occur in the discipline of psychology. In fact, if you find that you are only interested in conducting research with no consideration of its implications, or that you are only interested in conducting applied work with no consideration of its research basis, then you should consider pursuing a different major. Otherwise, you may face a long road of questioning the utility of the knowledge and skills you will acquire in your academic work in psychology.

Learning Independently

Another challenge students may confront is the degree of independent learning that must take place in the psychology major. In addition to the large amount of information that must be consumed, the academic work requires students to read sources of information and master difficult concepts. They must be able to grapple with complex ideas, language, methodologies, and analyses. Of course psychology majors are not expected to engage in these learning activities without the guidance and assistance of their professors. However, they must be able to tolerate the ambiguity and uncertainty that comes with this degree of independent learning. Perhaps the greatest consequence for students who struggle with this aspect of the academic work is falling behind. This typically occurs when students procrastinate on academic work that they know will be demanding in some way. Unfortunately, students who fall behind because they view the academic work as too difficult are then faced with the task of completing larger portions of this same work in order to recover.

Incorporating several strategies into your approach to academic work in the psychology major will improve your chances of success in adjusting to the type of learning that is required. First, examine your expectations for the level of independent learning you will need to do in your coursework. Work to combat any expectation you have for passive learning in which you merely attend lectures and casually read the assigned materials. Instead, ready yourself to be an active, engaged consumer of information, both within and outside of class. Second, ask for help when you need it. Although struggling with difficult concepts and ideas is an important part of independent learning in the major, recognize that there are limits to how much of a struggle this should be. Be willing to seek out the assistance of your professors and peers as part of your active learning. However, be sure that when you look for assistance that you have already put forth a concerted effort. Using others' help when you do not yet have a foundation for understanding the material is unlikely to contribute to your learning. Third, make it a top priority to stay up to date with your academic work. This is of course far easier said than done, but dedicating yourself to staying current with course readings and assignments will go a long way towards sustaining your motivation for independent learning, thereby bolstering your performance. When you do fall behind, commit yourself to recovering as soon as possible. For additional tips for managing the workload, refer to the section on academic strategies in Chapter 2.

Writing and APA Style

Much has been discussed about the poor state of students' writing abilities (e.g., Bartlett, 2003). Research from the National Center for Education Statistics (Snyder & Dillow, 2012) indicates that only 27% of high school seniors in the US are proficient writers, and 21% lack even basic writing ability. Such observations have contributed to calls for changes in how writing is taught (e.g., The National Commission on Writing in America's Schools and Colleges, 2003). Psychology students are not immune to these difficulties. In fact, research suggests that psychology students acknowledge that they typically lack the skills necessary to write proficiently in their academic coursework (McGovern & Hogshead, 1990). Many have come to college with inadequate writing skills, and others struggle to adjust to the specific writing expectations of their psychology courses.

Your success in adjusting to the writing demands of academic work in psychology can be enhanced by following several steps. First, strive to understand the role of writing in the learning objectives for psychology majors. One of the five APA learning objectives, that of Communication, focuses on writing skills, and all of the other goals have components related to or are often assessed via student writing. Writing is a key skill because both the research and applied endeavors in the field depend heavily on psychologists' ability to communicate effectively with each other and the individuals with whom they interact. As a result, undergraduate programs in psychology strive to help students become strong writers who appreciate the role of good writing in their academic and professional lives.

A second step to ensuring success in writing is to adopt an organized approach. Often students are intimidated by the scope of a writing assignment. The task of producing a substantial piece of writing that integrates outside sources of information, concepts, and theories in a clear, coherent manner can overwhelm them to the point that they avoid tackling the project. By not investing sufficient time and circumventing key steps in the process, some students consistently perform poorly on writing assignments. The most important strategy for countering this pitfall is to create a plan for completing the assignment and following it. Box 3.3 provides a sample guideline for writing literature review papers, a common undergraduate writing task, in an organized fashion.

A third step in adjusting to the writing demands of academic work in psychology is to understand the purpose and function of APA Style. Within a few minutes' time you can probably find several fellow psychology majors who will assert that writing papers in APA Style is the bane of their existence. But such frustration is largely born out of negative previous experience with using APA Style and a lack of appreciation for its real purpose. APA Style is merely an editorial style, or a set of rules and guidelines for preparing written text. The guidelines for this particular style are contained in the *Publication Manual of the American Psychological Association* (APA, 2010b), often referred to as the APA Manual. Other editorial styles exist, such as the Modern Language Association (MLA) and Chicago Manual of Style (CMOS), and chances are you have been exposed to one or more of

Box 3.3 *Steps for Organizing Literature Review Papers*

1. Select a general topic area consistent with your assignment.
2. Read information (e.g., empirical and review articles, textbook chapters) about this topic area.
3. Pinpoint your specific topic.
4. Identify and locate potential sources for your paper.
5. Read these sources for understanding their key ideas, taking notes in your own words.
6. Organize your thoughts on the topic and your notes from the sources according to content.
7. Outline the paper, adding as much detail from your notes as possible.
8. Pull additional information from sources as needed, finding additional sources when necessary.
9. Compose a draft of the paper.
10. Revise the draft in a repeated fashion.

them prior to having to use APA Style. Transitioning from one writing style to another can create some of the same difficulties as trying to learn a new language, but keep in mind why the different styles are needed and why learning to use them is important. Having everyone within a discipline adhere to the same rules for formatting, organization, expression, and citations facilitates communication and understanding. As a student of psychology, it is key that you learn this language because you will need to both read and produce writing that adheres to this editorial style.

Conducting Literature Searches

One aspect of the writing process that many students find challenging is searching the existing psychological literature for sources of information. Writing good papers in large part depends upon your ability to identify and locate excellent sources of information. Students who struggle to do this will perform poorly on writing assignments. The difficulties students experience in conducting literature searches often take one of several forms. At the beginning of their college careers, many students are unfamiliar with how to go about locating sources. Once they learn this process, most will then struggle to sort through the vast quantity of sources that are available. Even students who have learned how to focus their searches have difficulty deciding what sources are relevant to their paper.

Box 3.4   *Helpful Databases for Literature Searches in Psychology*

PsycINFO
Contains citations for and summaries of journal articles, books, book chapters, dissertations, and technical reports from the field of psychology as well as from other disciplines when relevant to psychological topics. The scope of the database is broad, including sources dating to the 1600s and numerous international journals.

PsycARTICLES
Contains full-text articles, as well as citations and summaries, from over 100 journals published by the APA. Many journals are provided starting with their first volume.

Psychology and Behavioral Sciences Collection
Contains full-text articles, as well as citations and summaries, from over 500 journals. The scope of the database goes beyond the field of psychology to include sources from psychiatry and anthropology, as well as sources pertaining to the topic of research methods.

As seen in Box 3.3, several steps precede the point at which you begin to identify and locate potential sources of information for your paper. Completing these steps is essential if your literature search is to be a success. Incorporating several other strategies into your approach will improve your chances of success. First, become familiar with the tools to use when attempting to locate sources. The best tools available are online databases. Thousands of these databases exist, and most are organized by the content and types of sources they contain. Entries, or listings of individual sources, in these databases contain information about the authors, title of the work, its source, and often a brief summary of the information contained within. There are three such databases that are particularly helpful to psychology students, and each is briefly described in Box 3.4. The libraries of most colleges and universities provide students with access to these and other databases for scholarly sources. In addition, many of these libraries set up the databases in such a way to facilitate your ability to acquire the actual source while searching. It may be immediately available in electronic form, or there may be links provided to help you locate the source at your institution or request it from other institutions.

Like all software, there is a learning curve associated with becoming proficient at using these databases to find what you need. Practice over time will greatly enhance your skill and the likelihood that you will come to see these databases as valuable tools rather than obstacles. As is the case with other online search engines, databases of scholarly works are driven by the type of search terms you enter. Search terms are often key words that pertain to your topic, and databases can be searched for all instances where these terms appear in any part of the source. However given the scope of most databases, such searches frequently return thousands of sources, which means the vast majority of these will be irrelevant to your paper and not useful. As a result, search terms must be focused more narrowly by combining multiple terms and/or searching for more specific information such as an author's name, part of the title, the name of the source, or the date of publication. The key to executing good and productive searches is your willingness to experiment with your search terms and build upon your sources by conducting multiple, evolving searches.

A third step in conducting good literature searches involves understanding how to use the results of your searches. Even well constructed searches often identify 100 or more sources that have relevance to your paper topic. Navigating these results can be overwhelming, but with practice students can learn to do this quite well. Results of searches are best examined in chronological order, starting with the most recently published (many databases automatically return results in this order). Start by reading the titles of sources and identifying those that seem relevant to your topic. Then examine the abstracts of these articles and again determine which are most relevant. Scan the text of those articles whose abstracts seem most promising, and identify the articles that provide the most useful information. Those identified articles will then need to be read carefully as you work to identify important concepts and ideas you wish to incorporate into your writing. Keep in mind that once you identify an article as a good fit for your topic, the sources used within this article may also prove to be helpful for your paper. But you need to obtain those sources and read them for yourself to determine their relevancy.

Strategies for Success

Although success in the psychology major is in large part determined by your ability to adjust to the nature of the academic work and deal with the challenges that arise, there are several broader steps you can take to support your progression toward earning the degree. This final section of the chapter describes three such general strategies for succeeding in the major.

Planning Courses and Degree Progression

One of the most helpful strategies you can undertake to ensure your success in and progression through the psychology major is to plan carefully how you will go about completing your degree requirements. Carefully planning the courses you will take has several advantages. It will provide you with a clear and accurate perception of exactly what you must do in order to graduate. Having this plan will also help keep you on track toward earning your degree. In addition, making the plan will assist you in selecting courses that will prepare you for the next step in your career.

The best way to go about planning your courses and degree progression is to first obtain the exact requirements for earning the psychology degree at your institution. These are typically accessible in the undergraduate catalog for your institution as well as through departmental materials. Many psychology departments provide students with a checklist of the degree requirements, and some institutions provide students with access to electronic records that document your progress in completing these requirements. The second step involves planning your entire college coursework, beginning with your first semester of college and going all the way through to the semester in which you will graduate. Your plan should focus on satisfying the degree requirements while adhering to all restrictions, such as prerequisites or sequencing of courses. You should also plan courses that meet your interests and prepare you for your plans after graduation. But remember that the plan will only be useful if it is realistic. Take into account both your previous academic history and other commitments that will compete for your time. For example, if you have struggled to complete successfully four or five courses per semester due to academic difficulties, family obligations, or work demands, then your planned coursework should accurately reflect what you are capable of completing in a term. Lastly, keep the plan and update it at the end of each semester. Do not be alarmed when you need to deviate from it due to a course not being offered or schedule conflicts. In fact, having the plan will greatly facilitate your ability to deal with such changes in ways that do not delay earning your degree.

Planning Relevant Experiences

After earning their degree, or in the late stages of their college careers, students majoring in psychology frequently indicate that they wish they had gained experience outside of the classroom. This typically occurs as students confront the fact that the employment or graduate school paths they are about to pursue require this type of experience or at least give priority to

Box 3.5 *Common Elements of Experience Outside the Classroom*

- Intern/Practicum Student:
  - ○ Provide general assistance in the operations of the organization
  - ○ Interact with customers/clients/patients of the organization
  - ○ Write reports summarizing organizational activities and/or gathered data
  - ○ Observe the work of professionals employed by the organization
  - ○ Complete training relevant to the operations of the organization
- Teaching Assistant:
  - ○ Administer/monitor exams
  - ○ Produce course materials (e.g., handouts, lectures, review sheets, quizzes, exams)
  - ○ Conduct study or review sessions
  - ○ Grade course assignments and record grades
  - ○ Assist the professor with class meetings, activities, demonstrations, and labs
- Research Assistant:
  - ○ Collect, score, code, enter, and analyze data
  - ○ Conduct literature searches and obtain source materials relevant to research studies
  - ○ Contribute to the development and design of new research studies
  - ○ Prepare materials for and participate in the presentation/publication of research results
  - ○ Maintain lab space and equipment
  - ○ Complete administrative tasks (e.g., make calls, process mail, schedule appointments)

individuals who have it. The three types of these experiences commonly available to students include internships and practica, research assistantships, and teaching assistantships. Box 3.5 provides a description of common activities within each of these experiences.

In addition to opening doors in your career pursuits, gaining experience outside of the classroom provides several benefits. It frequently provides students with a new perspective on their career aspirations. Some students feel that these experiences solidify their goals while others walk away having changed their minds about their career path. In addition, students who gain these types of experiences develop knowledge and skills that typically cannot be acquired through traditional coursework. Often these are among the skills that most appeal to employers and graduate schools. Finally, these experiences have a tendency to contribute to students developing a more mature and seasoned perspective on their academic and career goals. This resonates with employers and graduate schools that seek individuals with clear understandings of themselves and their goals.

Students in most psychology programs are informed of the benefits of gaining experience outside the classroom by their professors and advisors. Yet once students become engaged in their academic work, few of them seek it out and commit time to it. This is in part understandable because academic work likely has more immediate consequences (e.g., grades, graduation). But the consequences of not obtaining these relevant experiences can be even more significant in terms of their impact on your career. In addition, gaining experiences outside of the classroom can be a difficult and intimidating process for students because these opportunities must be actively sought out and pursued. This stands in stark contrast to the passive nature of selecting and registering for courses.

There are several things to keep in mind if you are seriously considering seeking experience outside of the classroom. First, recognize that there are limited opportunities to gain this experience and that you may be competing with peers for these positions. As such, your academic abilities, previous experience, and motivation will weigh heavily in determining whether or not you are selected. Second, understand that although these positions are occasionally advertised, students more often learn about them by actively seeking them out. Talk to peers who are involved in these activities and faculty members who work with research and teaching assistants to get a feel for what opportunities are available. Talk with organizations that offer internships or that you are interested in working with about the possibility for positions in the future. However, do your homework beforehand. Start your conversations with faculty members or potential internship sites by doing the following: (1) introduce yourself, (2) describe your interests in obtaining more experience, (3) demonstrate your knowledge of their work, and (4) inquire about potential opportunities.

Utilizing Available Resources

Psychology majors sometimes struggle needlessly to overcome challenges in their academic work. There are several valuable resources readily available in almost every psychology department that can be of assistance. This section highlights four such resources in an effort to encourage you to take greater advantage of them.

Perhaps the greatest resources students have at their disposal are the professors of their courses. Theses faculty members are certainly knowledgeable about the course material and assignments, but they also possess expertise on broader issues relevant to student success such as study skills, institutional resources, and degree requirements. These professors' varied teaching styles and approaches to courses can also be used to your advantage. Although striving to take courses from professors who you enjoy listening to and learning from is one component of this, you should also be taking courses from professors who can help you address weaknesses in your academic skills. For example, if writing, statistics, and/or public speaking are areas of weakness for you, talk to peers about which professors do an excellent job of teaching and guiding students in these areas. Resist the temptation to simply take courses from professors who do not emphasize these skills.

Besides the professors of your current courses, you should also view the other faculty members in your department as potential resources. Some of the faculty may have backgrounds in subfields that match your interests, or perhaps they attended graduate school at an institution that is of interest to you. In these cases, the faculty member can provide excellent information that you can use to guide your goal formation and decision making. Faculty members also may offer teaching and research assistantships that would allow you to gain the outside of class experience that employers and graduate schools value. Given the important role a faculty member in your department might play in your academic and career progression, it is vital that you keep your interactions with all faculty professional and focused.

Other important resources available to psychology majors are the various activities, programs, and organizations sponsored by psychology departments. Many academic departments regularly invite guest speakers to present on their research or other topics of interest. These events are typically open to anyone interested in attending. Departments also sponsor student groups such as Psi Chi, the International Honor Society in Psychology, or Active Minds, a mental health awareness and advocacy group. These organizations provide students with opportunities to work with their peers on various projects related to the discipline while gaining valuable experience in leadership and group work. Departments often also host research symposiums or conferences that feature student research projects. These events provide great opportunities for students engaged in research to showcase their work and for students considering such activities to learn about the opportunities that exist. If these types of activities or programs are not readily available at your institution, investigate whether they may be available to you at neighboring institutions.

Finally, the psychology department office likely provides several important resources that are helpful to students. The administrative staff is usually knowledgeable about the major, degree requirements, institutional policies and regulations, and resources available to students. The staff may also be your access point if you need to arrange a meeting with a faculty member, advisor, or the department chair. The office typically has printed materials and forms relevant to the major. Information is also frequently posted concerning graduate programs, internships, assistantships, and job opportunities. Many departmental offices maintain a small library of books that are useful for majors, including common textbooks, study guides, and career and graduate school preparation guides. Keep in mind that most departments maintain websites that provide some or all of this information in an online format, including faculty biographies and contact information, syllabi from courses, and announcements about events as well as opportunities for outside experiences (e.g., employment, internships).

Conclusion

The psychology major can be a challenging path to earning your bachelor's degree. Academic difficulties and obstacles will certainly arise at points along the way. Preparing to overcome these begins with developing an awareness of the issues involved. Understand the nature of the academic work in psychology and how this unique perspective and way of thinking will influence what you will be asked to learn as a student. Recognize that there are some common challenges that students encounter and that there are helpful strategies in minimizing the impact of these on your performance. Finally, learn that there are valuable resources at your disposal to help ensure your success in completing the major. Taking these steps will go a long way toward ensuring that psychology moves from simply being your major to being your degree.

Suggested Exercises

1. Familiarize yourself with the psychology faculty at your institution. Begin by studying their biographies, which are often available on the department website. If faculty members have their own websites or resources for learning more about their professional work, read this information as well. Begin to identify the faculty members who share your interests in terms of careers, research, and professional activities. Strive to get to know these people over time by taking multiple courses with them, seeking them out as advisors, and initiating conversations about their work.

2. Practice conducting a literature search and writing APA-style citations by taking the following steps:
    a. Select a topic of interest to you (e.g., memory problems with chronic alcohol use, infant language development, sleep disorders, treatment of autism spectrum disorder, stereotype formation), and choose two relevant terms to

use in conducting a search using PsycINFO. For example, if your topic was infant language development, you might conduct a search using the terms "language development" and "infants." Save the first 10 results.

b. Conduct a second search by altering the search terms. Using the above example, you might change "language development" to "language acquisition," or you might change "infants" to "infancy." Examine the first 10 results and compare them to the results you saved from the first step. Pay attention to the types of sources you find with each search and determine which are more relevant to your topic.

c. Refine your search terms further in order to generate results that are in line with your topic. Then choose five sources from the results. Select a mixture of articles, books, and book chapters. Write an APA-style reference entry for each of these sources using the APA *Publication Manual*. Note that many database browsers, such as EBSCOhost, will produce citations in APA Style that can either be copied or downloaded. However, these citations contain errors that must be corrected. Ask an experienced peer, writing consultant, or professor to look at your references and give you feedback.

Suggested Readings

Landrum, R. E. (2002). Maximizing undergraduate opportunities: The value of research and other experiences. *Eye on Psi Chi, 6*(2), 15–18.

Landrum, R. E., & Davis, S. F. (2014). *The psychology major: Career options and strategies for success* (5th ed.). Boston, MA: Pearson.

Silvia, P. J., Delaney, P. F., & Marcovitch, S. (2009). *What psychology majors could (and should) be doing: An informal guide to research experience and professional skills*. Washington, DC: American Psychological Association.

Resources

- APA Education Directorate – Pre-College and Undergraduate Resources: http://www.apa.org/ed/precollege/index.aspx
- Psi Chi, The International Honor Society in Psychology: www.psichi.org
- Active Minds: www.activeminds.org

References

American Psychological Association. (2010a). *Ethical principles of psychologists and code of conduct*. Washington, DC: Author. Retrieved from www.apa.org/ethics/code/index.aspx

American Psychological Association. (2010b). *Publication manual of the American Psychological Association* (6th ed.). Washington, DC: Author.

American Psychological Association. (2013). *APA guidelines for the undergraduate psychology major: Version 2.0*. Washington, DC: Author. Retrieved from http://www.apa.org/ed/precollege/about/psymajor-guidelines.pdf

Bartlett, T. (2003, January 3). Why Johnny can't write, even though he went to Princeton. *Chronicle on Higher Education*. Retrieved from http://chronicle.com/article/Why-Johnny-Can-t-Write-Even/35918

Boyack, K. W., Klavans, R., & Börner, K. (2005). Mapping the backbone of science. *Scientometrics, 64*, 351–374. doi:10.1007/s11192-005-0255-6

Cacioppo, J. T. (2013). Psychological science in the 21st century. *Teaching of Psychology, 40*, 304–309. doi:10.1177/0098628313501041

Fisher, C. B. (2003). *Decoding the ethics code: A practical guide for psychologists.* Thousand Oaks, CA: Sage Publications.

Gaither, G. A., & Butler, D. L. (2005). Skill development in the psychology major: What do undergraduate students expect? *College Student Journal, 39*, 540–552.

McGovern, T. V., & Hawks, B. K. (1986). The varieties of undergraduate experience. *Teaching of Psychology, 13*, 174–181.

McGovern, T. V., & Hogshead, D. L. (1990). Learning about writing, thinking about teaching. *Teaching of Psychology, 17*, 5–10.

National Commission on Writing in America's Schools and Colleges. (2003). *The neglected "R": The need for a writing revolution.* Retrieved from http://www.collegeboard.com/prod_downloads/writingcom/neglectedr.pdf

Snyder, T. D., & Dillow, S. A. (2012). *Digest of education statistics: 2012* (NCES 2014-015). Washington, DC: National Center for Education Statistics, Institute of Education Sciences, US Department of Education. Retrieved from http://nces.ed.gov/pubsearch/pubsinfo.asp?pubid=2014015

Chapter Four
Assessing and Developing Career Goals

Introduction

"What do you want to be when you grow up?" You likely remember being asked and providing an answer to this question as a child. Perhaps as an adult you have even found yourself posing the question to children. We find children's answers amusing given that they are more likely to offer plans for being a superhero or princess than a regional manager. But our amusement reveals as much about our own thinking in regard to careers as it does the child's. Children's career aspirations often clash with our adult sensibilities about how the world works, particularly in terms of the pressures that create a need to work and constrain our choice of careers.

As adults, our society emphasizes careers as a defining element of who we are. Getting to know another person routinely involves sharing information about each other's occupations. Knowing the answer to the question "What do you do?" helps us have a clearer sense of who the person is. But adults often do not answer questions about their careers as freely as they did as children. The question posed to children recognizes an inherent flexibility and open-ended quality to the child's career development. It is future oriented. Children respond by thinking about what it is that they would like to do, considering "jobs" they are familiar with, and then selecting one that seems like a good idea. In contrast, the question we pose to adults about their career seeks information about their present status. It is no surprise

Majoring in Psychology: Achieving Your Educational and Career Goals, Second Edition.
Jeffrey L. Helms and Daniel T. Rogers.
© 2015 John Wiley & Sons, Ltd. Published 2015 by John Wiley & Sons, Ltd.

then that adults respond by describing their current occupation, the organization they work for, and the nature of their work. Our assumption in these exchanges is that adults' careers are already determined and to some degree stable.

How does the transition occur from a child with wide open career possibilities to an adult with an established career? Most adults began with educational goals in mind (e.g., "I have to finish high school" or "I want to get a college degree"). While completing their education, or sometimes shortly thereafter, they consider their career goals. Once they take on a particular career, many later consider their life goals, often in response to feeling that their career is not helping them achieve these goals (e.g., "I wish I had more financial security" or "If only I had more free time to spend with my family"). This pattern of goal setting is common. Many individuals realize later in life that their education is restricting their pursuit of career goals, and their career is restricting their pursuit of life goals. Real-world circumstances lead many to pursue an education before carefully considering their career options. These same forces cause some to pursue a career before carefully considering their life goals. But because the order in which adults consider and develop these goals can have significant consequences, we would like to encourage you to approach your goals differently.

Career goals occupy a position of prominence throughout this text and are emphasized in this chapter. In fact, the chapter begins with a discussion of the nature and value of career goals. However, we also want to stress that career goals have little meaning or value in isolation from education and life goals. As a result, our approach to goal setting in this chapter asks you to consider your life goals first, career goals second, and educational goals third. For each area, you will be invited to complete a brief self-assessment exercise and then to respond to specific questions about your goals. We believe that the order in which these three areas are explored is key. Assessing your life interests and abilities facilitates forming life goals. Your life goals will then inform the assessment of your career interests and abilities, and in turn the formation of career goals. And finally, your career goals will inform the assessment of your educational interests and abilities, as well as the development of educational goals. You may have already established some educational and career goals without thinking in depth about life goals – this is fine. The approach we are suggesting is not strictly linear. We strongly encourage you to revisit goals in any of these areas as you have new experiences and your perspective changes. Begin to think about the development of these goals as an ongoing, lifelong process that can support both your career success and your overall well-being.

The Nature and Value of Career Goal Setting

Career Development Theories

Psychologists, along with researchers in several other fields, have been interested in the topic of career development for some time because it involves aspects of human development, functioning, and overall well-being. Their work has fostered the creation of multiple theories on the process of career development. Other researchers have used these theories to create methods of assessing career interests and techniques for guiding individuals in developing and pursuing career goals. Each theory views the process of career development differently by emphasizing diverse factors that influence an individual's selection of a career.

Career development theories can be placed into several categories. Trait or factor theories (e.g., Parsons, 1909) emphasize the role that an individual's personal characteristics play in their career choices. Individuals are thought to possess unique combinations of traits (e.g., abilities, values, personality, achievements, etc.), and careers are thought to require a unique set of factors for an individual to be successful. The match or mismatch between the two is believed to play a critical role in career development. Type theories (e.g., Holland, 1959) suggest that individuals adopt a few overall dispositions or tendencies in their life that make them drawn to careers that satisfy their unique needs. Individuals thus seek out occupations that allow them to express their skills in order to derive satisfaction. Developmental theories (e.g., Super, 1963) stress that career preferences develop and mature over time and are therefore subject to change. As individuals' self-concepts change with experience, their preference for and satisfaction with different types of careers also evolve.

Trait, type, and developmental theories play an important role in career development research and career counseling. However, another theory has garnered much attention of late. Social cognitive career theory applies several key concepts from psychology to account for how individuals typi-cally form and act on their career interests (Lent, Brown, & Hackett, 2002). Importantly, the theory accounts for multiple factors that influence career goals and actions, and it describes individuals as constantly adapting as these factors change (Lent, 2013). Box 4.1 provides a visual representation of the paths of influence between the major factors in social cognitive career theory. The notion that career interests lead to goals and goals lead to actions may seem intuitive. Yet, the model highlights two important sets of factors in this process that are often overlooked. Interests, goals, and actions are informed by several important factors, including our unique situation/

Box 4.1 *Social Cognitive Career Theory Model*

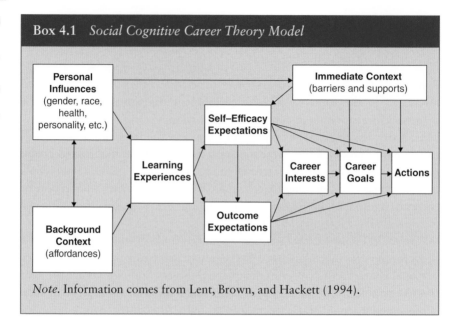

Personal Influences (gender, race, health, personality, etc.)

Immediate Context (barriers and supports)

Self–Efficacy Expectations

Learning Experiences

Career Interests

Career Goals

Actions

Background Context (affordances)

Outcome Expectations

Note. Information comes from Lent, Brown, and Hackett (1994).

context, our expectations for outcomes, and our beliefs in our own capabilities (i.e., self-efficacy). And the driving factor in shaping our expectations for outcomes and self-efficacy is our learning experiences. What these pieces of the model highlight is the significance of learning experiences in shaping how we assess our abilities and likelihood of success, which in turn help drive our interests, goals, and actual careers.

Each theoretical approach to career development recognizes that career goals are not selected in an arbitrary manner. Instead, these goals are dependent on many aspects of the individual and their unique set of experiences. Keep in mind that your personality, life circumstances, developmental stage, learning experiences, and beliefs about yourself all play a role in shaping your career goals.

Approaches to Career Goal Setting

Despite the rich theoretical diversity on the subject of career development, and the fact that these theories stress that careers are multi-determined, information presented to the general public about this topic is often overly focused on the career itself. Many of the books, websites, and questionnaires available on career goal setting focus exclusively on helping you identify a handful of careers that are supposedly the best fit for you. You might be wondering, "Isn't that the purpose of developing career goals?"

The answer is, in part, yes. Identifying careers that fit some aspects of you as a person is a worthy outcome. But those of you who have tried using these resources likely have had a more mixed reaction. Individuals often report that the process only confirms the career ideas they already had. Others report that the results are so at odds with their career ideas that they have no intention of further exploring the suggested careers. Still others might learn about career options they had not previously considered, and they then must explore these further. In all of these situations, individuals who engage in a process that only generates career options typically do not walk away from this experience with clear, well-developed career goals. As an alternative, an approach placing the selection of specific careers within a broader framework that establishes a variety of interrelated goals is more meaningful and provides the individual with greater control over the process.

Setting Career Goals as an Active Process

Assuming greater control over your career goals begins with forming them in as active a manner as possible. Too often individuals find themselves in particular careers as a result of circumstances rather than purposeful planning and choice. This has many potential consequences. First, individuals can feel locked into a career or career field when they lack the necessary skills to transition elsewhere or when they cannot afford to give up their current position to pursue additional goals. Second, individuals can dislike their careers when they feel that their jobs are forced upon them out of necessity and provide little to no satisfaction. If there are significant consequences, then why do individuals fail to actively develop career goals? Many take on careers out of financial necessity only to later find that this situation constrains their goal setting. Others find the active development of career goals to be an overwhelming endeavor. Many believe they do not have sufficient information about themselves and the job market to make such an important decision. They fear they will choose the wrong career path and come to regret the decision later.

Concerns over making an error in developing your career goals can be reduced if you begin to view the development of goals as an ongoing, evolving process. This approach is particularly important if you want to weather the sometimes dramatic changes that can occur in the job market. Table 4.1 presents data on several careers that have changed significantly over the past decade in terms of the workforce engaged in those types of activities. Numerous factors can bring about such changes. For example, advances in pharmaceuticals and a greater reliance on pharmacological interventions have led to an increased demand for the services of pharmacists and pharmacy technicians. Even greater reliance on technology in the workplace and as a means of communication with clients and customers has helped to continue the growth of computer support and public relations specialists. And increasing demands for assistance with personal, child, elder, and health care have led to increases in these related careers. But gains in technology have also led to a decrease in demand for other careers as products become more reliable,

Table 4.1 Change in Percentage of Workforce Employed in Careers between 2003 and 2013

Specific Careers	Change in Percentage of Workforce
Petroleum engineers	+162.7%
Nonfarm animal caretakers	+75.2%
Pharmacy technicians	+60.3%
Compliance officers	+47.9%
Computer support specialists	+47.0%
Food preparation and service, including fast food	+45.8%
Home health aides	+39.9%
Public relations specialists	+29.0%
Childcare workers	+20.5%
Registered nurses	+16.7%
Lawyers	+15.7%
Flight attendants	–6.7%
Editors	–7.3%
Automotive service technician and mechanics	–12.3%
Computer programmers	–22.5%
Carpenters	–33.6%
Travel agents	–34.7%
Telemarketers	–42.7%
Sewing machine operators	–43.0%
Switchboard and answering service operators	–43.8%
Word processors and typists	–49.2%
Advertising and promotions managers	–55.7%

Note. Percentage change calculated using data from "November 2003 National Occupational Employment and Wage Estimates," by United States Department of Labor, Bureau of Labor Statistics, 2005, retrieved from http://www.bls.gov/oes/2003/november/oes_nat.htm, and "May 2013 National Occupational Employment and Wage Estimates," by United States Department of Labor, Bureau of Labor Statistics, 2004, retrieved from http://www.bls.gov/oes/current/oes_nat.htm

production becomes more automated, and services and manufacturing can be accomplished at a greater distance often at a cheaper cost.

Changes in the demand for certain careers are sometimes gradual and easily forecasted. But other shifts are dramatic and unforeseen, such as those in response to economic downturns. This has led some to argue that individuals entering the workforce should anticipate changing careers, not simply jobs, multiple times in their working life (Bolles, 2013). This requires being prepared to change career goals as forces dictate without knowing exactly how and when these changes will occur. Individuals whose career goals are derived solely from their career aspirations are most at risk of being unable to shift with the changing occupational environment. In contrast, those who develop career goals through a careful self-assessment in which career goals are rooted in a larger understanding of self and interrelated goals will have less difficulty modifying their plans as needed.

The Value of Career Goals

In addition to providing grounding in the face of shifting and uncertain forces in the career environment, having well developed career goals provides other, less obvious benefits to individuals. For example, adolescents who have clear goals related to their abilities and future careers have better school attendance and fewer disciplinary issues (Oyserman, Terry, & Bybee, 2002). They also possess higher levels of self-esteem, even when self-esteem is rated by an outside observer (Chiu, 1990). College students who have developed specific career goals are more likely to act in ways that support their persistence in their education (Hull-Blanks et al., 2005). Among employees, those who set career and work goals experience better adjustment to their current employment situations (Kubota, 1982).

Establishing specific career goals may serve not only to help achieve those goals but also to foster one's overall health and well-being. For example, employees' satisfaction with their careers is correlated with both having obtainable goals and being committed to those goals (Roberson, 1990). Employees who form clear goals and have support for them have more positive attitudes about their work, and employees who are dissatisfied with their work are more likely to experience stress, conflict, and failure related to their career goals (Lee, Bobko, Earley, & Locke, 1991). The relationship between career goals and job satisfaction is important because a clear relationship exists between job satisfaction and physical and mental health (e.g., Cass, Siu, Faragher, & Cooper, 2003; Faragher, Cass, & Cooper, 2005).

Assessing Self and Developing Life Goals

Life goals are aspirations you have for yourself across your lifespan. They can be things you want to do or things that you want to make an integral part of your life. Examples include experiences you want to have, things you want to accomplish, or the type of person you want to be. If these goals sound broad and sweeping, that is by design. General goals can be channeled into a variety of specific activities as situations and resources allow. Importantly, individuals who form life goals report higher levels of subjective well-being (Headey, 2008). Expressing life goals in written or verbal form is also correlated with physical health and well-being (Harrist, Carlozzi, McGovern, & Harrist, 2007; King, 2001).

Formulating life goals may seem like a daunting task, especially when you might be trying to select a major, picking courses to take next semester, and working to fund your education and living expenses. The task should feel less overwhelming if you keep in mind that life goals often change, and they can become more specific over time. Keep in mind that generating life goals, even if they are fairly general at this time, will promote the formation of meaningful career goals.

Developing meaningful life goals is dependent upon having sound knowledge about one's self. Therefore, the first step should be a careful assessment of your various life interests and preferences. Many forms of self-assessment can lead to this end result. Examples include self-reflection, journaling, meditation, psychotherapy, and counseling. Certainly these methods cannot be duplicated within this chapter, but one component that they have in common – taking stock of one's life priorities – can be explored. Box 4.2 presents several common components of individuals' lives and asks you to rank them in order of their importance to you. This task is not intended to serve as a comprehensive self-assessment of life interests and preferences. Instead, it is designed to stimulate your thinking about these issues in a way that will assist in formulating life goals. The life components listed are general in nature and likely mean different things to different people. This allows you to think and respond to them in ways that best capture your unique approach to life. As with all of the assessment and goal setting tasks presented in this chapter, you should not feel constrained by the specific elements provided. Feel free to add your own components in order to best capture important areas of your life that are not represented.

There are also many ways to go about formulating life goals. We believe an excellent place to start is by reflecting on your personal interests, preferences, ideas, aspirations, etc., then considering how these translate into specific goals. Box 4.3 provides several questions, grouped into six domains, which are designed to stimulate your thinking about specific life goals. This

Box 4.2 *Self-Assessment of Life Interests and Preferences*

Instructions: Read the following list carefully and decide how important each element is in your life. Assign each element a ranking using the numbers 1 to 20, with "1" indicating the most important element in your life and "20" indicating the least important.

Appearance / image   _____
Autonomy / choice / control   _____
Contributing to or serving others / better society   _____
Creativity   _____
Faith / spirituality   _____
Family   _____
Health / wellness   _____
Interests / hobbies / pursuits   _____
Joy / fulfillment / inner peace   _____
Knowledge / expertise / wisdom   _____
Meaningful relationships / community   _____
Minimization of pain, disappointment, loss   _____
Money / financial status   _____
Power / influence / leadership   _____
Productivity / industriousness   _____
Recognition / admiration / fame   _____
Safety / security   _____
Self-awareness / self-understanding / insight   _____
Structure / predictability / stability   _____
Success / accomplishments / achievements   _____

list stops short of being exhaustive, but it is important not to feel overwhelmed when beginning this process. Remember to use your prioritized interests and preferences from Box 4.1 to guide your goal formation. Feel free to revise or add questions as you see fit, but respond honestly and thoughtfully to the items. You may want to keep a record of your ideas for reference before moving on to the next section.

It is important to keep in mind that variations in your life goals may or may not guide your decision about whether to major in psychology. Because the discipline is broad and includes many different subfields, individuals with widely differing life interests and preferences still find that pursuing an education in psychology meshes with their life goals. However, having a clearer sense of your life goals will help inform your thinking about careers, which in turn will help shape decisions you make about your education.

Box 4.3 *Questions to Stimulate the Formation of Life Goals*

Structure
- How much control will you have over your daily life?
- How much predictability will there be in your daily life?

Learning
- What types of knowledge or expertise will you gain?
- To what degree and in what ways will you engage the world and information about it?

Leisure
- What types of hobbies and activities will you pursue in your free time?
- What contributions or services will you provide to others?

Relationships
- What role will personal relationships (friendship and romantic) play in your life?
- What pattern of communication will you engage in with significant others?

Status
- What financial status will you obtain?
- What will be your physical and mental health status?

Environment
- What will be your living situation/home environment?
- What types of communities will you associate with and/or create?

Assessing Self and Developing Career Goals

Once you have started to clarify some of your life goals, it will be easier to recognize the tremendous impact they can have on your ideas about future careers. For example, an individual who develops life goals that give priority to family involvement and having a high level of stability in their daily life is unlikely to be satisfied in a career that requires extensive travel. This is not to say that career goals can never impact life goals. In fact, when some career opportunities present themselves, a reevaluation of life goals may be a prudent and necessary response. But even in these situations, you will be in a better position to make decisions about your career if you already understand how such shifts will affect your life goals.

Early in their lives, many individuals focus their time and effort on obtaining their career goals. This emphasis is often feasible because younger individuals are more willing to delay life goals for the pursuit of their career path. But when career and life goals come to be at odds, the result is often some level of dissatisfaction in the career. The best possible remedy for any such conflict is to ensure not only that your career goals are in line with your life goals but also that they actually support one another. For example, if one of your life goals is to obtain a particular financial status, then it is important to have a congruent career goal. The greater the synchrony between one's life and career goals, the more likely one's career experiences will be rewarding and fulfilling.

Allow the life goals you began developing in the previous section to serve as a foundation for now considering your career goals. As was the case with setting life goals, it is best to begin by assessing one's self in several important areas. Most individuals strive to pursue careers that they find intrinsically interesting, and most employers hire individuals who have the skills needed in a position. Therefore, working to identify and prioritize your career-relevant abilities will provide a good starting point for beginning to develop career goals. Box 4.4 presents a list of abilities and asks you to select and rank those that best fit you. The abilities are divided into categories that reflect the focus of these skills. You may find that your abilities are primarily within one category or that they branch across all three. Again, this task in isolation falls short of providing a thorough self-assessment of your career abilities and interests, but it should help stimulate your thinking about the topic in a way that will enhance your formulation of career goals. As with the previous exercises, feel free to add additional abilities to best capture your unique experiences.

Use your identified abilities from Box 4.4 as a starting point for beginning to formulate several career goals. Box 4.5 provides a few questions that address key areas of career goals. The questions are grouped into the same six domains used earlier to organize the life goal questions. Again, the list is far from exhaustive, so revise or add questions as you see fit. Be sure to record your ideas for reference as you continue to work toward developing specific goals.

Variations in your career goals will influence your decision about whether to major in psychology and, if so, what occupation to pursue. But by formulating career goals that are broader than simply identifying a desired occupation, you do not limit yourself to one particular educational path. In addition, the varied areas within the psychology field, as well as the related occupations at the bachelor's level and graduate level, are capable of satisfying a wide range of career goals. Rather than dictate

Box 4.4 *Self-Assessment of Career Related Abilities*

Instructions: Read the following list carefully and decide which of the career abilities best describe you. Select and rank your top 10 abilities using the numbers 1 to 10.

Working with Information	Working with People	Working with Things
Analyzing ____	Advising ____	Adjusting ____
Calculating ____	Assisting ____	Assembling ____
Classifying ____	Caring ____	Calibrating ____
Comparing ____	Conducting ____	Carrying ____
Compiling ____	Confronting ____	Composing ____
Connecting ____	Consulting ____	Constructing ____
Coordinating ____	Coordinating ____	Controlling ____
Creating ____	Counseling ____	Creating ____
Designing ____	Demonstrating ____	Designing ____
Developing ____	Enforcing ____	Disassembling ____
Diagnosing ____	Entertaining ____	Driving ____
Editing ____	Evaluating ____	Emptying ____
Examining ____	Influencing ____	Guarding ____
Experimenting ____	Initiating ____	Guiding ____
Expressing ____	Leading ____	Handling ____
Forecasting ____	Listening ____	Illustrating ____
Gathering ____	Mentoring ____	Installing ____
Inspecting ____	Motivating ____	Loading ____
Interpreting ____	Negotiating ____	Maintaining ____
Observing ____	Organizing ____	Manipulating ____
Organizing ____	Persuading ____	Monitoring ____
Perceiving ____	Providing ____	Moving ____
Planning ____	Representing ____	Performing ____
Presenting ____	Serving ____	Preparing ____
Reading ____	Sharing ____	Refining ____
Reporting ____	Speaking ____	Regulating ____
Researching ____	Supervising ____	Remodeling ____
Scheduling ____	Teaching ____	Repairing ____
Synthesizing ____	Training ____	Selling ____
Translating ____	Treating ____	Tending ____

your educational goals, your career goals should inform your thinking and decision making as you make choices about your education and training.

> **Box 4.5** *Questions to Stimulate the Formation of Career Goals*
>
> Structure
> - How much autonomy and independence will you have in your work life?
> - Will you be led/supervised/managed or will you lead/supervise/manage others?
>
> Learning
> - What types of skills will you need to acquire through ongoing training?
> - In what ways will your work challenge you?
>
> Time
> - What will your daily schedule or working hours be like?
> - How will your work impact your free time?
>
> Relationships
> - What type of people will you work with/around/for?
> - What role will relationships with coworkers play in your life?
>
> Status
> - What type of earnings and benefits will you receive?
> - In what ways will your work provide opportunities for you to advance?
>
> Environment
> - What will your work setting/environment be like?
> - How will your work impact your physical location (e.g., residence, commute, travel)?

Assessing Self and Developing Educational Goals

So far you have been working through tasks designed to help clarify your life and career goals. When this process begins to develop momentum, you may find yourself breathing a sigh of relief. Perhaps for the first time in your life you may begin to feel that you have a sense of direction and purpose in terms of your future career path. However, there is one final step to consider, that of assessing and developing your educational goals.

Because many careers require a minimum level of education, your ability to secure a particular career will be heavily influenced by your educational choices and accomplishments. At times these requirements only specify a particular degree or general area of training. For example, an entry-level management position may require a bachelor's degree with a major in business, human services, or a social science. But other careers can have more specific requirements. For example, positions as a clinical psychologist require a doctorate in clinical psychology, often from an accredited program, along with coursework and training in specific areas of practice. As a result, your developing career goals and interests may play a critical role in shaping your educational goals.

If you are already in college, you may be wondering, "What is the purpose in developing educational goals now?" Certainly you have already started your pursuit of certain educational goals, like graduating from college. But chances are your career interests and goals are still being formulated. As these goals become clearer, aspects of your education must change accordingly. In other words, the time that remains in your pursuit of a college degree is vital, and the goals you set now will help shape the outcome of these experiences. Also, many of you need to begin preparing for education beyond your bachelor's degree, regardless of whether this entails graduate or professional school immediately after college or at a later point in your career.

Although your career plans will have a substantial influence on your educational interests and goals, it is vital that you not allow them to be the sole determining factor. Students sometimes state that because they want a particular career that requires a certain level of education, then they must now seek that education. This certainly sounds logical, but the student who forms an educational goal in this manner is setting themselves up to fail. Students who enter college, graduate, and professional programs with this mindset are often not academically or mentally prepared to take on such a goal. Even if they possess the academic skills to succeed, viewing their education solely as "a means to an end" does not bode well for their sustaining the high levels of motivation and perseverance that these levels of education require.

Allow the life and career goals you began developing in the previous sections to serve as a foundation for now considering your educational goals. As with setting these previous goals, it is best to take some time before developing educational goals to assess your educational interests and abilities. One major factor to consider is your academic skills. Students can make full use of the academic skills they have by putting themselves in educational situations that maximize these resources. At other times the lack of particular academic skills can significantly affect the goals one develops and the pursuit of them. As a result, evaluating your academic skills can be a key element of conducting an assessment of your educational interests and abilities. Box 4.6 presents a list of skills that are critical to academic success at all levels. The task presented is for you to identify which of these skills are among your greatest academic

---

Box 4.6 *Self-Assessment of Academic Strengths and Weaknesses*

Instructions: Read the following list carefully. Identify which academic skills are strengths and which are weaknesses for you by marking them with an "S" for strength or a "W" for weakness. Then rank your three greatest strengths and your three greatest weaknesses from among those you identified, using the numbers 1 to 3.

Academic Skill	Strength or Weakness	Ranking
Accepting and using feedback	____	____
Completing exams or quizzes	____	____
Concentrating or focusing	____	____
Following directions	____	____
Giving presentations	____	____
Listening in class or being attentive	____	____
Managing time or workload	____	____
Organizing self and materials	____	____
Participating in class	____	____
Planning or prioritizing	____	____
Preparing for exams or quizzes	____	____
Reading and studying course materials	____	____
Relating effectively to peers	____	____
Relating effectively to instructors	____	____
Staying motivated	____	____
Taking notes in class	____	____
Using technology to gather information	____	____
Working in groups or teams	____	____
Writing or preparing written assignments	____	____

---

strengths and weaknesses. As with the previous self-assessment tasks, identifying strengths and weaknesses is just one part of a thorough self-assessment of educational interests and preferences, but it should stimulate your thinking about issues relevant to formulating educational goals.

Any self-assessment of one's academic abilities only partially captures the various factors that might shape your eventual educational pursuits. Yet, you can use your identified strengths and weaknesses as a starting point for beginning to formulate your educational goals. Box 4.7 provides several questions that address key areas of educational goals. The questions are grouped into the same six domains used earlier to organize the life and career goal questions. Again, the list is far from exhaustive, so revise or add questions as you see fit. Be sure to record your ideas for future reference.

Of the three areas of goals considered in this chapter, certainly your educational goals are the most likely to impact directly your decision of whether to major in psychology. But keep in mind that students pursuing a bachelor's degree in psychology can have vastly different educational experiences. The school you attend, courses you take, activities you engage in, and effort you exert will combine to produce your overall educational experience. Deciding on your major is only the beginning of this process, and thankfully you have much control over how these other elements of your education come together to support your career and life goals.

Box 4.7   *Questions to Stimulate the Formation of Educational Goals*

Structure
- How much autonomy and independence will you have in your educational life?
- How will your learning and progress be evaluated?

Learning
- What type of learning environment will you seek out (e.g., resources, class size, hands-on)?
- How academically rigorous will your education be?

Time
- How many years will you dedicate to pursuing your education and training?
- How much time during a week will you dedicate to pursuing your education and training?

Relationships
- What will your interactions with faculty/instructors be like?
- What role will relationships with peers play in your life?

Status
- What type of financial investment will you make in your education?
- What will be the reputation of the institution you attend?

Environment
- What will your institution's setting/environment be like?
- In what geographic location will you pursue your education?

Conclusion

Our goal in this chapter was to introduce you to the value of viewing life, career, and educational goals as interdependent. In addition, we gave you several suggestions and methods for beginning to think about your interests in each of these areas and how these inform the development of clear goals. For the most part, the other chapters of this book place emphasis solely on the area of career goals. However, we hope that as you continue reading about the various subfields of psychology, and the steps you can take to prepare for your career, that you keep this chapter in mind. Having a clearer sense of your life, career, and educational goals will enhance both your understanding of the information to come and the usefulness of it in helping you identify psychology-related careers that may be in your future.

Suggested Exercises

1. Familiarize yourself with the career services provided to students at your institution. Many colleges and universities have a career services center or office that provides helpful career-related information and assistance to students. These services are often "free" in that they are already covered by student fees. Develop an understanding of what types of resources they provide and, if possible, arrange a meeting with a career counselor to discuss your progress in developing career goals.
2. Complete several additional self-assessment tasks to supplement those provided in the chapter. Use these additional tasks to gather more information about your life, career, and/or educational interests and abilities as you work to further develop your goals. Many self-assessment tasks are available online either for free or for a small fee, but be cautious about how you interpret any feedback. Rather than view the results as definitive information about you or your career goals, view it as yet another piece of potentially helpful information to use in formulating goals for yourself. Several websites offer overviews of the numerous online self-assessment tools available, including:
   • Quintessential Careers: http://www.quintcareers.com/online_assessment_review.html
   • The Riley Guide: http://www.rileyguide.com/assess.html
3. Attend a career fair. Career fairs are typically organized by colleges and universities to provide students with opportunities to interact with area businesses and organizations. Fairs are often advertised by your institution's career services center or through the offices that coordinate student activities. If your institution has no information about career fairs, contact the career services centers of neighboring institutions to inquire about any upcoming fairs they are familiar with. Many students incorrectly believe that if they are not currently seeking a job, that they have nothing to gain from attending a career fair. But by attending you will learn about a variety of opportunities in your area that you may not have even known existed.

Suggested Readings

Curran, S. J., & Greenwald, S. (2006). *Smart moves for liberal arts grads: Finding a path to your perfect career.* Berkeley, CA: Ten Speed Press.

Pollak, L. (2012). *Getting from college to career* (Rev. ed.). New York, NY: HarperCollins.

References

Bolles, R. N. (2013). *What color is your parachute? 2014: A practical manual for job-hunters and career-changers.* Berkeley, CA: Ten Speed Press.

Cass, M. H., Siu, O. L., Faragher, E. B., & Cooper, C. L. (2003). A meta-analysis of the relationship between job satisfaction and employee health in Hong Kong. *Stress and Health: Journal of the International Society for the Investigation of Stress, 19,* 79–95. doi:10.1002/smi.959

Chiu, L. (1990). The relationship of career goal and self-esteem among adolescents. *Adolescence, 25,* 593–597.

Faragher, E. B., Cass, M., & Cooper, C. L. (2005). The relationship between job satisfaction and health: A meta-analysis. *Occupational and Environmental Medicine, 62,* 105–112.

Headey, B. (2008). Life goals matter to happiness: A revision of set-point theory. *Social Indicators Research, 86,* 213–231. doi:10.1007/s11205-007-9138-y

Harrist, S., Carlozzi, B. L., McGovern, A. R., & Harrist, A. W. (2007). Benefits of expressive writing and expressive talking about life goals. *Journal of Research in Personality, 41,* 923–930. doi:10.1016/j.jrp.2006.09.002

Holland, J. L. (1959). A theory of vocational choice. *Journal of Counseling Psychology, 6,* 35–45. doi:10.1037/h0040767

Hull-Blanks, E., Kurpius, S. E. R., Befort, C., Sollenberger, S., Nicpon, M. F., & Huser, L. (2005). Career goals and retention-related factors among college freshmen. *Journal of Career Development, 32,* 16–30. doi:10.1177/0894845305277037

King, L. A. (2001). The health benefits of writing about life goals. *Personality and Social Psychology Bulletin, 27,* 798–807. doi:10.1177/0146167201277003

Kubota, Y. (1982). An empirical study on the effect of career goal setting. *Japanese Journal of Experimental Social Psychology, 21,* 149–157. doi:10.2130/jjesp.21.149

Lee, C., Bobko, P., Earley, P. C., & Locke, E. A. (1991). An empirical analysis of a goal setting questionnaire. *Journal of Organizational Behavior, 12,* 467–482. doi:10.1002/job.4030120602

Lent, R. W. (2013). Social cognitive career theory. In S. D. Brown & R. W. Lent (Eds.), *Career development & counseling: Putting theory and research to work* (2nd ed.; pp. 115–146). New York, NY: Wiley.

Lent, R. W., Brown, S. D. & Hackett, G. (1994). Toward a unifying social cognitive theory of career and academic interest, choice, and performance. *Journal of Vocational Behavior, 45,* 79–122. doi:10.1006/jvbe.1994.1027

Lent, R. W., Brown, S. D., & Hackett, G. (2002). Social cognitive career theory. In D. Brown and Associates (Eds.), *Career choice and development* (4th ed.; pp. 255–311). San Francisco, CA: Jossey-Bass.

Oyserman, D., Terry, K., & Bybee, D. (2002). A possible selves intervention to enhance school involvement. *Journal of Adolescence, 25,* 313–326.

Parsons, F. (1909). *Choosing a vocation*. Boston, MA: Houghton Mifflin.

Roberson, L. (1990). Prediction of job satisfaction from characteristics of personal work goals. *Journal of Organizational Behavior, 11,* 29–41. doi:10.1002/job.4030110106

Super, D. E. (1963). Vocational development in adolescence and early adulthood: Tasks and behaviors. In D. E. Super, R. Starishevsky, N. Matlin, & J. P. Jordaan (Eds.), *Career development: Self-concept theory* (pp. 79–95). New York, NY: College Entrance Examination Board.

Chapter Five
Using your Bachelor's Degree
Preparing for the Job Market

Introduction

This chapter details a variety of issues related to preparation for employment upon graduation with a bachelor's degree. Topics covered include:

- work settings of recent graduates;
- what employers want from applicants for entry-level positions;
- how to develop what employers want (e.g., suggested coursework and experiences);
- finding entry-level positions;
- preparing job application materials (e.g., résumés and cover letters);
- preparing for and completing job interviews and considering offers; and
- starting salaries.

Before we jump into the topics, we would like to highlight a few points to keep in mind. First, as noted earlier in the book and as a reminder, the bachelor's degree in psychology can be seen from two distinct perspectives (a preprofessional degree and a liberal arts degree). The preprofessional degree mirrors, for example, the natural sciences in that to become a physician, dentist, surgeon, etc., you first earn your bachelor's degree in one of the sciences and then continue your education in medical/dental school. The corollary with psychology is that to become a psychologist you first earn your bachelor's degree in psychology then continue your education in graduate school. In this way, the student is using the bachelor's degree as a stepping

Majoring in Psychology: Achieving Your Educational and Career Goals, Second Edition.
Jeffrey L. Helms and Daniel T. Rogers.
© 2015 John Wiley & Sons, Ltd. Published 2015 by John Wiley & Sons, Ltd.

stone (i.e., a preprofessional degree). From the second perspective, the liberal arts degree provides the student with a well-rounded education in the humanities, fine arts, natural sciences, and social sciences. A liberal arts education provides the student the opportunity to gain general knowledge and critical thinking and communication skills that can be applied to a wide array of circumstances (i.e., job settings and opportunities). With this in mind, the vantage point of this chapter is using the bachelor's degree in psychology as a liberal arts degree; that is, using your bachelor's degree as a foundation for entering the job market immediately upon graduation.

Second, for those of you wishing to pursue graduate training immediately upon completion of the bachelor's degree, don't discount the information in this chapter. Many, if not most, of the suggestions and pointers offered are equally valid for those who want to pursue graduate training upon completion of the bachelor's degree and those who decide to continue their education at a later time.

Last, although this chapter addresses preparation for the job market with a bachelor's degree, keep in mind that these are general pointers, suggestions, and insights. For those wanting to enter the job market immediately upon graduation (which is the case for most students), don't forego the second half of this book mistakenly believing that working within the subfields of psychology is only open to those with graduate training and degrees. This belief is far from the truth! Many people work in the specialized subfields of psychology as support staff, technical assistants, etc. As a result, each of the subfield chapters includes an entire section on positions available to those with a bachelor's degree. Check them out!

Work Settings of Recent Graduates

What can you do with a bachelor's degree in psychology? The better question may be "What *can't* you do with a bachelor's degree in psychology?" Granted that this may be overstating it, but the truth is that a liberal arts degree in psychology puts you in a great situation for entry-level positions. Your degree program provides you with the opportunity to gain a well-rounded education in the humanities, fine arts, natural sciences, and social sciences. A liberal arts education provides the student the opportunity to gain general knowledge and critical thinking and communication skills that can be applied to a wide array of circumstances (i.e., job settings and opportunities). The opportunities provided by most psychology programs are due in no small part to guidance provided by the American Psychological Association (APA; 2013) via their Board of Educational Affairs Task Force on Psychology Major Competencies (Task Force). The Task Force developed (and regularly revises) a "set of optimal expectations for performance by undergraduates engaged in the study of psychology" (p. 3). The set includes five goals (along with associated subgoals) that most undergraduate psychology programs address and attempt to achieve via the curriculum offered to the psychology major. Some of the many skills noted in the goals are using scientific reasoning, conducting research, applying ethical standards, and demonstrating self-efficacy.

The opportunities provided by departments attempting to achieve the goals developed by APA (2013), placed the 108,986 students obtaining a bachelor's degree in psychology in 2011–2012 (US Department of Education, National Center for Education Statistics, 2013) in excellent shape for pursuing a variety of career paths upon graduation. Box 5.1 provides a sampling of the wide variety of entry-level positions possible with a bachelor's degree in psychology. We hope the box inspires some career ideas that you may not have considered. For additional ideas take a look at Appleby, Millspaugh, and Hammersley's (2011) *172 Careers of Interest to Psychology Majors*, which is available at http://teachpsych.org/resources/Documents/otrp/resources/appleby11.pdf. Remember that these are just *examples* of possible positions! It is not meant to limit your ideas or neglect other great entry-level career choices for those with a bachelor's degree in psychology. We also encourage you to review the positions in light of the information provided in the chapter on assessing and developing your career goals.

According to the National Science Foundation's (NSF; 2012) 2008 National Survey of Recent College Graduates, representation of recent recipients of bachelor's degrees in psychology significantly varied among the three main employment sectors. Approximately 27% of recent psychology graduates were employed in educational institutions. In its definition of educational institutions, NSF includes "elementary and secondary schools, 2-year and 4-year colleges and universities, medical schools, university-affiliated research organizations, and all other educational institutions" (p. 49). Approximately 8% of recent psychology graduates worked in the government sector. NSF "includes local, state, and federal government; military; and commissioned corps" in its definition of the government sector (p. 49). By far, the largest employment sector of recent recipients of bachelor's degrees in psychology is business/private industry at approximately 65%. This number includes both nonprofit organizations and those individuals who are self-employed. Additionally, NSF defines this sector as private industry and business which "includes all private for-profit and private not-for-profit companies, businesses, and organizations, except those reported as educational institutions" (p. 49).

> **Box 5.1** *A Sample of Various Entry-Level Positions Possible with a Bachelor's Degree in Psychology*
>
> - Activity leader
> - Admissions evaluator
> - Advertising sales representative
> - Alumni director
> - Applied statistician
> - Benefits manager
> - Caseworker
> - Child development specialist
> - Child welfare/placement caseworker
> - Claims supervisor
> - Coach
> - Community organization worker
> - Conservation officer
> - Corrections officer
> - Customer service representative supervisor
> - Department manager
> - Disability case manager
> - Employee relations specialist
> - Employment counselor
> - Employment interviewer
> - Financial aid counselor
> - Fund raiser
> - Health care facility administrator
> - Host/hostess
> - Human resource advisor
> - Loan officer
> - News writer
> - Occupational analyst
> - Patient resources and reimbursement agent
> - Personnel recruiter
> - Police officer
> - Preschool teacher
> - Probation/parole officer
> - Psychiatric aide/attendant
> - Psychiatric technician
> - Purchasing agent
> - Recreation leader
> - Recreational therapist
> - Research assistant
> - Retail salesperson
> - Sales clerk
> - Social services aide
> - Technical writer
> - Victims' advocate
>
> *Note.* Examples come from Appleby et al. (2011).

What Employers Want from Applicants for Entry-Level Positions

Although the types of employment and settings are varied, research strongly suggests that employers seek out particular skills and attributes in applicants. Before evaluating particular skills and attributes, however, employers often make a cut based on grade point average (i.e., GPA). According to their annual publication (*Job Outlook*), the National Association of Colleges and Employers (NACE; 2013) found that 67% of employers indicated that they would be

Box 5.2	*Top 10 Attributes Employers Search for in an Applicant's Résumé*

1. Written communication skills
2. Leadership
3. Analytical/quantitative skills
4. Strong work ethic
5. Ability to work in a team
6. Problem-solving skills
7. Verbal communication skills
8. Initiative
9. Detail oriented
10. Computer skills

Note. Information comes from *Job Outlook* (NACE, 2013).

screening applicants based on GPA. The majority (60%) would be using a 3.0 as the cut point. In other words, simply obtaining the degree is not sufficient to open the doors to the entry-level positions these employers are seeking to fill.

Once the GPA cut is made, employers will be looking more closely at the applicant's résumé for particular attributes. Box 5.2 provides a list of the top 10 attributes employers look for in applicants' résumés. As a result, it is not only important to develop these attributes but also to clearly convey them on your résumé.

Collegegrad.com (2011) presents a different but somewhat similar perspective on what employers want from new college graduates. The results of this survey produced 10 "characteristics that influence hiring decisions" (p. 4). The criteria with accompanying percentage of employers ranking it as "most important" are:

1. the student's major/degree (34%);
2. the student's internship/experience (24%);
3. the student's interview/communication skills (22%);
4. the college the student graduated from (8%);
5. the student's community service (4%);
6. the student's GPA (3%);
7. the student's personal appearance (2%);
8. the student's computer skills (1%);
9. the student's integrity/drive (1%); and
10. the student's passion (1%).

As can be seen from the criteria, 24% indicated that internships/experience is the "most important" criterion in evaluating new college graduates. It is second only to the student's major/degree (34%). In other words, experience counts! Summer jobs, part-time jobs, structured volunteer experiences, field practica, and internships/externships all provide opportunities to gain experience. Complementing the finding by Collegegrad.com is the 2013 NACE survey that found that approximately 74% of employers "prefer to hire candidates with relevant work experience" (p. 33).

But what about psychology majors in particular? Appleby (2000) developed a list of job skills that employers who interview psychology majors value. The job skills categories along with examples within each category are presented in Box 5.3. In sum and comparing them to other research findings, the skills valued in psychology majors were not much different from those noted earlier for liberal arts majors in general and all majors.

Box 5.3 *Job Skills that Employers Who Interview Psychology Majors Value*

1. Social skills
   a. Deals effectively with a wide variety of people
   b. Displays appropriate interpersonal skills
   c. Handles conflict successfully
   d. Works productively as a member of a team
2. Personal skills
   a. Shows initiative and persistence
   b. Exhibits effective time management
   c. Holds high ethical standards and expects the same of others
   d. Remains open-minded during controversies
3. Communication skills
   a. Listens carefully and accurately
   b. Speaks articulately and persuasively
   c. Writes clearly and precisely
4. Information gathering/processing skills
   a. Plans and carries out projects successfully
   b. Thinks logically and creatively
   c. Gathers and organizes information from multiple sources
5. Numerical/computer/psychometric skills
   a. Displays computer literacy
   b. Performs and interprets descriptive and inferential statistics

Note. Information comes from Appleby (2000).

How to Develop What Employers Want

Now we know what the research reveals about what employers look for in entry-level job applicants. However, knowing what attributes are valued is different from knowing how to develop them. As a result, we discuss possible strategies to developing some of the main skills consistently revealed in these research studies, keeping in mind that the skills developed and the methods used to develop them fit nicely on a résumé. Résumés are discussed later in this chapter.

Communication Skills (Verbal and Written)

Two of the most common ways to develop communication skills are writing integrative papers and reports and making oral presentations. Frequent opportunities exist to build and refine verbal and written skills in your undergraduate program. As is the case with most upper-level coursework and your research-oriented courses (e.g., Experimental Psychology), integrative papers and literature reviews are commonplace. If you are not a good writer or simply want to improve your writing skills, certainly take advantage of the resources at your university (e.g., writing centers).

Teamwork and Leadership Skills (Ability to Work in a Team Structure)

Teamwork and leadership skills can be developed inside a particular course and outside of coursework. Inside the classroom, group projects and activities can be utilized. Although not a favorite aspect for many students, employers' desire for this skill and professors' beliefs in the value of collaboration, support the use of group assignments. Teamwork and leadership skills can be developed outside of traditional coursework too. For example, involvement in a service project as a member of your psychology club or honor society is an opportunity to develop this skill and demonstrate your aptitude in this area. These organizations also often provide opportunities to serve in leadership positions like president, secretary, and treasurer. Importantly, NACE (2013) found that if you have the desired major an employer seeks, having held a leadership position often breaks a tie between applicants where all else is equal! In terms of specific coursework, courses in the areas of social psychology and industrial–organizational psychology often incorporate group activities, given the nature of these subfields.

Strong Work Ethic and Integrity

In many ways, a strong work ethic and integrity must be developed (i.e., demonstrated) over time. For example, consistent class attendance and participation demonstrate a commitment to the educational process. These qualities are also demonstrated through consistency, punctuality, and time consciousness. Arriving on time to class, completing assignments when due, etc. illustrate to those around you (e.g., the faculty who will be your future references) that you take your education seriously. The strength of your work ethic is also demonstrated by the quantity and quality of your work product. Do you do the minimum? Is it obvious that you are taking the course only because it is a "required" course? Enrolling and excelling in some of the optional coursework may demonstrate a strong work ethic too. Optional courses like practica and advanced research courses should be considered.

Initiative

Students show initiative when they seek out opportunities to get more experience and practice. Students who have initiative often go above and beyond the requirements of a particular course assignment. As a result, opportunities to demonstrate initiative abound in the undergraduate curriculum. Students who do the minimum in order to finish quickly give clearly negative information to their professors (i.e., their future references). Also, students who are not self-motivated or shy away from leadership opportunities lack initiative. Those students who need significant amounts of guidance (i.e., "hand holding") lack initiative typically. Taking advantage of extracurricular activities like leadership opportunities in the department clubs and organizations can demonstrate your initiative.

Interpersonal Skills (Works Well with Others)

A common question that is asked of references is how well a person relates to others, both peers and those in authority or supervisory positions. Is the student open to criticism and feedback? Is the student argumentative, always trying to get that missed point back on the exam? Does the student get along well with classmates? Professors and students alike have experienced having that one person in class who dominates the discussion or asks/answers all of the questions. In contrast to this, encouraging peers to offer their perspective and listening closely to those peers who may disagree with you demonstrates your skill in this area. Additionally, professors cannot comment on your behavior if you do not engage in class discussion or avoid department activities (e.g., club activities and fundraisers). Equally important, although professors generally love to interact with students (one of the great things about our jobs), professors certainly do not want to remember you for being the one that *required* tons of attention. In addition to learning about interpersonal skills in courses like Social Psychology, Family Psychology, and Group Psychology, working with a professor one-on-one on a research project or departmental project (e.g., a psychology club fundraiser) will provide the professor with an opportunity to observe your interactions with others (and them too!).

Analytical and Quantitative Skills

As seen in the research, employers are increasingly seeking entry-level job applicants who have analytical and quantitative skills. The desire for this set of skills puts psychology majors at an advantage when compared to most other liberal arts majors. Within your program you will have the opportunity to develop these skills within your courses on research methods, statistics, and experimental psychology. For those who have the opportunity at their institution, we encourage taking additional statistics courses and even minoring in statistics if possible. Directed study and work with faculty members on their research also provide excellent opportunities to develop and increase your analytical and quantitative skills.

What about coursework to prepare for entry-level positions in specific fields? In their article, Lloyd, Kennedy, and Dewey (1997) recognize that the majority of students entering the job market enter the business/private industry sector and that many students pursue employment in the human services sector as well. As a result, these authors provided suggestions for coursework to take for those interested in pursuing careers in these areas. In addition to suggested coursework in the business and economics disciplines, Lloyd et al. suggested courses like the Psychology of Women, Psychological Statistics, Industrial–Organizational Psychology, Applied Psychology, Social Psychology, and Field Practica for those students interested in the business sector. For those interested in the human services area, they suggested Child Psychology, Lifespan Development, Behavior Modification, Abnormal Psychology, Tests and Measurement, Field Practica, Substance Abuse, Psychology of Women, Theories of Personality, and Health Psychology.

Obviously, we realize that students can't take all of the suggested courses. There just isn't enough time! Regardless, knowing what potential employers want in applicants and knowing the associated coursework that may provide opportunities to develop those skills put you in a better place when selecting your coursework. Fortunately, regardless of which data are reviewed or highlighted, the typical curriculum associated with a bachelor's degree in psychology provides the opportunity to develop each of these qualities, putting you in a good place for entry-level positions upon graduation. Again though, the challenge for the student is to choose coursework wisely, keeping in mind his or her ultimate career goal.

Finding Entry-Level Positions

Now that you know what employers want, where do you find these entry-level positions? Before you start looking for positions, revisit your self-assessment completed in Chapter 4. Be guided by your values (i.e., how you really are) and not just how you think you "should" be. With this understanding in mind, begin your search.

Recruiting Methods

Although it may go without saying, there are effective methods and ineffective methods for searching for jobs. The same is true for the employers looking to fill entry-level positions. As a result, knowing information about employers' recruiting methods can shed light on what may be effective for the new or soon-to-be college graduate. NACE (2013) surveyed employers to find out more about their recruiting methods. In short, it is clear from the responses that employers are using technology and social media networks to identify potential new employees. However, employers have not given up on face-to-face recruiting opportunities. In fact, approximately 38% indicated that they will be attending *more* career fairs as part of their strategy. As is the case for many of us, we need to make the most of our limited time and busy schedules. As a result, knowing where employers are spending their time and money to identify potential new employees will prove useful in deciding where to spend your time!

Resources

Finding actual job openings can be difficult. This difficulty is due in no small part to the problem that many or even most job openings are not posted in the traditional manner. As a result, the majority of job openings may go unnoticed. In hopes of decreasing the problem of the "hidden job market," Box 5.4 lists a variety of resources and resource ideas, both traditional and nontraditional, to assist you in the job search.

As can be seen from the resources listed, jobs and opportunities will not likely come looking for you. Instead, you will have to go looking for them. This process, along with letting people know you are looking for a position

---

Box 5.4 *Job Search Resources and Where to Find Job Openings*

General job websites
- www.indeed.com
- www.careerbuilder.com
- www.glassdoor.com
- www.simplyhired.com
- www.monster.com
- www.collegegrad.com

Nonprofit jobs websites
- www.idealist.org
- www.opportunityknocks.org
- www.encore.org

Government employment websites
- www.usajobs.gov
- www.governmentjobs.com
- http://www.usa.gov/Citizen/Topics/Work_for_the_Government.shtml

Diversity-related employment websites, resources, networking opportunities
- American Foundation for the Blind – http://www.afb.org/Community.asp?Type=Employment
- Disabilities in the workplace – www.diversityworld.com
- National Gay and Lesbian Chamber of Commerce – www.nglcc.org
- General diversity-related online resources:
  o www.diversityinc.com
  o https://career.berkeley.edu/Infolab/Diversity.stm
- Transgender Workplace Diversity Network – transworkplace.ning.com

Local papers – Many post their classifieds online too.

University resources
- Career centers and libraries (Most universities have these resources.)
- Your professors

Community resources
- Employment agencies
- Temporary employment agencies

and establishing connections in the field that you want to pursue as a career, is called *networking*. Networking will serve you well in your endeavor to find that perfect job. In fact, networking is invaluable. The importance of networking is why sites like www.linkedin.com have become so popular in recent years. In fact, you may even decide to establish a presence on that networking site.

Preparing Job Application Materials: Résumés and Cover Letters

The two most important pieces of a job application are the résumé and cover letter. Both are always carefully and thoughtfully prepared. They are both always typed (i.e., never handwritten).

Résumés

There are two basic types of résumés, functional and chronological. The core part of the functional résumé is organized by skill type (e.g., sales experience, leadership experience, writing experience, and interpersonal experience). Box 5.5 provides an example of a functional résumé. The core part of the chronological résumé is organized by dates of activities (e.g., July 2014 – July 2015; July 2015 – present). Box 5.6 provides an example of a chronological résumé.

Regardless of the type of résumé, all résumés have the basic elements in common. First, a résumé should be one page long, no more. It should be printed on good quality white or off-white paper, not pink, powder blue, beige, purple, etc. (The same paper should be used for the cover letter too.) The résumé should be individually tailored to the position (not generic). When individuals mass-mail generic résumés and cover letters, it strongly indicates that care and attention to detail are not strong attributes of the applicant. Generic résumés and cover letters stand out from the crowd and not in a good way. In constructing the résumé and cover letter, action verbs should be used, display techniques should be consistent (e.g., Times New Roman size 12 font throughout), and abbreviations should be avoided. Some of the common headings within a résumé include:

Name and contact information.   As seen in the examples, this informa- tion is typically centered at the top of the résumé. Be prepared and will- ing to be contacted at all of these. In other words, if you don't want to be contacted at your current place of employment, do not include that

Box 5.5 *Example Functional Résumé*

Joyce E. Brawley
1000 St. John's Church Rd.
Kennesaw, GA 30144
(770) 555-5555
JoyceEBrawley@emailnowz.com

Career Objective

To obtain an entry-level position in the human resources area that utilizes my strong interpersonal and research skills.

Education

Your University, Atlanta, GA; Bachelor of Science in Psychology, May 2018
  Minors: Statistics and Human Services; GPA: 3.6/4.0; Graduated Cum Laude

Relevant Skills

- *Technical Skills* Extensive experience with SPSS Statistical Package and Microsoft Office (Word, Excel, PowerPoint, Publisher, and Access); Familiar with several web design software packages.
- *Writing Skills* Coauthored paper presented at regional psychology conference. Extensive experience with American Psychological Association Style, including writing empirically based papers. Helped develop, pilot, and analyze an employee satisfaction survey while on internship.
- *Organizational Leadership* Secretary for two years and President for one year of my university's psychology club. Headed the annual fundraiser two consecutive years in which over $10,000 was raised for battered women and abused children. Treasurer for 1 year for the Psi Chi chapter.

Employment

Your University, Atlanta, GA, 2016–2018 (Psychology computer lab assistant)
Ira's Summer Employment, Inc., Bates, GA, 2015 (File clerk)
Gene's Sunday Eatery, Clivetown, GA, 2013–2014 (Hostess and wait staff)
Signatory Stores of Heiko, Milledgeville, GA 2010–2013 (Retail staff)

Honors and Professional Society Memberships

Outstanding Undergraduate Psychology Major Graduate Award – 2017–2018
Psi Chi Honors Society – 2015–present
American Psychological Association (student affiliate) – 2014–present
Society for Human Resource Management (student member) – 2014–present

Availability

Immediate

Box 5.6 *Example Chronological Résumé* 89

Joyce E. Brawley
1000 St. John's Church Rd.
Kennesaw, GA 30144
(770) 555-5555
JoyceEBrawley@emailnowz.com

Career Objective

To obtain an entry-level position in the human resources area that utilizes my strong interpersonal and research skills.

Education

May 2018	Bachelor of Science in Psychology
	Minors: Statistics and Human Services
	Your University, Atlanta, GA; GPA: 3.6/4.0
	Graduated Cum Laude

Relevant Experience

August 2016 – May 2018   Your University, Atlanta, GA
Psychology Computer Lab Assistant

- Assisted students and faculty with American Psychological Association writing style, including writing empirically based papers
- Routinely used SPSS and Microsoft Office (Word, Excel, PowerPoint, Publisher, and Access)
- Occasionally used Dreamweaver web design software

August 2015 – May 2016   Your University, Atlanta, GA
Human Resources Intern

- Assisted in the development, piloting, and statistical analysis of an employee satisfaction survey
- Presented results to director of human resources
- Coauthored paper based on findings and presented it at a regional psychology conference
- Routinely interacted with administration, faculty, and employees in a professional role

August 2014 – May 2018   Psychology Club
Active Member

- President from 2017–2018, Secretary from 2015–2017
- Headed annual fundraiser for two consecutive years in which over $10,000 was raised for charity

Honors and Professional Society Memberships

Outstanding Undergraduate Psychology Major Graduate Award – 2017–2018

Psi Chi Honors Society – 2015–present (Served as treasurer from 2015–2016)

Society for Human Resource Management (student member) – 2014–present

American Psychological Association (student affiliate) – 2014–present

email/phone number/address. Additionally, only provide professional email addresses and phone voicemail messages. For example, a professional email address would be one with your name in it like IraGene@abcxyz.edu, not FunnyBunny21@abcxyz.edu. Also, a professional voice message on your voicemail does not include the latest pop song as an introduction. If you have a professional web page you may want to include it too. Some universities encourage or require students to develop a web page to display their writing samples, résumés, etc. On this point, you may want to do an internet search of yourself (e.g., Google, Facebook) to see what employers can find out about you. They will do this too! As a result, this would be a great time to make "private" those pages that you are allowed to secure from general public view or search engines.

Profile or career objective. This single sentence or phrase is typically located immediately after the contact information. If it takes the form of a profile, the content should provide a snapshot summary of your best qualifications (i.e., who you would be as an employee). If it takes the form of a career objective, the content should summarize your career goal(s). Decide which approach best suits your résumé and the types of positions to which you will be applying.

Educational background. This heading typically includes the degrees you have earned as well as those you are pursuing (e.g., BS expected May 2019). Along with the location of the university where you obtained your degree(s), you will also want to include your major, any minors, your grade point average, and any graduation honors (e.g., cum laude and summa cum laude).

Relevant experience. Due to space limitations, only relevant experience is noted/described. This section also varies based on the amount of your experience and the positions you seek. For example, you may include your multiple retail experiences for a management trainee position at a local store but not include it when applying to work at a daycare. In that situation you may highlight your volunteer experience with kids at a local community center.

Relevant skills. This section focuses on the specific skills you will bring to bear on the position. These skills may include your computer knowledge, writing skills, statistical knowledge (including software packages like SPSS), and foreign languages.

References. Depending on available space, you may provide a list of references and accompanying contact information for them. Sometimes, résumés only include an indication of references being available upon request. If names are included, always ask permission before listing them as references and give them notice of when and where you are sending your application/résumé.

Additional headings. Additional headings may include relevant extracurricular activities, military experience, honors societies, volunteer experiences, professional affiliations/memberships, and selected achievements. Obviously, not all headings will be used in each of your résumés. Instead, they will vary depending on the type of position and the skills you are trying to highlight. Regardless of the headings used, the information found in your résumé should be accurate. Even small inaccuracies can prove fatal for a job prospect.

Cover Letters

A cover letter always accompanies a résumé. An example of a cover letter is provided in Box 5.7. Cover letters consist of three main sections/paragraphs and are most often one page or less in length. The first section identifies why you are writing, what job you are applying for, and where you found information about the possible job opening. The second section (middle paragraph) relates your background to the position. At this point you reference the match between your skills, experiences, and goals and the organization's needs. Information on most organizations (e.g., their mission, history, business plan/goals) can be found online. Be specific and tailor the letter to the position. General, nonspecific, "template" letters reflect poorly on you and your interest in the company and position. The last paragraph/section

Box 5.7 *Example Cover Letter*

Joyce E. Brawley
1000 St. John's Church Rd.
Kennesaw, GA 30144
(770) 555-5555
JoyceEBrawley@emailnowz.com

June 27, 2018

Ira Amparo Longstreet, Jr.
State Human Resources Inc. of California
135-B Tango Place Rd. SW
Madera, CA 93636

Dear Mr. Longstreet,

Please let this letter and the attached résumé serve as my application for the human resource associate position at your company. I learned of this opening from an advertisement on your company's website.

Based on the information provided in the advertisement and information on your organization's website, it appears that there is an excellent fit between your needs and my background and career goals. According to the position description, you are seeking an individual with a bachelor's degree in psychology who has strong interpersonal skills, organizational experience, and a background in customer satisfaction survey development. As can be seen in the attached résumé, I graduated cum laude with my BS in Psychology last month. During my education I had the opportunity to intern in the university's human resources department. During that internship I helped develop, pilot, and analyze the results from an employee satisfaction survey. Based on the results, my supervisor and I developed a set of recommendations for the administration that would hopefully improve employee retention. I presented the findings to the director of human resources as well as at a regional conference. The skills developed through this internship match nicely with the background you desire.

My strong skills in working with others individually and in teams along with my desire to relocate to your area correspond well with the available position. I would appreciate the opportunity to speak with you regarding the position. Please feel free to contact me at 770-555-5555 or email me at the above address. I will touch base with you next week to make sure you received the application. I look forward to hearing from you in the near future.

Sincerely,
[Signature]
Joyce E. Brawley
Enclosure

should reiterate your interest in the company and position. At that point, you should state what you will do next (e.g., call or email to check on receipt of application, where the process stands, etc.) and invite the reader to contact you.

Keep Track of Where You Send Your Applications!

Given that most job seekers will send out lots of applications, it can be difficult to keep track of the specifics of positions. In addition to keeping copies of all applications, a good way to address potential memory glitches and keep your applications straight is to use a spreadsheet (e.g., using Microsoft Excel). In a spreadsheet, indicate the following for each application sent:

- contact person at the organization;
- address of the organization (Sometimes you may apply at more than one branch or location.);
- date the application was sent;
- response (Did they receive the application? Did they offer an interview?);
- job type (retail sales, managerial, human resources, etc.);
- salary (if known); and
- date decision to be made (if known).

Preparing For and Completing Job Interviews and Considering Offers

Preparing for the Interview

Before the interview, refresh your memory about why you applied for the position at this company. First, review the information on the position (e.g., the job advertisement). Second, review the information available on the company/program. Third, review your résumé and your application. Remember, each of your résumés and cover letters will be different, emphasizing only those skills and attributes pertinent to that particular position. Fourth, do a mock interview with your college's career center advisor/counselor. Most universities provide some form of coaching and preparation for interviews. (Note: Some of these services may also be available to graduates even years after they have graduated.) Fifth, practice in front of the mirror and role-play with friends who will provide *critical* feedback. Although it is nice to get positive feedback (especially the day of the interview), the days and weeks leading up to the interview should be focused on areas in need of improvement. Some practice interview questions are provided in Box 5.8. Another way to get feedback on your interviewing style is to video yourself

---

Box 5.8   *Practice Interview Questions*

Tell me what you know about our organization and the position.

What attracted you to our organization and the position?

Where do you see yourself in 5/10 years?

What background experience do you have?

What is your greatest strength?

What is your greatest weakness?

What do you think you will bring to the organization?

Tell me about a time when you had a conflict at work. How did you resolve it?[a]

Tell me about an ethical dilemma you have encountered in the past. How did you address it?[a]

We are interviewing quite a few people, why should we hire you?

Tell me about yourself.

What do you like to do in your spare time?

Is there anything else you would like us to know about you?

How has your background and education prepared you for the job you are seeking with us?

How would your previous employers/coworkers describe you and your work?

Do you have any questions about the organization or the position?

Note. [a]These behavioral-type interview questions are common. As a result, you should spend additional time preparing for this type of question.

as you will appear on the interview day and practice answering questions. Being videoed can create some anxiety, which might match the anxiety experienced on the interview day, allowing you the opportunity to find ways to manage the anxiety (e.g., deep breathing and practicing answers to common questions).

Although it is sad to say, appearance counts. As a result, in the days and weeks leading up to an interview, you will want to choose an outfit that fits the professional situation for which you are applying. Some pointers on appearance can be found at the University of North Carolina – Wilmington's Career Center internet site at http://uncw.edu/career/dressforsuccess.html (University of North Carolina – Wilmington, n.d.). In general, you will want to dress conservatively, wearing a dark suit, neat hair, minimal jewelry, and minimal make-up/cologne. In terms of your outfit, you will want to wear it prior to the interview so that you can ensure a comfortable fit.

The Day of the Interview

On the day of the interview, you should arrive early but not too early. You will want to allow plenty of time for traffic and parking problems. If you arrive too early for the interview (i.e., more than 15 minutes), take the time to review a copy of your application and the information you have on the organization and the person who will be interviewing you (if available). In terms of what to take with you to the interview, it is generally recommended that an interviewee have a notepad and pen, a copy of his/her application, several copies of an updated résumé (in case the person you are meeting with has not reviewed it), and a copy of your questions. Box 5.9 provides some ideas for questions you might ask.

Box 5.9 *Possible Questions to Ask a Potential Employer*

What is the financial outlook of the organization?
Where do you see the organization in 5/10 years?
What is the biggest challenge facing the organization?
Where in the hiring process are you?
When do you think a hiring decision will be made?
What do you like most about the organization?
How many applicants are you interviewing?
How would you describe the work atmosphere?

It is a given that you will be asked a variety of questions about your application and interest in the position and organization. Fortunately, your preparation through role-playing with friends and in front of the mirror has helped with this aspect of the interview. Additionally, there are generally typical questions that are asked by the interviewer that revolve around your strengths, skills, weaknesses, salary requirements, and career goals. However, you will also be expected to ask questions. Instead of having to think on your feet, having your questions prepared in advance can relieve some stress. Referring to your notes for this part and taking notes on answers to the questions are good ideas. It is difficult to remember what someone said hours, days, or weeks later given the stress of the interview day. Box 5.10 provides a list of some additional pointers for the interview.

After the Interview

After the interview is complete, send a thank-you note. Since most interviewees do not send one, it will set you apart in a good way. Depending on the situation, a note card or even an email will be sufficient. Calling the interviewer to deliver a thank you is not best. Unless you have genuine

---

Box 5.10 *Some Additional Interview Pointers*

- Demonstrate knowledge of the company/organization and the position.
- Be prepared to discuss your career plans.
- Show enthusiasm for the position (but not too much).
- Avoid evasiveness. Be direct with your answers when possible.
- Give eye contact, but do not stare.
- Be prepared to discuss your skills and experience, including limitations/weaknesses.
- Don't smell (i.e., too much perfume/cologne).
- Talk but not too much; engage in the conversation, but don't dominate it.
- Focus on the interview.
- Exude confidence, not arrogance.
- Eliminate street slang.
- Be honest, starting with your application and résumé.

Note. Some of the pointers come from Landrum and Davis (2013) and Martin (2013).

questions (e.g., you received another job offer and want to see where they are in their hiring process), it is best not to call.

Considering Job Offers

Be prepared for getting a job offer. In order to be prepared, you will want to have a minimum salary in mind, if you don't already. A good way to determine this amount is by developing a budget of your monthly expenses and multiplying these expenses by 12 to determine the yearly expenses. Once this number is calculated, multiple it by 1.35 to determine the approximate salary needed before taxes. Knowing this number can make the negotiation of salary easier. Websites like www.salary.com and www.payscale.com may also help with your estimations. Keep in mind that the salary offered is rarely the highest amount the employer can afford. Employers typically assume the potential employee will negotiate, and as a result, they will hold back some of the salary to allow for this negotiation. Additional things to consider when offered a job are:

- Will you be able to pay your bills?
- What is the work environment like? Is it friendly and collegial?
- What opportunities exist for raises and advancement?
- Will the company help with relocation expenses?
- What are the benefits? Do they include parking, health insurance, dental insurance, life insurance, and retirement?
- How is vacation and sick time accrued?
- What type of office space and equipment are provided?
- Is there administrative support?
- Are there professional development opportunities?
- Are the hours flexible or set?
- If the job involves a client load or caseload, what is it?
- What is the cost of living in the community where you will be living and working? (This varies greatly. We recommend using one of the cost-of-living calculators online to approximate the difference between where you currently live and where the new job is located.)

Starting Salaries

Don't think that we've forgotten about money! According to NACE's *Salary Survey* (2014), which is based on actual starting salaries as reported by approximately 400,000 employers, the average starting salary for new graduates with a bachelor's degree in psychology in 2013 was $37,400. Unfortunately, this number is significantly lower than the overall average starting salary of $45,633 for all students graduating with a bachelor's degree regardless of the field of study. However, this overall average of $45,633 could be skewed upward by some other disciplines like computer science (mean starting salary of $59,084) and engineering (mean starting salary of $62,564). Regardless, graduates in the humanities and social sciences do start at a lower salary on average when compared to their counterparts in other disciplines. However, even within the 2013 cohort of psychology bachelor's degree recipients, starting salaries varied depending on the industry where the new graduate started working. For new graduates working in "educational services," the average starting salary was $40,000. For those starting work in the "health care and social assistance" area, the average was $34,100. New graduates entering the workforce in "federal, state, and local government" positions averaged $41,600. Those entering the "professional, scientific, and technical services" area reported an average starting salary of $38,800. When evaluating these numbers, it's important to understand both that these are averages and that individual salaries are very dependent on the new graduate's qualifications. This last point deserves extra highlighting since you are in complete control of how you spend your time in college in taking advantage of the opportunities to develop qualifications that will set you apart from the "average!" The *qualifications* part is up to you!

Suggested Exercises

1. Using O*Net (www.onetonline.org), investigate three careers that interest you.
   a. What is the average salary for that position in your state?
   b. What are the typical work activities?
2. Based on your investigation in Suggested Exercise 1, choose the career that most interests you and do an informational interview of someone in that field. The following article by Crosby and Dillon (2010) will provide assistance with structuring the interview: http://www.bls.gov/careeroutlook/2010/summer/art03.pdf
3. Utilizing one of the internet resources listed in this chapter, find and investigate a current job opening that requires a bachelor's degree in psychology.
   a. What is the position?
   b. Where is it located?
   c. What are the application procedures?
   d. What is the salary?
4. Using the information in this chapter develop two résumés.
   a. Base your first résumé on your current experiences, background, and training.
   b. Base your second résumé on what you hope to accomplish by the time you graduate.

5. Using the information from this chapter, write a cover letter for a position in the field that you want to pursue.

Resources

*   Many universities have career web pages. These sites are often more trustworthy than the general internet findings. Here are two examples:
    *   https://careerctr.kennesaw.edu
    *   www.uncw.edu/career
*   Résumé resources on the internet – Be careful of online and paid services! We discourage using online and paid résumé services because they often use templates instead of tailoring a person's information to specific jobs. In contrast, we recommend your university career center. Most university career centers will help you with résumé writing. Some helpful resources available online are:
    *   Crosby and Liming (2009): http://www.bls.gov/careeroutlook/2009/summer/art03.pdf
    *   http://jobsearch.about.com/od/resumewriting/qt/writeresume.htm
    *   www.rileyguide.com
    *   www.eresumes.com
*   General job search and preparation resources:
    *   www.monster.com
    *   www.quintcareers.com
    *   www.collegegrad.com
    *   www.indeed.com
*   Psi Chi – The International Honor Society in Psychology has dozens of brief articles on career preparation. Go to this link and click on *Eye* under the Publications drop down menu at the top. Once at the *Eye on Psi Chi* site, browse the current and past issues for lots of great information on career and educational preparation: www.psichi.org.
*   O*Net Resource – www.onetonline.org: This resource provides a wide variety of information on occupations.
*   CareerOneStop – www.careeronestop.org: This site is sponsored by the US Department of Labor and offers employment information and career resources for students, job seekers, and businesses.
*   CareerZone – https://www.careerzone.ny.gov: The site boasts that it is "the place to explore careers related to your strengths, skills, and talents."
*   *Career Outlook* (formerly known as the *Occupational Outlook Quarterly*) – http://www.bls.gov/careeroutlook/: Bureau of Labor Statistics' quarterly publication of occupation-related information. Articles include:
    *   *What can I do with my liberal arts degree?* (Gehlhaus, 2007–2008) http://www.bls.gov/careeroutlook/2007/winter/art01.pdf
    *   *Internships: Previewing a profession* (Jones, 2006) http://www.bls.gov/careeroutlook/2006/summer/art02.pdf
    *   *Employment interviewing: Seizing the opportunity and the job* (Crosby, 2000) http://www.bls.gov/careeroutlook/2000/Summer/art02.pdf

- Lantz, C. (2011). *Psychology student employability guide: From university to career*. York, UK: The Higher Education Academy Psychology Network. Link: https://www.heacademy.ac.uk/sites/default/files/Employability_Guide_0.pdf Topics covered include:
  - career planning and decision making;
  - getting work experience;
  - creating a résumé; and
  - networking.

References

American Psychological Association. (2013). *APA guidelines for the undergraduate psychology major: Version 2.0.* Washington, DC: Author. Retrieved from http://www.apa.org/ed/precollege/about/psymajor-guidelines.pdf

Appleby, D. (2000, Spring). Job skills valued by employers who interview psychology majors. *Eye on Psi Chi, 4*(3), 17.

Appleby, D. C., Millspaugh, B. S., & Hammersley, M. J. (2011). *An online resource to enable undergraduate psychology majors to identify and investigate 172 psychology and psychology-related careers.* APA Division 2 – Society for the Teaching of Psychology's Office of Teaching Resources in Psychology. Retrieved from http://teachpsych.org/resources/Documents/otrp/resources/appleby11.pdf

CareerOneStop. (n.d.). Retrieved from www.careeronestop.org

CareerZone. (n.d.). Retrieved from www.careerzone.ny.gov

Collegegrad.com. (2011). 2011 top entry-level employers survey: Executive summary. Retrieved from http://www.collegegrad.com/docs/Top-Employers-Executive-Summary.pdf

Crosby, O. (2000, Summer). Employment interviewing: Seizing the opportunity and the job. *Occupational Outlook Quarterly, 44*(2), 14–21. Retrieved from www.bls.gov/careeroutlook/2000/Summer/art02.pdf

Crosby, O., & Dillon, T. (2010, Summer). Informational interviewing: Get the inside scoop on careers. *Occupational Outlook Quarterly, 46*(2), 22–29. Retrieved from http://www.bls.gov/careeroutlook/2010/summer/art03.pdf

Crosby, O., & Liming, D. (2009). Resumes, applications, and cover letters. *Occupational Outlook Quarterly.* Retrieved from www.bls.gov/careeroutlook/2009/summer/art03.pdf

Gehlhaus, D. (2007–2008, Winter). What can I do with my liberal arts degree? *Occupational Outlook Quarterly, 51*(4), 3–11. Retrieved from http://www.bls.gov/careeroutlook/2007/winter/art01.pdf

Jones, E. (2006, Summer). Internships: Previewing a profession. *Occupational Outlook Quarterly, 50*(2), 16–18. Retrieved from http://www.bls.gov/careeroutlook/2006/summer/art02.pdf

Landrum, R. E., & Davis, S. F. (2013). *The psychology major: Career options and strategies for success* (5th ed.). Upper Saddle River, NJ: Pearson.

Lloyd, M. A., Kennedy, J. H., & Dewey, R. A. (1997, August 28). *Suggested courses to develop skills that prospective employers want.* Retrieved from http://www.psywww.com/careers/suggest.htm

Martin, C. (2013). *Steer clear of interviewers' pet peeves.* Retrieved from http://career-advice.monster.com/job-interview/interview-preparation/interviewers-pet-peeves/article.aspx

National Association of Colleges and Employers. (2013). *Job outlook 2014*. Bethlehem, PA: Author.

National Association of Colleges and Employers. (2014, January). *Salary survey: Starting salaries for new college graduates: Data reported by employers*. Bethlehem, PA: Author.

National Science Foundation, National Center for Science and Engineering Statistics. (2012). *Characteristics of recent science and engineering graduates, 2008. Detailed statistical tables NSF 12-328*. Arlington, VA: Author. Retrieved from http://www.nsf.gov/statistics/nsf12328

University of North Carolina – Wilmington Career Center (n.d.). *Dress for success*. Retrieved from http://uncw.edu/career/dressforsuccess.html

US Department of Education, National Center for Education Statistics. (2013). *Table 318.30: Bachelor's, master's, and doctor's degrees conferred by post-secondary institutions, by sex of student, and discipline division: 2011–12*. Retrieved from http://nces.ed.gov/programs/digest/d13/tables/dt13_318.30.asp

Chapter Six
The Preprofessional Degree
Preparing for Graduate School

Introduction

As noted earlier, the undergraduate degree can be viewed from two perspectives. The first views the bachelor's degree in psychology as a liberal arts degree. The student pursuing this path has the primary goal of entering the job market upon graduation. The second perspective views the bachelor's degree in psychology as a preprofessional degree. This is similar to the trajectories of pre-dental, pre-medicine, and pre-law that many students follow as undergraduates. As such, the student taking the preprofessional view of the bachelor's degree in psychology has the primary goal of gaining admission to graduate school either immediately upon graduation or at some point in the future. Although these perspectives have much in common (e.g., the same curriculum to complete the bachelor's degree), preparation issues significantly differ between the two. This chapter addresses some of those differences with the goal of helping students on the preprofessional path make the most of their undergraduate experience by preparing for the competition involved in applying to graduate school and for the demands of being a student in a graduate program. Topics addressed in this chapter include deciding to go to graduate school and making the necessary preparations, such as choosing the best courses, making good grades, gaining research experience, gaining field/work experience, establishing a mentoring relationship, getting involved in professional organizations, getting involved on-campus, and getting involved in the community.

Majoring in Psychology: Achieving Your Educational and Career Goals, Second Edition.
Jeffrey L. Helms and Daniel T. Rogers.
© 2015 John Wiley & Sons, Ltd. Published 2015 by John Wiley & Sons, Ltd.

Is Graduate School Right for You?

Before getting into specific graduate school preparatory issues, we would first like to examine graduate school from a broader perspective. As discussed in the chapter that focuses on applying to graduate school, the application process is no easy task and neither is graduate school itself. In fact, the *10-year* doctoral completion rate is only 65.1% for psychology (Council of Graduate Schools PhD Completion Project, 2008). Given the difficulty, why should someone want to go to graduate school? The most obvious reason is that almost all of the specialized skills associated with psychology are taught and acquired *only* at the graduate level (e.g., program evaluation, employer/employee consultation, counseling, psychotherapy, psychological testing, and advanced research skills). The undergraduate degree in psychology provides the solid foundation for the acquisition of these skills at the graduate level. The second part of this book spends considerable time reviewing the graduate-level skills learned in the specific subfields of psychology. In short, there are a number of skills learned in graduate school that make the process not only worthwhile but also very enjoyable. Salazar and Frincke (2005) note 15 skills developed and improved during graduate training, regardless of the subfield studied. These skills include understanding group dynamics, objective thinking, ability to argue and defend different viewpoints, computer skills, and the scientific method. Box 6.1 provides a list of all 15 skills.

Another, often overlooked reason to complete graduate training is employment status and prospects. A survey of recent doctorate recipients reported an unemployment rate of 6% (Michalski, Kohout, Wicherski, & Hart, 2011). Although seemingly high, this percentage is significantly better when taken in light of the economic downturn in 2008 and the double digit unemployment levels for many graduates. Furthermore, 72% of those surveyed indicated that the employment position they currently held was their first choice. In terms of how long it took to find employment, 44% found their current position prior to completing their graduate program, and 29.1% found their position within 3 months. Only 11.1% took more than 6 months to find their current position. Last but definitely not least, respondents to the survey indicated an overall positive level of satisfaction with their current position.

Even given these very positive attributes, how do you know if graduate school is right for you? Over the years, authors have attempted to provide some guidance to students trying to answer this question (e.g., Fretz & Stang, 1988; Keith-Spiegel & Wiederman, 2000; Kuther, 2011). All urge students who are considering graduate study to be honest with themselves.

Box 6.1 *Skills Developed and Improved During Graduate School*

- Ability to function in various roles/environments
- Teaching skills (inside and outside the classroom)
- Interviewing skills
- Public speaking skills
- Computer skills
- Ability to argue and defend different viewpoints
- Scientific method skills
- Research methods, data analysis, and statistic skills
- Ability to integrate information from multiple sources
- Ability to evaluate information/data critically
- Ability to understand group dynamics
- Ability to appreciate and work with differing viewpoints
- Ability to accept criticism and rejection
- Objective thinking skills
- Ability to tolerate and work with ambiguity

Note. Information comes from Salazar and Frincke (2005).

For example, it takes a great deal of self-motivation and strong organizational skills to succeed in graduate school. Because these are generally viewed as positive attributes, students may tend to indicate that they possess these qualities at a high level when in reality they do not. For such a weighty decision as whether or not to attend graduate school, an inaccurate self-assessment would be a mistake as it sets you up for failure. To assist with making an accurate evaluation of your readiness for graduate school, Box 6.2 provides some personal qualities and behaviors to consider when making your decision. We provide them with the hope that you will pursue the path that is the best fit for you.

Course Selection

Tailoring your course selection to match those courses required or preferred by graduate programs is a wise move. The American Psychological Association (APA; 2014) annually publishes a text titled *Graduate Study in Psychology* (GSP). It is an excellent resource for students investigating different graduate school programs in psychology. Historically, GSP included information on courses that were required or recommended by specific

Box 6.2 *Twenty Personal Qualities, Attitudes, and Behaviors Consistent with Graduate Training*

How accurately do the following qualities and behaviors describe you?

1. Comfortable living below the poverty line
   - Although many programs offer tuition remission and stipends, rarely is the stipend enough to prevent having to substantially adjust one's standard of living and/or borrow money.
2. Enjoys writing
   - Most courses require extensive writing assignments. Interestingly, graduate school professors often given a *maximum* length to term papers as opposed to the minimum lengths frequently provided to undergraduates.
3. Enjoys doing research
   - Depending on the type of program, the majority of your time outside of your regular coursework will be spent conducting research for your professors, working on your own research (e.g., your master's thesis or doctoral dissertation), and helping colleagues with their research. (By "research" we mean things like doing literature reviews, designing and conducting experiments, gathering and managing data, statistically analyzing data, and writing up the results.)
4. Good with statistics
   - Most programs require at least a couple of advanced statistics courses. Some require one each semester. Regardless, students will need to use and understand statistics on a regular basis in their research activities.
5. Enjoys reading psychology books and journals
   - Background reading consumes significant amounts of time. This reading involves not only course materials but also reading related to your research and training. This reading often includes large amounts of original empirical research. Luckily, it is typically in an area you enjoy!
6. Can delay gratification (short-term and long-term)
   - Graduate students often make difficult decisions, putting off personal preferences for necessities that serve their ultimate goals. For example, it is not uncommon for graduate students to:
     a. study instead of going out or watching television;
     b. eat at home instead of at restaurants; and
     c. opt for cheaper living accommodations (e.g., have roommates, live in university housing).

7. Enjoys studying for hours at a time (e.g., 6–8 hours per session, multiple times per week)
    - Although graduate students certainly have fun, a significant part of their time is spent studying. When not in class or in their lab working on research, they are often studying. Unlike many of the courses you will have in your bachelor's program, graduate school is a building process in which you are required to retain information not only for the test but also for the duration of the program and your career.
8. Can easily concentrate
    - Successful graduate students are able to focus their attention on a particular course, project, situation, etc., even though other forces may be impinging on them (e.g., a noisy room-mate, personal issues, neighbors, television).
9. Organized
    - Graduate school requires the ability to get and stay organized. This ability is especially important given the large quantity of material to be learned and increased time commitments.
10. Gets above average/excellent grades
    - Most graduate programs do not allow any Cs. In fact, the expectation is 'A' work in all courses. Bs, although sufficient in most programs, suggest that you may be struggling.
11. Desires graduate training not because of status (e.g., "being called Dr.")
    - The novelty of being called "Doctor" soon wears off. More times than not, when someone calls you "doctor," they need/ want something from you. If status is a goal, there are much easier paths than graduate school.
12. Desires graduate training not because of an imagined high salary
    - Although salary is significantly greater with a graduate degree, few areas of psychology command top salaries relative to other careers. Industrial–organizational psychology is an exception.
13. Strong desire to learn
    - Without a strong desire to learn, it is very easy to get side-tracked from your ultimate goal of a graduate education.
14. Has strong interpersonal skills
    - Graduate students routinely interact with a variety of individu-als. Interpersonal skills are very important in dealing with fellow

graduate students, research participants, professors, clients/patients, department staff, and your own students (for those who are teaching assistants).

15. Can receive and respond effectively to critical feedback
   - As a graduate student, you will receive vast quantities of critical feedback from faculty mentors, supervisors, and peers. With the feedback comes the expectation that you will remedy any weakness immediately.

16. Enjoys school and the school environment (i.e., class, library, labs)
   - Graduate students spend the majority of their time in the academic environment. There are few escapes beyond holidays with family. Oftentimes your social activities and even your roommates are program-related.

17. Driven to accomplish
   - Graduate students are expected to be self-starters. Very little hand-holding is provided. In fact, the more supervision required for some activities, the more negatively you may be viewed by the professors. There is an expectation that you will seek out answers on your own and not rely on or look first to your professors.

18. Devoted to the discipline
   - Graduate students in psychology develop a clear and strong identity within the discipline. Although doing this may in part be self-protective because they have invested a lot of themselves in the graduate school venture, it is uncommon to find a graduate student who is not clear in his or her commitment to the discipline.

19. Does not mind (enjoys) giving presentations
   - Graduate students routinely give presentations. These include presentations in their own graduate courses, undergraduate courses they teach, and at research conferences.

20. Can tolerate ambiguity
   - As you are learning in your undergraduate program, psychology is not a clear cut science. Ambiguity is a cornerstone to the discipline. Graduate students must tolerate and in some cases embrace this aspect. For some subfields of psychology (e.g., clinical psychology), decisions that affect people's lives must be made even in the face of uncertainty.

graduate programs. Although still an excellent resource for other information, GSP discontinued inclusion of this specific information in recent years. Fortunately in a recent study, Lawson, Reisinger, and Jordan-Flemming (2012) reviewed the websites of all graduate departments listed in the then-current GSP. Results clearly indicated that Statistics was overwhelmingly the most preferred course, regardless of the type of program (i.e., clinical, experimental, industrial–organizational, educational–school, or mixed programs). Statistics was listed by 91.8% of the programs. Collapsing across all program types, Research Methods came in second at 74.4%. Not surprisingly, they also found that courses like Abnormal Psychology were preferred more by clinical and counseling psychology programs than by experimental or industrial–organizational psychology programs. Although similar studies in the past (Lawson, 1995; Smith, 1985) indicated courses like Statistics and Research Methods to be highly valued, certain courses that were historically preferred (e.g., History and Systems, Sensation and Perception) were less desired in the more recent study's findings.

In terms of preferences of specific types of programs, Lawson et al. (2012) found that the top six most preferred psychology courses by the clinical and counseling psychology programs were Statistics (88.1%), Abnormal (73.8%), Research Methods (73.1%), Developmental (46.9%), Personality (46.3%), and Biopsychology (33.1%). The top six for educational and school psychology were Statistics (86.7%), Research Methods (75.6%), Developmental (64.4%), Abnormal (44.4%), Testing (35.6%), and Personality (31.1%). The top six courses for industrial–organizational psychology programs were Statistics (92.9%), Research Methods (60.7%), Social (25%), Cognitive (17.9%), Testing (14.3%), and Personality (14.3%). The top six courses preferred by experimental psychology graduate programs were Statistics (96.2%), Research Methods (81.1%), Biopsychology (18.9%), Cognitive (18.9%), Developmental (15.1%), and Learning (15.1%).

In addition to choosing your psychology coursework wisely, you should also choose your nonpsychology coursework wisely. We discourage taking "fluff" courses like Badminton or Bowling. This advice is not commentary on whether these are challenging or fun courses, it simply is a reminder that graduate programs will review your undergraduate transcript as a record of your learning. If you must take these types of courses, wait until your very last semester so that they do not appear on your transcripts submitted with your graduate school applications. Graduate faculty who review applications tend to view these courses as a waste of valuable time, time that could have been spent doing research or minoring in a related area. For example, electives in the math and natural sciences areas are strongly encouraged. In fact, we recommend filling at least a portion of your electives with several courses in statistics. Most math departments offer upper-level courses in statistics. As another example, if you want to pursue a graduate degree in animal behavior, physiological psychology, or neuroscience, we would recommend biology and chemistry coursework as electives.

Timing of your coursework is also important. As discussed in the next chapter, some graduate programs require applicants to take the Psychology Subject Test (a standardized test developed by the Educational Testing Service). As the name indicates, this test covers all areas of psychology. Students usually take it during the fall semester of their senior year, immediately prior to applying to graduate school programs for admission the following fall semester. As a result, students are strongly encouraged not to postpone taking the "harder" psychology courses (e.g., Cognitive Psychology, Sensation and Perception, Physiological Psychology) until their senior year. Doing so will put you at a significant disadvantage when taking this test. Even if the graduate programs you want to attend do not require it, graduate faculty will want to see excellent grades in these upper-level courses on your transcript. This means that you will need to complete at least some of them in time so that they show up on your transcript. Moreover, we encourage seeking opportunities to accentuate your courses through additional work. For example, many universities have an honors program or college that allows students to explore required (and additional) coursework in more depth. Exceeding the required minimum in your coursework demonstrates your commitment to education.

An additional timing issue is starting your major coursework early. We recommend beginning your coursework for the psychology major your first semester of college by taking Introductory or General Psychology. Lower-level coursework is often required prior to taking any of the upper-level coursework. Additionally, you will want to take your research foundation coursework (e.g., Research Methods, Experimental Psychology, and Statistics) as early as possible. This is important because faculty will generally not allow you to work with them on research projects until you have successfully completed the research foundation coursework. Discussed in a later section of this chapter, research experience is almost always the number one ranked criterion when evaluating graduate school applicants (e.g., Lawson, 1995).

Students also have concerns about withdrawing from courses. Although the preference is for students to have no withdrawals on their transcript, students should have no more than one or two withdrawals at most. The reason for this preference is that withdrawals indicate one of two possible personal attributes of the student. First, it may indicate that the student took on more responsibility than he/she could handle. Not knowing your limits is not a good attribute. Second, a withdrawal may indicate that the student could not do the work. Given the significant increase in difficulty of graduate work, not being able to successfully complete an *undergraduate* course is not a good sign for later success in graduate school. In short, withdrawals only signal and draw attention to potential negative attributes.

Grades and Grade Point Average

A student's grades and grade point average (GPA) are very important pieces of the graduate school application. As a result, it is imperative to begin your undergraduate career strong and stay strong. In other words, it is difficult to raise a low GPA. The next question students almost always ask is, "What is a *good enough* GPA?" Although it varies by program, research indicates that the average *minimum* required overall GPA of applicants in 2003–2004 was 3.11 for doctoral programs and 2.92 for master's programs (Norcross, Kohout, & Wicherski, 2005). The associated *minimum* required Psychology GPA was 3.17 for doctoral programs and 3.05 for master's programs. However, the minimum required is often significantly different from what is actually accepted. In fact for these same years (2003–2004), the study found that the *actual* overall GPA was 3.54 for applicants accepted to doctoral programs and 3.37 for applicants accepted to master's programs. For some programs (e.g., Clinical Psychology PhD programs), the *actual* overall GPAs can be close to 4.0. These findings hold true (and may have increased some) in more recent years too. According to the recent GSP (APA, 2014), median GPA for those accepted to master's programs was 3.49. Those accepted into doctoral programs had a median GPA of 3.62. Knowing this information, students will often mistakenly opt to take "fluff" courses to raise their GPAs. As noted in the previous section, this is unwise. The reason it is unwise is that graduate school faculty expect (and verify) that the GPA a student has is based on an adequate, if not rigorous, curriculum/coursework. Also, keep in mind that calculation of your GPA when applying to graduate school includes all undergraduate coursework at all universities attended. This includes the summer course you took at the local community college. Your GPA also includes the grade you received in the course you "retook" for a higher grade plus the grade in the original course. It also includes your first semester of college before you transferred to your current college. In short, it includes *everything*. The GPA that graduate schools want you to report is all inclusive. As you think about maintaining or improving your GPA, remember that earlier chapters in this book provide some concrete strategies for improving the likelihood of success in college and in the psychology major.

Research Experience

In addition to objective criteria (e.g., GPA and test scores), nonobjective criteria (e.g., letters of recommendation, personal statements, and interviews) are also used to evaluate applicants to graduate programs. Research experience is one of these nonobjective criteria. In fact, experience helping professors with their research projects and experience collaborating with a professor on your own research idea are excellent preparation for graduate school. Box 6.3 provides a list of some of the benefits of engaging in research.

Appropriately enough, the importance of research experience is verified by research studies. Smith (1985), Lawson (1995), and Norcross et al. (2005) reviewed the importance of having this experience when applying to graduate school. All three studies relied on analysis of data provided in the GSP. Regardless of the years reviewed or whether reviewing master's or doctoral programs, research experience was rated very highly.

Two additional studies surveyed graduate school faculty. Keith-Spiegel, Tabachnick, and Spiegel (1994) surveyed 123 graduate faculty members regarding the importance of a host of nonobjective criteria. Research experience resulting in authorship credit in a peer-reviewed publication received the highest overall rating (i.e., a 4.45 out of a possible 5). In a more recent survey of faculty involved in selecting students for graduate study in forensic psychology, research activity received a mean of 2.94 out of a possible 3 in importance (Helms & Mayhew, 2006). In fact, its mean clearly placed it as the most important nonobjective criteria in the study, ahead of letters of recommendation and

---

Box 6.3   *The Benefits of Research Experience*

- Acquire knowledge and skills outside of the classroom (i.e., applied, hands-on experience)
- Work individually with a faculty member
- Contribute to the scientific literature/advance science (including possible authorship credit)
- Exposure to research techniques
- Enhance project management and teamwork skills
- Practice written and oral communication skills by preparing articles for submission to journals and conferences and presenting at conferences
- Establish a mentoring relationship

Note. Information comes from Landrum (2002).

personal statements. In summary, it appears that regardless of the research methodology used, research experience enjoys a place at the top in terms of its evaluative importance for graduate school applicants. It is important to highlight the fact that this finding remains consistent over time.

So how do you get involved in research? First, you will want to begin early. Because relationships with faculty take time to develop and research takes time to complete, your first year of college is not too early to begin. Learn about your professors' research by reading their biographies on the department website and reading some of their recent publications. Talk with students who are currently conducting research to learn about their experiences. Check with your department to see if there is a centralized process (e.g., an application) for starting a research experience. Introduce yourself to professors who you might want to work with, making sure to communicate your interests in obtaining research experience and your knowledge of their specific research. Some advanced students, undergraduates and graduates, may need help with their research studies too. Offer to collect and enter data for a professor or advanced student. Offer to gather background literature for his or her study. These initial activities will demonstrate your commitment to research and increase the likelihood that a faculty member will include you in his or her later projects as well as work with you on developing your own project. Also, you will want to branch out and work with multiple faculty members too. As discussed in the next chapter, you will need at least three letters of recommendation to accompany your applications to graduate school. You will want to make sure that at least two of the three faculty members who write letters for you will be able to address your research experience first-hand.

An additional point needs to be kept in mind. Students often start gaining research experience too late (e.g., their last year). As a result, they do not have time to advance through the process of assisting a professor to developing/completing their own study. Because research studies take time to complete, beginning a study during your last year will likely not result in a completed project before it is time to send out graduate school applications. (Most applications are due in late November and December for admission the following fall semester.) Also, Kaiser, Kaiser, Richardson, and Fox (2007) found that not all research experiences are valued equally by graduate programs. The results of their survey clearly indicated that research experiences that resulted in being an author or coauthor on a publication and presenting at a professional conference outranked other types of research experiences. In short, bringing the research project to fruition and disseminating the results are very important. Given that seeing an article accepted and actually published can take a year or more after submission to a journal, and given that deadlines for some conference submissions can be 6 months or more in advance of the actual conference, getting started early is imperative. Fortunately, you know this now, which puts you ahead of many of your competitors.

Internships, Field Practica, and Work Experience

Internships, field practica, and work experience can be valuable points of reference not only for the student but also the graduate faculty reviewing the student's application. Graduate faculty members routinely hear from perspective students via applications or in communications that they are really interested in this particular area of psychology, whatever *this* area is. When faculty members ask these students *how* they know they are interested in this area, they often receive a blank stare or an equally unsophisticated response of "I just know." As you already know, intuition does not hold much value in this field as a way of knowing something. On the other hand, a student who can support his or her interest in a particular field with first-hand experience of working with a particular population (e.g., children) or in a particular setting (e.g., a correctional environment) places herself or himself above the pack of other applicants or interviewees. Walter (2007) provides the following six benefits in pursuing internship, field practica, and relevant work experience:

1. clarification of interests and goals;
2. skill development;
3. networking opportunities;
4. enhances graduate school applications;
5. allows application of what has been learned; and
6. increases awareness of strengths and weaknesses.

Opportunities to gain experience are typically available to those students who are genuinely interested. Oftentimes, departments have internship or field practicum courses, and university career services centers and faculty have connections in the community to jumpstart an experience. Opportunities vary from being an undergraduate teaching assistant for those with the goal of entering academe to being a behavioral technician at a program for children with developmental disabilities for those interested in being a clinical or school psychologist. Even in universities that do not have these types of opportunities, community settings often have volunteer programs (e.g., psychiatric hospitals). Regardless, you will want an experience that provides ample supervision and structure. Unstructured and unsupervised activities typically do not carry much weight on graduate school applications.

Additionally, given time and financial demands, some students have found paying jobs in related settings that prove useful to their eventual career goals. For those who take time off before going to graduate school, working in a field that is directly related to the graduate program you wish to pursue is very important. Last but not least, a supervisor of your field-related work is a possible source for another letter of recommendation.

Mentoring

A mentor is a person who is able to provide ongoing direction to a novice seeking to enter the same field. In academe, a mentor is a professor who guides the student through his or her education, always keeping in mind the student's career goals. The guidance provided by a mentor is based not only on experience but also on what the research has shown to be helpful when pursuing certain goals (e.g., encouraging research experience). In searching for a mentor and beginning a mentoring relationship, a student should keep in mind three characteristics: interpersonal skills, personal attributes, and professional competencies (Appleby, 1999). Box 6.4 lists the four components of each characteristic.

Box 6.4 *Characteristics and Components of an Effective Mentor*

Interpersonal skills
- Caring and encouraging
- Promoting and sponsoring
- Supporting and protecting
- Challenging and demanding

Personal attributes
- Mature and wise
- Friendly and optimistic
- Admired and respected
- Trustworthy and dependable

Professional competencies
- Qualified and competent
- Experienced and seasoned
- Knowledgeable and informative
- Professionally involved and active

Note. Information comes from Appleby (1999).

Although comfort with the mentor should come first, the student will do well to choose a mentor in a field similar to what he or she wants to pursue. For example, although a clinical psychologist could provide some excellent general perspectives on preparing for graduate school in social psychology, a better resource and potential mentor would be a social psychologist. In this example, the social psychologist would likely be more familiar with the available training programs and have connections to graduate faculty in the social psychology area. In looking at Box 6.4, you might be thinking that deciphering who might be a good mentor is impossible or at least too complicated and time consuming to be useful. However, a few tools can help you measure a potential mentor in advance.

1. Base part of your decision on having had the mentor as a professor.
2. Gravitate to the more challenging and demanding professors.
3. Seek out the professors who generally work with students.
4. Focus on those professors who produce (i.e., professors who have students regularly presenting at conferences and being accepted into graduate schools).

These four pointers should make the process significantly easier for you.

Getting Involved in Professional Organizations

Membership in a professional organization provides many and varied opportunities for the undergraduate student. Unfortunately, Koch (2006) notes that many students join professional organizations simply to list them on their vita or résumé. However, students interested in really getting involved in their respective field are encouraged to join and get active. In fact, most professional organizations provide student memberships at significantly reduced cost.

One of the benefits to joining a professional organization as a student member includes eligibility to apply for travel awards and research grants specifically for students. For example, the RISE Research Award from the Association for Psychological Science (APS) aims "to cultivate scholarly research in psychological fields related to socially and economically underrepresented populations, as well as to acknowledge outstanding research conducted by student members" (APS, n.d.). Submissions for this award are reviewed by student members. As a result, even though you may not submit a grant/award proposal you could volunteer to review other students' proposals. Experience providing feedback to colleagues/peers, especially in regard to research, is an excellent skill to highlight on a graduate school application. APS's Student Caucus may have a representative already on your campus. To find out, refer to the web link listed in Box 6.5. If your campus does not have a representative, this is another opportunity for you to become involved!

Benefits of belonging to a professional association also include the opportunity to network with other students and professors at other universities. Most student memberships also include the organization's publications. For example, student affiliates of the APA receive the association's main journal, the *American Psychologist*, as well as their monthly magazine, *Monitor on Psychology*. These publications give you the opportunity to stay abreast of some of the current happenings in the field.

Because it may be more difficult to get involved in the larger national associations (e.g., APA), the APA divisions, the regional psychological associations, and the state/territory/provincial psychological associations may provide an opportunity for involvement. Box 6.5 provides links to some resources to get you started. Granted this type of activity is not as highly valued as research experience. However, being actively involved in a professional organization clearly demonstrates your current and long-term commitment to the field. This commitment is especially visible when your activity level in the organization is high and has occurred for an extended period of time (i.e., more than a year).

Getting Involved on Campus

Similar to professional organizations, getting involved on campus by being active in psychology-oriented clubs and honor societies demonstrates commitment to the field. This commitment and involvement will be noticed by the faculty members in your department, including those who will be writing letters of recommendation for you. The two most common student organizations are a psychology club and Psi Chi – The International Honor Society in Psychology. For those students at junior and community colleges, Psi Beta – The National Honor Society in Psychology for Community and Junior Colleges is sometimes available. Although most psychology clubs do not have requirements for membership, the honor societies do. These requirements include completion of a certain number of psychology courses and a minimum 3.0 GPA on a 4.0 scale. If you do not have Psi Chi or Psi Beta at your university or college, consider starting a chapter. The first author (Helms) was a founding member of the Psi Chi chapter at his undergraduate university. Involvement in one of these organizations is typically

Box 6.5 *Professional Organizations* 117

National organizations
- American Psychological Association – http://www.apa.org/students
- Association for Psychological Science (APS) – www.psychological science.org
- Association for Psychological Science – Student Caucus – http://www.psychologicalscience.org/apssc

Regional associations
- Eastern Psychological Association – www.easternpsychological.org
- Midwestern Psychological Association – www.midwesternpsych.org
- New England Psychological Association – www.newenglandpsy chological.org
- Rocky Mountain Psychological Association – www.rockymountain psych.org
- Southeastern Psychological Association – www.sepaonline.com
- Southwestern Psychological Association – www.swpsych.org
- Western Psychological Association – www.westernpsych.org

APA divisions
- Fifty-four divisions of the APA devoted to specific interest areas (e.g., Psychotherapy, Addictions, and Developmental Psychology).
- A list of all divisions along with links to their respective websites can be found at: http://www.apa.org/about/division.html

Diversity-related organizations
- Asian American Psychological Association – aapaonline.org
- Association of Black Psychologists – www.abpsi.org
- Society for the Psychological Study of Lesbian, Gay, and Bisexual Issues – www.apadivision44.org
- Society for the Psychological Study of Men and Masculinity – http://www.apa.org/divisions/div51
- Society for the Psychology of Women – http://www.apa.org/divisions/div35
- Society for the Psychological Study of Culture, Ethnicity, and Race – division45.org

State/territory/provincial psychological associations
- A list of all state/territory and provincial psychological associations with links to their respective websites can be found at: http://www.apa.org/practice/refer.html

International psychological associations
- A list of international psychological associations with their respective web sites and contact information can be found at: http://www.apa.org/international/directories/international-orgs.aspx

more accessible and readily identifiable in comparison to external professional organizations. However, the same principle applies; simply being a member is not enough. The student must be active. Fortunately, opportunities to serve in student organizations that are related to psychology are usually available. Some of the opportunities include being an officer (e.g., president, treasurer) and participating in fundraising activities (e.g., raising money for a local charity).

Community Service and Extracurricular Activities

Although potentially beneficial educationally, most graduate programs do not rate community service and extracurricular activities very highly when evaluating graduate school applicants. In fact, these activities are generally last in the rankings (Norcross et al., 2005). This does not mean that these activities are not given any value. Regardless, given time and resource limitations, students are encouraged to focus their efforts on research experiences first and the other activities noted in this chapter prior to devoting time to activities in this realm (e.g., fraternity or sorority involvement).

Suggested Exercises

1. Using your department's web page, investigate two psychology faculty members who may be potential mentors to you. Helpful questions to answer might include:
   a. In what area of psychology is his/her degree?
   b. What research does he/she do?
   c. Has she/he published any articles? (If so, find a recent one and read it.)
   d. Does she/he ever work with students? If so, how can you tell?
   e. Does his/her research interest you?
   Based on your investigation, contact the professor you are most interested in working with, introduce yourself and your interests, demonstrate your familiarity with their research, and inquire about possible opportunities to assist on a project.
2. Access a copy of your university's student handbook or catalog that includes descriptions of the courses offered throughout the university. Based on your ultimate educational and career goals, plan out the remainder of your undergraduate education. Be sure to include courses in the areas recommended in this chapter (e.g., upper-level Statistics courses).

Box 6.6 *Timeframe of Suggested Activities for Preparing for Graduate School*

First year
- In addition to focusing on your university's general education coursework, complete lower-level psychology coursework.
- Begin taking the required math and science coursework along with statistics coursework.
- Begin attending department activities (e.g., join and participate in the psychology club).
- Get involved with research by discussing opportunities with professors.
- Identify a potential mentor by observing her or his activities inside and outside the department.
- Attend a local/state/regional psychology conference.

Second year
- Complete the research foundation coursework (e.g., Research Methods and Experimental Psychology).
- Increase your research activity.
- Join Psi Chi and become involved in its activities.
- Join a professional association and become involved.
- Discuss with a faculty member the possibility of developing your own research idea.
- Attend another local/state/regional psychology conference.

Third year
- Take the majority of your upper-level psychology coursework in preparation for the Graduate Record Exam Psychology Subject Test.
- Hold an office in Psi Chi or the Psychology Club.
- Become involved with RISE in APS or a similar research-oriented activity.
- Complete first research study with a professor and present it at a conference.
- Work with your professor to submit a manuscript to a peer-reviewed journal.
- Begin work with another professor on research.

Fourth year
- Continue research activities with at least two professors.
- Present another study at a conference.

- Work with your professor to submit the new research to a peer-reviewed journal.
- Complete a field practicum, teaching assistantship, internship, etc.
- Maintain level of activity in the organizations.

Note. Specific information on the application process and timeframe is provided in Chapter 7.

3. Use Box 6.2 "Twenty Personal Qualities, Attitudes, and Behaviors Consistent with Graduate Training" for this exercise. Rate each of the personal qualities on a scale from 1 (Not at all like me) to 5 (Absolutely like me). Sum your ratings for a total ranging from 20–100. Answer the following questions.
   a. Does the number surprise you?
   b. How does it compare to your peers?
   c. Which qualities are most like you?
   d. Which are least like you?
   e. Which do you think will be the most difficult for you as a graduate student?
   f. Which are areas that you could significantly improve during the remainder of your undergraduate education?

Suggested Readings

American Psychological Association. (2007). *Getting in: A step-by-step plan for gaining admission to graduate school in psychology* (2nd ed.). Washington, DC: Author.

Buskist, W., & Burke, C. (2007). *Preparing for graduate study in psychology: 101 questions and answers* (2nd ed.). Malden, MA: Blackwell.

Keith-Spiegel, P., & Wiederman, M. W. (2000). *The complete guide to graduate school admission: Psychology, counseling, and related professions* (2nd ed.). Mahwah, NJ: Lawrence Erlbaum Associates.

Resources

- APA Science Directorate: Lists resources to help undergraduate students find research experiences and internships: http://www.apa.org/science/undergradopps.html
- Psi Beta – The National Honor Society in Psychology for Community and Junior Colleges: www.psibeta.org
- Psi Chi – The International Honor Society in Psychology: www.psichi.org
   o *Eye on Psi Chi* Magazine (http://www.psichi.org/?page=eye_main): regularly provides career-related and graduate school preparation resources

References

American Psychological Association. (2014).*Graduate study in psychology: 2014*. Washington, DC: Author.

Appleby, D. (1999, Spring). Choosing a mentor. *Eye on Psi Chi, 3*(3), 38–39.

Association for Psychological Science. (n.d.). *RISE research award*. Retrieved from http://www.psychologicalscience.org/index.php/members/rise/research-award

Council of Graduate Schools PhD Completion Project. (2008). *Program completion and attrition data*. Retrieved from http://www.phdcompletion.org/quantitative/book1_quant.asp

Fretz, B. R., & Stang, D. J. (1988). *Preparing for graduate study in psychology: Not for seniors only!* Washington, DC: American Psychological Association.

Helms, J. L., & Mayhew, L. L. (2006). *Undergraduate preparation for graduate training in forensic psychology*. APA Division 2 – Society for the Teaching of Psychology's Office of Teaching Resources in Psychology. Retrieved from http://teachpsych.org/resources/Documents/otrp/resources/helms06.pdf

Kaiser, J. C., Kaiser, A. J., Richardson, A. J., & Fox, E. J. (2007, Winter). Perceptions of graduate admission directors: Undergraduate student research experiences: Are all research experiences rated equally? *Eye on Psi Chi, 11*(2), 22–24.

Keith-Spiegel, P., & Wiederman, M. W. (2000). *The complete guide to graduate school admission: Psychology, counseling, and related professions* (2nd ed.). Mahwah, NJ: Lawrence Erlbaum Associates.

Keith-Spiegel, P., Tachnick, B. G., & Spiegel, G. B. (1994). When demand exceeds supply: Second-order criteria used by graduate school selection committees. *Teaching of Psychology, 21*, 79–81. doi:10.1207/s15328023top2102_3

Koch, C. (2006, Fall). Student memberships lead to greater opportunities in psychology. *Eye on Psi Chi, 11*(1), 27–28.

Kuther, T. L. (2011). *The psychology major's handbook* (3rd ed.). Belmont, CA: Cengage.

Landrum, R. E. (2002, Winter). Maximizing undergraduate opportunities: The value of research and other experiences. *Eye on Psi Chi, 6*(2), 15–18.

Lawson, T. J. (1995). Gaining admission into graduate programs in psychology: An update. *Teaching of Psychology, 22*, 225–227. doi:10.1207/s15328023top2204_2

Lawson, T. J., Reisinger, D. L., & Jordan-Flemming, M. K. (2012). Undergraduate psychology courses preferred by graduate programs. *Teaching of Psychology, 39*, 181–184. doi:10.1177/0098628312450430

Michalski, D., Kohout, J., Wicherski, M., & Hart, B. (2011, May). *2009 doctorate employment suvey*. Washington, DC: American Psychological Association's Center for Psychology Workforce Analysis and Research. Retrieved from http://www.apa.org/workforce/publications/09-doc-empl/report.pdf

Norcross, J. C., Kohout, J. L., & Wicherski, M. (2005). Graduate study in Psychology: 1971 to 2004. *American Psychologist, 60*, 959–975. doi:10.1037/0003-066X.60.9.959

Salazar, M., & Frincke, J. (2005, April). *Yesterday, today, and tomorrow; Careers in Psychology: 2005, What students need to know*. Paper presented at the annual convention of the Western Psychological Association, Portland, OR.

Smith, R. A. (1985). Advising beginning psychology majors for graduate school. *Teaching of Psychology, 12*, 194–198. doi:10.1207/s15328023top1204_2

Walter, T. J. (2007, Spring). The undergraduate psychology internship: Benefits, selection, and making the most of your experience. *Eye on Psi Chi, 11*(3), 24–26.

Chapter Seven
The Preprofessional Degree
Applying to Graduate School

Introduction

In the last chapter, we began the discussion of how you can prepare during your undergraduate years for graduate training in psychology. We continue that discussion in this chapter by taking the process to the next level. This chapter examines the procedures and expectations typically involved in successfully applying to graduate school. Topics include preparing for entrance exams (i.e., the Graduate Record Exam and Psychology Subject Test), selecting appropriate graduate programs, preparing vitae and statements of intent, preparing application materials, interviewing, and making decisions about the program's fit with your goals and interests. Most of the steps in the application process must be carefully sequenced, and many of them require significant amounts of time for preparation. Box 7.1 provides a suggested timeline for organizing and planning these activities.

The Subfields of Psychology

Before diving into the application process, it is important for you to begin narrowing your interest areas. Unlike the general nature of undergraduate training in psychology, graduate programs are typically specialized. As a result, you will need to select programs based in part on their ability to train you in a particular subfield of psychology. To help you accomplish this task

Majoring in Psychology: Achieving Your Educational and Career Goals, Second Edition.
Jeffrey L. Helms and Daniel T. Rogers.
© 2015 John Wiley & Sons, Ltd. Published 2015 by John Wiley & Sons, Ltd.

Box 7.1 *Timeline for Applying to Graduate School*

Junior Year

Fall and Spring Semesters
- Take advanced psychology courses (e.g., Physiological Psychology, Psychological Testing, Cognition, Perception). These will help prepare you for the Psychology Subject Test.

Spring Semester
- Study for the GRE General Test and Psychology Subject Test.

Summer Semester
- Take the GRE General Test.
- For the programs in which you are interested (the initial 40–50 programs), review professors' publications as well as the other variables listed in Box 7.3.

Senior Year

August
- Narrow down your list of programs to the top ones (approximately 20–25). Review each remaining program in more detail.
- Order and inspect a copy of your transcript to ensure that it is error-free.
- Develop your vita and an initial personal statement that can provide you with a starting point.

September
- Contact professors at the graduate programs to see if they are taking students for the following year.
- Finalize your list of schools to which you will apply (approximately 10–15).
- Develop a file for each program in order to keep all information together.
- Fine-tune your vita and personal statement. Get lots of feedback!
- Deliver packets of information to the faculty who will be writing your letters of recommendation.

September/October
- Take the Psychology Subject Test.
- Order official transcripts.
- Have GRE scores sent to programs.

Early November	• Retrieve letters of recommendation.
Mid November – December	• Finalize your applications and make a copy of each for the program's respective file.
	• Submit your applications.
	• Verify that applications were received.
January – Mid March	• Wait.
	• Interview.
	• Wait some more. (Don't forget your current coursework! It can preoccupy you as you wait!)
	• Develop some back-up plans in case you receive no offers.
April 1	• This is the deadline for offers from graduate schools.
April 15	• Submit your decision to the graduate schools on (or preferably before) this date.
Post-April 15	• Email your letter writers regarding your decision, thanking them for their letters and assistance.

we have listed here some of the main subfield areas of psychology. Although each of these areas is covered in more detail in the second part of the book, a brief description is provided here to give you some ideas as you begin exploring various graduate programs. However, the list is by no means complete. In fact, the book *Graduate Study in Psychology* (GSP) by the American Psychological Association (APA; 2014a) lists dozens of areas of study in its index. For now, we will focus on these.

Experimental Psychology

Experimental psychology is the scientific study of psychological phenomenon. The two major organizations devoted to experimental psychology are the Association for Psychological Science (APS; www.psychologicalscience. org) and APA Division 3 – Experimental Psychology (http://www.apa.org/divisions/div3).

Developmental Psychology

Developmental psychology is the scientific study of "age-related changes that occur as a person progresses from conception to death" (Weiten, 2008; p. 306). Three of the major organizations devoted to developmental psychology are APA Division 7 – Developmental Psychology (http://www.apadivisions.org/division-7), the Society for Research in Child Development (www.srcd.org), and APA Division 20 – Adult Development and Aging (http://www.apadivisions.org/division-20).

Social Psychology

Social psychology is the scientific study of the "influences that people have upon the beliefs and behaviors of others" (Aronson, 2004; p. 5). The major organization devoted to this subfield is APA Division 8 – Society for Personality and Social Psychology (www.spsp.org).

Cognitive Psychology

Cognitive psychology is the scientific study of how people think. It includes contributions from the diverse areas of memory, language processing, and decision making. Two of the major organizations devoted to cognitive psychology are the Cognitive Neuroscience Society (www.cogneurosociety.org) and the Cognitive Science Society (cognitivesciencesociety.org).

Physiological Psychology

Physiological psychology (also known as biological psychology and behavioral neuroscience) is the scientific study of the biology of behavior. To learn more about this subfield visit APA's Division 6 – Behavioral Neuroscience and Comparative Psychology (http://www.apadivisions.org/division-6).

Industrial and Organizational Psychology

Industrial and organizational (I/O) psychology is the scientific study of people in work/business organizations. I/O psychology is both a research and applied field of study. The major organization devoted to this subfield is APA's Division 14 – Society for Industrial and Organizational Psychology (www.siop.org).

Clinical Psychology

Clinical psychology integrates theory, science, and practice in an effort to "understand, predict, and alleviate maladjustment, disability, and discomfort" and to "promote human adaptation, adjustment, and personal development" (Society of Clinical Psychology, n.d.; http://www.apa.org/divisions/div12/aboutcp.html). The major organization devoted to clinical psychology is APA's Division 12 – Society of Clinical Psychology (www.div12.org).

Counseling Psychology

Counseling psychology integrates theory, science, and practice in an effort to promote "personal, educational, vocational, and group adjustment in a variety of settings" (Society of Counseling Psychology, 2014; http://www.div17.org/about). In addition to information provided later in the text, more information about counseling psychology may be found at APA's Division 17 – Society of Counseling Psychology (www.div17.org).

School Psychology

School psychology is "concerned with the science and practice of psychology with children, youth, families; learners of all ages; and the schooling process" (APA, 2014a; http://www.apa.org/ed/graduate/specialize/school.aspx). The two major organizations devoted to school psychology are APA Division 16 – School Psychology (http://www.apadivisions.org/division-16) and the National Association of School Psychologists (www.nasponline.org).

Educational Psychology

Educational psychology is the subfield of psychology devoted to improving "curriculum design, achievement testing, teacher training, and other aspects of the educational process" (Weiten, 2008; p. 18). APA's Division 15 – Educational Psychology is the major organization devoted to this subfield (www.apadiv15.org).

Exercise and Sport Psychology

Exercise and sport psychology is "the scientific study of the psychological factors that are associated with participation and performance in sport, exercise, and other types of physical activity" (APA Division 47, 2014; http://www.apadivisions.org/division-47/about/resources/what-is.aspx).

Two of the major organizations devoted to exercise and sport psychology are APA's Division 47 Exercise and Sport Psychology (http://www.apadivisions.org/division-47) and the Association for Applied Sport Psychology (www.appliedsportpsych.org).

Health Psychology

Health psychology is an interdisciplinary field devoted to promoting, improving, and maintaining healthy functioning as well as preventing and treating illness. Two of the major organizations devoted to this area of study are APA's Division 38 – Health Psychology (www.health-psych.org) and the Society of Behavioral Medicine (www.sbm.org).

Neuropsychology

Experimental neuropsychology develops and clinical neuropsychology applies knowledge of brain–behavior relationships to human problems. APA's Division 40 – Clinical Neuropsychology (www.div40.org) and the British Psychological Society – Division of Neuropsychology (http://www.bps.org.uk/networks-and-communities/member-networks/division-neuropsychology) are devoted to this area of study.

Forensic Psychology

Bartol and Bartol (1999) define forensic psychology as:

> both (a) the research endeavor that examines aspects of human behavior directly related to the legal process…and (b) the professional practice of psychology within, or in consultation with, a legal system that encompasses both criminal and civil law and the numerous areas where they interact. (p. 3)

The main organization devoted to this area is APA Division 41 – American Psychology-Law Society (http://www.apadivisions.org/division-41).

Deciding on the Type of Graduate Education

The four levels of graduate education are certificate, master's, specialist, and doctoral. We describe each of these levels as well as the types of degrees within each level where applicable. We will begin at the graduate certificate level and move up to the highest level of education available in the social sciences, the doctorate.

Graduate Certificates

Graduate certificates are offered in a variety of areas (e.g., geropsychology, conflict resolution, psychopharmacology). The certificate programs are generally a year long. These programs allow individuals to gain additional education in a specified area. Certificate programs often do not provide specific skills training. Rather, they provide additional coursework in a circumscribed area and typically at the beginning graduate level. When specific skills training is a part of the program, students usually must already possess a graduate degree prior to enrollment. This requirement helps ensure a base level of knowledge and expertise. Regardless, graduate certificates are not graduate *degrees*. However, they may give you additional background in an area that will make you more attractive to potential employers when compared with someone with a bachelor's degree or someone without the additional coursework.

Master's Degrees

Master's degrees are offered in all areas of psychology. These programs are typically two years long, although applied programs (e.g., clinical psychology and counseling psychology) may take additional time due to practicum requirements. Two types of master's degrees are available. These are the Master of Arts (MA) and the Master of Science (MS) degrees. Historically the MS degree required significantly more research experience than an MA degree, but these lines are much blurrier now. However, be cautious of programs that do not help students build a strong research foundation (e.g., requiring a thesis). Not all master's degree programs require a thesis (an independent research project that the student develops, carries out, and defends). If you plan on continuing your education at the doctoral level either immediately upon graduation or at a later time, you will want to choose a master's program that requires a thesis.

Master's degree programs are also designated as terminal or nonterminal. Terminal master's degree programs are not a part of a doctoral program at that institution and as such prepare the individual to enter the job market upon graduation. This does not mean that individuals in a terminal master's degree program cannot continue their education at the doctoral level. In fact, terminal master's degree programs are sometimes excellent *proving grounds* for students. Because terminal master's programs often have lower entrance requirements than doctoral programs (APA, 2014a), students who may not have the best GPAs or enough research experience may opt to apply to master's programs to gain or improve their standing. Keep in mind though that even the median GPA of students admitted to terminal master's degree

---

Box 7.2 *Reasons to Pursue a Master's Degree First*

- Low grade point average (GPA)
- Weak/low Graduate Record Exam (GRE) scores
- Limited research experience
- Limited clinical experience
- Uncertain about career goals
- Missed deadlines for doctoral programs
- Weak letters of recommendation
- Limited background in psychology

Note. Information comes from Norcross, Sayette, and Mayne (2008).

---

programs was a robust 3.5 (APA, 2014a). Box 7.2 lists some reasons given by Norcross, Sayette, and Mayne (2008) to obtain a master's degree first instead of proceeding immediately to a doctoral program.

Nonterminal master's degree programs are part of a doctoral program and as such students will typically continue with their studies until they earn their doctorate (at the same university, in the same program). For nonterminal master's degree programs, students usually either enter a doctoral graduate program and earn their master's degree along the way or they enter the master's program and near its completion apply to continue on in the doctoral program. This is very common in the field of psychology.

Specialist Degrees

The specialist degree can be either a specialist in psychology (PsyS) or a specialist in education (EdS). The EdS degree is significantly more common and dominates this level. In general, the specialist degree is an expanded master's degree program. This typically 3-year-long program is found almost exclusively in the school psychology domain. It often comprises 2 years of practica and coursework, 1 year of full-time internship in a school environment, and a final project. The project is generally an expanded form of a thesis research study. Detailed information on the field of school psychology (including necessary education and training) may be found in the second part of the book.

Doctoral Degrees

There are three types of doctoral degrees in psychology: the doctor of philosophy (PhD), doctor of psychology (PsyD), and doctor of education (EdD) degrees. Although the EdD is offered in a few counseling psychology and developmental psychology programs, the PhD and PsyD degrees are the most common doctoral degree programs in psychology. As a result, this section will focus on the PhD and PsyD degrees. Regardless of the type, the doctoral degree is the highest degree available in psychology. Although postdoctoral training and programs are common (especially in the applied areas), the doctoral degree is the final step possible in the formal education process.

Non-health service provider subfields of psychology. For the non-health service provider subfields of psychology (e.g., experimental psychology, social psychology, developmental psychology), doctoral programs lead to the PhD degree and tend to last approximately 4–5 years. The majority of the time in the respective program is spent in one of two activities, coursework and research. Given the scientific basis of psychology, coursework tends to center on the respective research findings in the area of study and expanding research methodology skills, including advanced research methodology and statistics coursework. Outside of coursework, much time is devoted to research activities, your own and your major professor's research. The term *major professor* refers to the professor who accepted you into the program or with whom you have established a mentoring relationship. As such, the major professor directs much of your work, including course selection and your dissertation. The dissertation is the large research study that you complete prior to graduating with your doctorate. Although approved and supervised to some extent by your major professor, the development of the ideas behind your dissertation and bringing the study to fruition are your responsibility. Additionally and once completed, you must defend your dissertation in front of a committee comprising your major professor and other faculty members. A successful defense is the final hurdle to obtaining your doctorate in most programs.

Health service provider subfields of psychology. Different training models exist for the health service provider subfields of psychology (i.e., clinical psychology, counseling psychology, and school psychology). Although covered in more detail later in Chapter 10, this information bears mentioning here due to its importance. There are three general training models for professional clinical psychology programs. These models have been adopted to greater and lesser degrees by the other two applied health service provider subfields within psychology (counseling psychology and school psychology). The three models are the Boulder Model, the Vail Model, and the Academy of Psychological Clinical Science (APCS) Model.

In 1949, the Conference on Training in Clinical Psychology was held in Boulder, Colorado (Matthews & Anton, 2008). Named after the host city, the Boulder Model for training clinical psychologists was developed in which students would be well trained in both clinical research skills and application skills. The incorporation of these two definitive aspects of the field is also referred to as the scientist–practitioner model.

In 1973, the National Conference on Levels and Patterns of Professional Training in Psychology met and endorsed the practitioner–scholar model (Matthews & Anton, 2008). Often referred to as the Vail Model (so named after this conference's host city), this model proposed that training in clinical application skills could dominate the doctoral training, placing significantly less emphasis on research skills and production. The Vail Model, or practitioner–scholar model, is analogous to the practitioner models of medicine (MD), dentistry (DMD), and veterinary medicine (DVM). Programs adopting this model would focus on training students to be consumers of research more than producers of research. By the time the conference met, the first program utilizing this model had already begun at the University of Illinois in 1968. Although the University of Illinois program is no longer around, several other early programs still train students in this manner today (e.g., Widener University since 1970, Baylor University since 1971, and Rutgers University since 1973). Interestingly, many still view the PsyD degree, which sprung from this model, as being "new" even given a 45+ year history. Today, there are over 70 APA-accredited PsyD programs (APA, 2012). We will discuss accreditation later in the chapter.

As alluded to in the previous paragraph, to reduce confusion, Peterson (1976) argued that programs training practitioners should award the PsyD degree and those programs training scientists/researchers should award the PhD degree. This differentiation was not sufficient for some in the clinical psychology subfield and resulted in the development of the Academy of Psychological Clinical Science (APCS; 2014). The dissatisfaction resulted from what some saw as a departure from the scientific basis of clinical psychology. Sometimes referred to as the "Super Boulder Model," programs subscribing to the model commit heavily to the clinical research enterprise in training graduate students. A current listing of these programs may be found at the APCS website (http://www.acadpsychclinicalscience.org/doctoral-programs.html).

As you are thinking about this information please keep in mind that with the possible exception of the APCS model, strict adherence to these models by individual programs is rare. Each program ends up putting its own unique stamp on its training. Basically, clinical psychology programs vary in their balance of the two themes (practice and research training). In fact, it may be additionally or even more informative for you to ask the programs in which you are interested what percentage of the training is devoted to practice (e.g., learning and practicing psychotherapy and psychological assessment) and what percentage is devoted to research endeavors (e.g., statistics coursework, research laboratory work, data collection and analysis, research publication/presentation). The answer will likely provide you with important information as you select programs to pursue.

Finding Available Graduate Programs

One of the early steps to selecting a graduate program is to review what programs are available. Several resources can help you in your quest. These include:

- *Graduate Study in Psychology* (GSP; APA, 2014a) – Produced annually, this publication provides a listing of graduate programs in psychology. For many programs, it includes such information as accreditation status, application information and statistics, financial assistance available, student progression, and placement of students upon graduation. GSP also provides an index that lists programs by subfield and by geographic location.
- Academy of Psychological Clinical Science (http://www.acadpsychclinical science.org/doctoral-programs.html) – This website provides a listing of programs that adhere to the APCS Model. Links to the member programs are provided when available.
- Psychological Clinical Science Accreditation System (PCSAS; 2014; www.pcsas.org) – Although separate, this accreditation system is closely aligned with the APCS. PCSAS was incorporated in 2007 and accredits clinical psychology programs that adhere to a rigorous clinical science model of training. Accredited programs are listed on their website.
- APA division websites – Many of APA's divisions provide lists of programs in their respective areas. A list of links to the various APA divisions may be found at http://www.apa.org/about/division
- *Insider's Guide to Graduate Programs in Clinical and Counseling Psychology* (Norcross & Sayette, 2014) – This guide provides reports on clinical and counseling psychology programs. The reports include information on research areas, clinical opportunities, theoretical orientation of faculty, statistics of recent applicants, and average length of time to complete program. The reports also provide information on a program's balance between practice and research.
- Chapters 8–15 – When available, the chapters in the second part of this text cover careers in the respective subfields and provide information on where to find programs.

Evaluating the Graduate Programs You Find

As you can see from reviewing any of the resources noted in the previous section, there is a wide variety of graduate programs available in psychology. As a result, evaluating the array of programs that pique your interest may be difficult and cumbersome. To help with the evaluative process, we suggest the creation of a data file in which you can organize the program information important to you. Box 7.3 provides a list of possible variables to consider. Once you have your data file or spreadsheet formatted with the variables of interest to you, begin filling in the blanks. Although many data points are easily filled, evaluating the meaning of some of these variables may be more difficult. Because of this, we provide some pointers to help in your evaluation of the personal meaning of the information.

Application and Acceptance Rates

Number of applications to a program and the program's acceptance rate are easily understandable variables. The information they provide can be invaluable. In fact, acceptance rates are significantly different based on program type. For example, research-oriented programs (e.g., experimental psychology) have fewer applications and higher acceptance rates (although still rigorous), while practice-oriented PhD programs have larger numbers of applications and lower acceptance rates. The acceptance rates for research-oriented programs (although improving), vary considerably (Norcross & Kuhle, 2011). For doctoral programs in social and personality psychology, approximately 12% of applicants are accepted (Mulvey, Michalski, & Wicherski, 2010). This rate is contrasted with the 36% of applicants accepted into quantitative psychology doctoral programs (Mulvey et al., 2010).

In terms of clinical psychology doctoral programs, freestanding PsyD programs (i.e., those that are not affiliated with a university, although they may use "university" in their name) accept approximately 50% of their applicants, university-based PsyD programs accept approximately 35% of their applicants, practice-oriented clinical PhD programs accept approximately 16% of their applicants, clinical PhD programs with equal emphasis on practice and research accept approximately 14% of their applicants, and research-oriented clinical PhD programs accept approximately 7% of their applicants (Norcross, Ellis, & Sayette, 2010). Looking at the information in a different way, the higher the acceptance rate the higher the likelihood you will get into the program. From another perspective, the higher the acceptance rate, the higher the likelihood that people who are not qualified will get into the program. The reason this last piece of information is so important

Box 7.3 *Potential Program Variables to Review*

- School reputation
- Geographic location
- Degree(s) granted (MA, MS, EdS, PhD, PsyD, EdD)
- Field of study (e.g., developmental psychology, social psychology)
- Areas of specialization or tracks
- Balance between research and practice (mainly for applied psychology programs)
- Any required undergraduate coursework
- Diversity representation in faculty and students
- Number of applications
- Number of offers
- Number of incoming students
- Mean/median GRE Verbal score
- Mean/median GRE Quantitative score
- Mean/median GRE Analytical Writing score
- Mean/median Psychology Subject Test score
- Mean/median GPA
- Mean/median psychology GPA
- Mean/median last 2 years GPA
- Number of program faculty
- Theoretical orientation (for clinical/counseling programs)
- Percentage of students receiving full tuition waiver
- Percentage of students receiving assistantship only
- Percentage of students receiving both full tuition and assistantship
- Annual cost of the program (considering tuition waivers/assistantships)
- Research areas available
- Name of faculty member you are interested in working with
- Grant activity
- Personal interview required/optional
- Teaching experience available
- Percentage of students applying for internship accepted to APA accredited site (clinical/counseling/school psychology only)
- Percentage of students licensed (applied programs only)
- Mean/median time to completion of program
- Placement of students upon graduation (e.g., academe, research institutes, practice)
- Attrition rate
- Accreditation (regional and APA)

is that being accepted into and even graduating from a program is not the end of the story. You will also need to find a job, and for those in the clinical, counseling, or school psychology fields, you will also need to get licensed. Although this piece is covered in another chapter, suffice it to say that students from PsyD programs with higher acceptance rates have significantly lower scores on the tests necessary for licensure compared to PhD graduates (Kupfersmid & Fiola, 1991; Maher, 1999). In fact, the correlation between the mean score on the Examination for Professional Practice in Psychology (EPPP; the national licensing exam) and a program's acceptance rate is –.64 (Templer & Arikawa, 2004). Unfortunately, there also appears to be a comparative decline in scores for PsyD program graduates on the test over the years compared to their PhD counterparts (Templer, Stroup, Mancuso, & Tangen, 2008).

This information does not mean that you should not apply to PsyD programs. Remember, the first author (Helms) has a PsyD degree. Rather, it means that the higher the acceptance rate, the lower the quality/rigor of the program generally, resulting in graduates not prepared for the rigors of the licensure process or the professional practice of psychology. These concerns are so real that one of the original proponents of the Vail Model strongly encouraged a merciless evaluation of existing programs with implicit hope that weak, ineffectual, and poor programs be eliminated (Peterson, 2003). Given the time, energy, and financial resources expended by students for their educations, we eagerly welcome this prospect.

Grade Point Average (GPA)

Research indicates that the average *minimum* required overall GPA of applicants in 2003–2004 was 3.11 for doctoral programs and 2.92 for master's programs (Norcross, Kohout, & Wicherski, 2005). The associated *minimum* required Psychology GPA was 3.17 for doctoral programs and 3.05 for master's programs. However, the minimum required is *significantly* different from what is actually accepted. In fact for these same years (2003–2004), the study found that the *actual* overall GPA was 3.54 for applicants accepted to doctoral programs and 3.37 for applicants accepted to master's programs. As reported in more recent data, the median GPA was 3.5 for those admitted to master's programs and 3.63 for those admitted to doctoral programs (APA, 2014a). For some programs (e.g., clinical psychology PhD programs), the *actual* overall GPAs can be close to 4.0. In summary, you will want to look at the statistics of students admitted to the program in recent years. If your GPA is substantially lower than the mean or median listed (i.e., more than .2 points lower), you probably will not be a viable candidate. Additionally, our experience tells us that students often inaccurately believe that *desire* to go to graduate school will somehow make up for GPA or GRE inadequacies. Succinctly put, this is not the case.

Graduate Record Exam and the Psychology Subject Test

Although it leaves a bad taste in most students' mouths, standardized admissions tests are an important part of the application to graduate school. The importance is predicated on its ability to compare students from a wide variety of educational experiences. For example, is a 3.8 GPA at your undergraduate institution equivalent to a 3.8 GPA at neighboring institutions? What about across different majors within your institution? Some variations can even occur in the same major at the same institution. Think about a fellow psychology major you may know who only takes the "easy" professors and the "easy" electives. Is comparing your GPA to this peer's a fair assessment of your academic abilities? Now you're getting a sense about why it is important to have a measure that is consistent across individuals and across situations. The General Test (sometimes referred to as simply the GRE) and the Psychology Subject Test of the Graduate Record Exam (GRE) are the two examinations most often required by psychology graduate programs in an effort to level the playing field.

The General Test of the Graduate Record Exam (GRE) is a computer-based exam developed and marketed by the Educational Testing Service (ETS; 2014a). The General Test consists of three components: quantitative reasoning, verbal reasoning, and analytical writing. In 2011, the scoring system for both the quantitative and the verbal reasoning components changed from a range of 200–800 points with 10-point increments to a range of 130–170 points with 1-point increments. Statistics for GRE scores often add these two component scores together to produce a total score, ranging from 260–340. The analytical writing component, introduced in 2002, has a score range from 0–6 and is scored in half-point increments. Because of the somewhat complex nature of the scoring employed by ETS and the recent transition to a different score range, you are encouraged to visit the ETS website for information on how to interpret your scores (http://www.ets.org/gre/revised_general/scores/understand).

According to ETS (2014c), the verbal reasoning component of the General Test is intended to measure examinees' abilities to:

- "analyze and draw conclusions from discourse; reason from incomplete data; identify author's assumptions and/or perspectives; understand multiple levels of meaning, such as literal, figurative, and author's intent

- select important points; distinguish major from minor or relevant points; summarize text; understand the structure of a text
- understand the meanings of words, sentences, and entire texts; understand relationships among words and among concepts." (http://www.ets.org/gre/revised_general/about/content)

In terms of the quantitative reasoning component, ETS (2014c) says that it is intended to measure examinees' abilities to:

- "understand quantitative information
- interpret and analyze quantitative information
- solve problems using mathematical models
- apply basic mathematical skills and elementary mathematical concepts of arithmetic, algebra, geometry, and data interpretation." (http://www.ets.org/gre/revised_general/about/content)

The question that students often ask about the quantitative reasoning component of the GRE is whether you can use a calculator. The answer is that there is an onscreen calculator that you can use.

According to ETS (2014c), the analytical writing component measures examinees' abilities to:

- "articulate complex ideas clearly and effectively
- support ideas with relevant reasons and examples
- examine claims and accompanying evidence
- sustain a well-focused, coherent discussion
- control the elements of standard written English." (http://www.ets.org/gre/revised_general/about/content)

In terms of graduate school applications, 80% of master's programs and 97% of doctoral programs in psychology require the General Test (APA, 2014a). Because of the relatively recent conversion to the new scoring range of 130–170 for the Verbal and Quantitative Reasoning sections, some programs are still reporting at least a portion of their data in terms of the older 200–800-point scale. However, this is beginning to change. According to GSP (APA, 2014a) the median score for those admitted to master's programs was a GRE Verbal score of 154 on the new scale (510 on the old scale) and a GRE Quantitative score of 150 on the new scale (591 on the old scale). Additionally, the median score for those admitted to doctoral programs was a GRE Verbal score of 158 on the new scale (577 on the old scale) and a GRE Quantitative score of 154 on the new scale (668 on the old scale). Keep in mind that these median scores are derived from both applied psychology and experimental psychology programs. The median General Test scores for applied psychology programs tend to be significantly higher than median scores for experimental psychology programs. This leads to another important point. Programs will sometimes report *minimum* required scores. The minimum requirement is *rarely* enough to attain an admission offer. In fact, the minimum required score is often far below that of those students who are actually admitted to the program. As a result, we encourage you to review mean/median scores for students who have actually been recently admitted to the programs. Programs regularly provide this information online along with other information about their programs.

For the Analytical Writing component, Briihl and Wasieleski (2007) reported that only 35% of psychology graduate programs utilized the score in their admission decisions. However, this may change in coming years as familiarity with this relatively new GRE component increases. In other words, you will still want to study and do your best on it!

The Psychology Subject Test of the GRE is currently a paper and pencil test given three times a year (ETS, 2014b). Although the specific dates change annually, the testing months are typically April, September, and October. Students often choose the October administration because it allows enough time to submit scores to graduate programs as well as enough time into the fall semester to learn some of the advanced coursework covered by the exam that they may be currently taking. For actual test dates, visit www.gre.org.

The Psychology Subject Test has three content areas that cover all areas of psychology with varying degrees of emphasis (ETS, 2014b). It consists of approximately 205 questions with five answer options. When scored, the test produces two subscores, experimental and social, that range from 20–99 and a total score that ranges from 200–990. According to ETS (2014b), the three content areas that feed into the two subscores along with respective topics and percentage of questions on the test are:

- Experimental subscore area
  - accounts for approximately 40% of the questions; and
  - covers learning, language, memory, thinking, sensation, perception, and physiological psychology.
- Social subscore area
  - accounts for approximately 43% of the questions; and
  - covers clinical and abnormal psychology, lifespan development, personality, and social psychology.

- Other areas
  - o account for approximately 17% of the questions; and
  - o cover general areas (e.g., history and industrial–organizational psychology), measurement, and research methodology.

APA (2014a) reported that 13% of doctoral and 6% of master's psychology programs require the Psychology Subject Test. Based on data from GSP (APA, 2014a), the median score for those admitted to master's programs was 682. For those admitted to doctoral programs the median score was 686.

In terms of associated costs for the tests, the General Test costs approximately $200, and the Psychology Subject Test costs approximately $150. However, the costs do not stop here. An official report of your scores must be sent to the graduate programs. These cost approximately $30 per report per school. These costs are certainly disincentives to take the tests more than once. However, many students do retake the tests (especially the General Test) in the hope of obtaining a higher score. According to ETS (2014a), scores do typically increase when the test is retaken. Keep in mind that, generally speaking, an additional few points on your score will probably not make a difference in your viability for a program. Students mistakenly hope that scoring those additional few points will help them reach the required minimum or the average of incoming students for the last year. We have already covered the issue with the required minimum (i.e., ignore those scores). As for meeting the mean or median score of incoming students, some of these students surpassed this score and others fell short. In other words, it is unlikely that a few points will make a difference unless the program uses a cutoff score when considering applications. If it is known that the program uses a cutoff score (and you know what it is), retaking the test to clear the cutoff makes sense, especially given the ability to select which scores will be sent to programs.

ETS (2014d) recently introduced a service whereby a student can select which set or sets of scores to send to a program (if the test is taken more than once). Obviously, this creates a big incentive to attempt the test multiple times (and pay the multiple administration and scoring fees). However, we caution students who plan to take the test multiple times that they should prepare for each administration and not simply take it haphazardly with the hope that they will get a better score. Not only is the haphazard approach unlikely to produce results, but it is also costly financially.

In terms of preparing for the General Test, there are hundreds of books, online resources, and programs that can help in your preparation. However, we do give the warning that some of the strategies available are costly and unproven. As a result, buyers beware! Regardless, some of the basic tried and true strategies include taking as many practice tests as possible (and under test-like conditions), memorization of vocabulary that has been on the test in the past, improving writing skills for the analytical writing component, and practicing basic algebra and geometry skills.

In terms of the Psychology Subject Test, you have been preparing for this test for your entire undergraduate education. However, you will need to prepare much more. One mistake students make is that they wait until their last semester or final year to take the "harder" psychology coursework (e.g., physiological psychology, cognitive psychology). As a result, much of the information on the test will be completely unfamiliar. Our suggestion is to take as much of the core psychology coursework prior to your senior year and save your electives for the senior year. Additionally, studying your textbooks and taking as many practice Psychology Subject Tests as possible will likely prove useful.

Students also ask about how much time they should spend preparing for the tests. In general we recommend a concerted weekly effort for 6 months. For the first month or so, you may only devote a few hours every other day for the test. This amount will increase to every day as the test approaches. You will want to note that we mean intense studying during these times and not simply light reviews of the components.

Stipends vs. Loans vs. Eventual Salary

Most good graduate programs provide some level of financial assistance to their students. Financial assistance can come in the form of:

- Tuition waivers: No tuition is charged by the university. Sometimes registration and other fees still apply but are minimal by comparison.
- Research assistantships: You will work in a faculty member's research lab in exchange for a stipend (i.e., a certain amount of money that can help defray educational costs and living expenses).
- Teaching assistantships: You will teach undergraduate courses in exchange for a stipend. Under supervision, you may teach a variety of in-demand undergraduate courses such as Introductory Psychology and Research Methods.
- Scholarships: Due to your undergraduate academic record and GRE scores (relative to other incoming students) you may receive additional financial awards as incentives for you to attend a program.

Unfortunately, not all programs offer these types of assistance. In fact, some programs report providing financial assistance, but when you read the fine print, all they provide is access to student loans or an extremely small percentage of students are awarded stipends or assistantships (e.g., only one or two students get small stipends or partial tuition waivers). In reviewing the variables on programs, the percentage of students receiving tuition waivers, assistantships, or both considered in conjunction with the typical size of this funding will give you insight into a program's financial commitment to students. In general, good programs will not admit students that they are unable to support at least partially.

In terms of the data, Michalski, Kohout, Wicherski, and Hart (2011) reported that 68% of those earning a doctorate in psychology in 2009 had debt related to their education when they graduated. However, the differences in debt level are striking (and disturbing to some) when viewed through the lens of program type. Seventy-eight percent of those in the practice-oriented subfields (e.g., clinical psychology) and 48% of those in the research-oriented subfields (e.g., social psychology) reported some level of debt. For those in the practice-oriented subfields, the median level of debt was $80,000. For those in the research-oriented subfields, the median level of debt was $32,000. That's a huge difference! For those receiving their PsyD degree, the median debt level was $120,000! This is up $20,000 from their survey 2 years prior. For those receiving their PhD in clinical psychology, the median debt level was $68,000. This was an increase of $13,000 over 2 years.

The message we encourage you to take away from this variable is in relation to eventual salary. Loans must be repaid, and at this level of debt a substantial chunk of your salary will go directly to your loans for many years (decades) after graduation. It is also important to compare debt level to expected salary. In the same survey noted earlier, Michalski et al. (2011) noted that the median starting salary for those new doctorates was $64,000. Out of context, this amount seems quite substantial. For those graduating with substantial debt potentially due in part to non-supportive programs (e.g., programs not offering tuition waivers), this amount diminishes rapidly. Also, consider what other debt you might normally take on after completing a graduate degree (e.g., buying a home, starting a business) and how those options might be impacted by existing student loan debt. We urge careful consideration of these issues because our experience is that some students are blinded by their desire to attend graduate school…at any cost. This can be compounded by programs that prey on this desire.

Research

This variable refers to both the amount of research required and the type of research occurring in the graduate program. The type of research is rather straightforward. What topics are the faculty members pursuing? This information is often readily available via the faculty member's web page or via a literature search for his or her publications. A program's web page may also have a link to the respective faculty member's vita, a rich source of information. (Developing your own vita is discussed in an upcoming section of this chapter.)

In terms of the amount of required research and reminiscent of the discussion of the various models of training, some programs require heavy amounts of research and others require very little. In reviewing the faculty in the program, some insight into this variable may come from the faculty member's website. For example, and if listed, do the faculty members co-author papers, posters, and publications with students? If so, how many do they collaborate on each year? Some programs have a website devoted to current graduate students' activities. This resource can provide information too. An additional piece to consider is the outlet for their publications. Are they publishing in the top journals in the field?

Once this information is compiled, you will need to decide how important research productivity and experience are to you. If you plan on pursuing a research-oriented career (e.g., academe), the heavier the research requirements, and the more plentiful the opportunities to conduct research in graduate school, the better it will be for you in the long run.

Grant Activity

Closely tied to the research area, grant activity is an important variable to consider. Grant activity refers to the number, monetary amount, type (government or private), and duration of financially sponsored activities of faculty members. Large, multi-year government grants are a sign of stability for a research program and the associated faculty. It can signify to you that the program will be able to financially support you in your studies. Depending on the program, the stipend that pays you for your teaching assistantship, research assistantship, or tuition waiver may come directly from a grant.

Time to Complete Program

Program websites often describe the intended or designed length of their program. As we noted, typically research-oriented programs are 4–5 years long and practice-oriented programs are 5–6 years long. However, the program's intended curriculum may not match the average length of time it takes its students to actually complete the program. In truth, the described curriculum can be aspirational rather than typical. As a result, it will be more informative for you to find out the average length of time for a student to complete the program. This information is available in most resources including GSP (APA, 2014a).

Attrition Rate

Not surprisingly, not everyone that starts a graduate program completes the training. This fact is referred to as a program's attrition rate. When programs do a good job of selecting qualified students who fit their program and supporting them along their development, attrition rates will be extremely low (and even 0%). Yet even for programs that do a good job selecting appropriate students and supporting them, some students may still leave the program. The reasons students leave a program are varied and include such issues as:

- Change of interest – The student decided that the field of study was not for him/her.
- Academic issues – The student was not able to maintain adequate academic standing. For most graduate programs adequate standing is a 3.0 minimum GPA. In reality, most students typically earn all A's.
- Asked to leave – Students may be asked to leave a program. Typical reasons for these "requests" are poor collegiality, personal problems affecting quality of work, and ethical infractions. Being asked to leave is rare but does occur.
- Personal and financial reasons – Life circumstances sometimes prevent completion of a program.
- All But Dissertation (ABD) – Completion of the large independent research project (i.e., the dissertation) often prevents individuals from finishing their program in a timely manner. Although most will eventually complete their dissertations, some will remain in a state of limbo for years until the program terminates their standing. Most programs allow only a limited amount of time to complete your degree (e.g., 10 years from the start of a program).

Teaching Experience

Because many individuals completing their doctoral degree will pursue careers in academe, teaching experience will be important. Although some programs ensure that all students have some experience in the classroom, other programs provide the experience only as an option or even not at all. Depending upon the types of academic positions sought after graduation, teaching experience may be essential. This experience is most valued when you serve as the instructor of record, and not just a teaching assistant, for multiple courses.

Placement of Students in Internships

For those of you interested in the applied subfields of school psychology, counseling psychology, and clinical psychology, a year-long predoctoral internship will conclude your doctoral training. The application process is extremely competitive, and not all applicants are matched to positions. In fact, there are not enough sites for everyone that applies. The Association of Psychology Postdoctoral and Internship Centers (APPIC) administers the matching process for internship. Information on APPIC is available on their website at www.appic.org. Of the 4,335 applicants participating in the 2014 internship match process, 3,458 applicants were successfully matched. Some of the applicants withdrew from the process (294), and some were unmatched (583). In other words, a little over 20% of the applicants did not get matched. In terms of evaluating programs, good programs typically hover around 100% of their students getting matched to internships. To more finely evaluate programs, it is also enlightening to see how many of their students got their first or second choice of internship site. Additionally, it is important to note that large, freestanding PsyD programs match at significantly lower rates than smaller, university-affiliated PhD programs (APPIC, 2012). Remember, you cannot finish your degree until you complete the internship. Because the match takes place only once a year, without an internship match, you will be spending another year waiting around for the next match. Information about a program's match rate is readily available on most programs' web sites and via the APPIC website.

Placement of Students after Graduation

Graduate programs are proud of their students' accomplishments. This includes where their students go on internship and postdoctoral training and where they are employed. As a result, most programs provide this information readily. For your evaluation purposes, if most of a program's students end up in clinical environments and you want to pursue an academic career, this information may sway your decision to apply. The opposite may also be true of a program. If you want to practice and the school prepares students for careers in academe, it may not be a good match for you.

Licensure of Students after Graduation

For students applying to clinical, counseling, and school psychology doctoral programs, licensure of students upon graduation and completion of postdoctoral training is a key issue. Knowing what percentage of students in the program become licensed *and* how quickly is critical. In general, all students in applied programs should become licensed as psychologists upon completion of the appropriate requirements. The additional factor that is equally important to evaluate is the number of times it takes for a program's students to pass the required exams. What percentage of your students passes the licensure exams on the first try? What is the average score of your students on the national exam (i.e., the EPPP)? Most states institute a passing score of 70% on the EPPP. Obviously, programs whose students routinely take more than one attempt and whose EPPP average hovers around 70% or lower are programs to avoid. We can't imagine a worse feeling than completing all of the educational requirements for licensure (doctorate and postdoctorate) and not being able to pass the licensure exams due to poor training. Important to reiterate from earlier, EPPP scores are significantly lower for PsyD programs than traditional PhD clinical programs (Templer & Arikawa, 2004). As a result, you will need to be even more diligent when evaluating PsyD programs in this regard.

APA Accreditation

Closely tied to the previous section on licensure, APA accreditation of doctoral programs in clinical, counseling, and school psychology is extremely important. In fact, you will be unable to get licensed as a psychologist in many states/jurisdictions if you do not graduate from an APA-accredited program. In terms of evaluating a graduate program in one of these subfields of psychology, APA accreditation is a starting point. It is an indication that the program meets *minimum* standards. In other words, knowing a program is accredited is the starting point and not the ending point. Additional points to evaluate are how long the program has been accredited and when the next site visit is. This information is found in every December issue of the *American Psychologist*.

Geographical Location

Although geographical location may be important to you (e.g., staying close to family), this is not something that is considered by graduate programs. In fact, you will be competing for your place in graduate school with people from all over the country (and perhaps the world). Also, geographical locations that are less desirable may provide you with a better chance of admission. Others may not apply in such large numbers and when they apply may not accept an offer of admission. We encourage you to keep this in mind as you apply…broadly.

In summary, as you are evaluating programs that interest you, be sure to assess your own qualifications. How well do you match their criteria? *Desire* to pursue graduate education will not overcome poor or mediocre qualifications. The additional point to consider is whether graduate school is right for you. Can you pursue your desired career without graduate training? Other parts of the book can help with this piece.

Selecting Programs to Pursue

Keeping the above characteristics in mind, review 40–50 programs from one of the resources noted earlier. The review should include familiarizing yourself with all of the variables noted in Box 7.3 for each program and all of the information available on the programs' websites. Once your review is complete and for the 20–25 that "float" to the top for you, email to see if the professors you are interested in working with at the school are taking students for the coming year. (Because this information is sometimes on the program's website, be sure to check there before emailing.) Contacting professors should be done at the beginning of the fall semester of your senior year. Be careful! Your email should be extremely thoughtful and professional. In fact, we recommend having your undergraduate mentor or one of the faculty members who will be writing a letter of recommendation for you read it prior to sending it. Some schools do not have a mentor model but rather admit a group of students who decide within the first year or so of the program with whom they would like to work. Touching base with those professors with whom you are interested in working is still not a bad idea.

When it's time, which is typically November or December for doctoral programs and a little later for master's programs, we strongly recommend applying to 10–15 programs. Based on the information you have collected on the 20–25 programs that "floated" to the top (given the professors will be taking students for the upcoming year), we recommend the following break down for the 10–15 to which you will apply:

- Half of your applications should be to programs where you *exceed* the statistics of their recent admissions (i.e., last 2 years).

- A quarter of your applications should be to programs where you *meet* the statistics of their recent admissions (i.e., last 2 years).
- A quarter of your applications should be to programs where you are *slightly below* the statistics of their recent admissions (i.e., last 2 years).

This strategy will hopefully cover your bases by providing coverage of *dream* programs and *back-up* programs.

Preparing Vitae – An Essential Part of Your Application Packet

Although vitae are similar to résumés, there are important differences. Unlike résumés, vitae provide the "complete" story. Unlike résumés, which should not be more than one page, vitae can be 20, 30, or more pages for professionals who have been in the field for some time. For the student applying to graduate school, his or her vita will likely be three to four pages. To clarify, these three to four pages assume 1-inch margins on all sides, single-spaced line spacing, and Times New Roman size 12 font. The pages should be devoted to accomplishments and pertinent information, not fluff! With the exception of the "Career Objective" heading, which is almost never used in vitae, the potential headings noted in our discussion of résumés will generally fit for vitae too. However, you will also want to include additional information/headings regarding your research experiences and psychology and psychology-related coursework. In terms of research experiences, this section includes such information as papers and poster presentations given at conferences, publications, and any research assistance you provided to others (e.g., data entry or administering research protocols for a faculty member). All of your presentations and publications should be in correct APA format.

In terms of listing coursework, the psychology coursework you should list is evident (i.e., all psychology courses). The psychology-related coursework you list will depend on your interest area. If you are pursuing an industrial–organizational psychology graduate program, your coursework in business and advanced statistics would be listed. If you are pursuing clinical psychology graduate programs, your coursework in advanced statistics would be listed. Box 7.4 provides an example vita. We encourage you to seek lots of feedback on the layout of your vita and the information you include. Additional examples of vitae may be found online. Your professor may even let you take a look at his or her vita as a model.

Box 7.4   *Example Vita*

Michele Amparo Ashley
100-B Chastain Rd. Apt. #123
Kennesaw, GA 30144
(555) 555-5555
MicheleAmparoAshley@emailnow.com

Education

May 2018 (anticipated)   **Bachelor of Science in Psychology**
Kennesaw State University
Kennesaw, GA
Current GPA: 3.82
Current Psychology GPA: 4.0
Last 2 Years GPA: 4.0

Publication

Ashley, M. A., & Smith, L. P. (2016). LGBT student attitudes in introductory psychology courses. *Undergraduate Studies in Sex Research, 15,* 316–328.

Conference Presentations

Ashley, M. A., & Helms, J. L. (2016, April). *Differences between students and the community: Attitudes toward sexual orientation minorities.* Paper presented at the annual Georgia Undergraduate Research in Psychology conference, Kennesaw, GA.

Ashley, M. A., & Smith, L. P. (2016, May). *Student gender attitudes: The inside is worse than the outside.* Poster session presented at the annual Association for Psychological Science conference, Ann Arbor, RI.

Other Research Experiences

Careen, Z. L. (2014, March). *Gender inequity in psychology programs.* Poster session presented at the Gender Studies in Psychology annual conference, Jacksonville, FL. (Assisted Dr. Careen with survey administration and data entry.)

Careen, Z. L. (in progress). *Rankings of developmental psychology programs.* Unpublished research, Kennesaw State University, Kennesaw GA. (Assisted Dr. Careen with data entry and coordinated all students involved in the project.)

Fall 2014 – Spring 2015 **Lab Member,** Animal Behavior Lab
Kennesaw State University
Faculty Mentor: Dr. Dorothy Williamson

Research projects: Influence of environmental factors on the procreation of rats including relative birth weight of offspring
Responsibilities: Coordinated data collections by first-year psychology students, maintained rat colony, data analyses, managing and developing online survey databases, recruiting participants, submitting IRB proposals.

Clinical Experience

Fall 2014 – present

Behavior Therapist
Atlanta, GA
Supervisor: Dr. Oloe V. Veins
Description: Part-time position working with children who are diagnosed with pervasive developmental disorders (e.g., Asperger's and Autism).
Responsibilities: Duties include administering behavioral protocols developed by the psychologists on staff.

Teaching Experience

Fall 2015

Undergraduate Teaching Assistant
Life-span Developmental Psychology
Supervisor: Dr. Roxanne Buddie
Responsibilities: Developing materials for class, website construction, providing evaluative feedback on student work, answering questions, and tutoring students.

Research Application and Writing Skills

SPSS
SAS
Microsoft Office Products (Excel, PowerPoint, MSWord)
APA Format

Honors and Awards

Fall 2015

Outstanding Undergraduate Teaching Assistant Award
Department of Psychology, Kennesaw State University

| April 2016 | First Place for Paper Presentation: Georgia Undergraduate Research in Psychology (GURP) Conference |
| Fall 2013 – Spring 2016 | President's List and Dean's List (Every Semester) |

University Involvement and Leadership Experience

Fall 2013 – present	**Psychology Club**
	President (Fall 2013 to present)
	Coordinated the 2013 and 2014 annual charity benefit, which raised over $5,000 each year.
Fall 2014 – present	**Psi Chi**
	Treasurer (Fall 2014 through Spring 2015)

Professional Affiliations

2014 – present	**American Psychological Association** *(Student Affiliate)*
2014 – present	**Association for Psychological Science** *(Student Affiliate)*
2014 – present	**Association for Psychological Science Student Caucus**
	APS Student Caucus Campus Representative Program, Kennesaw State University Campus Representative (2014–present)
	APS Student Caucus, RISE Research Award Committee member (2014–present)

Coursework

Psychology Coursework*	**Related Coursework**
General Psychology	Elementary Statistics
Careers in Psychology	Advanced Statistical Analysis
Research Methods in Psychology with Lab	Human Communications
	Biology I and II
Experimental Psychology with Lab	Anatomy and Physiology I and II
	Contemporary Health Issues
Life-Span Developmental Psychology	Deviance and Social Control
	Sociology of Mental Illness
Abnormal Psychology	Family Health and Human Sexuality
Social Psychology	
Theories of Personality	Social Organization
Learning and Conditioning	Juvenile Delinquency
Perception	Honors Directed Study

Physiological Psychology
Psychopharmacology
Introduction to Counseling
   Psychology
Field Practicum in Psychology
Senior Seminar in Psychology

Honors Colloquium I and II
Honors Senior Capstone
Experience

Psychology GPA: 4.0

Current Research and Interest Areas

Gender Issues in Psychology and Law
Sexual Orientation Minorities
Gender Issues in Health Psychology

Hobbies

Playing the ukulele, hiking, bicycling, surfing, and cooking.

References

Dr. Mary L. Careen
Assistant Professor
Department of Psychology
Kennesaw State University
Kennesaw, GA
(555) 555-5555
drcareen2@kennesaw.edu

Dr. Jameson L. Pinero
Associate Professor
Department of Psychology
Kennesaw State University
Kennesaw, GA
(555) 555-5555
drpinero@kennesaw.edu

Dr. Hans Christian Heiko
Professor
Department of Psychology
Kennesaw State University
Kennesaw, GA
(555) 555-5555
drheiko@kennesaw.edu

Statements of Intent and Admissions Essays

With mean ratings of 2.63 and 2.81 out of a possible 3 for master's programs and doctoral programs, respectively, the importance of the statement of intent to admissions committees cannot be overestimated (Norcross et al., 2005). The statement of intent is also called the statement of purpose and personal statement. Regardless of the label used, the statement is an indication of:

- your academic background and how it has prepared you for graduate study in this specific field (e.g., research experience);
- why you want to attend graduate school in general;
- why you want to attend that *specific* graduate program (e.g., the match between the program and your research/practice interest areas);
- which faculty you are interested in working with in terms of research; and
- your ultimate goal upon graduation (i.e., career goals).

In fact, these points can form an outline for your statement in terms of information to cover. Although there will be similarities among the letters to the different programs, each statement should be specific to the program of interest. Nothing speaks more negatively than a canned, nonspecific, generic letter. The thinking on the recipient's end will be, "If he or she couldn't take enough time to personalize the information for our program, then he or she must not be that interested."

On second thought, although it is still extremely negative, there is something even worse than a generic letter. A statement that is not grammatically accurate is probably the "kiss of death" for your application. Given that you have "all the time in the world" to construct this statement, including getting lots of feedback from your faculty and peers, even one minor error may be perceived as a lack of attention to detail and sloppiness (not good attributes for a potential graduate student). As a result, always remember that this statement (as well as all of your application materials) is a writing sample. In this vein, statements should be in a highly legible font (e.g., Times New Roman size 12) with 1-inch margins and double-spaced (unless single-spaced is allowed). If single-spacing is allowed, take advantage of it! But remember, no fluff is allowed. In truth, programs often specify a maximum length (e.g., two to three pages, double-spaced) so there is little room for "fluff." If no length is specified, three to four pages should be the goal. In terms of length, use the maximum length indicated as the general required length (without exceeding it). Appleby and Appleby (2007) provide some additional "kisses of death" for your personal statement in Box 7.5.

> **Box 7.5** *Four Kisses of Death for Your Personal Statement*
>
> - **"Avoid references to your mental health."** – This may raise concern about your ability to function as a graduate student.
> - **"Avoid excessively altruistic statements."** – A strong need to help others may be seen as a stronger desire than to perform research and other required foundational activities.
> - **"Avoid providing excessively self-revealing information."** – This may suggest a problem with appropriate and healthy interpersonal boundaries.
> - **"Avoid inappropriate humor, attempts to appear cute or clever, and references to God or religious issues when these issues are unrelated to the program to which you are applying."** – This may be interpreted as both an indication of inappropriate boundaries and a lack of awareness of the seriousness of the process.
>
> *Note.* Information comes from Appleby and Appleby (2007; p. 21).

In addition to requiring a personal statement, many programs also require answers to other essay questions. These essays tend to require short answers (e.g., one page or less) and focus on certain aspects of the program or your qualifications (e.g., "Which area of research interests you most and why?"). The same level of seriousness, care, and preparation should be given to these answers as was given to your personal statement.

On a final but related note, both Appleby and Appleby (2007) and Bottoms and Nysse (1999) strongly urge students not to misinterpret the "personal" nature of the required statements and essays. In this situation, *personal* should not in any way be construed as meaning private. In fact, it should instead be defined as your *professional* statement of purpose. In other words, it is inappropriate to discuss personal issues like mental health, your philosophy of life, or religion. This type of information may doom your application to the reject pile. For more information on statements of intent and example essays, we encourage you to access the web resources given at the end of the chapter.

Letters of Recommendation

Applications to graduate school require letters of recommendation from individuals who know you well in relation to your professional and academic life. Most programs require three letters of recommendation.

These letters should be from professors who know you well and have worked with you personally (e.g., on research projects or on student organization activities). All letter writers would preferably be psychologists (i.e., your professors). At least two of them absolutely need to be psychologists. We would recommend that at least two of the three are professors with whom you have collaborated on research. Having individuals who do not know you well (e.g., a professor who you have only worked with in a class or two) write letters suggests to the admission's committee that you were not actively involved in your education. Furthermore, if your interaction with a professor consists only of coursework (i.e., you took a class or two with the professor), the information provided in such a letter likely can readily be found on your transcript in the form of your grades. In other words, you want to have letters from professors who have taught you in coursework and who have worked with you outside of class on significant projects.

A question we often get from students is about letters from nonpsychology professors or psychologists outside of academe (i.e., practicing applied psychologists in the community). Nonpsychology professors and psychologists outside of academe are often unfamiliar with what is valued in the graduate school application process due to no experience or dated experience. As a result, their letters may be more (unintentionally) harmful than helpful. The question that admissions' committees may ask is why did you not have your psychology professors write letters, with the implication that you did not have good relationships with them or were not involved. This impression is certainly not something you want to convey!

In terms of logistics relevant to letters of recommendation, you will want to allow your recommenders at least 4–6 weeks to write the letters (excluding weekends, holidays, and school breaks). In this vein, you will want to give faculty deadlines that are relative to when you will send the application and not when the application deadline occurs. Faculty may misinterpret the application deadline as their due date, making your application late and often not considered further in the process as a result.

Because graduate programs want your recommenders to comment on such attributes as creativity, leadership, ability to accept criticism, ability to work independently, research skills, writing ability, etc., most recommenders will want you to waive your right to read the letter. Faculty may feel freer in their evaluations of these attributes, and the letter may carry more weight as a result. In fact, some faculty will not write letters when students do not waive their right to read the letters. In other words, we recommend waiving your right. The truth is that you should trust your writers or ask

> **Box 7.6** *Materials Included in a Packet for the Faculty Providing You with Letters of Recommendation*
>
> - A short cover letter indicating the contents of the packet and the agreed upon date that you will return to pick up the letters
> - A checklist of all programs with information on due dates, type of program, any special information (e.g., "This is my top choice because of the research they do on heart disease.")
> - A copy of your vita
> - A chronological list highlighting the courses and significant activities/interactions you had with the letter writer
> - A copy of your personal statement (the generic one that is nonspecific to a program is sufficient)
> - An unofficial copy of your transcript
> - An unofficial copy of your GRE and Psychology Subject Test scores
> - Any required recommendation forms
> - Web addresses/links (along with passwords) to recommendation forms that must be filled out online
> - A preaddressed envelope for the recommendation form and letter (stamped if the faculty member has to mail it himself or herself) for each program as appropriate

someone else. Your recommenders should be genuinely excited to write that strong positive letter of recommendation for you. Hesitation in agreeing to write a letter should indicate a less than strong letter may be on the horizon. If this is your feeling, we encourage you to seek another recommender because mediocre letters, as well as strong positive letters with even a small negative, can put your application in the "reject" pile. Box 7.6 lists materials to include in a packet to each of your letter writers. We encourage you to be cognizant of these tips. Recommenders do not like disorganization, a characteristic they will be commenting on in the letter. Including the information in a binder with dividers separating the different programs is an excellent idea. Emailing the packet of information via attachment may also be helpful to your letter writer. All of this work communicates organizational skills and respect and understanding of the cumbersome process of letter writing.

The Graduate School Application Packet

As noted in Mayhew's "10 Tips from a Successful Applicant," proper and professional preparation of your application packet is extremely important. Some important points on the packet include:

- Send materials all at once. If possible, send everything together (including letters of recommendation and official transcripts). This will decrease the likelihood of materials getting lost.
- Send your packet at least 2 weeks before the deadline. This will ensure that it arrives on time. Plus, if it does not arrive for some reason, you have time to submit another packet before the deadline. Not meeting the deadline is an extremely negative sign. In fact, your materials are not likely to be reviewed at all. Although, your application fee will still be processed.
- Submit all of your materials in a nice neutral folder that has your name and contact information neatly typed on the front. This provides not only a professional presentation but also a mechanism to keep all of your materials together.

We encourage you to review Mayhew's *Tips* for additional pointers. Box 7.7 provides a checklist of contents to include in your packet. We strongly encourage you to use this as a guide. In summary, your application packet must be impressive enough that they want to invite you for an interview or make you an offer.

Interviewing

Most graduate programs in the applied psychology subfields (i.e., clinical, counseling, school, and industrial–organizational) require an interview. In fact, 93% of clinical psychology and counseling psychology programs require some type of interview prior to an offer of admission (Oliver, Norcross, Sayette, Griffin, & Mayne, 2005). Research-oriented subfields (e.g., social, developmental, experimental) generally do not require interviews. Interviews can take place on the phone, in person, or both. In terms of clinical and counseling psychology programs, Oliver et al. indicate that 27% require an in-person interview, 62% prefer an in-person interview, 4% require a telephone interview, and 7% do not require an interview. Because interviews are costly (airfare, hotel, car rentals, food), you will want to keep

> **Box 7.7** *Checklist for Preparing the Application Packet for Submission – Making the Right Impression*
>
> - Cover letter:
>   - Indicating that this is your application to their graduate school
>   - Indicating to which program you are applying (since most departments have multiple programs). Note: Even if a department has more than one program in which you are interested, you should only apply to one program. Applying to more than one makes you look indecisive.
>   - Indicating the contents of your application
>   - Requesting that they mail the enclosed postcard when your application is complete
> - Vita
> - Copy of your GRE General Test and Psychology Subject Test Scores (original is sent by ETS)
> - Official copy of your transcripts in a sealed envelope (and signed/stamped over the seal) – If the program requires transcripts to be sent by the school, include a photocopy of your transcripts in the packet.
> - Writing samples – maximum of two – possible examples include:
>   - Copy of a publication you authored or co-authored
>   - Copy of your senior thesis
>   - Copy of a research article you authored and submitted for publication
>   - Copy of a poster you presented
>   - Copy of a research article you presented at a conference
> - Copies of publications and conference presentation handouts
> - Personal statement (remember: Times New Roman size 12 font; proofread)
> - Application forms
> - Additional essays required by the program
> - Self-addressed stamped postcard for them to mail when your application is complete
> - Letters of recommendation in sealed envelopes (signed over seal), unless required to send them separately

this in your mind as you work out your budget for the interview season. Some programs acknowledge this expense and assist with housing (e.g., current students volunteer to let applicants sleep on their couches). Although you may request a telephone interview if you are unable to travel for an interview, you will want to understand that this puts you at a disadvantage relative to others who interview in-person. As a result, we strongly encourage attending an in-person interview when invited.

Suggestions Specific to In-Person Interviews

Before beginning these suggestions and to eliminate redundancy, we encourage you to review information about attire (e.g., wearing a business suit) and preparation (e.g., doing a mock interview and reviewing program materials and your application) provided earlier in the book. That information applies here too. Keeping these suggestions in mind, you can focus yourself during the course of the interview day (or days) on that information most important to you (i.e., Is this program right for me?). During the course of the interview day(s), you will likely meet with faculty and students in both formal and informal settings. Regardless of the setting, you are being evaluated continually, including by the current students. Therefore, you will want to be aware of your behavior in all of these settings (e.g., limiting alcohol use at a dinner or social event).

Some applicants are blessed with multiple interview offers. However, multiple interview offers have their own downside. Because interviews are generally conducted on Fridays in later January, February, and early March, overlap may occur in interview dates. Although some programs provide alternative interview dates for students with scheduling conflicts, others do not. As a result, you may be in the position of needing to rank the two or three programs with conflicting interview dates and request phone interviews with the ones coming in second and third. Regardless of the stress, count yourself lucky to have such a situation arise!

Suggestions Specific to Telephone Interviews

For telephone interviews, you will still want to prepare, including ensuring a distraction-free environment for the interview. For the interview, you will want to make sure you are dressed as you would be in an in-person interview (helps remind you of the importance of the call) and have your materials (e.g., application, program information, biographies of those who are calling if known) laid out in front of you (to reduce paper shuffling while on the phone). Norcross et al. (2008) suggest preparing a telephone card (i.e., a single sheet of paper that notes specifics of the program). These specifics should include:

- name of the university and program;
- faculty research interests;

- faculty you would like to work with and why;
- questions you have for the program (see Box 7.8 for possibilities); and
- why you are interested in the program.

Having this information readily available on each program to which you applied is not a bad idea. This will help you in case a program calls you without warning and wants to talk with you at that moment.

For both phone and in-person interviews, you will want to convey a sense of enthusiasm about the program. This excitement can be displayed via your knowledge of the program and the program's faculty members (including their research programs and publications). Enthusiasm is communicated not only by your answers to their questions but also by the questions that you ask. Box 7.8 provides some examples of potential questions you may be asked and that you might ask as well. In general, your preparation for the interview should include a list of questions for the individuals you will meet, including the current students. Furthermore, engaging your interviewer in a discussion of his or her research interests and how those interests match yours is an excellent goal for the interaction.

Thank You Notes

Once all interviews with a particular program are complete (whether the interview was in-person or via telephone), we encourage you to send a thank you note to those involved in your interview. Send the note immediately as programs tend to make decisions about offers relatively soon after the interview day(s) conclude. Both thank you note cards and emails are generally acceptable in the academic environment. In fact, a professional email thank you may work best in terms of timeliness. The note should indicate your continuing, genuine interest in the program and your enjoyment of the interview day(s). Sending a thank you note is, generally, the last contact you will have with a program before decisions and offers are made by the program. As a result, you will want to ensure that the note is professional.

Making Your Decision

In our experience, admission offers are made relatively soon after interviews are complete. As a result, offers typically begin being made in late February and continue until April 1. All offers (along with financial assistance accompanying an offer) must be made by April 1. Although you may accept an

Box 7.8 *Potential Questions for Graduate School Interviews*

Questions by you:
- What percentage of your students publish before they graduate?
- Is there any formal training for teaching?
- How are most students funded?
- What are your current research studies?
- In what research projects are your students currently involved?
- What courses do your students assist with teaching this semester?
- What is the first-attempt pass rate for your students on the licensure exams? (applied programs only)
- Where do your students find employment?
- What is the typical class size?
- How often do you meet with your graduate students?
- What are the student–professor relationships like (i.e., collegiality)?
- At which conferences do students regularly present?
- Is financial support available for travel to conferences?
- Are summer stipends available?
- What community placements are available for practica?
- What is the biggest strength of the program?
- If you could change something about the program, what would that be and why?

Questions for you
- Why are you interested in our program?
- What made you decide on this subfield of psychology?
- What do you know of my (the interviewer's) research program?
- What research studies are you interested in conducting?
- What is your theoretical orientation? (applied programs only)
- What research background/experiences do you have?
- What applied experiences do you have? (applied programs only)
- What do you plan on doing upon receiving your graduate degree?
- What do you think will be your biggest challenge in graduate school?
- What do you like to do for fun/to relax?
- What questions do you have for us?

offer before April 15, you are allowed until April 15 to make your decision. After April 15, positions not filled/accepted may be offered to others. Given the stress associated with a decision of this magnitude, we encourage you to rank order the offers you receive. Some of the variables you may want to consider in your ranking include many of the attributes that helped you narrow your original list (see Box 7.3). We also encourage you to talk with family, your undergraduate mentor, and your letter writers. These individuals continue to be invested in your success and want the right fit for you and your career goals.

Once you have arrived at your decision, make it! When you notify the graduate program of your acceptance (by postal mail or via email depending on the program's preference), you will then want to notify the other programs that are continuing to consider you. Releasing your other offers allows those programs to offer your spot to someone on their "wait list." By releasing your spot, you will make someone very happy! Last but not least, thank your letter writers and let them know your decision.

Plan B: What if I Don't Get In?

As is obvious from the percentage acceptances for programs noted earlier, not everyone that applies to graduate school will get an offer to attend. Even if you followed every suggestion given by us and others, success is not guaranteed (although our experience suggests that the likelihood is increased). As a result, you will want to develop an alternative plan. Our main suggestion for a "Plan B" is to consider applying to master's programs instead of doctoral programs if you do not have a master's degree or if you did not apply to them already. Beyond the possibility of simply having "bad luck," the likelihood is that there are reasons that a student did not get an offer. These reasons can include:

- applying to only high-ranked programs;
- not applying widely enough (geographically or otherwise);
- low GPA/GRE relative to the mean/median of a program's recent acceptances; and
- no research experience.

In thinking about your alternative plan, we encourage you to sit with a trusted faculty member who you believe will provide unadulterated critical feedback and suggestions. Give yourself a breather before you do this though. April 16 may be too soon for some. However, in terms of the suggestion of applying to master's programs, some master's programs have late deadlines. As a result, you may consider applying immediately.

10 Tips from a Successful Applicant

Laura L. Mayhew
University of South Florida

Kudos to you for considering graduate school! The admission requirements and application process can seem daunting, but don't let that deter you from pursuing your goals. With forethought, organization, and taking advantage of any and all resources available to you, you can be fully prepared, and the application process can go smoothly...and hopefully lead to an admission offer! Here are some suggestions to help you with your preparations.

1. Consider your options...and really consider a multitude of them. Although you may have very specific ideas regarding what you want to do in your career and what programs you want to pursue, allow some flexibility. For example, if you are pursuing a research-oriented degree, don't immediately dismiss a program because a professor's line of research doesn't perfectly match with your interests. Graduate school is a training period, and you can always tailor your research (or practice, teaching, etc.) more specifically to your liking when you complete your graduate studies.

2. Be a superstar student, and study your tush off for the GRE to earn high scores. Like it or not, GPA and GRE scores are always considered in graduate admissions. Although minimum and average GPAs vary among programs, you need to do well in your undergraduate coursework for admission to (and success in) most graduate programs. Start now! You can't build a stellar GPA in one semester. Similarly, GRE score requirements vary by program, but you want to do as well as you can. And, in order to do your best you need to study, study, STUDY, and practice, practice, PRACTICE. In addition to studying the specific test areas (e.g., learning GRE-quality words, reviewing math concepts, practicing analytical writing), take as many practice tests as you can get your hands on.

3. Professor who??? Get to know your professors. In order to get strong positive recommendation letters it helps if your professors actually know who you are! Take and excel in multiple classes with the same professors, put in extra face time with them outside of

class (e.g., drop in during office hours to discuss coursework and graduate school), and get involved with professors' projects. Besides increasing the possibility of getting stellar recommendations you might actually learn a thing or two (a lot of these folks tend to be pretty smart).

4. Research! Research! Research! Although the importance of research experience varies among programs, it is essential for many PhD programs, and it probably won't hurt your chances with programs that emphasize other experiences. Apply for research assistantships in professors' laboratories, or, if there aren't structured labs, ask your professors what upcoming projects they have and inquire how you can contribute. Also consider approaching a professor about a directed study or completing a senior thesis... and always look for opportunities to present (or even better, publish) your research.

5. In a similar vein, get experience! Practical or clinical experience is important to some programs. Participate in practicum opportunities if your department offers them. Entry-level employment and structured volunteer experience in your field (including research-based positions) can be impressive to admissions committees. In addition, get involved with your department's psychology club and Psi Chi. Become a student affiliate of professional organizations in the field. The

Association for Psychological Science Student Caucus (APSSC) is a great international organization in which to get involved. Unlike some other professional organizations, the APSSC offers many opportunities for undergraduates. These types of experiences are great for professional activities you could encounter in your career and look great on your vita to boot!

6. Apply to a LOT of schools with varying degrees of entrance/requirement difficulties. Again, flexibility is important. There are many people who want to go to graduate school in the same area in which YOU are interested. In other words, competition is stiff, and admission is never guaranteed. To increase your chances for admission don't limit yourself to only top-tier programs. Find out where you stand (i.e., your attributes vs. the programs' statistics), and apply to a variety of programs where you meet and exceed the typical student's credentials plus some of those dreamy programs where you might not be quite up to par.

7. Contact professors at the schools you are considering before applying. Find out whether or not the professors plan to take students (if it is a mentor-based program) for the upcoming year. This information is often posted on programs' websites, but the contact can benefit you by putting your name "out there." A professor might give you just a bit of

extra consideration when your application packet arrives because of the prior contact with you. An email also serves as an opportunity to show genuine interest in the professor's work. Who doesn't like to hear accolades about their work? Similarly, you may try to get in touch with students in a program with questions you may have. Students' opinions of applicants can sometimes influence acceptances, and they can give you a perspective you'll likely want to hear. After all, your goal is to be in their position next year, right?

8. Be sure your application materials are organized and professional, and seek the opinion of multiple professors to ensure the quality. Your application is the graduate program's first impression of you, so make sure it looks professional! Ask multiple professors to review and help you tweak your personal statement and vita. They will know what admissions' committees value. Place all required application materials in a folder, and include photocopies of materials that may have been sent separately (e.g., transcripts, GRE scores). You also want to make sure your application was received, but don't call. Instead, include a self-addressed stamped postcard with the name of the university on it for staff to send to you upon receipt of your application.

9. Prepare for interviews. Many programs require interviews prior to an admission offer. An interview is your chance to impress the faculty. Prepare stellar answers to common interview questions. Also, prepare questions that you want to ask them! Having your own questions is important because it shows that you are really interested. Read up on the faculty's publications, and be prepared to discuss your possible contributions to their research program. Prepare questions to ask students because you will likely be spending time with them (and being interviewed by them) at dinners or in other less formal situations. Remember to ask about anything that would be relevant to your consideration of spending several years at this place (unless, of course, you are concerned about the bar/club scene! Save that for later, not the interview!).

10. If at first you don't succeed, try, try, try again. You will HAVE to be persistent as a graduate student. So, if you don't get accepted the first time you apply, consider it an opportunity to build up your persistence skills! Get more experience, seek guidance, work on your application materials, and go for it again in the next round!

I hope you find these tips useful in your pursuit of even higher higher education. Good luck!

Note. Laura L. Mayhew earned her bachelor's degree in psychology from Kennesaw State University and received the University System of Georgia Board of Regents' Academic Recognition Scholar Award (2005–2006). She earned her master's degree and is currently a doctoral candidate in the Clinical Psychology PhD program at the University of South Florida. Laura's predoctoral internship is at the Bay Pines VA Healthcare System. Her research is predominantly in the health psychology area.

Suggested Exercises

1. Using one of the resources noted in the chapter, identify two programs in your area of interest. Develop an Excel or SPSS file based on the variables listed in Box 7.3 and fill in the spreadsheet for each of the programs.
2. Using the sample vita and other resources identified in this chapter as a guide, create the vita that you would like to have when you apply for graduate school. (Once completed, let it serve as a guide for your undergraduate activities!)
3. Using one of the programs you identified in the first exercise, develop a mock application. (Applications can often be downloaded. If not, choose a similar program that does have a downloadable application.) As part of the application, develop a cover letter and statement of intent specific to that program.

Suggested Readings

American Psychological Association. (2007). *Getting in: A step-by-step plan for gaining admission to graduate school in psychology*. Washington, DC: Author.

American Psychological Association. (2014a). *Graduate study in psychology: 2014*. Washington, DC: Author.

Buskist, W., & Burke, C. (2007). *Preparing for graduate study in psychology: 101 questions and answers* (2nd ed.). Malden, MA: Blackwell.

Keith-Spiegel, P., & Wiederman, M. W. (2000). *The complete guide to graduate school admission: Psychology, counseling, and related professions* (2nd ed.). Mahwah, NJ: Lawrence Erlbaum Associates Publishers.

Norcross, J. C., & Sayette, M. A. (2014a). *Insider's guide to graduate programs in clinical and counseling psychology: 2014/2015 Edition*. New York, NY: Guilford.

Resources

Program Rankings

Please note that these rankings tend to change quickly. They are provided only as a beginning point, not as an ending point!

- PhDs.org
  Description: "Rank the top 238 psychology graduate programs in the US using the latest National Research Council data."
  Link: http://www.phds.org/rankings/psychology

- The Gourman Report
  Description: Ranking of US psychology PhD programs by area.
  Link: http://www.socialpsychology.org/ggradoth.htm

Statement of Purpose Resources

- Accepted.com
  Description: Provides examples and do's and don'ts for writing your statement of purpose for graduate school.
  Link: http://www.accepted.com/grad/personalstatement.aspx
- Massachusetts Institute of Technology – Career Services
  Description: Provides pointers on graduate school admission essays and statements as well as examples (although mainly in the engineering field).
  Link: http://web.mit.edu/career/www/workshops/gradschool/statement.html
- University of California – Berkeley – Career Center
  Description: Provides pointers on graduate school admission essays and statements.
  Link: http://career.berkeley.edu/Grad/GradStatement.stm
- Asher, D. (2012). *Graduate admissions essays: Write your way into the graduate school of your choice* (4th ed.). New York, NY: Ten Speed Press.

Vita Preparation

- Landrum, R. E. (2005, Winter). The curriculum vita: A student's guide to preparation. *Eye on Psi Chi, 9*(2), 28–29, 42.
  Link: http://www.psichi.org/?092EyeWin05dLandrum

General Resources

- Psi Chi – The International Honor Society in Psychology
  Description: Publishes *Eye on Psi Chi*, a magazine with topical and timely articles on such issues as preparing for graduate school, getting research experience, and preparing for entrance exams.
  Link: www.psichi.org
- About.com – Graduate School (by Tara Kuther)
  Description: Information on topics like letters of recommendation, admissions essays, and preparing for the GRE.
  Link: gradschool.about.com
- Social Psychology Network: Online Psychology Career Center
  Description: Information on topics like preparing a vita (including examples) and letters of recommendation. Also provides useful links to additional resources like program rankings.
  Link: www.socialpsychology.org

References

Academy of Psychological Clinical Science. (2014). *Mission*. Retrieved from http://acadpsychclinicalscience.org/mission

American Psychological Association. (2012). *Commission on Accreditation: 2012 annual report online: Summary data: Doctoral programs.* Washington, DC: Author. Retrieved from https://www.apa.org/ed/accreditation/about/research/2012-doctoral-summary.pdf

American Psychological Association. (2014a). *Graduate study in psychology: 2014.* Washington, DC: Author.

American Psychological Association. (2014b). *Public description of school psychology.* Retrieved from http://www.apa.org/ed/graduate/specialize/school.aspx

American Psychological Association – Division 47 – Exercise and Sport Psychology. (2014). *What is exercise psychology and sport psychology?* Retrieved from http://www.apadivisions.org/division-47/about/resources/what-is.aspx

Appleby, D. C., & Appleby, K. M. (2007, Spring). How to avoid the kisses of death in the graduate school application process. *Eye on Psi Chi, 11*(3), 20–21.

Aronson, E. (2004). *The social animal* (9th ed.). New York, NY: Worth.

Association of Psychology Postdoctoral and Internship Centers. (2012). *2012 APPIC match: Survey of internship applicants.* Retrieved from http://www.appic.org/Match/MatchStatistics/ApplicantSurvey2012Part2.aspx

Association of Psychology Postdoctoral and Internship Centers. (2014). *2014 APPIC match statistics.* Retrieved from http://www.appic.org/Match/MatchStatistics/MatchStatistics2014Combined.aspx

Bartol, C. R., & Bartol, A. M. (1999). History of forensic psychology. In A. K. Hess & I. B. Weiner (Eds.), *Handbook of forensic psychology* (2nd ed., pp. 3–23). New York, NY: John Wiley & Sons.

Bottoms, B. L., & Nysse, K. L. (1999, Fall). Applying to graduate school: Writing a compelling personal statement. *Eye on Psi Chi, 4*(1), 20–22.

Briihl, D. S., & Wasieleski, D. T. (2004). A survey of master's-level psychology programs: Admissions criteria and program policies. *Teaching of Psychology, 31,* 252–256. doi:10.1207/s15328023top3104_5

Educational Testing Service. (2014a). *About the GRE Revised General Test.* Retrieved from http://www.ets.org/gre/revised_general/about?WT.ac=grehome_greabout_b_130807

Educational Testing Service. (2014b). *Psychology test.* Retrieved from http://www.ets.org/gre/subject/about/content/psychology

Educational Testing Service. (2014c). *Test content and structure.* Retrieved from http://www.ets.org/gre/revised_general/about/content

Educational Testing Service. (2014d). *The ScoreSelect option.* Retrieved from http://www.ets.org/gre/revised_general/about/scoreselect

Kupfersmid, J., & Fiola, M. (1991). Comparison of EPPP scores among graduates of varying psychology programs. *American Psychologist, 46,* 534–535. doi:10.1037/0003-066X.46.5.534

Maher, B. A. (1999). Changing trends in doctoral training programs in psychology: A comparative analysis of research-oriented versus professional-applied programs. *Psychological Sciences, 10,* 475–481. doi:10.1111/1467-9280.00192

Matthews, J. R., & Anton, B. S. (2008). *Introduction to clinical psychology.* New York, NY: Oxford University Press.

Michalski, D., Kohout, J., Wicherski, M., & Hart, B. (2011, May). *2009 doctorate employment survey.* Washington, DC: American Psychological Association. Retrieved from http://www.apa.org/workforce/publications/09-doc-empl/report.pdf

Mulvey, T. A., Michalski, D. S., & Wicherski, M. (2010). *2010 graduate study in psychology snapshot: Applications, acceptances, enrollments, and degrees awarded to master's- and doctoral-level students in U.S. and Canadian graduate departments of psychology: 2008-2009.* Retrieved from www.apa.org/workforce/publications/10-grad-study/report-applications.pdf

Norcross, J. C., & Kuhl, B. X. (2011, Summer). New probabilities of admission into graduate psychology programs. *Eye on Psi Chi, 15*(4), 21–22.

Norcross, J. C., & Sayette, M. A. (2014). *Insider's guide to graduate programs in clinical and counseling psychology: 2014/2015 Edition.* New York, NY: Guilford.

Norcross, J. C., Ellis, J. L., & Sayette, M. A. (2010). Getting in and getting money: A comparative analysis of admission standards, acceptance rates, and financial assistance across the research-practice continuum in clinical psychology programs. *Training and Education in Professional Psychology, 4,* 99–104. doi:10.1037/a0014880

Norcross, J. C., Kohout, J. L., & Wicherski, M. (2005). Graduate study in psychology: 1971 to 2004. *American Psychologist, 60,* 959–975. doi:10.1037/0003-066X.60.9.959

Norcross, J. C., Sayette, M. A., & Mayne, T. J. (2008). *Insider's guide to graduate programs in clinical and counseling psychology: 2008/2009 Edition.* New York, NY: Guilford.

Oliver, J. M., Norcross, J. C., Sayette, M. A., Griffin, K., & Mayne, T. J. (2005, March). *Doctoral study in clinical, counseling, and combined psychology: Admission requirements and student characteristics.* Poster presented at the 76th annual meeting of the Eastern Psychological Association, Boston, MA.

Peterson, D. R. (1976). Need for the doctor of psychology degree in professional psychology. *American Psychologist, 31,* 792–798. doi:10.1037/0003-066X.31.11.792

Peterson, D. R. (2003). Unintended consequences: Ventures and misadventures in the education of professional psychologists. *American Psychologist, 58,* 791–800. doi:10.1037/0003-066X.58.10.791

Psychological Clinical Science Accreditation System. (2014). *Welcome.* Retrieved from www.pcsas.org

Society of Clinical Psychology. (n.d.). *What is clinical psychology?* Retrieved from http://www.apa.org/divisions/div12/aboutcp.html

Society of Counseling Psychology. (2014). *About Division 17.* Retrieved from http://www.div17.org/about

Templer, D. I., & Arikawa, H. (2004). Concerns about professional schools. *American Psychologist, 59,* 646–647. doi:10.1037/0003-066X.59.7.646

Templer, D. I., Stroup, K., Mancuso, L. J., & Tangen, K. (2008). Comparative decline of professional school graduates' performance on the Examination for Professional Practice in Psychology. *Psychological Reports, 102*(2), 551–560. doi:10.2466/PRO.102.2.551-560

Weiten, W. (2008). *Psychology: Themes and variations* (7th ed., Briefer version). Belmont, CA: Thomson.

Part II
The Subfields of Psychology

Chapter Eight
Careers in Research
Experimental, Developmental, Social, Cognitive, and Biopsychology

Introduction

The scientific process forms the core of psychology. Because all psychologists are trained in how to design research, gather and analyze data, and consider the implications of results, research-based careers occur in every subfield of the discipline. Because so many psychologists with diverse areas of focus are involved in research, it is impossible to capture all the variations within and among these careers in a single chapter. However, for several subfields in psychology, the likely careers almost always include a substantial research emphasis. Although these research-intensive subfields are quite varied in their focus and methods, we think that an overview of them as a group can provide you with a sense of what these types of careers entail.

Before turning to various research-oriented careers in the field, let us first consider a key question. What is research? Research involves gaining knowledge about the world around us in a specific way. Although we gain knowledge daily by reasoning about situations, accepting the view of authority figures, or experiencing things first-hand, each of these methods of understanding is prone to error and bias. In contrast, research uses methods and techniques specifically designed to ensure that the knowledge gained is objective. Scientists across different fields of study use research methods and techniques to answer questions relevant to their work. Psychologists use research to answer questions about behavior. Even though these questions stem from their own curiosity, psychologists allow the data they gather to answer their questions rather than relying on intuition, logic, authority, or personal experience.

Majoring in Psychology: Achieving Your Educational and Career Goals, Second Edition.
Jeffrey L. Helms and Daniel T. Rogers.
© 2015 John Wiley & Sons, Ltd. Published 2015 by John Wiley & Sons, Ltd.

Research is a creative endeavor full of excitement and possibilities. Despite this, undergraduate psychology majors do not typically rank the research-intensive subfields high among their future career goals (Gallucci, 1997). This lack of interest appears to be in place even before students select psychology as their major. For example, new majors indicate that they do not expect research and statistics to be a priority in their psychology courses (McGovern & Hawks, 1986). Apparently many students choose the psychology major while still unfamiliar with what the field entails. In fact, many students have a misconception that the field involves only applied work in mental health (Webb & Speer, 1985). Yet approximately one third of the doctoral degrees granted in psychology in the US between 2002 and 2012 were in the five research-intensive subfields considered in this chapter (National Science Foundation, 2013). Students' lack of understanding about the role of research in the field likely stems from limited contact with psychologists who are doing this work. As a result, few students can conceptualize what a research-oriented career in psychology would be like, and a portion of those students may be missing out on a career opportunity that could be an excellent fit for their interests and goals. Changing this perception begins with being better informed.

Defining the Subfields

Experimental Psychology

Experimental psychologists' expertise is in conducting psychological research. It is true that conducting research is emphasized in all areas of psychology. In fact, training in research methodology, experimentation, and statistics will be a core part of your education as an undergraduate student studying psychology. If you choose to pursue a graduate degree in psychology, these same areas will be points of emphasis regardless of the subfield you choose. But experimental psychologists pursue a subfield that places the ability to design and conduct psychological research at the forefront of their training. In order to give you a better sense of the kinds of research these psychologists might conduct, Box 8.1 lists several research questions that experimental psychologists have sought to answer in recent years.

Because their research skills and expertise are general enough to be applied to a variety of topics, experimental psychologists are not restricted to conducting research in any one area. However, most do choose a specialty or concentration for their career while in graduate school. Graduate programs in experimental psychology, and the faculty who guide them, often

Box 8.1 *Questions Addressed by the Research of Experimental Psychologists*

- How do certain characteristics of a task/challenge/problem affect one's success in completing it?
- What visual features facilitate the detection of emotions in facial expressions?
- What are the implications of increased use of and reliance on technology?
- What contextual and individual factors would lead an eyewitness to falsely identify an innocent suspect?
- How do people make decisions when presented with information that contradicts their beliefs?
- What practice or rehearsal schedules should be followed in order to maximize learning?
- What characteristics of a stimulus contribute to the conditioning of fear?

have a particular research focus. Students attending the programs develop knowledge in these areas while becoming experts in general research methods. This can be a confusing point for undergraduate students because their professors who are trained as experimental psychologists may or may not identify themselves as such. For example, one professor may identify herself as an experimental psychologist while another states he is a cognitive psychologist. Yet, both could conduct research on essentially the same topic.

Reading the research literature is a good way to gain additional understanding of the types of research being conducted in psychology and the careers of the individuals involved in this research. For each of the subfields discussed in this chapter, we will summarize elements of a recent research article to further demonstrate the rich diversity of topics investigated in the field. For example, Chen, Minson, Schöne, and Heinrichs (2013) investigated the commonly held notion that maximizing eye contact is an effective strategy when trying to persuade others. They conducted two studies in which participants (listeners) observed videos of individuals (speakers) expressing a range of views on social and political topics that are widely debated or controversial. The researchers used eye-tracking technology to measure where listeners looked during the videos and self-report instruments to measure the degree of change in listeners' own attitudes about the topic. In the first study, listeners watched the videos with no restrictions.

The researchers found that the more listeners looked at the speaker's eyes, the less they were persuaded to change their attitude on the topic. In the second study, listeners were instructed to either focus on the mouths or eyes of the speakers. The researchers found that the listeners making direct eye contact were less persuaded to change their attitudes. The results of the study shed light on nonverbal tactics that might facilitate or inhibit persuasion. In addition, the study demonstrates how knowledge gained from psychological science can at times contradict knowledge gained from relying on intuition, authority figures, personal experience, and reasoning.

Developmental Psychology

Developmental psychologists' expertise is in the scientific study of human development. Emotional, cognitive, and physical development are all areas of potential focus. In their research, developmental psychologists keep two broad themes in mind. First, they view development as occurring across the lifespan. Important changes take place at all ages, not just in childhood and adolescence. Second, they view development from a global perspective. Change always occurs within a specific context, and what happens developmentally in one culture might not occur in the same way within a different culture. To better understand the types of research developmental psychologists might conduct, Box 8.2 provides several examples of research questions that have received attention in recent years.

Box 8.2 *Questions Addressed by the Research of Developmental Psychologists*

- What types of experiences can hinder the normal progression of language development?
- What components of peer relationships play a role in risky behavior and decision making for adolescents and young adults?
- How do the events of normal aging affect life satisfaction?
- How does the quality of the relationship between a child and parent affect the child's relationships as an adult?
- What factors contribute to young children's ability to think about and visually recognize themselves?
- What role do characteristics of the environment play in older individuals' responses to stress?
- How does direct experience with a task, or the lack of it, affect a child's ability to complete it in the future?

Studying human development is a complex task. Change at any point in a person's development is dependent upon a host of factors such as genetics, physiology, nutrition, education, personality, culture, and environment. Developmental psychologists must understand something about each of these sources of influence. Their particular research interests might only concentrate on a select few, but they are likely to collaborate with professionals who possess expertise on the others. Although most developmental psychologists continue to be focused on research in their careers, increasing numbers of them are also pursuing applied endeavors. These psychologists often conduct research on interventions designed to address a developmental issue. For example, they may design a program to address language delays in preschoolers and then evaluate its effectiveness in various settings.

As one example of research within the developmental psychology subfield, consider a study by Tardif, Fletcher, Zhang, Kaciroti, and Marchman (2008). The researchers investigated the idea that infants all over the world first acquire and use object-naming nouns when learning to speak rather than other parts of speech. They recruited the caregivers of children between the ages of 8 and 16 months from English, Mandarin, and Cantonese speaking households. The caregivers reported the words the child was speaking. Analysis of these lists revealed strong similarities. Words for daddy, mommy, bye, uh-oh, woof, and hi were among the top 20 most common words in all three languages. In addition, the researchers found strong similarities in the types of words that were spoken. Yet rather than find a universal bias for using object-naming nouns, the authors discovered that the strongest consistency across cultures was for words pertaining to people. The results highlight the combined role that genetics and culture play in language acquisition in human development.

Social Psychology

Social psychologists' expertise is in understanding human behavior as it occurs within social contexts. Their research focuses on how humans' thoughts, actions, and feelings are influenced by various aspects of the social environment. They also investigate how humans relate to one another in these environments. Social psychologists interested in individual behavior examine both the characteristics of an individual that influence his/her social interactions and how these characteristics in turn are shaped by the social group. Other social psychologists focus more exclusively on group behavior. Their interests often focus on how group characteristics and actions affect members and how group behavior and decision making can differ from that of an individual. Box 8.3 provides several examples of research questions that have received attention in recent years from social psychologists.

Box 8.3 *Questions Addressed by the Research of Social Psychologists*

- What factors contribute to whether an individual finds someone else to be attractive?
- How does the nature of our social experience with other groups influence the ways in which we apply attitudes, beliefs, and judgments to members of those groups?
- How much influence do others' expressed perceptions of an event have on an individual's perception of the same event?
- What factors make stereotypes more or less resistant to change?
- What aspects of a salesperson's behavior have the greatest influence on a customer's decisions?
- Does exposure to interpersonal violence foster subsequent aggressive behavior?
- Why do some individuals confess to a crime they did not commit?

Social psychology has much in common with other subfields including clinical, counseling, cognitive, and personality psychology. In fact, psychologists in each of these areas investigate topics related to behavior in social contexts such as aggression, stereotypes, interpersonal relationships, and attributions. The research of social psychologists can similarly have direct applications at the societal level. For example, knowledge in social psychology might be used to develop a school-based program to reduce bullying or a public health campaign to reduce smoking. Knowledge about how consumers make individual judgments might be used to enhance the marketing of a product or help increase a population's use of mass transportation.

To provide an example of the kind of research that is possible within social psychology, consider a recent study by Goff, Jackson, Di Leone, Culotta, and DiTomasso (2014). The researchers investigated whether the social category of "children" (i.e., small physical size, innocence, need for protection) is applied to Black boys differently than it is applied to their peers. In a series of studies, both undergraduate students and police officers served as participants by examining and responding to written and visual stimuli that asked them to report on their perceptions about a target individual. In general, the findings across the studies suggested that in comparison to their peers, Black boys are more likely to be misperceived as being older and are more likely to be perceived as having greater guilt, or less innocence. The results indicated that these differences in the way adults perceive children based on race may begin when the child in question is around the age of 10. In their studies with police officers, the researchers found support for how these phenomena might combine with an officer's implicit attitudes toward Black males to increase the likelihood of actually behaving in ways that perpetuate racial disparities in the criminal justice system. The Goff et al. (2014) study also serves as an excellent example of how the research-oriented subfields in psychology often overlap in focus, in this case combining the elements of attitudes, perception, cognitive processing, and awareness of development as they pertain to a social phenomenon.

Cognitive Psychology

The expertise of cognitive psychologists consists of understanding human and nonhuman animals' mental processes. These mental processes are often the foundations for acquiring and using information, and they involve a host of diverse skills and abilities. As a result, cognitive psychologists can investigate a wide range of topics pertaining to the processes that allow information to either be taken in, processed, stored, retrieved, or expressed. Each of these processes can function at varying levels of effectiveness. As a result, some cognitive psychologists strive to understand how these processes can be facilitated while others focus on how they are hindered. To help you conceptualize the types of research cognitive psychologists might conduct, Box 8.4 provides several examples of questions that researchers have focused on in recent years.

Box 8.4 *Questions Addressed by the Research of Cognitive Psychologists*

- What factors contribute to distortions in memory?
- How do features of one's language shape the ability to think about certain concepts?
- What elements of multimedia-based instruction facilitate learning?
- What factors stimulate or discourage flexibility and creativity in thinking?
- What types of information are most often relied on to solve problems?
- What role does imagination play in transferring a piece of information into memory?
- What factors contribute most to the comprehension of text when reading?

Given cognitive psychologists' interests in topics such as attention, information processing, perception, memory, reasoning, language, and communication, the overlap between this subfield and other disciplines has grown in recent years. It is now quite common to find cognitive psychologists collaborating with colleagues in education, cognitive science, medicine, linguistics, and computer science. In addition, many cognitive psychologists investigate topics that have an applied focus. For example, research on factors that facilitate or hinder learning and memory can be used to improve human performance. Components of educational and occupational training programs borrow heavily from the cognitive psychology research literature.

To better demonstrate the vast potential in cognitive psychological research, consider a recent investigation conducted by Lucas, Bridgers, Griffiths, and Gopnik (2014). The researchers investigated how young children and adults might differ in their abilities to learn about causal relationships between objects. Acquiring rules for possible cause and effect relationships between objects allows individuals to make inferences about the world around them, specifically how similar objects might relate. This process of acquiring knowledge and generalizing it to similar situations facilitates understanding and interacting with the environment. For the study, the researchers recruited undergraduate students and 4- and 5-year-olds. They presented the participants with objects of various shapes (the potential causes) that when used correctly triggered lights and music from a device (the effect). Participants first observed an event that gave information about a potential cause–effect relationship between shapes and the device. They were then asked to judge the ability of shapes to elicit an effect and to work with a new set of shapes to attempt to trigger the device. Preschoolers tended to solve the task more quickly, which led the researchers to conclude that younger children have greater flexibility in their thinking about cause and effect. They suggested that adults' previous experience acts as a bias and slows their acquisition and application of new information about cause–effect relationships, especially when that information is atypical or unusual compared to their previous learning. In other words, children likely pay greater attention to the evidence that is immediately available to them about a cause–effect relationship, whereas adults are more likely to discount that information in favor of previous learning. The Lucas et al. (2014) study provides a good example of how cognitive psychology research can cross into related areas of study (e.g., developmental) and have implications for applied endeavors (e.g., teaching and learning).

Biopsychology

Biopsychologists' expertise is in exploring the links between behavior and biology. These links can be investigated from a variety of perspectives. As a result, this specialty area includes and/or overlaps with the work of physiological psychologists, behavioral neuroscientists, and cognitive and clinical neuropsychologists. What distinguishes biopsychologists from other psychologists studying similar topics are the methods used in their research. They apply biological principles in studying the links between biological functioning and behavior. Consequently, they spend time investigating such topics as neuroanatomy, neural communication, pharmacology, endocrine functioning, and genetics. In order to give you a better sense of the kinds of research biopsychologists might conduct, Box 8.5 lists a few research questions that these psychologists have sought to answer in recent years.

Biopsychologists are interested in establishing how biological systems affect behavior and how behaviors affect biological systems. Emphasis is given to understanding how these interactions normally occur and how they occur when there are interfering factors at work. For example, some biopsychologists investigate the impact of disease processes, such as Parkinson's or schizophrenia, on the body. Others examine the influence that substances, such as medications or environmental toxins, have on biological and behavioral processes.

As an example of the types of research that are possible within the biopsychology subfield, consider a study by Kleykamp, Jennings, Sams, Weaver, and Eissenberg (2008). The authors investigated the effectiveness of nicotine patches in helping individuals stop smoking. Participants in the study smoked

---

Box 8.5 *Questions Addressed by the Research of Biopsychologists*

- How can sensitivity to pain be altered?
- What neurotransmitters are involved in the various forms of mental illness?
- What psychological and environmental factors influence immune functioning?
- What role do hormone levels play in mood?
- How do certain genetic conditions affect motor control?
- What are the short- and long-term effects of stress on the body?
- How do sleep patterns and the effects of sleep deprivation change with age?

at least 15 cigarettes per day and had smoked for at least 2 years. They completed four trials on separate days, during which they received nicotine patches with varying dosage levels. For each trial, the participant had refrained for smoking for the prior 8 hours. During the trial they completed computerized assessment measures and provided blood samples in order to measure nicotine levels. Several hours into each trial, participants were allowed to smoke as they wished. The results indicated that the use of a nicotine patch reduced some of the symptoms that regular smokers experience when they do not smoke. The patches also diminished some of the effects of smoking, such as heart rate increase, and lowered the intensity and frequency of smoking. The authors found no differences for these effects between male and female participants. In conclusion, the authors noted that although nicotine administration appears to be a useful aid in efforts to stop smoking, the presence of nicotine in the system alone is not sufficient to eliminate all of the symptoms that occur with smoking abstinence. This suggests that the symptoms smokers experience when they do not smoke are only partly based on nicotine withdrawal. Other non-nicotine factors (e.g., the action of smoking, the smell of a lit cigarette) may also play a role in withdrawal symptoms.

The Work

Because the psychologists who pursue careers in research come from diverse subfields and have diverse interests, it is impossible to briefly describe the nature of this work in all of its possible forms. Instead we will describe some of the characteristics and issues that are common across all research-oriented careers in the field. In doing so, we hope to provide a clearer sense of the activities, settings, salaries, and employment issues that are part of the professional lives of psychologists who pursue careers in research.

Core Activities

Most experimental, developmental, social, cognitive, and biopsychologists seek out their careers because they are interested in learning more about a specific topic through conducting research. As a result, most plan to spend the bulk of their professional lives engaging in the scientific process. But these careers frequently involve the closely related activities of administration as well as teaching and supervision.

Research. Research is a process of discovery. Researchers begin with a question about a particular topic then gradually gather more and more evidence to help answer that question. Importantly, the evidence that is discovered is eventually shared with colleagues in the field who allow this new knowledge to guide and inform the types of questions they are asking in their own research. Over time, this process yields an increasingly sophisticated knowledge base that informs additional research. Eventually this research may begin to impact our daily lives in a direct manner. Psychologists who pursue careers in research do so because they enjoy this endeavor.

The research conducted by psychologists can be classified as either basic or applied in nature. The goal of basic research is to advance our understanding of some topic. For example, a developmental psychologist might seek to understand the age at which children can classify or categorize certain types of objects. A cognitive psychologist might explore how characteristics of presented stimuli affect memory for that information. The knowledge that basic research generates answers questions about how something works. This knowledge typically sparks additional research. In contrast, the goal of applied research is to use existing knowledge for a specific purpose, typically to solve a real-world problem. To extend the previous examples, consider that the developmental psychologist who gains knowledge about children's object categorization later conducts research on the effects of teaching children these strategies. The cognitive psychologist who gains an understanding of how the features of presented material affect memory later investigates whether varying the layout of textbooks improves learning. Although some psychologists conduct both basic and applied research, most spend their careers pursuing one or the other.

Teaching and supervision.   Psychologists who pursue research careers are involved in generating new knowledge. Because this research is often conducted in academic settings, many of them also teach and supervise students who are pursuing a psychology degree. Typically these psychologists teach courses within their area of expertise. At the undergraduate level they teach courses that provide a general overview of their subfield. At the graduate level they teach courses specific to their particular interests. For example, a cognitive psychologist might teach an undergraduate course titled "Introduction to Cognitive Psychology" and graduate courses titled "Pattern Recognition and Analysis" and "Neurolinguistics." Many of these psychologists also supervise undergraduate and graduate students' research. They use their expertise in the subfields and in conducting research to guide student learning. In turn, these students assist psychologists in their research. These mutually beneficial relationships play an important role in the research careers of psychologists and the training of future psychologists.

Administration. Some research careers in psychology include less direct involvement in the research process. Psychologists with expertise in a specific area can be responsible for overseeing research conducted by other professionals. Often this type of activity occurs within an agency that provides grant funding for research. Before such funds are given, the proposed research projects must be carefully reviewed. The projects are then subject to reviews while the research is being conducted and after the project is complete. Many companies that conduct research also depend upon administrators to oversee this work. These types of administrative roles are best filled by individuals who possess expertise in the research process and the skills necessary to work with diverse groups of people. Research-oriented psychologists often fit this description well.

Settings

Experimental, developmental, social, cognitive, and biopsychologists must carry out their careers in settings that can support their research, including the physical facilities and the money necessary to complete projects successfully. Colleges, universities, and medical schools are some of the most common settings providing this support, as evidenced by the fact that approximately 68% of recent graduates from doctoral programs in the research-intensive subfields of psychology are employed in these settings (American Psychological Association [APA], 2011). Psychologists working in these settings often have responsibilities that consist of teaching, research, service, and administration. Although most of these individuals work in psychology departments, others are employed in related departments such as cognitive science, biology, education, psychiatry, business, neurology, and statistics. These occupations involve numerous challenges and rewards that are unique to this setting. Additional information on them is provided in Chapter 16.

Approximately 26% of recent graduates in the research-oriented subfields of psychology are employed full-time in private sector and government positions (APA, 2011). These positions can include responsibilities as a researcher or administrator depending on the specific setting and nature of the work. Many psychologists are hired into these positions because their expertise, either in a particular subject or with a particular methodology, will be of benefit to the organization as it pursues areas of research. Some of these psychologists function as analysts or database managers by overseeing the collection and analysis of large data sets to answer questions related to a company's goals. Others may function in the role of consultants who guide the development and design of new research. Still others in government positions might conduct research or help craft policies and initiatives related to their area of expertise.

Salaries

The salaries earned by experimental, developmental, cognitive, social, and biopsychologists vary widely based on the type of career they pursue and the setting in which they work. According to the US Department of Labor (2014), 80% of psychologists outside of the clinical, counseling, or industrial–organizational subfields earned an estimated annual salary between $42,550 and $117,090, with a median income of $91,140. Much of the variation within these estimates stems from the discrepancy that often exists between academic or government positions and those in the private sector. Typically the private sector positions command a higher salary. However, advanced positions in academic and government settings can include salaries that rival those of the private sector positions.

Employment Issues

Finding employment in a research-oriented career in psychology is heavily dependent upon the funding available to the institutions that offer such positions. It might also depend upon a particular institution's current financial status. For example, universities that are well funded either by the state or through private endowments may hire many faculty members in the same year that neighboring universities are struggling to keep the positions they currently have. Similar disparities among government agencies can occur based on trends in the research fields as well as changes in the funding allocated. Private sector positions depend more heavily on current economic conditions and the degree to which a company is willing to fund research positions at a given time. The message here is that in research careers, employment opportunities and the security of the positions are dependent upon the funding sources supporting the research. It is also important to keep in mind that in all types of settings, research careers will carry expectations for productivity. Companies may expect that a certain number of projects be completed by a deadline. Academic positions may be dependent upon the researcher securing sufficient funding through grants and producing a certain number of publications in a period of time. Although productivity expectations are a reality of most careers, they can be particularly challenging in research positions given that the research process is by its nature unpredictable.

Training and Preparation

Earning a Degree

The primary goal of graduate programs in experimental, developmental, social, cognitive, and biopsychology is to prepare students to be independent researchers. Despite studying different topics and populations, using varying methodologies, and pursuing diverse career paths, all of these future psychologists strive to leave graduate school with the knowledge and skills to conduct their own research.

Doctoral programs. Doctoral programs in these subfields of psychology within the US vary in availability. There are approximately 100 doctoral level programs each in the areas of cognitive, developmental, social, and biopsychology/neuroscience, and approximately 50 doctoral programs in experimental psychology (APA, 2013). Each program within a given subfield will vary in terms of the topics emphasized, the faculty's expertise, and the training offered. Each of these factors combines to affect the nature of the careers that graduates of these programs pursue. One variation that is often of immediate concern to undergraduates trying to select a program is the amount of funding provided to graduate students. Typically graduate programs in the research subfields provide substantial financial support to students, often in the form of tuition waivers, stipends, and assistantships. These programs do so because the research-intensive nature of the training supports the research of the faculty, who can in turn secure grant funding to support the program. Thus these programs seek to pay students for the work they contribute. In addition, these funding sources are one way that programs attract and recruit the best students. For a more detailed overview of these issues, refer to Chapter 7.

Master's programs. Although often fewer in number than doctoral programs, master's level programs exist in experimental, developmental, social, cognitive, and biopsychology. The largest number is in experimental psychology (APA, 2013). Graduates of master's level programs in the research-intensive subfields typically either seek employment that utilizes their training or pursue a doctoral degree. Many of these programs strive to train students with one of these two outcomes in mind. Programs that offer a terminal master's degree often train students who intend to seek employment following graduation. Programs that offer a non-terminal master's degree train students who intend to seek additional education at the doctoral level. Although some programs identify themselves accordingly, others are less clear. Inquiring about what recent graduates of the program are currently doing will often provide the best indication of what the training will best prepare you to do. However, keep in mind two important things about master's level programs in experimental, developmental, social, cognitive, and biopsychology. First, a master's degree in one of these areas does not make you a psychologist. Instead, your career options will be in research-oriented positions that will tap your quantitative, statistical, and writing skills. Second, although completing a master's degree may make you more attractive as a candidate to a doctoral program, most do not grant course credit for a prior master's degree. Instead, they will expect you to complete the bulk of the training they offer in their doctoral program.

Postdoctoral training. Postdoctoral training is a common element in exper-imental, developmental, social, cognitive, and biopsychologists' education. Recent data indicated that just over 30% of all new graduates of doctoral programs in these subfields immediately pursue postdoctoral training (APA, 2011). Postdoctoral training serves as an important period of time in which these new psychologists hone their skills and begin developing their own research programs. In addition, many employers prefer to hire individuals who have research experience beyond their graduate school training.

Preparing for Graduate Training as an Undergraduate

If the subfields of experimental, developmental, social, cognitive, and biopsychology are of interest to you for your future career, there are several things you can do as an undergraduate student to prepare. Most important among them is focusing on developing your knowledge through coursework and your skills through research experience.

Coursework. To prepare for graduate study in a research-intensive sub-field of psychology, you must first and foremost be highly successful in your required courses covering the topics of statistics, research methods, and experimental design. The concepts and skills addressed in these courses are the basis of careers in research. Therefore, you should not only excel in but also enjoy these courses. In addition, most psychology departments offer upper-level courses in the areas of cognitive, developmental, social, and biopsychology. Outside of psychology, students interested in these career areas should strongly consider taking courses in the natural sciences, particularly biology and chemistry. These courses provide additional train-ing in both the scientific process and knowledge that relates to scientific inquiries in psychology. Finally, additional coursework in statistics can be of great benefit.

Activities. Hands-on research experience is invaluable for any student considering graduate training in a research-intensive subfield of psychology. You will develop a feel for what a research career would be like and will have the opportunity to decide if this type of work is the best fit for you. Such experience often provides students with a clearer sense of their specific interests in the field. Graduate programs that train students in the research-oriented areas of psychology tend to believe that having research experience prior to graduate school is a must. They understand that such experience leads students to be more informed in their selection of a subfield. In addition, having a strong record of research experience speaks volumes about a student's potential as a graduate student.

Working in Research-Related Areas with a Bachelor's Degree

As discussed in several previous chapters, the bachelor's degree in psychology can be thought of as either a liberal arts or preprofessional degree. If you are interested in a research-oriented career in psychology, you should view your undergraduate education as preparation for pursuing the doctoral degree. Although students with sufficient research training and proficiency can secure employment in a research-oriented career with a bachelor's or master's degree, the level of autonomy and control they will have over the research they conduct will be limited. The authority to design and oversee research, as well as to seek grant funding, typically resides only with doctoral level professionals. However, some psychology students choose to pursue research-oriented careers with less education because they find the work inherently rewarding and/or they view such additional experience as an important step in their career path.

Research Assistant or Lab Technician

Employment as a research assistant or lab technician involves responsibility for aspects of ongoing research projects. These positions are often available with institutions or companies that have active, ongoing research programs that require numerous employees to manage and operate them. Often there are tiers of researchers with varying responsibilities consistent with their training and expertise. At the bachelor's level, research assistants often are responsible for the day-to-day maintenance and upkeep of laboratory space and equipment. In addition, many have data entry and database management duties. If they have relevant experience, research assistants might be involved in data collection through conducting interviews, administering questionnaires, taking measurements, or obtaining specimens. According to the US

Department of Labor (2014), the median salary estimate was $38,310 for research assistants in the social sciences and $44,200 for technicians in the life, physical, and social sciences.

Data Entry and Analysis

Bachelors' level positions that are focused on data entry and analysis are also available with some institutions and companies. Students with strong quantitative, statistical, and computer skills would be eligible for such positions. The job duties often entail working with research or analyst teams to compile and examine data in order to answer questions that are essential to the successful functioning of the organization. Positions as analysts sometimes require experience and/or expertise in a specific area (e.g., accounting for budget analysts, computing technology for database analysts). According to the US Department of Labor (2014), the median salary estimate was $28,470 for data entry keyers and $60,800 for market research analysts.

Advertising and Sales

Many bachelor's level positions sought by psychology majors are in for-profit settings. For example, those with specific interests in the social psychology subfield might seek positions in the areas of advertising or sales. These areas allow for applications of social psychological principles toward the goals of predicting and influencing consumers' behavior. With a bachelor's degree, these positions are likely to be in the areas of account representatives, managers, and direct sales. According to the US Department of Labor (2014), the median salary estimate was $45,830 for advertising sales agents, $37,200 for retail sales supervisors, and $39,800 for real estate sales agents.

Teacher

Psychology majors who are drawn to the developmental subfield area but who are seeking to find employment with a bachelor's degree might want to consider teaching. Teaching positions provide an opportunity to engage with students at various points in their development and have an impact on their learning. In addition, teachers often play a substantial role in their students' growth in many other areas, including social and emotional development. Although undergraduate psychology programs do not equip students with the background and skills necessary to earn a teaching certification, many public school districts allow individuals to begin teaching while they work to complete their certification. According to the US Department of Labor (2014), the median salary estimate was $19,600 for childcare workers and $53,590 for elementary school teachers.

An Insider's Perspective

Testing the Waters

Marie Balaban, PhD
Eastern Oregon University

As you consider a research-related career, your undergraduate training should include learning to read research and learning to do research.

Getting your Feet Wet:
Reading Research
Textbook authors synthesize information from a wealth of sources to explain controversies or distill conclusions. For example, are the pros and cons of reaching puberty early or late, with respect to peers, different for girls than for boys? You read the textbook authors' interpretation of the research findings, but some results seem contradictory. Psychology majors should develop skills in finding, understanding,

and evaluating original sources. You might grow skeptical about a conclusion after examining a study's methods or you might be convinced after reading a carefully controlled study.

Primary research typically refers to published journal articles that report the work's background, methods, results, and discussion. Wading through primary sources can be challenging and may require reading the paper more than once. Authors use jargon intended for experts in the field, and advanced statistical analyses can be confusing. Look at the tables or figures to find key results and at the first part of the discussion to find the authors' description of their findings.

Reading one article often leads to related sources. Reading research is like navigating a mystery: what has been done, why, and what questions are propagated as you explore further? If you enjoy this process, then perhaps a research career is right for you!

A more general reason to read primary research sources is to build your confidence for using these kinds of sources in future circumstances. Perhaps you'll want to look up current information on a treatment in sports medicine or research on family relationships for adopted children. Knowing how to look beyond the popular information will be a valuable asset.

Diving In: Doing Research

Most psychology majors quickly discover that hands-on research experience is important on a practical level for graduate school and career preparation. At a deeper level, the process of discovery can be exciting. Seek out research opportunities and start early (perhaps sophomore year). Ask faculty if they need a research assistant. Find out whether your program offers opportunities for individual student research projects. Do you have a question to explore? The topic that you investigate does not have to be the topic you eventually pursue in graduate school or a career. One former student of mine completed an excellent, detailed project on parsing language in adults, and then earned a PhD in child clinical psychology. During your undergraduate years, you might work with more than one faculty member or you might stay in one research lab.

Participating in research gives you the chance to find out whether you like delving into a research question. You may find that, like the rest of us, you will make mistakes and learn from them. Another former student of mine unwittingly photocopied only one side of a two-sided temperament questionnaire, and used it throughout a study; the results could not be scored or used. That was a harsh lesson to face! Being a research assistant also gives you a "home"

within your psychology department and connections – with professors, postdoctoral fellows, graduate students, or other undergraduates. The ripple effect from these connections can be long-lasting if you pursue a research career.

You might present your research at a student conference, co-author a presentation at a professional conference, or co-author a publication. You'll also gain expertise in some of the following skills: using library databases, understanding research ethics and informed consent procedures, using software for collecting data, using spreadsheets, making graphs, using and interpreting statistical programs, and designing posters for presentations. All of these accomplishments are good practical qualifications for graduate school or careers. Moreover, perhaps your research findings will make a splash by providing insight that advances the field of psychology as well as the next wave of textbooks.

Note. Dr. Marie Balaban is a developmental psychologist and a professor of psychology at Eastern Oregon University. She has authored over 25 peer-reviewed journal articles on the topics of infant sensation, perception, and cognition, as well as psychophysiological measurement. Dr. Balaban teaches courses on development, cognition, sensation and perception, emotion, and statistics.

Professional Spotlight

Cynthia L. Pickett, PhD

Education:

- Bachelor of Arts (BA) in Psychology from Stanford University (1994)
- Master of Arts (MA) in Social Psychology from Ohio State University (1996)
- Doctor of Philosophy (PhD) in Social Psychology from Ohio State University (1999)

Position:

Associate Professor of Psychology at the University of California, Davis

Description of Position:

My time is split between conducting research and teaching. I maintain an active program of research involving several graduate students and undergraduate research assistants on topics such as social identity, the self, social cognition, and intergroup relations. I teach undergraduate and graduate courses on these topics as well.

Most Significant Professional Accomplishment:

I was named by the Association for Psychological Science as a "Rising Star" in psychology.

Favorite Publication:

Pickett, C. L., Bonner, B. L., & Coleman, J. M. (2002). Motivated self-stereotyping: Heightened assimilation and differentiation needs result in increased levels of positive and negative self-stereotyping. *Journal of Personality and Social Psychology, 82,* 543–562. doi:10.1037/0022-3514.82.4.543

Areas of Research:

I investigate self, social identity, social cognition, and intergroup relations.

Professional Memberships:

- Association for Psychological Science
- Society of Experimental Social Psychology
- Society for Personality and Social Psychology
- Social Psychology Network

Most Rewarding Aspect of Your Career:

I love the scientific process of developing and testing hypotheses, and it is great that in academia one can choose the questions that one pursues. I also find teaching to be a fun and rewarding experience. I enjoy exposing students to new theories and ideas and trying to get them as excited about the material as I am.

> **Words of Advice to the Student Who is Interested in Your Subfield:**
> If possible, try to get involved in research at your undergraduate institution. It will give you a new appreciation for how social psychologists study social behavior and test their theoretical models.

Suggested Exercises

1. Think for a moment about some aspect of human behavior that has piqued your curiosity in recent days. Perhaps you observed an aggressive driver, children playing a game, or a couple interacting. Formulate a question about some aspect of what you observed. Now look to the research literature and see what is known about the question you formulated. Based on what you find in your search, revise your question. Observing behavior, generating questions, and examining the literature are all part of the scientific process that occurs in psychological research, and they are great ways of fostering your research ideas.

2. Identify the faculty members in your psychology department whose backgrounds are in experimental, developmental, social, cognitive, or biopsychology. Select one whose research area interests you and ask them to provide you a reference for a research article that is important in their subfield. Read the article and develop one or two questions about it. Consider posing these questions to the faculty member, either in person during their office hours or by email. Inquiries and conversations such as these are important in helping you determine what areas of research you find compelling.

3. Investigate opportunities for gaining research experience. Some departments of psychology post openings for research assistant positions in a faculty member's lab. In other departments these positions can only be discovered by having conversations with faculty members about opportunities to assist them. Keep in mind that even research experience outside of your area of interest can be valuable in helping you decide if a research career in psychology is right for you. If opportunities within your department are limited, consider contacting faculty members in other departments or at neighboring institutions to ask about volunteering in their research labs.

Suggested Readings by Topic Area

Experimental Psychology

Healy, A. F., & Proctor, R. W. (Eds.). (2013). *Handbook of psychology: Vol. 4, Experimental psychology* (2nd ed.). Hoboken, NJ: Wiley.

Mandler, G. (2007). *A history of modern experimental psychology: From James and Wundt to cognitive science*. Cambridge, MA: The MIT Press.

Developmental Psychology

Lerner, R. M., Easterbrooks, M. A., & Mistry, J. (Eds.). (2013). *Handbook of psychology: Vol. 6, Developmental psychology* (2nd ed.). Hoboken, NJ: Wiley.

Liben, L. S. (Ed.). (2008). *Current directions in developmental psychology* (2nd ed.). Boston, MA: Allyn & Bacon.

Social Psychology

Ruscher, J. D., & Hammer, E. Y. (Eds.). (2008). *Current directions in social psychology* (2nd ed.). Upper Saddle River, NJ: Prentice Hall.

Tenne, H. A., & Suls, J. M. (Eds.). (2013). *Handbook of psychology: Vol. 5, Personality and social psychology* (2nd ed.). Hoboken, NJ: Wiley.

Cognitive Psychology

Levitin, D. J. (Ed.). (2002). *Foundations of cognitive psychology: Core readings.* Cambridge, MA: The MIT Press.

Spellman, B. A., & Willingham, D. T. (Eds.). (2004). *Current directions in cognitive science.* Upper Saddle River, NJ: Prentice Hall.

Biopsychology

DeVries, A. C., & Nelson, R. J. (2008). *Current directions in biopsychology.* Englewood Cliffs, NJ: Prentice Hall.

Nelson, R. J., & Mizumori, S. J. Y. (2013). *Comprehensive handbook of psychology: Vol. 3, Behavioral neuroscience* (2nd ed.). Hoboken, NJ: Wiley.

Resources by Topic Area

Experimental Psychology

- Society of Experimental Psychology – Division 3 of the APA
  ○ http://www.apa.org/divisions/div3
- Association for Psychological Science
  ○ www.psychologicalscience.org

Developmental Psychology

- Developmental Psychology – Division 7 of the APA
  ○ http://www.apadivisions.org/division-7
- Adult Development and Aging – Division 20 of the APA
  ○ http://www.apadivisions.org/division-20

Social Psychology

- Society for Personality and Social Psychology – Division 8 of APA
  ○ www.spsp.org
- Society of Experimental Social Psychology
  ○ www.sesp.org

Cognitive Psychology

- Cognitive Science Society
  - http://cognitivesciencesociety.org/index.html

Biopsychology

- Behavioral Neuroscience and Comparative Psychology – Division 6 of APA
  - http://www.apadivisions.org/division-6/index.aspx

References

American Psychological Association. (2011). *2009 doctorate employment survey.* Washington, DC: Author. Retrieved from http://www.apa.org/workforce/publications/09-doc-empl/index.aspx

American Psychological Association. (2013). *Graduate study in psychology 2014.* Washington, DC: Author.

Chen, F. S., Minson, J. A., Schöne, M., & Heinrichs, M. (2013). In the eye of the beholder: Eye contact increases resistance to persuasion. *Psychological Science, 24,* 2254–2261. doi:10.1177/0956797613491968

Gallucci, N. T. (1997). An evaluation of the characteristics of undergraduate psychology majors. *Psychological Reports, 81,* 879–889. doi:10.2466/pr0.1997.81.3.879

Goff, P. A., Jackson, M. C., Di Leone, B. A. L., Culotta, C. M., & DiTomasso, N. A. (2014). The essence of innocence: Consequences of dehumanizing Black children. *Journal of Personality and Social Psychology, 106,* 526–545. doi:10.1037/a0035663

Kleykamp, B. A., Jennings, J. M., Sams, C., Weaver, M. F., & Eissenberg, T. (2008). The influence of transdermal nicotine on tobacco/nicotine abstinence and the effects of a concurrently administered cigarette in women and men. *Experimental and Clinical Psychopharmacology, 16,* 99–112. doi:10.1037/1064-1297.16.2.99

Lucas, C. G., Bridgers, S., Griffiths, T. L., & Gopnik, A. (2014). When children are better (or at least more open-minded) learners than adults: Developmental differences in learning the forms of causal relationships. *Cognition, 131,* 284–299. doi:10.1016/j.cognition.2013.12.010

McGovern, T. V., & Hawks, B. K. (1986). The varieties of undergraduate experience. *Teaching of Psychology, 13,* 174–181. doi:10.1207/s15328023top1304_1

National Science Foundation. (2013). *Doctorate recipients from U.S. Universities: 2012* (NSF 14-305). Retrieved from http://www.nsf.gov/statistics/sed/2012/

Tardif, T., Fletcher, P., Liang, W., Zhang, Z., Kaciroti, N., & Marchman, V. A. (2008). Baby's first 10 words. *Developmental Psychology, 44,* 929–938. doi:10.1037/0012-1649.44.4.929

US Department of Labor. (2014). *May 2013 national occupational employment and wage estimates.* Retrieved from http://www.bls.gov/oes/2013/may/oes_nat.htm

Webb, A. R., & Speer, J. R. (1985). The public image of psychologists. *American Psychologist, 40,* 1063–1064. doi:10.1037/0003-066X.40.9.1063.b

Chapter Nine
Careers in Industrial and Organizational Psychology

Introduction

As humans, we spend a large portion of our lives engaged in work. How we function as employees is influenced by such factors as our personality, skills, motivations, knowledge base, attitudes, and previous work experiences. As workers, we are also affected by the characteristics of the work itself. Relationships with coworkers, the nature of the tasks, interactions with superiors, compensation, and environmental conditions all impact the work experience. Industrial–organizational psychologists, subsequently referred to in this chapter as I/O psychologists, spend their careers investigating this important part of human existence. Their focus is the well-being of the employee and the organizations that employ them.

Many undergraduate students are interested in the subfield of I/O psychology. Data show that 9.7% of all master's degrees and 3.9% of all PhDs granted in psychology in the US are in the I/O subfield (American Psychological Association [APA], 2014). Part of the draw for students is the diversity of topics explored. Box 9.1 provides a brief list of some of the many issues that I/O psychologists seek to address in their work. Another attractive component for students is the combination of scientific and applied endeavors in the subfield. I/O psychologists address the issues described in Box 9.1 by conducting scientific research and applying these findings to real-world situations in the workplace. This emphasis has led some to describe I/O psychology as the subfield that seeks to maximize human capitol.

Majoring in Psychology: Achieving Your Educational and Career Goals, Second Edition.
Jeffrey L. Helms and Daniel T. Rogers.
© 2015 John Wiley & Sons, Ltd. Published 2015 by John Wiley & Sons, Ltd.

> **Box 9.1** *Common Topics Addressed by I/O Psychologists*
>
> - Facilitating major changes to the organization, structure, or mission of a company
> - Gathering, evaluating, and responding to customer satisfaction data
> - Selecting the most effective and efficient methods for recruiting and hiring new employees
> - Creating a work environment that ensures employee productivity and satisfaction
> - Determining which candidates for a position or promotion are the most qualified
> - Reducing employee stress, turnover, absenteeism, burnout, and low productivity
> - Building collaborative and cooperative work teams
> - Evaluating or appraising employees' work
> - Decreasing incidents of harassment, discrimination, and conflict
> - Increasing employee motivation, dedication, and commitment

Defining the Subfield

The industrial and organizational elements in the name of this subfield reflect more about its history than its current practice. In the past, I/O psychologists often focused on either the industrial or the organizational aspects of issues involved in the intersection between psychology and the workplace. Psychologists in the US first adopted the term industrial psychology when they began assessing workers' vocational interests and abilities (Bryan & Vinchur, 2013). Greater focus on the organizational aspects of businesses and the workplace followed due in part to the influence of social psychology and changes in business culture (Highhouse, 2007). In recent decades, the divide between industrial and organizational elements of the field has steadily decreased. Present day I/O psychologists increasingly focus on both sets of issues. Many have come to see the previous divide as somewhat artificial. In fact, I/O psychologists outside of the US often refer to themselves as work, occupational, or organizational psychologists, and I/O psychologists inside the US have at several points considered adopting a new title (Highhouse & Schmitt, 2013). Despite the momentum to shed the old divisions in the subfield, an introduction to the work of I/O psychologists is still aided by an overview of how the industrial and organization components of their work can differ.

Industrial Psychology

Industrial psychology concentrates on the individual employee and his or her behavior. As a result, the activities involved in this area are often referred to as personnel psychology. The emphasis of industrial psychology is on assisting companies and organizations in structuring the individuals who engage in their work. In doing so, I/O psychologists help companies select and place employees, evaluate them as they work, and train them to improve their performance.

Selection and placement.   Companies of all shapes and sizes struggle to know who to place into a vacant position. This dilemma occurs for new hires from the outside and for hires and promotions from within. Many companies develop their own methods for accomplishing this task. However, these can vary widely, and their effectiveness is often unknown. For example, some companies leave the hiring and promoting decisions in the hands of executives or administrators. Although these individuals may have a good grasp for the operations of the company and have experience in making such decisions, they could be biased in how they evaluate candidates. Despite their best intentions, they might simply not have the knowledge or skills to select the candidates who will perform the best in the position. In contrast, other companies use more elaborate systems of applications, interviews, and tests. But having data on and consistency across applicants is still no guarantee that the ones who rise to the top in this process will perform the best in the position.

I/O psychologists assist in hiring and promotion situations by bringing their expertise to bear on the selection process. First, they obtain a thorough understanding of the position that needs to be filled. Second, they devise and implement methods of obtaining information about candidates in order to determine how well they fit the position requirements. This might include recruiting tools, screening measures, applications, interviews, and assessments. The assessment component varies depending on the nature of the position, but common areas of focus include cognitive abilities, work-related knowledge and skills, physical abilities, personality, honesty/integrity, and interpersonal skills. Importantly, I/O psychologists use assessment techniques that are reliable, valid, and effective. This is critical given that the assessment process can be costly, especially for companies who normally use less scientific methods. However, the payoff for these companies can be substantial if the I/O psychologist is able to help them save resources, make the hiring process fairer, and increase the rates of successful hires.

Performance evaluation and appraisal. Once employees are hired, there is a need to periodically gauge the effectiveness of their work. Information about employees' performances influences how the company perceives them. An appraisal might lead the company to alter an employee's compensation package, provide them with additional training, or adjust the degree of supervision given. Information about performance also ultimately plays a role in the company's decision to retain, terminate, or promote an employee. I/O psychologists devise and implement methods for obtaining this type of information through performance evaluations. They begin by establishing the criteria that the company deems important for its employees. I/O psychologists then implement systems for evaluating and tracking employee performance over time.

Training and education. Once employees are working in their positions and their performances are being evaluated, often there is a need to provide training and education to assist them in acquiring new knowledge and skills. This is necessary if employees have areas of weakness, but it also becomes vital when they are asked to take on new tasks or responsibilities outside their expertise. I/O psychologists help companies assess employees' needs for training and education, often as a part of ongoing performance evaluations. They also assist with the development and implementation of training programs by establishing and/or leading courses and workshops. Some I/O psychologists focus solely on training executive-level employees, often referred to as executive coaching, in order to expand their administrative and managerial skills. Much of the emphasis in traditional training and education programs is placed on improving the productivity and effectiveness of the employee in their current position. However, I/O psychologists are increasingly assisting companies with training employees for the possibility of future promotions. Termed succession planning, this process assists companies in dealing with vacancies at the executive and management levels by having an established network of potential candidates trained and screened for these positions.

Organizational Psychology

Organizational psychology concentrates on the workplace, or the behavior of the company as a whole. The focus is on how characteristics of the organization affect productivity and the well-being of the company. I/O psychologists who do this work help companies evaluate and organize themselves by examining such issues as their inherent structure, leadership, environment, worker satisfaction, and organizational change.

Organizational structure. Whether it is carefully planned or simply emerges as a byproduct of their decision making, all companies have inherent structure. I/O psychologists assist companies in evaluating their structure and implementing changes designed to improve productivity. For example, a company's management structure will dictate how information is communicated, problems are addressed, and decisions are made. Or the structure of work teams will determine how responsibility for problems and successes are shared. I/O psychologists can also assist companies in dealing with structures that may be somewhat outside of the business itself such as relationships with labor unions or community organizations. Although not entirely internal to the company, these relationships can play a major role in productivity and the ability of the company to accomplish its goals effectively.

Leadership. Throughout most of the time that I/O psychology has existed as a subfield, much research and applied efforts have focused on the issue of leadership. As a result of this knowledge base, I/O psychologists can assist companies with understanding the types of leadership styles that are the most effective in different situations. They help implement leadership training in which managers and supervisors are exposed to leadership theories and guided in applying them in their work. In some situations, I/O psychologists might assist a company with restructuring their leadership by altering such things as the types of responsibilities held and the chain of command.

Environment. The overall climate of the workplace can have a substantial effect on the productivity of individual employees and the company as a whole. I/O psychologists often assess organizational climates and facilitate changes to address problems. Among the common areas of focus are the degree of emphasis on health and safety, the reduction and management of stress, and the improvement of channels of communication. Improving an organizational environment also means attending to the worker's sense of community and their commitment to the company. I/O psychologists can help address some of the threats to a cohesive and productive climate such as harassment, discrimination, and unethical conduct.

Job satisfaction and commitment. Two of the biggest threats to productivity for companies occur when workers are dissatisfied with their jobs and are uncommitted to the organization. Employee dissatisfaction and lack of commitment can fuel problems such as absenteeism, turnover, and customer dissatisfaction. I/O psychologists work to help companies boost employee satisfaction and commitment by evaluating and altering the factors that contribute to these conditions. In particular, they work to help structure employees' pay and benefits in ways that promote a sense of fairness and justice. Environmental or climate changes can also go a long way to improving employees' satisfaction with their job. For example, incentive programs that reward employees for their productivity through the allocation of additional compensation, prizes, vacation time, or perks within the company can help create satisfied and committed employees.

Organizational change and development. Given the ever changing marketplace and situational demands that arise, companies periodically adjust their practices, structures, and positions. Often these adjustments must be made in response to conditions or factors that are thrust upon the organization. I/O psychologists can be of great help to companies undergoing such changes. In particular, organizations that are going through mergers, acquisitions, relocations, downsizing, and expansion must successfully weather these changes to stay in business. These events can lead to dramatic changes in the structure, leadership, and environment of a company. Just as I/O psychologists assist stable companies with these issues, they can assist companies in flux by creating strategic plans for adjustments and monitoring their success.

Legal and Policy Issues

Because there can be a host of legal issues involved in the hiring, firing, promotion, and evaluation processes, issues of policy in the workplace are a common concern for I/O psychologists. Problems in these areas often arise with respect to an individual employee, but creating policies that prevent such problems takes place at the organizational level. As such, the area of legal and policy issues is another example of how I/O psychologists' work can no longer be easily divided into industrial or organizational topics. These psychologists assist companies in dealing with policy issues when they arise in specific situations and preparing for them to occur in the future. They often train management to carry out their business while adhering to the law. They also help companies craft internal policies and guidelines to reduce the occurrence of these problems. Finally, other I/O psychologists assist companies once a problem has already occurred by guiding their actions to address it and/or assisting with legal cases where the company's actions are being challenged.

The Work

Core Activities

I/O psychology is a broad subfield encompassing issues ranging from hiring a single employee to guiding an organization through massive restructuring. The psychologists who engage in this work typically approach these issues either as a consultant, an administrator, or a researcher. In order to provide a glimpse of the diversity of these careers, Box 9.2 provides a few examples of recent positions advertised for I/O psychologists. The careers that I/O psychologists select shape the types of activities in which they engage.

Consultation. Consulting refers to the act of providing one's expertise to an individual or organization, typically in exchange for compensation. Individuals from a wide variety of professions engage in consulting. Although

---

Box 9.2 *Recent Openings in the I/O Psychology Subfield*

Position:	**I/O Senior Manager, Global Testing Leader**
Setting:	The Proctor & Gamble Company
Responsibilities:	Plan and lead development of testing solutions for human resources, legal, and management divisions, including all aspects of job analysis and employee assessment, selection, and training. Apply advanced statistics to analyze business data. Provide expert advice to internal groups and develop external, professional connections.
Position:	**Assistant Professor**
Setting:	Auburn University
Responsibilities:	Maintain an active research program publishing in I/O areas, teach undergraduate and graduate courses in area of specialization, and support the outreach efforts of the I/O graduate program.
Position:	**Consultant – Global Alliances**
Setting:	Hogan Assessment Systems
Responsibilities:	Serve as a consultant and account manager for clients who utilize the company's selection, development, and leadership assessment tools. Provide project management, consulting, training and education, and product support.

psychologists from all subfields serve as consultants, it is I/O psychologists who most often conduct their professional careers in this role. Consultants in I/O psychology provide their clients with assistance on personnel and organizational issues. Some are retained as consultants for extended periods of time, during which time they may advise a company on any relevant issues that arise. Others are retained only to help the company deal with a specific issue, such as hiring for a particular job or helping guide the organization through a transition in leadership. Because consultants are sought after and paid for their expertise, they often travel to where there is demand for their services. In addition, there is an expectation that once these services are provided, the relationship will end. Of course, companies that have successful experiences with I/O psychologists as consultants routinely hire them again for other issues that arise in the future.

Administration.   Some I/O psychologists choose to work within organizations in administrative positions rather than from the outside as consultants. The descriptions of these positions vary and can include such titles as director, vice president, or manager of such areas as human resources, development, testing, employee relations, talent management, or training. These psychologists are typically seen as the experts in an organization on the worker, workplace, and productivity issues. The nature of I/O psychologists' training means that these positions will typically involve other administrative responsibilities as well. So in addition to assisting the company with assessing and implementing important changes, the I/O psychologist who works within the organization often is responsible for a team of employees who help carry out these changes and evaluate them over time.

Research.   Because I/O psychology is a subfield that emphasizes both science and applied practice, many I/O psychologists choose to focus their careers on conducting research. These psychologists are experts in research methods, experimental design, and statistical analyses of data related to the intersection of psychology and business. Because many of them conduct their research in organizational settings, they are often experts in confidentiality and ethical issues involved in collecting data in the workplace. Their research concentrates on personnel and organizational issues that impact productivity such as assessment techniques, training programs, environmental factors, and leadership models. This research is essential to creating new techniques for applying psychological principles to the workplace and for evaluating the effectiveness of existing techniques. The dissemination of this information through publications keeps I/O psychologists informed. Box 9.3 provides a sampling of journals that publish I/O psychology research.

Box 9.3 *Journals that Publish I/O Psychology Research*

- *Journal of Applied Psychology*
- *Personnel Psychology*
- *Academy of Management Journal*
- *Academy of Management Review*
- *Organizational Behavior and Human Decision Processes*
- *Journal of Occupational and Organizational Psychology*

Settings

Given the diversity of their work, I/O psychologists carry out these activities in a variety of settings. Of those earning doctoral degrees, the largest portion, approximately 69%, are employed in business, organization, or government settings (APA, 2011). Some of these I/O psychologists own and operate their own private sector consulting business through which they provide services to companies and individuals. However, a large portion work for regional, national, and multinational consulting firms (Khanna & Medsker, 2007). These psychologists provide their expertise on personnel and workplace issues from within the company or government agency rather than as outside consultants. As a result, they are often responsible for the design, implementation, and evaluation of a host of initiatives and processes related to employee selection, placement, and evaluation, and organizational training, structure, and environment. Approximately 24% of I/O psychologists are employed in academic settings. Their responsibilities often include teaching, research, service, and administration, though some may be hired only to teach or conduct research. Although many of these I/O psychologists are employed in departments of psychology, a large number hold positions in schools of business, management, or engineering.

Salaries

The salaries earned by I/O psychologists depend largely on the type of work they perform and the setting in which it is conducted. According to the US Department of Labor (2014), 80% of I/O psychologists earned an estimated annual salary of between $49,570 and $140,390, with the median income for these psychologists being $80,330. An APA salary survey suggests that I/O psychologists with less than five years of experience report a mean income of approximately $90,109 in consulting firms and $75,833 in business or industry; those with 10–30 years of experience report a mean income of approximately $164,347 in consulting firms and $147,501 in business or industry (Finno, Michalski, Hart, Wicherski, & Kohout, 2010). These figures place I/O psychologists among the highest wage earners of all the subfields in psychology. Although this fact may in part contribute to students' interest in I/O psychology, it is important to consider the advantages and disadvantages of the factors that impact these wages. I/O psychologists as a group often command a higher salary because a sizeable portion of them work as consultants in either large consulting firms or private practices. As is the case with all professionals who work in professional practices, the income potential typically exceeds that of careers in business, academic, or government settings. But consultation work involves parallel risks given that one's income can be heavily influenced by market forces such as competition and the demand for one's services. I/O psychologists who work in organizations and businesses, as well as those who hold academic positions in schools of business, also tend to receive a higher salary. Otherwise, these organizations and institutions risk losing these professionals to lucrative consulting practices. In addition, when the expertise and services that I/O psychologists provide to businesses and institutions have a direct impact on productivity and profits, these savings typically translate into higher salaries.

Employment Issues

Given the nature of their work, I/O psychologists' careers can be dramatically impacted by numerous societal and economic factors. Although virtually all individuals' careers are dependent upon their performance, I/O psychologists in consulting and business settings are directly engaged in activities with the goals of improving productivity and efficiency. In essence, their work is intended to have a direct and positive impact on a company's financial bottom line. Because profitability is a primary interest of businesses, companies that hire I/O psychologists expect to see a return on this investment. Without it, not only might the I/O psychologist's current position be at stake, but their professional reputation and ability to secure future positions could also be in jeopardy.

Shifts in the characteristics of employees and the market require I/O psychologists to adjust their techniques. For example, increased globalization in the business market has meant that I/O psychologists must be prepared to assist companies with issues that arise from having an international presence. Consider the difficulties involved in structuring a company's leadership, communication, environment, assessment techniques, selection processes, and evaluation procedures when its workforce becomes multinational. Even companies whose operations remain within the US need assistance as their workforce ages and becomes increasingly diverse.

The technological advances of the last few decades have led to rapid changes in the nature of work and the ways that most companies conduct business. These advances have contributed to the extinction of some positions and the creation of others that did not exist only a few short years ago. In addition, workers who continue to engage in the same type of work now do so in different ways, including working from home. These changes have impacted not only the types of issues I/O psychologists assist companies with but also the ways in which they do so. For example, the activities of employee selection and evaluation have become increasingly automated. For some I/O psychology consulting firms, the bulk of their work involves providing client companies with systems for managing their personnel and human resources issues.

Training and Preparation

Degree Options and Licensure

Careers in most subfields of psychology require a doctoral degree. For the subfields that involve applied work with clients and patients in the general public (e.g., clinical psychology, neuropsychology), these psychologists must obtain a professional license from the state within which they practice. Without it, they cannot refer to themselves as psychologists or engage in the practice of psychology while working with the public. (For a more detailed discussion of licensure as a psychologist, see Chapter 10.) As a result, I/O psychologists who intend to refer to themselves as psychologists and engage in the practice of psychology when working with clients must be licensed in most states. However, there are two scenarios in which an individual might engage in a career that is related to I/O psychology yet not seek licensure. First, some individuals with doctorates in I/O psychology opt not to be licensed if the work they engage in does not constitute the practice of psychology (e.g., academic careers, directing or managing human resource activities). Second, some individuals obtain master's degrees in I/O psychology or related areas and as a result are not eligible for licensure as a psychologist. The individuals in both of these scenarios are able to conduct applied work in business settings, often using concepts and methods that are relevant to I/O psychology. But this is allowable only if they do not refer to themselves as psychologists, do not engage in the practice of psychology (i.e., use psychological principles and techniques to observe, evaluate, or modify behavior), and do not engage in practices that could pose a threat of harm to the public (Sackett, Thomas, Borman, & Champion, 1995). Given this situation, master's degrees in I/O psychology and related disciplines have become an increasingly popular option for individuals seeking careers in this area.

Some key individuals in the I/O psychology subfield support the requirement of licensure for I/O psychologists given the limitations on the practice of unlicensed individuals and the confusion that can occur about their expertise (e.g., clients must understand that those without a license are consultants, not psychologists). In their model licensure act, which many states use as a guide in crafting licensure laws and regulations, the Association of State and Provincial Psychology Boards (ASPPB) characterizes I/O psychology as a practice area, noting that corporations and organizations can be clients who receive psychological services (ASPPB, 2001). The Society for Industrial and Organizational Psychology (SIOP) maintains a policy on the licensure issue. That policy currently describes a context-dependent approach that asserts the following: (1) when the applied and research work of I/O psychologists is not unique to psychology, does not constitute the practice of psychology, and does not pose potential harm to the general public, licensure may not be necessary; and (2) when a state requires certain areas of I/O practice to be conducted by licensed psychologists, licensure may be necessary (SIOP, 1996). Although there are competing perspectives on the importance of licensure for this subfield, and to a large degree the nature of the work and its context will dictate the need for licensure, our perspective is that it is typically best to adhere to the higher standards in the field and obtain licensure in order to ensure the greatest range of flexibility in providing services and reduce potential confusion.

Far more than making you eligible for licensure, the type of degree you earn reflects the nature and extent of your training. Therefore, the degree will have a direct impact on the types of jobs you are qualified to seek. Currently, the majority of I/O psychologists have doctoral degrees. With this level of education and training they can work in virtually any area of I/O psychology. Because this degree has been the standard in the field for some time, master's level programs were for years ignored by mainstream I/O psychology (Trahan & McAllister, 2002). But demand for master's level training options, both from potential students and employers of graduates, continued to grow. As a result, the number of programs available expanded. This situation caused SIOP (1994) to create guidelines for master's level programs. Guidelines had existed for some time for doctoral programs (for the current version, see SIOP, 1999), so these were adapted for the master's level. Table 9.1 presents an overview and comparison of these guidelines. Keep in mind that master's programs not only emphasize fewer guidelines

Table 9.1   Summary of Guidelines for Doctoral and Master's Programs in I/O Psychology

Guidelines	Doctoral	Master's
General Knowledge and Skills:		
• Consulting and business skills	x	
• Ethical, legal, and professional contexts of I/O psychology	x	x
• Fields of psychology	x	x
• History and systems of psychology	x	x
• Research methods	x	x
• Statistical methods/data analysis	x	x
Content Areas:		
• Attitude theory, measurement, and change	x	x
• Career development	x	
• Consumer behavior	x	
• Criterion theory and development	x	x
• Health and stress in organizations	x	
• Human performance/human factors	x	
• Individual assessment	x	
• Individual differences	x	x
• Job evaluation and compensation	x	
• Job/task analysis and classification	x	x
• Judgment and decision making	x	
• Leadership and management	x	
• Organization development	x	x
• Organization theory	x	x
• Performance appraisal and feedback	x	x
• Personnel recruitment, selection, and placement	x	x
• Small group theory and team processes	x	x
• Training: theory, program design, and evaluation	x	x
• Work motivation	x	x

than doctoral programs, but they also provide less depth of coverage of those guidelines that overlap with doctoral programs. Research has found that for the most part the master's level programs in I/O psychology are meeting these guidelines (Trahan & McAllister, 2002).

Variations in Graduate Programs

Graduate programs that offer degrees in I/O psychology and related fields identify themselves with a variety of titles. Box 9.4 provides a list of some of the more common program names. Although there is a degree of similarity

Box 9.4 *Common Titles of Graduate Programs in I/O Related Areas*

- Applied Psychology (with a concentration in I/O Psychology)
- Human Resources (and Management)
- I/O Psychology
- Organizational Behavior/Evaluation/Development/Analysis/Management
- Organizational Psychology
- Social and Organizational Psychology

across the education and training provided by these programs, do not overlook the meaning behind these titles. Typically these names reflect the basic focus or orientation of the program, and it is this focus that will serve as the foundation for your future career. Once you complete one of these training programs, remember that you should only identify yourself according to your training and licensure status. For example, if you earn a doctoral degree from a graduate program in I/O psychology and hold a license as a psychologist, you should describe your education and training as being in I/O psychology and should identify yourself as a psychologist. If you hold a degree (doctoral or master's) from a graduate program in organizational behavior and do not hold a license as a psychologist, you should describe your education and training as being in organizational behavior and should not identify yourself as a psychologist.

Earning the Degree

As with most graduate degrees, doctoral and master's degrees in I/O psychology and related areas involve multiple components of training. Formal coursework serves as a foundation of these programs, ensuring students possess essential knowledge in areas such as research methods, statistical analysis, and ethics. As a result, coursework is often heaviest for students at the start of their graduate training. As they advance, graduate students take on greater amounts of independent study. They also begin to engage in supervised experiences that are designed to promote learning through active engagement and skill acquisition. Depending on the nature of the graduate program and its learning objectives, supervised experiences can focus on training and skill building in either research or applied endeavors. Many graduate programs in the I/O psychology subfield also place emphasis on students gaining on-the-job training through internship and apprenticeship experiences. Often students work for a semester or two in a research, business, or consultation setting. These experiences allow them to observe professionals engaged in the work and begin to apply their developing skills.

Preparing for Graduate Training as an Undergraduate

As an undergraduate student considering the possibility of pursuing graduate training in I/O psychology or a related area, it is important to keep in mind that there are things you can and should be doing to prepare. In particular, the coursework and activities you engage in now can affect graduate programs' interest in you in the future.

Coursework. Given the variations we have discussed within programs in the I/O psychology subfield, it is difficult to establish absolute recommendations for undergraduate coursework that will best prepare you for graduate level training. However, there are core courses in most undergraduate psychology curriculums that are judged to be vital for students aspiring to enter I/O psychology graduate programs. These courses, as well as relevant course areas outside of psychology, are listed in Box 9.5. Notice that although courses in research, leadership, and organizational issues are important, students also benefit from a solid background in behavior, diversity, social psychology, and business.

Box 9.5 *Recommended Undergraduate Coursework for I/O Psychology*

Courses Areas Within Psychology	Course Areas Outside of Psychology
• Research methods	• Statistics
• Experimental psychology	• Business/management
• Industrial/organizational psychology	• Human resources
• Psychological testing	• Computer science
• Career development	
• Motivation and leadership	
• Group dynamics	
• Ethics	
• Cross-cultural psychology	
• Learning and behavior	
• Social psychology	

Activities. Training at both the master's and doctoral levels in I/O psychology involves a strong emphasis on research methods and statistical analysis. As a result, these programs are particularly interested in students who not only have the necessary coursework in these areas but also have experience conducting research. For undergraduate students, this experience is best gained by working closely with a faculty member either to assist them with their research or to conduct independent research of your own. Because many schools do not have I/O graduate programs and I/O faculty are not as commonly found in undergraduate psychology departments, faculty who conduct research in I/O psychology often are not readily accessible to undergraduate students. As a result, you should consider working with a non-I/O psychology faculty member if you find their research interesting and relevant. Often faculty who focus on social, cognitive, and clinical psychology topics are engaged in projects that overlap with I/O psychology. Another option is to consider seeking research experience outside of your own department. Faculty in business programs or in neighboring graduate psychology departments may be engaged in I/O psychology-related research and might be willing to allow you to assist.

In addition to research training and experience, some graduate programs in I/O psychology value students having had experience in business settings. Internship experiences, whether through formal programs in your department or informally created through your own initiative, can be helpful in securing such experience. Consulting firms that engage in I/O psychology and related practices may provide such positions. Finally, employment in human resources or closely related areas can also serve as a valuable experience in preparation for graduate school.

Working in Areas Related to I/O Psychology with a Bachelor's Degree

As discussed in earlier chapters, the bachelor's degree in psychology can be thought of as a liberal arts degree or a preprofessional degree. As such, it does not automatically qualify you to enter a particular career field nor does it provide you with a defined set of skills that employers easily recognize and value. Instead, your ability to secure employment in an area related to I/O psychology with only a bachelor's degree will in large part depend upon you gaining relevant experience as an undergraduate, identifying positions for which you qualify, and effectively conveying your knowledge and skills to potential employers. There are a number of career and employment opportunities that incorporate aspects of I/O psychology. Many of these bachelor's level careers allow for working directly with businesses to address employee and organizational issues. The most common options include management and human resources positions.

Management

Leadership positions within organizations often provide a rewarding career with considerable opportunity for advancement. Students who are interested in I/O psychology because of its emphasis on structuring the individual worker and organization might find that management positions provide opportunities to have an impact in these areas. The responsibilities of a given management position will of course vary based on the nature of the organization and the job description, but involvement in employee selection, evaluation, and training, as well as input into organizational structure and environment, are common. According to the US Department of Labor (2014), the median salary estimate was $95,600 for all types of managers, $108,540 for sales managers, and $82,310 for administrative services managers.

Human Resources

Human resource professionals are responsible for a wide array of tasks within businesses and organizations. Traditionally human resource departments managed the technical details of recruiting, hiring, promoting, firing, and compensating employees. This included completing necessary paperwork and maintaining up-to-date information about each employee. In recent years the responsibility of human resource professionals has expanded to include greater authority in decision making about personnel matters. In addition, many of these departments are now in charge of employee assessment, training, and evaluation procedures. With the expanding role of human resources within companies and institutions, the types of positions available have also grown. Individuals who work in human resources now hold a variety of titles, including benefits coordinator, personnel administrator, and human resources associate. In addition, training and certification programs for human resource positions are now common and play a large role in one's ability to secure certain positions and salaries. According to the US Department of Labor (2014), the median salary estimate was $56,630 for human resources specialists, $101,490 for compensation and benefits managers, and $100,800 for human resources managers.

An Insider's Perspective

The Flexibility of the Doctoral Degree in I/O Psychology

Russell E. Johnson, PhD
Michigan State University

I can remember back to when I was a senior undergraduate student and knowing that I wanted to study I/O psychology in graduate school, so the decision to apply to I/O graduate programs was an easy one. What was not easy, however, was figuring out exactly what I wanted to do *after* earning a graduate degree in I/O psychology. Did I want to focus on research and teaching as a professor at a university or college? Did I want to work in the "real world" as an internal or external consultant for a private company or work for a public organization like the government or military? Although I was about to receive a BA in psychology, these were difficult questions to answer without having had any in-depth training in I/O psychology.

Fortunately, earning a doctoral degree in I/O psychology prepares students for all of those aforementioned careers, whether it is as a professor, consultant, or human resource manager. Thus, one important source of flexibility for people with doctoral degrees in I/O psychology is the various employment opportunities that are available to them. This is especially true given that people's career aspirations sometimes change during graduate school (e.g., from initially wanting to be a professor to ultimately being a consultant).

I/O psychologists are trained according to the scientist/practitioner model, which provides students with the knowledge and skills to conduct research and interpret findings, as well as the knowledge and skills to apply research findings to actual problems that plague companies and employees. For example, as a graduate student, I was exposed to research concerning various employee abilities and dispositions that influence job performance (e.g., cognitive ability, personality). I then had opportunities to apply this knowledge, for example, by developing selection tests that identified the highest performing employees from a pool of job applicants. As it turned out, I particularly enjoyed the research and teaching aspects of my graduate training, so I ventured down the path to become a professor of I/O psychology. Furthermore, with a PhD in I/O psychology, there is also flexibility in deciding what academic department to work in (e.g., psychology, management, industrial relations, etc.). However, had it turned out that I did not enjoy lecturing and conducting experiments, it would have been possible for me to transition into a job working as an internal or external consultant instead. This degree of career flexibility provided by graduate training in I/O psychology is a luxury that does not extend to all disciplines.

A second source of flexibility is the wide range of topics available for study by I/O psychologists. Because I/O psychology represents the application of psychological theories and principles to the workplace, any and all topics studied by psychologists are fair game. For example, social psychology research on topics like group influences (e.g., groupthink) and social relations (e.g., prejudice) are applied to the workplace by I/O psychologists. I/O psychologists also make use of cognitive psychology research on topics like learning (e.g., practice effects) and decision-making (e.g., heuristics). As a final example, developmental psychology research informs I/O psychologists about the physical and psychological changes that employees undergo as they age and transition into retirement. Thus, the field of I/O psychology is flexible because it draws from a broad range of perspectives, each of which contributes something unique to understanding work organizations and their employees. If exposure to a variety of topics within psychology and having numerous career options sound appealing to you, then pursuing graduate training in I/O psychology is worth considering!

Note. Dr. Russell Johnson is an industrial–organizational psychologist and an associate professor of management at Michigan State University. Previously he was part of the psychology faculty at the University of South Florida. He has authored over 50 peer-reviewed journal articles on such topics as motivation, leadership, organizational justice, and work attitudes and perceptions. In 2013, Dr. Johnson received the Distinguished Early Career Contributions Award for Research from the Society for Industrial and Organizational Psychology. Dr. Johnson teaches undergraduate and graduate courses on organizational behavior and human resource management.

Professional Spotlight

John Chan, PhD

Education:

- Bachelor of Arts (BA) in Psychology from Emory University (1998)
- Master of Arts (MA) in Industrial/Organizational Psychology from the University of Tennessee (2001)
- Doctor of Philosophy (PhD) in Industrial/Organizational Psychology from the University of Tennessee (2003)

Position:

Global Practice Leader – Talent Architect & Analytics

Description of Position:

In my current role, I am part of the Global Leadership and Talent Team that oversees the identification and development of senior leaders globally. More specifically, I work with a global team of talent management professionals to identify high potential individuals in the organization and help give greater insight into their development needs using psychometric assessment tools. The role is also responsible for the development of talent analytics such as matching the global talent management strategy along with business metrics to create specific measures to evaluate the success of the different talent programs. One other responsibility in this role is managing the organization's global talent management system, which serves as the central knowledge base that is used for specific talent analytics and research.

Most Significant Professional Accomplishment:

One area that I focus on is the gender diversity gap in senior leadership/executive positions in organizations. In my last few roles, I have been able to not only raise the awareness of the gender gap but also show the importance and value of having a gender diverse senior leadership team through matching talent analytics and business results. Seeing organizations and leaders that I work with change their thinking and attitude on the importance of having a diverse leadership team is an accomplishment that I continually strive for.

Favorite Publication:

Paddock, J. R., Joseph, A. L., Chan, F. M., Terranova, S., Manning, C., & Loftus, E. F. (1998). When guided visualization procedures may backfire: Imagination inflation and predicting individual differences in suggestibility. *Applied Cognitive Psychology*, *12*, S63–S75. doi:10.1002/(SICI)1099-0720(199812)12:7<S63::AID-ACP600>3.0.CO;2-S

Areas of Research:

- Comparisons of optimism and its effects on workplace productivity and job burnout
- Innovation: How best to identify and nurture this trait
- Gender diversity in senior leadership teams and business results

Professional Memberships:

- American Psychological Association
- Association for Psychological Science
- Society for Industrial Organizational Psychology

Most Rewarding Aspect of Your Career:

The most rewarding aspect of my career is helping organizations realize the importance and value of creating effective talent management processes to identify high potential individuals and develop their people. Being able to connect business results with psychometric data from individual leaders is very satisfying in validating the work that we do. On a more personal level, helping someone understand what they want from their professional life and working with them to grow personally and professionally in the workplace is also very rewarding for me.

Words of Advice to the Student Who is Interested in Your Subfield:

Find out as much as you can about I/O psychology and all the different directions it can take you. There is a wide variety of positions in this field so get a head start on your career by engaging in internships as early and often as possible (even just to do data entry). The I/O field is relatively small so take the time to network with everyone in the field; you are bound to run into the same people again in your career. Be open to and look for international career opportunities as it will give you great exposure to other cultures and experiences that will be priceless in your career.

Suggested Exercises

1. Select a major business or organization and learn about how it currently operates in areas relevant to I/O psychology. For example, if you select a major retail chain, seek to learn about how it selects employees, evaluates employees' work, trains its leaders, or structures the work environment. Information may be readily available about some of the larger companies as books and articles are often written about their history, transformations, and current business practices. If possible, talk with employees of the company to gain an inside perspective.
2. Locate a job advertisement for a human resources position that you could potentially qualify for as an undergraduate student. Investigate the responsibilities associated with the position, as well as those of the department in which you would work. Consider whether such a position might provide good experience to help you decide if I/O psychology is right for you or prepare for graduate school in the subfield.

3. Identify a consulting firm that provides I/O psychology and/or related services to organizations and learn about the types of services they provide. The majority of these firms maintain a strong web presence in order to effectively market themselves. Contact a consultant within the firm and inquire whether they would be willing to correspond with you about their job and the educational path they took to arrive at their current position.

Suggested Readings

Hedge, J. W., & Borman, W. C. (Eds.). (2008). *The I/O consultant: Advice and insights for building a successful career*. Washington, DC: American Psychological Association.

Kuther, T. L. (2004). *Your career in psychology: Industrial/organizational psychology*. Pacific Grove, CA: Wadsworth.

Lowman, R. L. (Ed.). (2006). *The ethical practice of psychology in organizations* (2nd ed.). Washington, DC: American Psychological Association.

Northouse, P. G. (2013). *Leadership: Theory and practice* (2nd ed.). Los Angeles, CA: Sage.

Resources

- Society for Industrial and Organizational Psychology – Division 14 of APA
  o www.siop.org
- Society for Consulting Psychology – Division 13 of APA
  o http://www.apadivisions.org/division-13/index.aspx
- Society of Human Resource Management
  o www.shrm.org
- National Human Resources Association
  o www.humanresources.org

References

American Psychological Association. (2011). *2009 doctorate employment survey*. Washington, DC: Author. Retrieved from http://www.apa.org/workforce/publications/09-doc-empl/index.aspx

American Psychological Association. (2014). *Graduate study in psychology 2014*. Washington, DC: Author.

Association of State and Provincial Psychology Boards. (2001). *ASPPB model act for licensure of psychologists*. Retrieved from http://www.asppb.org/publications/model/act.aspx

Bryan, L. K., & Vinchur, A. J. (2013). Industrial-organizational psychology. In D. K. Freedheim & I. B. Weiner (Eds.), *Handbook of psychology, Vol. 1: History of psychology* (2nd ed.; pp. 407–428). Hoboken, NJ: Wiley.

Finno, A. A., Michalski, D., Hart, B., Wicherski, M., & Kohout, J. L. (2010). *Salaries in psychology 2009: Report of the 2009 APA Salary Survey*. Washington, DC: American Psychological Association. Retrieved from http://www.apa.org/workforce/publications/09-salaries/index.aspx

Highhouse, S. (2007). Where did this name come from anyway? A brief history of the I/O label. *The Industrial-Organizational Psychologist, 45*(1), 53–56.

Highhouse, S., & Schmitt, N. W. (2013). A snapshot in time: Industrial-organizational psychology today. In N. W. Schmitt, S. Highhouse, & I. B. Weiner (Eds.), *Handbook of psychology, Vol. 12: Industrial and organizational psychology* (2nd ed.; pp. 3–13). Hoboken, NJ: Wiley.

Khanna, C., & Medsker, G. J. (2007). *2006 income and employment survey results for the Society for Industrial and Organizational Psychology.* Retrieved from http://www.siop.org/bookspubs.aspx

Sackett, P., Thomas, J., Borman, W., & Champion, M. (1995). Proposed revision of SIOP policy on licensure: Call for comments. *The Industrial-Organizational Psychologist, 33*(1), 12–20.

Society for Industrial and Organizational Psychology, Inc. (1994). *Guidelines for education and training at the master's level in industrial/organizational psychology.* Arlington Heights, IL: Author.

Society for Industrial and Organizational Psychology, Inc. (1996). *Policy on licensure.* Retrieved from http://www.siop.org/tip/backissues/tipjul96/campion1.aspx

Society for Industrial and Organizational Psychology, Inc. (1999). *Guidelines for education and training at the doctoral level in industrial/organizational psychology.* Bowling Green, OH: Author.

Trahan, W. A., & McAllister, H. A. (2002). Master's level training in industrial/organizational psychology: Does it meet the SIOP guidelines? *Journal of Business and Psychology, 16,* 457–465. doi:10.1023/A:1012881209342

US Department of Labor. (2014). *May 2013 national occupational employment and wage estimates.* Retrieved from http://www.bls.gov/oes/2013/may/oes_nat.htm

Chapter Ten
Careers in Clinical Psychology and Counseling Psychology

Introduction

Which area in the field of psychology interests you most in terms of a future career? When undergraduate psychology students are asked this question, the majority respond with clinical psychology or counseling psychology (Gallucci, 1997). The popularity of these subfields is heavily influenced by two factors. First, clinical psychology and counseling psychology enjoy far greater exposure in day-to-day life and the media than the other subfields. As a result, you are more likely to come in contact and be familiar with clinical and counseling psychologists given the nature of their work. Second, a large portion of psychology students report that their career interests are influenced by a desire to "help people." Although vague and insufficient as a reason to sustain one's educational and career goals in the field, this statement typically reflects a wish to work directly with others in a treatment context. Once they understand that only a few of the subfields within psychology involve applied work with individuals seeking mental health treatment, some students choose to focus their interests in these areas.

The notion that the entire field of psychology involves applied work in mental health is a common misperception (Webb & Speer, 1985). As you have learned in other chapters of this book, there are numerous subfields in psychology that have no focus on mental health whatsoever. In addition, all areas in the field, including clinical psychology and counseling psychology, engage in scientific research. But this misperception is not entirely without basis. Consider that the popularity of the clinical and counseling psychology subfields among

Majoring in Psychology: Achieving Your Educational and Career Goals, Second Edition.
Jeffrey L. Helms and Daniel T. Rogers.
© 2015 John Wiley & Sons, Ltd. Published 2015 by John Wiley & Sons, Ltd.

undergraduate students translates into greater numbers of individuals pursuing these careers. For all doctoral degrees granted in psychology in the US between 2002 and 2012, 35% were in clinical psychology and 13% were in counseling psychology (National Science Foundation, 2013). Given the popularity of these subfields, a thorough exploration of them and the various training and career issues involved should prove informative as you consider your future career options in the field.

Defining the Subfields

Clinical psychology and counseling psychology are applied subfields because the work conducted in these areas has direct applications to human functioning. But being applied in focus is not enough to distinguish these areas from other applied subfields (e.g., health psychology, industrial–organizational psychology). What is unique to the clinical and counseling psychology subfields is a focus on improving human functioning by understanding and alleviating psychological dysfunction and distress.

The clinical and counseling psychology subfields emphasize the integration of science, theory, and practice. Clinical or counseling psychologists might spend the bulk of their work day conducting research or providing services to patients, but regardless of their focus they remain mindful of how all three areas contribute to their understanding. For example, a clinical psychologist conducting a psychological evaluation must be aware of the latest research and theory pertaining to the assessment measures being used and the questions being answered. Likewise, a counseling psychologist researching the prevalence of mental illness among college students must understand the theoretical foundations of the topic, the research methodology and statistical analyses required, and the implications for those who may provide treatment to this population.

Thus far we have discussed the subfields of clinical and counseling psychology as if they are one and the same, but they are not. As a student you may encounter sources of information that will claim that the two subfields are either indistinguishable or, as is more often claimed, that the differences are so small that it is not worth trying to draw a distinction. Unfortunately for students who are attempting to select a subfield of interest, develop career goals, and contemplate graduate training, such overgeneralizations are not helpful. There are indeed distinct differences in the clinical and counseling psychology subfields, and these differences have implications for the graduate training and professional careers of students who select them.

The Society of Clinical Psychology defines clinical psychology as integrating theory, science, and practice in an effort to "understand, predict, and alleviate maladjustment, disability, and discomfort" and to "promote human adaptation, adjustment, and personal development" (http://www.apa.org/divisions/div12/aboutcp.html). The Society of Counseling Psychology defines counseling psychology as integrating theory, science, and practice in an effort to help people "improve their well-being, alleviate distress and maladjustment, resolve crises, and increase their ability to function better in their lives" (http://www.div17.org/about/what-is-counseling-psychology). Both definitions encompass the diverse activities of clinical and counseling psychologists, which include researching, teaching, assessing, diagnosing, treating, consulting, and supervising. And both definitions seem to describe a similar focus in this work. This is because clinical and counseling psychologists share an integrative approach and share the goal of improving human functioning. But their emphasis in doing so varies. Clinical psychologists tend to concentrate on understanding psychological symptoms, distress, and disorders, with the goal of developing and providing interventions that treat these conditions. Counseling psychologists tend to concentrate on understanding human adjustment with the goal of developing and providing interventions that return patients to their normal functioning and promote growth. These distinctions are subtle, especially for those who are not involved in the subfields. But, they translate into significant differences in terms of the professional practice and training of these psychologists. For the remainder of the chapter, we will largely be discussing these two subfields together given their similarities. However, in areas where important distinctions occur, we will outline these differences.

The Work

Core Activities

Given the breadth of their training, it is difficult to briefly describe the work that clinical and counseling psychologists engage in without omitting large segments of some of these individuals' professional activities. However, the bulk of their activities can be divided into four general categories: practice, research, administration, and teaching and supervision.

Practice. The term practice is typically used in reference to activities that involve providing direct services to patients. This is sometimes referred to as clinical or applied work and can involve such activities as treatment, assessment, and consultation. When clinical and counseling psychologists provide treatment services, they usually conduct psychotherapy or counseling sessions

Table 10.1   General Comparisons between Psychotherapy and Counseling

	Psychotherapy	*Counseling*
Severity of problem	More severe	Less severe
Nature of problem	Longer in duration, internal to self, affects many areas in life	Shorter in duration, external to self, affects some areas in life
Focus of treatment	Relieve symptoms and distress, cure the underlying problem	Aid in adjustment, restore to normal functioning, growth
Nature of treatment	Longer-term, applying specific treatment techniques	Shorter-term, supportive, providing guidance and advice

with individuals, couples, families, or groups. Psychotherapy and counseling involve the application of psychological and counseling theories to create treatment interventions that reduce patients' distress, improve their capacity to cope, and enhance their well-being. Important differences exist between these interventions in terms of the types of problems that are conducive to each and the interventions typically applied. These differences are summarized in Table 10.1.

Consider how two patients, both experiencing depression, might be best served by seeking either psychotherapy or counseling. Patient A experiences a wide array of depressive symptoms that are intense and long-lasting. The symptoms have been present since adolescence, and although they fluctuate at times in response to life events, often the symptoms appear to occur without any relation to Patient A's current experiences or situational factors. Patient B experiences only a few depressive symptoms, and they have primarily only occurred since the death of a close friend a few months earlier. Patient B's symptoms also appear to be in large part influenced by situational factors such as stress at work and reminders of the friend's death. Although both patients in these scenarios would likely benefit from psychotherapy or counseling, the severity and nature of the depressions suggest that Patient A is a better candidate for psychotherapy and Patient B is a better candidate for counseling.

Clinical psychologists are more apt to provide psychotherapy, and counseling psychologists are more apt to provide counseling. However, the types of treatment these psychologists provide are based largely on their training, the settings in which they practice, and the needs of their patients. The differences between psychotherapy and counseling are generally agreed upon in the field, but consumers of these services, as well as clinical and counseling psychologists themselves, often use the terms more loosely. In addition, a patient might engage in both psychotherapy and counseling at various stages of a treatment or at different times in his or her life.

Assessment is also a core part of clinical and counseling psychologists' practice. Assessment refers to any type of formal evaluation of a patient, typically through the use of standardized tests and interview techniques. Psychological assessments differ from other types of assessments in their use of psychological principles, tests, and techniques to observe, evaluate, and draw conclusions about an individual or group's behavior. Psychological assessments are performed in order to answer specific questions about a patient and his or her functioning. Often these questions pertain to determining a diagnosis, making recommendations for treatment, or generating information about the functioning of symptoms. Although some elements of the practice of clinical and counseling psychology are not unique to these subfields (e.g., other mental health professionals conduct psychotherapy or counseling), performing psychological assessments has generally been exclusive to the work of clinical and counseling psychologists, with a few exceptions. In fact, the practice and valuing of assessment has been a cornerstone of the clinical and counseling psychology subfields. Assessment tools and approaches vary widely, but most clinical and counseling psychologists are trained in designing assessments, conducting them, interpreting the results, providing feedback, and authoring written reports that integrate the findings. Their proficiency with assessment and the degree to which they use it in their practice varies based on their training and the settings in which they work.

Most clinical and counseling psychologists also engage in consultation as part of their practice. Consultation involves offering opinions and recommendations on the basis of one's expertise. Clinical and counseling psychologists most often provide consultation to fellow mental health professionals regarding the treatment or assessment of a patient. This is a vital part of their professional work because it allows professionals to combine their expertise in the service of providing the best care. Clinical and counseling psychologists also offer consultation to individuals outside of the mental health field. For example, they may provide expert opinions to attorneys regarding a case that involves mental health issues.

In some limited instances, clinical and counseling psychologists can prescribe psychotropic medications as part of their professional practice. These psychologists must have specialized training, which typically includes coursework in physiology, biochemistry, and neuroscience, as well as extensive supervised experience and the successful completion of a national certification exam. Currently only two states in the US, New Mexico and Louisiana, allow psychologists with such training to prescribe. However, many others have considered similar legislation since the mid 1980s. The movement in large part grew out of a US Department of Defense demonstration project that successfully trained psychologists to prescribe psychotropic medications. Supporters of this move argue that clinical and counseling psychologists, given their expertise, are in an excellent position to integrate psychotropic medications into the overall treatment of a patient's mental illness. Others note that patients often have difficulty accessing psychiatric care, particularly in rural areas and when uninsured. Having some psychologists prescribe might help alleviate this problem. Opponents of the move have argued that even with specialized training, psychologists would lack the necessary knowledge and experience to prescribe safely. Others have cautioned that such a move would further shift mental health treatment to a biological model that relies on medications as the primary mode of treatment rather than psychological or social interventions. The controversy and debate around granting prescriptive authority to specially trained psychologists will continue to develop as additional states consider this type of legislation.

Research. Compared to practice, the design and conduction of research plays a more varied role in the work of clinical and counseling psychologists. This is in large part due to the fact that graduate programs in these subfields differ in their emphasis on research methodology and conducting original research. At a minimum, clinical and counseling psychologists should be trained to be highly sophisticated consumers of psychological research. Such training would equip them to be able to locate, read, understand, evaluate, and apply new scientific research to their applied work. At the other end of the spectrum, some clinical and counseling psychologists devote their entire careers to conducting research. The majority of clinical and counseling psychologists fall somewhere between these two extremes.

Clinical and counseling psychologists engage in diverse research projects, but their training and expertise yield several common areas of focus. One involves investigating various treatment and assessment techniques. This might include developing new psychotherapy techniques or assessment tools, or it could involve evaluating the effectiveness of established ones. Another research area consists of seeking to better understand psychological disorders by investigating their symptoms, prevalence, development, and impact. Still other clinical and counseling psychologists focus their research on issues that are central to the professions, such as the training of future psychologists, supervision, and ethical decision making. For examples of these and other types of research, Box 10.1 lists several journals that publish clinical and counseling psychology research.

Box 10.1 *Journals that Publish Clinical and Counseling Psychology Research*

- *Psychotherapy: Theory, Research, Practice, Training*
- *Journal of Consulting and Clinical Psychology*
- *Journal of Counseling Psychology*
- *Clinical Psychology: Science and Practice*
- *Journal of Abnormal Psychology*
- *Psychological Assessment*
- *Assessment*
- *Journal of Personality Assessment*

Administration. Clinical and counseling psychologists who are involved in administration typically oversee and manage both the operations of mental health treatment facilities and the staff who provide services within these facilities. Administration responsibilities are more likely to be a part of clinical and counseling psychologists' careers when they are employed in large settings such as outpatient and inpatient clinics. In addition, administrative activities are more often given to individuals who have substantial experience in the field.

Teaching and supervision. Many clinical and counseling psychologists teach and supervise students either in undergraduate institutions, graduate programs, or medical schools. Even those who spend most of their careers providing treatment and assessment services will at times teach a course in order to have variety in their work life, stay in touch with developments in the field, and give back to the profession. Supervision is a special form of teaching. It involves overseeing the work of students and trainees who are learning to provide psychotherapy, counseling, and assessment services. Many clinical and counseling psychologists provide supervision because they understand that this type of mentoring plays a central role in trainees' development into competent psychologists.

Theoretical Orientation

Many factors determine what types of activities clinical and counseling psychologists engage in and the ways in which they conduct their work. One significant source of influence on the work of these psychologists is their theoretical orientation. Theoretical orientation refers to the theory, or combination of theories, that a clinical or counseling psychologist adopts. Psychological theories are often broad and complex in their details, but at their core they offer a framework for understanding human behavior. In other words, these theories are models for how one might think about human behavior, its development, and how it can be modified. Some of the more common theoretical orientations include cognitive–behavioral, psychodynamic, humanistic, existential, relational, self-psychology, family systems, object relational, interpersonal, and solution-focused. Because of their complexity, the various theories complement each other in some areas and conflict in others. As a result, most clinical and counseling psychologists identify best with one or two theories. These ideas guide their understanding of and response to patients' unique experiences, and they guide the types of research questions asked.

Despite the substantial role of clinical and counseling psychologists' theoretical orientation in their practice and research, students interested in these subfields often have limited understanding of how one's particular theoretical orientation comes to be. One significant source of influence is the graduate program in which these psychologists are trained. Programs usually have a dominant theoretical orientation that flows from the orientations of the faculty. During training, students often adopt the orientation in which they are immersed. Although theoretical orientations are robust and can persist over time, some clinical and counseling psychologists experience shifts in their orientations during their careers.

Settings

Given the diversity of their training, clinical and counseling psychologists seek employment in a variety of settings. The most common among these are private practices, outpatient clinics, inpatient clinics or hospitals, academic institutions, and government and business.

Private practices and outpatient clinics. When students envision working as a clinical or counseling psychologist, many first imagine doing so in a private practice. However, only approximately 9% of clinical and counseling psychologists work in an independent practice setting immediately after graduation, including group-owned practices and community-based clinics (American Psychological Association [APA], 2011). Individuals who pursue private practice often do so because of the autonomy that comes with owning one's own business. Most enjoy a great deal of control over their time and income. However, as with owning a business in any field, private practice in psychology comes with complications, which will be discussed later.

Outpatient settings are typically clinics that patients visit for mental health services and then leave. Outpatient clinics tend to be significantly larger than private practices. Many clinics have a dozen or more professional staff including clinical and counseling psychologists, psychiatrists, counselors, and social workers. Many outpatient clinics have a particular focus or emphasis in the services they provide (e.g., substance use disorders, anxiety disorders, eating disorders). In structuring themselves in this way, these clinics ensure that they maintain a strong patient base and are able to provide services to a large number of patients. Outpatient clinics can be freestanding, similar to a large private practice, or affiliated with larger institutions such as hospitals or managed care organizations. In addition, many counseling psychologists work in outpatient clinics within universities and colleges, providing services to members of the campus community and at times helping to train future mental health professionals.

Academic. Approximately 28% of clinical and counseling psychologists are employed full-time in academic institutions immediately after graduation (APA, 2011). The largest portion of these is employed in university or college settings where their responsibilities may consist of teaching, research, service, and administration. Other clinical and counseling psychologists are employed in medical school settings where they participate in the education of physicians, provide treatment to patients, and conduct research. The nature of academic positions in psychology is explored in detail in Chapter 16.

Hospitals and inpatient clinics. Approximately 26% of clinical and counseling psychologists are employed full-time in hospital or inpatient settings immediately after graduation (APA, 2011). Inpatient settings are those in which patients seek mental health services that require residing in the treatment facility for a period of time. These settings are often necessary when the particular problem a patient is experiencing is too severe to be treated or assessed in a private practice or outpatient clinic. Some clinical and counseling psychologists prefer to work in these settings because their expertise lies in assessing and treating severe mental illness. Other psychologists are drawn to these settings because they enjoy the fast pace and unpredictability that often accompanies this work. These settings also tend to promote a high degree of collaboration among professionals from different disciplines, often in the form of treatment teams that are responsible for patient care.

Government and business. Approximately 27% of clinical and counseling psychologists are employed full-time in business or government settings immediately after graduation, with just under half of these working within managed care insurance companies (APA, 2011). These settings vary widely based on the nature of the business or government agency, but clinical and counseling psychologists are often hired in these environments to apply their expertise in a management or oversight capacity.

Salaries

The salaries earned by clinical and counseling psychologists depend largely on the type of work they perform and the setting in which it is conducted. According to the US Department of Labor (2014), 80% of clinical and counseling psychologists earned an estimated annual salary between $39,020 and $112,380, with a median income of $67,760. As with all professions, earnings vary according to geographic region as well as rural and urban settings. Recent trends in the mental health fields have had a substantial effect on clinical and counseling psychologists' income. Among these trends, two are noteworthy for their dramatic impact on not only salaries but also professional activities: managed care and master's level mental health professionals.

Massive health care reforms initiated in the US in the 1970s radically altered the ways in which the health care insurance system allocates resources to patients and reimburses professionals for providing services. Since then, the traditional indemnity insurance plans that reimbursed psychologists for the service they provided have by and large been replaced with managed care plans that reimburse only for contracted services at predetermined rates. Managed care organizations utilize numerous cost control strategies to maximize their profits. These strategies have contributed to greater competition among clinical and counseling psychologists for patients and greater willingness to provide services for reduced fees (Hayes, Barlow, & Nelson-Gray, 1999). In controlling costs, managed care organizations have also sought the services of master's level mental health providers because these professionals are often willing to accept lower reimbursement rates corresponding to their education and training levels. As a result, clinical and counseling psychologists who wish to provide services through certain managed care plans have been forced to accept increasingly lower rates as the number of master's level mental health providers has grown. Both of these consequences have only further elevated the competition for patients and membership on managed care panels, meaning psychologists have less ground for negotiating their rates and the types of services they offer.

Surveys of licensed psychologists have found that 80% report that managed care has had a negative impact on their work and careers (Phelps, Eisman, & Kohout, 1998). Additional studies have revealed that psychologists whose caseloads include more managed care cases report that they work longer hours, experience more stress and emotional exhaustion, receive less supervision, and are less satisfied with their incomes (Rupert & Baird, 2004). So why are psychologists working with managed care at all? First, managed care did address substantial problems in the mental health care system related to rampant costs. Many psychotherapy and counseling treatments previously were conducted with little to no oversight or quality control. Second, managed health care allows for larger numbers of individuals to have access to some form of mental health care that they might not otherwise be able to afford. Last, being an approved provider for managed care organizations often leads to a more predictable flow of new patients and referrals.

Employment Issues

Clinical and counseling psychologists enjoy flexibility when they are on the job market. Those with the most extensive training have the option of working in almost any environment, including inpatient, outpatient, academic, correctional, education, government, business, research, nonprofit, and private practice settings. Those with less extensive training, or training that is focused intently in only one or two areas, will have fewer options but will be more attractive to employers seeking specific skills. To demonstrate the range of employment options, Box 10.2 provides summary information from several recent job ads for clinical and counseling psychologists.

Among the employment issues that clinical and counseling psychologists face, the most significant have their impact on applied practice. As noted in the previous section on salaries, changes in insurance can have significant effects on the practice work of clinical and counseling psychologists. Beyond implications for reimbursement, salaries, and competition, insurance changes can also affect the types and nature of services psychologists provide. Two significant events in this arena bear mentioning. First, in an effort to strengthen insurance coverage of mental health care, federal legislation in 1996 and 2008 sought to require parity, or equivalence, between the coverage that insurers provide for medical and mental health care. The implementation of the law has proved problematic as insurers and employers sometimes found ways to circumvent the requirements. Second, the 2010 Patient Protection and Affordable Care Act brought about substantial changes in the regulation of health insurance. This included the requirement of mental health and substance abuse treatment coverage for insurance policies sold in the health insurance marketplaces and the coverage of preventative measures, such as depression screenings.

Box 10.2 *Recent Openings in the Clinical and Counseling Psychology Subfields*

Position: **Research Scientist**
Setting: Hazelden Foundation, Minnesota
Responsibilities: Formulate, design, and implement clinical research projects related to addiction treatment; oversee data collection; direct and supervise research staff, assistants, and graduate students; prepare and submit grant proposals and research manuscripts.

Position: **Assistant Professor**
Setting: Western Michigan University
Responsibilities: Teach undergraduate courses in psychology, behavior analysis, and areas of expertise; maintain a research and scholarship program in area of expertise; secure external grant funding; mentor graduate students in behavior analysis and clinical psychology programs.

Position: **Pediatric Clinical Psychologist**
Setting: Shriners Hospital, Illinois
Responsibilities: Consult with treatment teams on inpatient and outpatient child and adolescent cases primarily involving orthopedic conditions and spinal cord dysfunctions; analyze data and prepare manuscripts on grant-funded research projects related to spinal cord dysfunctions.

Position: **Psychologist**
Setting: US Army Medical Service Corps
Responsibilities: Evaluate and treat mental and behavioral disorders among soldiers and their families; implement and coordinate prevention and mental health promotion programs; supervise mental health staff and units; consult with commanders; conduct research on mental health topics of military importance.

Despite high health costs and spending, the US typically ranks far behind other developed nations in health outcomes (Murray & Frenk, 2010). And despite efforts to expand the availability of mental health treatment through insurance regulation and reform, most individuals' mental health issues are still treated in primary care (e.g., family physician) settings. As a result of these and other factors, health experts are discovering the need for a more integrative approach to improve the quality and effectiveness of primary care by fully addressing the biological, psychological, and social factors that influence patients' diseases, disorders, symptoms, recovery, and health behaviors (McDaniel & deGruy, 2014). Part of this shift involves an expanded role for mental health experts in primary care settings. Some psychologists have worked to articulate the nature of psychology practice in primary care settings in an effort to ensure that the field will play a role in this important transition in health care (e.g., McDaniel et al., 2014).

A different set of employment issues arises for those clinical and counseling psychologists who seek to establish a private practice. Owning and operating a private practice offers a number of benefits including greater control over your time, income, and the nature of your work. But much like owning any other business, private practices have their own set of complications. They can be costly to operate because you as the owner become fully responsible for all operating expenses, including purchasing facilities and maintaining them. Although some clinical and counseling psychologists do all of their own scheduling, billing, and paperwork, many find this time-consuming and hire staff to assist in this work. Any employees of the practice then become the responsibility of the owner. Like all businesses, private practices are subject to economic conditions and the public's desire for the products or services being offered. Owners of private practices must manage their resources well and be prepared to both weather changes in the market and respond to them by changing their approach. Because of these issues and potential problems, many clinical and counseling psychologists work together to establish private practices in order to share the costs, time, and risks involved. Still others will work for an established private practice, typically paying a percentage of their income in order to enjoy some of the benefits without having to be responsible for managing the business.

Related Careers

Before moving forward with a closer examination of how clinical and counseling psychologists are trained for their careers, it is important to note that there are a variety of careers outside of the psychology field that also engage in applied work regarding human behavior. In particular, there are several that are directly involved in mental health issues. Before making decisions about you own career goals, you should understand the similarities and differences in these careers and those in clinical and counseling psychology.

Psychiatrists.   Psychiatrists conduct research and/or provide services in the areas of diagnosis and treatment of mental illness. Like all other physicians, they are first trained in medical school and then receive more focused training in their specialty area during residency. Because the core of their training is in medicine, psychiatrists approach the diagnosis and treatment of mental illness using a medical model, meaning they apply treatments to alleviate identified symptoms and diagnosed conditions. Although psychiatrists previously provided psychotherapy as one form of treatment, and some still do, most now use psychotropic medications as their primary method for treating mental illness.

Clinical social workers.   Clinical social workers are concerned with the effects of social problems and strive to improve the human condition. Their training typically includes a master's degree in social work with an emphasis on clinical or applied interventions. One source of confusion about the profession of clinical social work stems from the fact that some jobs, particularly within government agencies and nonprofit organizations, may carry a title of social worker. However, individuals who occupy these positions may or may not be required to have the same level of education and training required for clinical social workers. The core of clinical social workers' training is in social theory and its applications within a societal system, particularly with regards to illness and dysfunction. Given the scope of this focus, their professional activities are diverse and include interventions at individual, group, community, and societal levels. These interventions are usually designed either to help individuals access social services (e.g., medical care, housing, job assistance) or to provide services directly (e.g., counseling). Depending on their training and activities, social workers can be employed in a variety of settings including hospitals, justice systems, government agencies, nonprofit organizations, and private practices.

Counselors and therapists.   Because the terms "counselor" and "therapist" are widely applied to a variety of professions and endeavors, this category is the most diverse within the related careers. Generally speaking, counselors and therapists in the mental health arena provide counseling and therapy services of some type to individuals and groups. The training and occupations of these professionals determine what specific services they provide. Common areas of concentration in the counseling field include school counseling, mental health or professional counseling, and addictions counseling. Common areas of concentration in the therapy field include marriage and family therapy, occupational therapy, and recreational therapy. The training required for these careers varies based on the nature of the work, but typically a master's degree in the field is required.

There are similarities between clinical and counseling psychologists and these related careers, but the differences matter greatly. The distinct training and backgrounds of each of these professionals leads them to think in highly divergent ways about human behavior and how it is best changed. Consumers of mental health services who struggle to distinguish between clinical social workers, counselors, therapists, psychiatrists, and psychologists will fail to appreciate the different approaches these professionals adopt and the unique expertise they offer. As a result, consumers may not seek out the professional that is best suited to understand and provide assistance with their particular problem. Likewise, if you have interest in a mental health-related career but fail to investigate or understand these distinctions, you run the risk of selecting a career path based not on desired expertise but on less pertinent factors such as salaries, ease of graduate school acceptance, and time spent in training.

Training and Preparation

Earning the Degree

In order to practice or direct research, clinical or counseling psychologists must earn a doctoral degree in psychology. There are two degree options: the doctor of philosophy degree (PhD) and the doctor of psychology degree (PsyD). Because both degrees are at the doctoral level, they have several components in common. Thus, if you are considering training to be a clinical or counseling psychologist, regardless of which degree you pursue, you can expect to have these elements as part of your graduate education.

Earning a doctoral degree in clinical or counseling psychology requires completing relevant coursework. Most doctoral programs in these subfields require students to complete courses in foundational areas such as development, assessment, ethics, research methods, physiology, statistics, and treatment. Coursework is heaviest at the beginning of graduate training, but it soon decreases as more time is invested in gaining applied experience. Applied training is started under the watchful eyes of supervisors. As this training advances, students gradually take on more applied experiences with increasing difficulty and less restrictive supervision. Depending on the emphasis of the particular graduate program, students pursuing a doctoral degree will often assist faculty with their research and ultimately engage in some type of independent research project. Although this project is typically an empirical research study, or dissertation, a few graduate programs allow students to complete literature reviews or case studies to satisfy this requirement. Because these alternatives to the traditional dissertation do not provide for training in conducting empirical research, they are not suited for students who intend to incorporate any level of research activity into their careers.

Doctoral degree options. The existence of the PhD and PsyD degrees is the result of figural events in the history of the field. The clinical and counseling psychology subfields first emerged at the beginning of the 20th century when groups of psychologists who studied human behavior began to apply this knowledge in order to improve human functioning. These early clinical and counseling psychologists separated from colleagues who resisted this move toward applications of psychological science; yet they remained firmly entrenched in the scientific basis of their work. After decades of applying psychological theory and research to practice, clinical and counseling psychologists established the first set of training standards in 1949. Known as the Boulder Model, these standards emphasized the need to prepare clinical and counseling psychologists for both practice and research careers. To accomplish this goal, training programs were based in university settings that could support research. All students were required to complete a final project that was research based, which resulted in a PhD. The PhD is an academic degree that can be earned in most disciplines. Those who earn a PhD possess not only in-depth knowledge about a particular subject but also expertise in how to gather and generate additional knowledge about the topic. The Boulder Model called for training programs to provide as much funding as possible for students and to keep the number of students low in order to maximize mentorship opportunities.

In the 1960s, pressure was mounting to create an alternative training model. This pressure arose because many students were interested in clinical and counseling psychology careers that would focus exclusively on providing treatment and assessment services rather than conducting research, teaching, and supervision. This new model would train psychologists to be skilled consumers of research but would stop short of training them to conduct research. Instead, it would focus more on the development of practice skills. As a result of this pressure, the Vail Model was officially recognized in 1973, and the PsyD degree was created to reflect the difference in expertise these psychologists would have. In the years since, the distinctions between the Boulder and Vail Models have become less stark. Other models for training have emerged, and graduate programs in the clinical and counseling psychology subfields now offer varying degrees of emphasis in applied and research training. Many PsyD programs now offer much less research training than the Vail Model ever intended, while some offer much more.

Some PhD programs are offering much less applied training than the Boulder Model ever intended, while others offer much more. The best measure of the type of training a program offers is a thorough examination of the program's training components and an evaluation of the psychologists they produce.

The PhD and PsyD degrees primarily differ in the nature of the training involved, and additional information about these degree options is contained in Chapter 7. In practice, these differences translate into several other important distinctions, which will be discussed in a later section of this chapter. But one important difference to consider at this point is how the degree is viewed. Just as the first clinical and counseling psychologists were disparaged for their efforts to apply psychological theory and research to working with patients, the PsyD degree model was initially disparaged for its relative lack of research training and skills. Concerns focused on the extent to which this altered training might adversely affect the PsyD holders' efforts to secure employment. Studies investigating this potential bias have in large part found no support for it (Hershey, Kopplin, & Cornell, 1991). However, this is confounded by the fact that holders of the PhD and PsyD degrees tend to seek employment in different types of settings (Gaddy, Charlot-Swilley, Nelson, & Reich, 1995). For example, the vast majority of clinical and counseling psychologists who are employed in academic settings hold the PhD degree. This is likely due to the fact that academic positions typically require some level of research production from faculty, and in general psychologists trained in PsyD programs are unlikely to possess the research experience or interest to pursue these positions.

Master's degrees.　Master's degrees in clinical or counseling psychology are available in some graduate programs. However, because a doctorate is required to be licensed and practice as a clinical or counseling psychologist, these master's degree programs have been the subject of debate. Individuals who earn these degrees are usually able to engage in limited practice activities as long as they are supervised by a doctoral-level professional. In other states, they may qualify for licensure and independent practice as a professional counselor or mental health counselor, but not as a psychologist.

The lack of a terminal master's degree option in clinical or counseling psychology that would lead to independent practice often puzzles students. Historically there has been pressure for the field to create this option, but many clinical and counseling psychologists resisted it out of concern that such an option would involve reduced training standards. As a result, clinical and counseling psychologists continue only to be educated at the doctoral level. Partly in response to this, a host of master's degree options have emerged in other fields to meet demand for a master's level entry into mental health careers. Some clinical and counseling psychologists are pleased that the training standards for entering the field were preserved. Others have criticized this move by noting that had a master's option been created, these mental health professionals would have a background in psychology and psychologists would have likely retained control over how these individuals are trained.

Predoctoral internship.   In addition to coursework, applied experiences, and an independent project, students pursuing doctoral degrees in clinical or counseling psychology typically must complete a predoctoral internship. The predoctoral internship is a year-long experience in which students work full-time providing treatment and assessment services. Because this experience comes after students have completed their graduate education, with the exception of the dissertation or final project, the internship serves as a capstone to the student's applied training. While on internship students have the opportunity to learn new skills and further refine the skills they have already acquired.

Predoctoral internships vary widely in terms of experiences, settings, workload, and compensation. The majority of internship sites are approved by an organization known as the Association of Psychology Postdoctoral and Internship Centers (APPIC). APPIC coordinates the application and selection process that matches students with their most desired internship sites, and vice versa. A major concern about this process in recent years has been the shortage of APPIC-approved internship sites compared to the number of students seeking positions. In 2014, 20% of the students seeking an internship site were unmatched, which was an improvement over the 24% and 26% unmatched in 2013 and 2012, respectively (APPIC Board of Directors, 2014). This imbalance has existed for some time as a result of reduced internship sites and increased numbers of students seeking internship placements (Keilin, Baker, McCutcheon, & Peranson, 2007). The number of sites has reduced in recent years due to the costs of offering training programs, and the number of students is growing due to the increase of professional schools in psychology and the number of students they train each year (Kaslow & Keilin, 2006). Although professionals in the field are working to address this problem, it is likely to persist for some time and may affect students who are interested in pursuing the doctoral degree in clinical or counseling psychology.

Variations in Graduate Programs

Graduate programs in clinical and counseling psychology vary in two important ways: the emphasis placed on research versus applied experience and the overall quality of the training. The balance between research and applied training is a variable that graduate schools readily disclose. They are invested in having students who will be satisfied with the training experiences they offer, so they are clear in their program descriptions as to what extent students are expected to conduct research versus applied work. Graduate schools are far less clear in describing the quality of their training. This is in part a result of having limited data available that compare the quality of various clinical and counseling psychology programs in a reliable and valid manner. As a result, graduate schools often do not have a clear idea of how the quality of their training compares to other programs. However, several factors that are known to these programs greatly impact training quality. These include the level of institutional and external funding for the program, the expertise of faculty, the resources provided to students, and the success of students in securing internship placements, licensure, and employment.

There are two basic types of graduate programs in clinical and counseling psychology: university-based and professional school programs. University-based programs are affiliated with and housed in established universities and colleges. Their training programs are most closely aligned with the traditional scientist–practitioner model that results in the PhD. The professional school programs are housed in institutions established for the purpose of educating and training clinical and/or counseling psychologists. These institutions can either be university affiliated, meaning they have some relationship to an established university or college, or freestanding, meaning they operate independently of any university or college. The professional school programs are most closely aligned with the scholar–practitioner model that results in the PsyD, although some university-based programs offer the PsyD as well.

In addition to training philosophy, some of the starkest differences in these two types of programs are related to how they are funded. University-based programs receive funding through the budgets of their home institutions. In addition, the faculty in these programs are typically involved in research that is supported by external sources of funding. These grants support research but also help support the needs of the program. Professional school programs are in a different position. Because many are freestanding or only loosely affiliated with a university or college, they typically receive limited or no financial support from other institutions. In addition, the faculty in these programs seldom engage in research that generates grants. It is important that students who are considering graduate school in clinical or counseling psychology understand these differences. Many of these have been discussed in the literature (e.g., Norcross, Castle, Sayette, & Main, 2004), and some are summarized in Table 10.2. They will

Table 10.2 Differences in Graduate Programs in Clinical and Counseling Psychology

	University-Based Programs	Professional School Programs
Training model	Scientist–practitioner	Scholar–practitioner
Degrees offered	PhD, some PsyD	PsyD
Acceptance rates	14%	41%
Receiving full financial assistance	72%	18%
Students enrolled each year	9	33
Securing accredited internships	93%	74%

Note. Information comes from Norcross et al. (2004).

have a real and immediate impact on your chances of being selected for a program and the financial costs of attending. They will have a less immediate impact on the training you receive. They may have a longer term impact on the skills and abilities you acquire, and as a result, the types of employment you will seek.

The APA is the organization that accredits doctoral programs in clinical psychology and counseling psychology. The APA has established training standards that all accredited programs must follow, including specific requirements for coursework, applied training, and research experience. The purpose of accreditation is to provide some consistency among graduate programs while ensuring that graduates have a certain level of knowledge and expertise required to enter the career field. Graduate programs must apply for APA accreditation and then be reviewed by the APA at great depth. Because programs can change over time, programs must regularly prove that they meet the APA standards or risk losing their accreditation status. Programs that are not APA accredited fall into several categories. Some are quality programs that for some reason have opted not to pursue APA accreditation. Others may be working to ensure that their program meets the standards so that they can apply in the near future. Still, other programs lacking APA accreditation simply cannot meet the standards. Some have attempted and been denied, and others had their accreditation suspended or revoked. Others, often because of lack of resources, are unable to offer the types of training experiences the APA requires. Given the meaning of a program's accreditation status, it should come as no surprise that APA-accredited doctoral programs in clinical or counseling psychology are among the most competitive of all graduate programs in terms of admissions.

How important is it to attend a graduate program that has APA accreditation? For students who opt to attend an unaccredited program, there are two consequences to consider. First, the training components that are lacking in these programs may place you at a disadvantage for securing a predoctoral internship, postdoctoral training, and employment, particularly when you are competing against individuals who attended APA-accredited programs. Second, some states will not grant a license as a psychologist to an individual who attended a graduate program that lacked APA accreditation. Other states will allow these individuals to take additional coursework or gain additional training experiences in order to satisfy the licensure requirements, but this varies by state. As a result, attending an unaccredited program may greatly restrict your (and even eliminate many) employment opportunities.

Licensure

To better understand the way professional licensure works, think for a moment about a driver's license. The state in which you live has established rules that require the possession of a valid, current driver's license in order to operate a motor vehicle. Obtaining a driver's license involves proving that you have met these requirements. Most states restrict the age of the driver and their driving ability. After individuals earn a driver's license, their behavior while using the license is also restricted. They must occasionally renew their license and prove their eligibility. They must obey rules and laws that govern their driving behavior, including what types of vehicles they are allowed to drive. Failing to follow these restrictions can result in the loss of the license. Can an individual operate a motor vehicle without a license? Of course they can, but they usually do so in violation of the law and thereby place their ability to earn a license in jeopardy.

All licensure processes work much like a driver's license, and many different professionals must be licensed in order to offer services to the public. This licensure process has three main purposes. First, it protects the public by ensuring that only those professionals who are qualified to provide these services do so. Second, it regulates the practice of a profession. By requiring a license to do something, the state is then able to establish standards for earning the license and can monitor the actions of the professional. Third, requiring a license protects the use of a title. Most states license clinical psychologists and counseling psychologists with the general title of "psychologist" or "licensed psychologist." This is typically done so that different types of applied psychologists (e.g., clinical, neuro, industrial–organizational, school) can be licensed under the same process. State laws prohibit individuals who do not hold a license as a psychologist from referring to themselves as such. This protects consumers of services from being misled and ensures that all licensed professions are protected from having unqualified individuals market themselves as something they are not.

Because states establish the laws and rules that guide the professional licensure process, the requirements for licensure vary from state to state. This can produce problems for psychologists who obtain licensure in one state and then relocate to a state with stricter licensing requirements. Although there have been efforts in the field to improve cooperation among states in recognizing each others' licenses, a process known as reciprocity, progress in this area has remained slow. Despite the differences between states' licensing requirements, there are some fairly common components to the licensure process for clinical and counseling psychologists. Licensure as a psychologist always requires a doctoral degree in one of the applied areas of psychology. In addition, all states require some amount of postdoctoral training experience where one's work is supervised by a licensed psychologist. The states differ widely in the hours that are required. Some require only 1,000 hours and allow hours accumulated during the predoctoral internship to count toward this requirement. At the other end of the spectrum, some states require 4,000 hours of postdoctoral experience, all of which must be accumulated after the degree is earned. All states require satisfactory completion of the national licensing exam, or the Examination for Professional Practice of Psychology (EPPP). Again, states vary in what they determine is a passing score, though minimums of between 70–80% correct are typical. Many states have additional requirements that are not as consistent. For example, some have state-level exams that address their specific laws and rules. These exams are typically either in a written or oral form and focus on state laws and ethical practice. Extensive information about the licensure process for psychologists, as well as the requirements for each state, can be accessed through the Association of State and Provincial Psychology Boards' website (www.asppb.net).

Professional licensure is a critical issue in the related mental health careers of professional counseling, clinical social work, and marriage and family therapy. The licensure process is similar in structure to that for clinical or counseling psychologists. Each state establishes its own requirements, and the degree of uniformity on a national level varies by profession. However, the components of specified education, training, supervision, and exam performance are present in most cases.

A license to practice psychology, as well as other mental health professions, must be maintained. Typically this involves renewal, and most states currently require licenses to be renewed every two years. In addition to paperwork and fees, renewal often involves documenting or attesting that one has completed any requirements that are in place for renewal. The most common requirement is continuing education requirements. States establish a minimum amount of additional training and education that psychologists must complete in order to renew their licenses. Most states also specify certain types of training that must be obtained (e.g., ethics, diversity) and the ways in which it can be acquired (e.g., workshops, self-study, conferences).

Another key component of maintaining one's license is ensuring that the license is not revoked as a result of failure to adhere to the rules and guidelines that regulate the practice of the profession. The most common reasons that states revoke a psychologist's license are for violations of professional ethics. Many states have adopted all or parts of the APA Ethical Principles of Psychologists and Code of Conduct into their state law or regulations, meaning that any violation is subject to both ethical and legal consequences. Still, other licenses are not maintained because psychologists fail to renew them or to complete the required continuing education. In addition, many states have established rules that allow for the revocation of professional licenses for behavior that is seen to be incongruent with professional practice, such as felony convictions, crimes of moral turpitude, and defaulting on student loans or child support payments.

Preparing for Graduate Training as an Undergraduate

Because many of the issues discussed thus far take place when selecting a graduate program and completing training, you may feel that they are far removed from your position of beginning to consider clinical or counseling psychology as a career option. But be aware that there are also factors you should be attending to as an undergraduate because they will have bearing on your ability to enter graduate programs in these subfields.

Coursework. We have already established that clinical and counseling psychology programs differ considerably in their emphasis on research and applied training. As a result, absolute recommendations for the types of courses that best prepare you for these programs are not realistic. However, there are core courses in most undergraduate psychology curricula that are judged to be vital for students aspiring to enter clinical or counseling psychology graduate programs. These courses, as well as

> **Box 10.3** *Recommended Undergraduate Coursework for Clinical and Counseling Psychology*
>
> | Courses Areas Within Psychology | Course Areas Outside of Psychology |
> | --- | --- |
> | Research methods | Statistics |
> | Experimental psychology | Natural sciences (chemistry and biology) |
> | Abnormal psychology | Business/marketing/accounting |
> | Clinical or counseling psychology | Computer science |
> | Testing, measurement, or psychometrics | Human services |
> | Ethics | |
> | Theories of personality | |
> | Life-span developmental psychology | |
> | Learning and behavior | |

relevant course areas outside of psychology, are listed in Box 10.3. Note that although courses pertaining to psychopathology and assessment are excellent choices, students also benefit from a background in the scientific foundations of the field and in various approaches to human behavior.

Activities. All students interested in graduate school are concerned about what types of experiences they should have that will prepare them and make their applications more desirable. There is much advice on this topic in the literature, and there are empirical studies that have surveyed graduate programs in psychology to determine what factors are most important when they are seeking new graduate students (e.g., Norcross, Kohout, & Wicherski, 2006). Typically these graduate programs report that the most important components in a student's application are their letters of recommendation, personal statements, and GPA. From there, the student's interview, research experience, and GRE are the next group of important factors. Extracurricular activities and experience gained through internships and/or employment are typically the least valued components of a student's application. Although these data reflect application components desired in all types of graduate programs in psychology, students interested in applying to clinical or counseling psychology programs should pay close attention to these findings. Those with limited time or resources to devote to preparing for graduate study will be best served by concentrating on their academic performance, developing a clear statement of their purpose and goals in pursuing graduate education, and cultivating relationships with faculty that might yield strong letters of support.

Working in Areas Related to Clinical or Counseling Psychology with a Bachelor's Degree

As discussed in earlier chapters, the bachelor's degree in psychology can be thought of as a liberal arts degree or a preprofessional degree. If you are interested in a career as a clinical psychologist or counseling psychologist, you should approach your undergraduate education as preparation for pursuing the doctoral degree. No matter how much coursework or exposure you have as an undergraduate to theories and applied practices of clinical and counseling psychologists, it is vital that you recognize that your education and expertise in this area is severely limited. As such, no undergraduate student in psychology should ever attempt to offer applied psychological services to another person. Few students would ever think of doing so. However, many others are far less cautious about casually attempting to diagnose disorders among friends and family or offering recommendations about behavioral problems and treatment. Under no circumstance is such action appropriate. The potential for harm is substantial, and you must recognize the highly limited nature of your knowledge and experience base in these areas.

But what are undergraduate students who have interests in the clinical or counseling psychology subfields to do if they do not intend to pursue a graduate degree? Certainly there are excellent mental health career options at the master's level in other disciplines such as social work, counseling, and therapy. But what about those individuals who will seek employment with their bachelor's degree, either as a career or in preparation for later attending graduate school? There are a number of career and employment opportunities that tap aspects of clinical and counseling psychology. Some students are initially dissatisfied with them because they do not allow one to provide counseling or therapy. Once they understand that doing so always requires a graduate degree, they often are open to reevaluating these options. Many of these bachelor's level careers allow for working directly with individuals who are experiencing distress or difficulties in functioning, just not in directly providing treatment services. In addition, some of these careers involve interactions with individuals where the goal is to provide help and make a positive impact in another person's life. The most common options include mental health technicians/aides and human/social service specialists.

Mental Health Technician/Aide

Mental health technicians/aides often go by a variety of job titles, including psychiatric technician/aide or residential counselor/assistant. The work varies, but typically these positions involve large portions of time spent in direct contact with patients who are receiving mental health treatment, often in an inpatient, residential, or camp setting. Patients who are living at a treatment facility are experiencing the types of problems that require extensive supervision and assistance. Mental health technicians/ aides are involved in the entire spectrum of the patient's daily routine. These professionals often know the patients well and are in the best position to monitor their behavior and response to treatment. Therefore, although mental health technicians/aides cannot provide treatment in the form of therapy or medication, they play an integral role in facilitating patients' overall care and advising the treatment teams. According to the US Department of Labor (2014), the median salary estimate was $25,120 for psychiatric aides, $29,880 for psychiatric technicians, and $24,520 for residential advisors.

Human/Social Service Specialists

Human/social service specialists also go by a variety of job titles, including social worker, consultant, specialist, case manager, and patient liaison. The work varies, but most of these individuals are involved in some type of coordination of services between a patient or client and an agency that serves them. Some human/social service specialists are in nonprofit settings and may be involved in community outreach, management of charitable cases, and coordination of services for individuals in need. Others are employed by local and state governments to ensure that services are being adequately delivered to the public. This might involve direct work with clients who are in need of services that government agencies can provide. But it might also involve monitoring the performance of businesses that provide these services, such as the regulation of childcare centers. According to the US Department of Labor (2014), the median salary estimate was $29,230 for human service assistants and $40,050 for community and social service specialists.

An Insider's Perspective

A Science of Heart and Mind

Robert McGrath, PhD
Fairleigh Dickinson University

People are sometimes surprised when they learn that even though I am a clinical psychologist I no longer provide clinical services. This is not because I do not value what psychotherapy can do for people. It can be a magical and moving experience, and I am proud that in some cases I profoundly affected another person's life for the better. Since early in my education, though, I was always drawn primarily to the potential for clinical psychology as a science.

The biggest problem I faced when I first began to develop a research program was how to pick just one topic to study. Clinical psychologists study a host of interesting issues. Just thinking of the colleagues with whom I work now, they are investigating topics as varied as the role mood plays in college students' alcohol abuse, how to improve treatment for eating disorders, and the best methods for predicting whether incarcerated criminals are likely to offend again.

My own research focuses on how best to measure psychological concepts. Perhaps that seems like a dry topic to settle on, but it depends how you look at it. For me, it combines an intellectual interest in science with a romantic notion that we can learn how to read and understand what is in another person's heart and mind more effectively. That strikes me as pretty fascinating.

That is what I find special about a career as a researcher in clinical psychology: bringing the techniques of science to bear on questions about what it means to be human, and how to improve the human condition. Thanks to recent advances in genetics, brain imaging, and cognitive research, I think we are on the verge of a new era in terms of understanding the causes of unhappiness and discontent, and how to help those people who need it. I do not know how clinical psychology will evolve in response to this new knowledge, but I am proud that it will be guided by the research that is being done by research clinical psychologists.

Note. Dr. Robert McGrath is a clinical psychologist and professor of psychology in the School of Psychology at Fairleigh Dickinson University in Teaneck, NJ, where he is the Director of the MS Program in Clinical Psychopharmacology. Dr. McGrath has authored over 200 peer-reviewed journal articles and conference presentations and serves as the Lead Consultant for Test Development for the VIA Institute on Character.

Professional Spotlight

Kimberlyn Leary, PhD, ABPP

Education:
- Bachelor of Arts (BA) in Psychology from Amherst College
- Master of Arts (MA) in Psychology from the University of Michigan
- Doctor of Philosophy (PhD) in Clinical Psychology from the University of Michigan
- Graduate of the Michigan Psychoanalytic Institute
- Masters in Public Administration (MPA) from the Kennedy School of Government, Harvard University

Position:
Chief Psychologist and Director of Psychology and Psychology Training at Cambridge Health Alliance; Associate Professor of Psychology at Harvard Medical School

Description of Position:
I direct the Division of Psychology in a large, urban medical center that is also a teaching hospital, where I work with our psychology faculty to design and implement clinical training experiences for practicum students, interns, and postdoctoral fellows. As a professor, I teach both psychology interns and fellows (as well as a medical students), engage in research and writing, present at conferences, and work collaboratively with colleagues. I also teach undergraduate students and in programs of continuing education for physicians, psychologists, and lawyers.

Most Significant Professional Accomplishment:
I feel honored to have the opportunity to serve as a leader. Leadership is an activity and consists of mobilizing others to engage in collaborative work toward shared goals. Thus, the most significant work I am doing now is engaging the psychologists in our system to do the work that is most meaningful toward our goal of teaching and training psychologists to care for patients who need help.

Favorite Publication:
Leary, K., Pillemer, J., & Wheeler, M. (2013, January/February). Negotiating with emotion. *Harvard Business Review, 91,* 96–103.

Areas of Research:
My scholarly work is at the intersection of leadership, negotiation, and clinical psychology. I am researching and writing on collaborative, relational problem solving across different sectors. This work aims to be attentive to the multicultural contexts

in which problem solving occurs. I am interested in helping people to resolve conflict more effectively – whether that conflict is within a person, between neighborhoods, or among international players.

Areas of Practice:

In my private practice, I offer psychoanalysis, psychodynamic therapy, and integrative therapies aimed at helping people with focal problems.

Professional Memberships:

As a member of the American Psychoanalytic Association, I chair the program committee and have sat on several national task forces. As a member of American Psychological Association, I have served as treasurer of the Women, Gender, and Psychoanalysis section in Division 39 (Psychoanalysis).

Most Rewarding Aspect of Your Career:

The most wonderful part of my professional life is the chance to learn with and from very talented, creative, and inspiring people – among them my colleagues, my students, and my patients. I love that being an effective psychologist obliges you to keep learning.

Words of Advice to the Student Who is Interested in Your Subfield:

Think big, follow your heart, but remember real work takes place one step at a time! Over the course of a career – if you are lucky – your interests will change. Listen to what your heart tells you and allow yourself to take reasonable chances. It is not possible to do everything that interests you all at once, but it may well be that you do many different things over the course of your career. Treat your career as an adventure.

Suggested Exercises

1. Contact a current graduate student who is pursuing a doctorate in clinical or counseling psychology in order to pose questions you have about training in these subfields. Many graduate programs provide email addresses for their graduate students, and many of these students are willing to answer specific questions that a potential applicant might have.
2. Interview a clinical or counseling psychologist who is working in a setting you have not previously considered as part of your career goals (e.g., hospital, prison, government, university, military). Think about your particular interests in clinical and counseling psychology and what settings these interests could be applied to.
3. Investigate a research opportunity within your undergraduate program or one at a neighboring institution. Contact a faculty member whose research interests you and have a conversation with them about what they typically look for in an undergraduate research assistant. Use the information they provide you to consider the following two questions:

   - Would you be willing to work with them at some point in the future?
   - What steps do you need to take to ensure that they would want you to work for them?

4. Investigate a volunteer opportunity within an area hospital or residential treatment center. Larger hospitals often have volunteer centers and allow some choice in the areas you work (e.g., psychiatric unit or mental health outpatient clinic). These experiences can often help focus your career goals.

Suggested Readings by Topic Area

Clinical Psychology and Counseling Psychology Careers

Gelso, C. J., Williams, E. N., & Fretz, B. R. (2014). *Counseling psychology* (3rd ed.). Washington, DC: American Psychological Association.

Kuther, T. L. (2005). *Your career in psychology: Clinical and counseling psychology.* Belmont, CA: Wadsworth Publishing.

Plante, T. G. (2011). *Contemporary clinical psychology* (3rd ed.). Hoboken, NJ: Wiley.

Graduate School in Clinical and Counseling Psychology

Norcross, J. C., & Sayette, M. A. (2014). *Insider's guide to graduate programs in clinical and counseling psychology.* New York, NY: Guilford Press.

Mental Health Care Issues

Mechanic, D., McAlpine, D. D., & Rochefort, D. A. (2013). *Mental health and social policy: Beyond managed care* (6th ed.). Boston, MA: Allyn & Bacon.

Thornicroft, G., Ruggeri, M., & Goldberg, D. (Eds.). (2013). *Improving mental health care: The global challenge.* Malden, MA: Wiley-Blackwell.

Resources

- Society of Clinical Psychology – Division 12 of the APA
  - www.div12.org
- Society of Counseling Psychology – Division 17 of the APA
  - www.div17.org
- Division of Psychotherapy – Division 29 of the APA
  - www.divisionofpsychotherapy.org
- Psychologists in Independent Practice – Division 42 of the APA
  - www.division42.org
- Association of Psychology Postdoctoral and Internship Centers (APPIC)
  - www.appic.org
- Association of State and Provincial Psychology Boards
  - www.asppb.net

References

American Psychological Association. (2011). *2009 doctorate employment survey.* Washington, DC: Author. Retrieved from http://www.apa.org/workforce/publications/09-doc-empl/index.aspx

APPIC Board of Directors. (2014). *2014 APPIC match statistics – Phase 1*. Retrieved from http://www.appic.org/Match/MatchStatistics/MatchStatistics2014PhaseI.aspx

Gaddy, C. D., Charlot-Swilley, D., Nelson, P. D., & Reich, J. N. (1995). Selected outcomes of accredited programs. *Professional Psychology: Research and Practice, 26*, 507–513. doi:10.1037/0735-7028.26.5.507

Gallucci, N. T. (1997). An evaluation of the characteristics of undergraduate psychology majors. *Psychological Reports, 81*, 879–889.

Hayes, S. C., Barlow, D. H., & Nelson-Gray, R. O. (1999). *The scientist practitioner: Research and accountability in the age of managed care* (2nd ed.). Needham Heights, MA: Allyn & Bacon.

Hershey, J. M., Kopplin, D. A., & Cornell, J. E. (1991). Doctors of psychology: Their career experiences and attitudes toward degree and training. *Professional Psychology: Research and Practice, 22*, 351–356. doi:10.1037/0735-7028.22.5.351

Kaslow, N. J., & Keilin, W. G. (2006). Internship training in clinical psychology: Looking into our crystal ball. *Clinical Psychology Science and Practice, 13*, 242–248. doi:10.1111/j.1468-2850.2006.00031.x

Keilin, W. G., Baker, J., McCutcheon, S., & Peranson, E. (2007). A growing bottleneck: The internship supply–demand imbalance in 2007 and its impact on psychology training. *Training and Education in Professional Psychology, 1*, 229–237. doi:10.1037/1931-3918.1.4.229

McDaniel, S. H., & deGruy, F. V., III. (2014). An introduction to primary care and psychology. *American Psychologist, 69*, 325–331. doi:10.1037/a0036222

McDaniel, S. H., Grus, C. L., Cubic, B. A., Hunter, C. L., Kearney, L. K., Schuman, C. C.,…Bennett Johnson, S. (2014). Competencies for psychology practice in primary care. *American Psychologist, 69*, 409–429. doi:10.1037/a0036072

Murray, C. J. L., & Frenk, J. (2010). Ranking 37th – Measuring the performance of the U.S. health care system. *New England Journal of Medicine, 362*, 98–99. doi:10.1056/NEJMp0910064

National Science Foundation. (2013). *Doctorate recipients from U.S. Universities: 2012* (NSF 14-305). Retrieved from http://www.nsf.gov/statistics/sed/2012

Norcross, J. C., Castle, P. H., Sayette, M. A., & Mayne, T. J. (2004). The PsyD: Heterogeneity in practitioner training. *Professional Psychology: Research and Practice, 35*, 412–419. doi:10.1037/0735-7028.35.4.412

Norcross, J. C., Kohout, J. L., & Wicherski, M. (2006). Graduate admissions in psychology I: The application process. *Eye on Psi Chi, 10*(2), 28–29, 42–43.

Phelps, R., Eisman, E. J., & Kohout, J. (1998). Psychological practice and managed care: Results of the CAPP practitioner survey. *Professional Psychology: Research and Practice, 29*, 31–36. doi:10.1037/0735-7028.29.1.31

Rupert, P. A., & Baird, K. A. (2004). Managed care and the independent practice of psychology. *Professional Psychology: Research and Practice, 35*, 185–193. doi:10.1037/0735-7028.35.2.185

US Department of Labor. (2014). *May 2013 national occupational employment and wage estimates*. Retrieved from http://www.bls.gov/oes/2013/may/oes_nat.htm

Webb, A. R., & Speer, J. R. (1985). The public image of psychologists. *American Psychologist, 40*, 1063–1064. doi:10.1037/0003-066X.40.9.1063.b

Chapter Eleven
Careers in Educational and School Psychology

Introduction

Consider for a moment as an undergraduate student how much of your life has been spent in the pursuit of education. From kindergarten through the completion of high school, you likely spent 30–40 hours per week at school with additional time at home devoted to reading, studying, and completing assignments. Some of you even began your formal education earlier by attending programs such as pre-K and pre-school. Now that you are in college, the hours spent in the classroom have decreased, but the time devoted to learning remains high. In fact, many of you may feel as though the time you have to devote to your families, friends, and work is more often than not being consumed by the demands of your education. For those of you contemplating earning a graduate or professional degree, this course of education could take an additional 2–8 years and often requires your full attention and devotion. With education playing such an enormous role in the lives of so many, it seems as though the field of psychology would have much to contribute to our understanding of the education process and the experiences of students. In fact, the field has been and continues to be closely involved in these educational endeavors, particularly through the work of educational and school psychologists.

The subfields of educational and school psychology are popular career options for students. Approximately 15.9% of all master's degrees and 9.5% of all doctoral degrees granted in psychology in the US are in one of these two subfields (American Psychological Association [APA], 2014). In a

Majoring in Psychology: Achieving Your Educational and Career Goals, Second Edition.
Jeffrey L. Helms and Daniel T. Rogers.
© 2015 John Wiley & Sons, Ltd. Published 2015 by John Wiley & Sons, Ltd.

survey of educational and school psychologists, many indicated that personal experiences with an educational or school psychologist during their childhood or adolescence helped shape their interest (Graves & Wright, 2007). Others noted that the opportunity to work closely with student populations was an important factor in their decision to pursue this career.

Defining the Subfields

Educational and school psychologists share a common overall focus. The foundation of their work centers on situations in which learning takes place. However, these subfields diverge when choosing what areas and topics within the learning process that they address.

Educational Psychology

The subfield of educational psychology is defined by its focus on the educational process. Educational psychologists are interested in how humans learn in educational settings. This includes an interest in both the teaching, or instructional, side of the process and the learning side. For the most part, educational psychologists approach these topics as theorists and researchers. They seek to generate new knowledge that can address psychological factors in the educational process.

Psychology in the US has always been linked to the topics of learning and teaching. Many of the founding figures in American psychology, such as William James, G. Stanley Hall, Edward Thorndike, and John Dewey, offered research, observations, and contributions to our knowledge of educational processes. Outside of the US, other leading figures in the field, such as Alfred Binet and Jean Piaget, viewed educational processes as fertile ground for developing their ideas about human learning, intelligence, and development.

Educational psychologists address a wide array of topics in their efforts to expand our knowledge of the teaching and learning process. Much of their work has been heavily influenced by dramatic shifts over the last 50 years in our understanding of human cognition. Currently educational psychologists examine factors in student learning such as motivation, intelligence, study habits, organization, perseverance, and response to success or failure. Others investigate aspects of instructional methods such as learning outcomes, teaching materials, curricula, assessment methods, and the use of technology and media. Still other educational psychologists study the impact of environmental variables such as student–teacher ratios, class composition, and classroom management.

School Psychology

The subfield of school psychology is defined by its focus on assisting students with particular needs. School psychologists work to improve students' well-being by addressing developmental, emotional, social, and academic problems that interfere with their education. Unlike educational psychologists who tend to approach educational issues as researchers and theorists, school psychologists are more likely to serve in the role of practitioners who work directly with individual students. School psychology differs from school counseling or guidance counseling in its emphasis on helping those students who are experiencing the most significant problems relative to their learning and education.

School psychology in large part developed out of the applied work of clinical and counseling psychologists and the focus of educational psychologists. Perhaps the single most influential event on the current state of school psychology occurred in 1975 with the passage of the Education for All Handicapped Children Act (Fagan & Wise, 2000). This piece of federal legislation led to the emergence of special education in the public school systems. The requirements placed new demands on schools to assess and respond to the needs of students who might be experiencing some type of disability. As a result, school districts across the country worked in the years that followed to implement requirements for providing special education resources to qualifying students. One result of these events was a doubling of the number of school psychologists between 1970 and 1980, and another doubling by the early 1990s (Reschly, 2000).

The topics of focus for school psychologists have expanded in recent decades as the laws guiding schools' handling of students with special needs have evolved. Many school psychologists concentrate on factors that contribute to student difficulties such as adjusting to school, academic achievement, mental health, substance abuse, social relationships, and life stress. But by far the single biggest issue that school psychologists address is students with special needs such as physical, emotional, and learning disabilities. School psychologists are involved in the assessment of these students and the coordination of special education programs designed to assist them. Although their primary focus is the needs of children who are experiencing these problems, school psychologists often consult with teachers and administrators about issues relevant to these students such as managing classroom behavior and structuring school environments.

The Work

Core Activities

Educational and school psychologists engage in activities consistent with their positions and responsibilities. Typically these activities are defined by the nature of the position and the setting in which the work is done. But much of this work falls into one of five categories: research, intervention, assessment, program evaluation, and consultation. To provide a glimpse into the diversity of career opportunities available, Box 11.1 provides a summary of several recent job advertisements in the educational and school psychology subfields.

Research. The subfields of educational and school psychology are engaged in conducting research and applying the findings of this research to real-world settings. In general, educational psychologists tend to pursue research careers, and school psychologists tend to pursue applied careers. Because educational psychologists are experts in teaching and learning processes, their research focuses on the design and evaluation of educational programs. They often evaluate methods of instruction and learning, develop new instructional techniques, and influence theories and approaches to the learning process. School psychologists are experts in assessment and intervention for individual students experiencing difficulties in educational settings. Given this, their research concentrates on creating new techniques of assessment, evaluating the effectiveness of interventions, and investigating the nature of student difficulties. For educational and school psychologists engaged in research, the dissemination of this information through publications is essential to having new information influence future research and educational practices. Box 11.2 lists several journals that publish research in these subfields.

Assessment and interventions. Educational and school psychologists place great value on the careful assessment and evaluation of situations before intervening. School psychologists are more likely to conduct assessments at the individual level by working with a student to evaluate the nature of her or his current academic, social, emotional, and/or physical difficulties. Given their focus on students with special needs, school psychologists spend a large portion of their time conducting assessments to determine what, if any, special services are needed in order for a child to succeed in a school setting. This includes assessing intellectual abilities, aptitudes for learning, achievement, social and emotional functioning, and mental health status.

Box 11.1 *Recent Openings in the Educational and School Psychology Subfields*

Position: **School Psychologist**
Setting: Springfield Public Schools, Oregon
Responsibilities: Conduct comprehensive educational, psychological, and functional behavioral evaluations; know and help implement research-based curricula, instructional practices, and behavioral supports; facilitate instructional team meetings; practice cultural competency and respect diversity; and work effectively with students, staff, and parents.

Position: **Assistant Professor, Educational Psychology**
Setting: University of New Mexico – Department of Individual, Family, and Community Education
Responsibilities: Collaborate with educational psychology faculty; teach graduate courses in educational psychology, especially in advanced educational statistics and research methods; conduct research; advise graduate students; and provide support to students and faculty in the use and application of statistical and research methods.

Position: **Assistant Professor, School Psychology**
Setting: University of Iowa – Department of Psychological and Quantitative Foundations
Responsibilities: Collaborate with school and counseling psychology faculty; teach graduate courses and supervise practicum placements related to the topics of academic and/or social adjustment, problems in school settings, and special education eligibility and management; and direct aspects of program operations.

Position: **Director of Assessment and Faculty Development**
Setting: Rowan University Cooper Medical School, New Jersey
Responsibilities: Develop and maintain the systematic plan of evaluation and assessment for the medication education program; develop and implement plans for faculty development; organize medical education research activities; supervise the creation, collection, maintenance, and analysis of data relevant to educational outcomes and accreditation report writing; and oversee responsibilities related to assessment and curriculum matters.

> **Box 11.2** *Journals that Publish Educational and School Psychology Research*
>
> Educational Psychology
>
> - *Educational Psychologist*
> - *Journal of the Learning Sciences*
> - *Learning and Individual Differences*
> - *Review of Educational Research*
> - *Journal of Educational Psychology*
> - *Learning and Instruction*
>
> School Psychology
>
> - *Journal of School Psychology*
> - *School Psychology Review*
> - *School Psychology Quarterly*
> - *School Psychology International*
> - *Journal of Psychoeducational Assessment*

Because school psychologists so frequently engage in applied work, they are more likely than educational psychologists to provide direct interventions in educational settings. These interventions include such activities as providing counseling to students struggling with academic, social, emotional, and family problems. Typically these problems come to the attention of school psychologists because they interfere with the student's academic performance. Other interventions include creating behavioral management plans that teachers and parents can use to help a student decrease problematic behaviors and increase desired behaviors. Interventions that occur on a larger scale include workshops and courses provided to groups of students on topics such as social skills, anger management, study habits, and coping. Some school psychologists also play a key role in the event of a crisis in the school, community, or life of a student. They guide administrators, teachers, and parents on how to best assist students in understanding and coping with such events.

Program evaluation.　Given their focus on teaching and learning processes, educational psychologists are more likely to conduct evaluations at a program level. These evaluations consist of investigating the nature of instructional and learning programs and determining their effectiveness. The results can be used to identify and implement appropriate strategies to improve educational processes. School psychologists engage in program evaluations as well, but typically only in situations where gathering information about an academic program or environment will help serve individual students. This might include evaluating the effectiveness of a special education or behavior management program in terms of its ability to address the particular needs of a student.

Consultation. Educational psychologists often serve in the role of consult-ants given their broad expertise in instructional and learning methods. Schools, businesses with education and training centers, and companies that develop educational materials, frequently seek consultation regarding their practices and products. The educational psychologist's role is to help the organization understand what is and is not effective in the design and delivery of instructional information and in the learning process. For school psychologists, consultation often comes in the form of collaborating with other professionals regarding the well-being of a student. They consult with teachers, administrators, parents, physicians, and mental health providers about the nature of a child's difficulties and the recommended interventions. Their goal is to find effective solutions to learning and behavior problems by gathering as much information as possible and strengthening working rela-tionships between important figures in the child's life. School psychologists also consult with educational staff to address and prevent student difficulties. Prevention efforts often involve implementing programs to address bullying, acceptance of diversity, substance abuse, and peer relationships.

Settings

Educational and school psychologists are employed in a variety of settings. Data on employment settings for new school and educational psychologists are presented in Table 11.1 (APA, 2011). Note that these data do not include the large numbers of school psychologists who earn the specialist's degree (discussed later); however previous research (Curtis, Grier, Abshier, Sutton, & Hunley, 2002) indicated that the employment settings of all school psychologists are comparable.

Salaries

In reporting data on the salaries of school psychologists, the US Department of Labor (2014) groups this career in with clinical and counseling psycholo-gists. These data indicate that 80% of these psychologists earned an estimated annual salary between \$39,020 and \$112,380, with the median income being \$67,760. Several factors contribute to the variations in salary, including the type of school (e.g., public vs. private, rural vs. urban) and its funding source (e.g., strong vs. weak tax base). A school psychologist's level of education and years of experience, as well as the level of administrative responsibilities in their position, also help determine salary. Valid salary information for educational psychologists alone is difficult to obtain, but given the settings in which they typically work, the median salary of

Table 11.1 Employment Settings for Educational and School Psychologists

	Educational Psychologists	School Psychologists
Academic settings	66.7%	23.2%
Schools and other educational settings	30.6%	60.7%
Independent practice	2.8%	1.8%
Direct/human services (hospitals, clinics)	0%	3.6%
Government and business	0%	8.9%

non-clinical, -counseling, -school, and -I/O psychologists provides an estimate at $91,140 (US Department of Labor, 2014). The APA salary survey indicates that the mean salary of psychologists in academic positions in departments of education is approximately $83,285 (Finno, Michalski, Hart, Wicherski, & Kohout, 2010).

Employment Issues

Educational psychologists engage in work that often requires funding to support the evaluation and development of new programs and instructional techniques. As funding sources rise and fall with changes in the economy and mission of funding agencies, educational psychologists may find that the feasibility of their work also changes. Those who work in school settings or provide direct services may face the additional pressure of needing to select and implement educational procedures that produce positive results. An additional issue that has shaped the careers of educational psychologists in recent years has been the enormous influence of technology on instructional and learning methods. The ways in which teachers and students present, consume, and generate information has changed radically with the advancement of computer technology, the internet, and digital media. Most educational psychologists have welcomed this exciting shift in educational research and theory given its potential to transform instructional and learning processes.

Because school psychologists' activities are determined by current legislation and requirements placed on schools, their positions are often tied to funding for these services. Some school systems and districts look to save money by expanding the caseloads of school psychologists. Although some schools may have one or more school psychologists dedicated to serving their students, often these positions are shared across several schools in a district. Less populated areas may be limited to a single school psychologist across an entire county. These high caseloads and shifting environments can at times contribute to a sense of isolation from fellow professionals. Despite efforts to spread their responsibilities, many schools and districts are in dire need of psychologists to provide services to students. In fact, a shortage of school psychologists has existed for some time and is expected to continue into the near future (Curtis, Hunley, & Grier, 2004). This shortage has come at a time when student populations have been changing dramatically in terms of demographic variables such as race, ethnicity, and socioeconomic status. The difficulties of responding to these changes have been further exacerbated by a lack of diversity among school psychologists, who in recent years have been predominantly Caucasian and female (Curtis, Grier, & Hunley, 2004).

Training and Preparation

Degree Options, Certification, and Licensure

The path to becoming an educational psychologist is fairly straightforward in that a doctoral degree is required. In contrast, school psychologists can hold degrees at the master's, specialist, or doctoral levels. Because most careers in psychology require a specific degree, the presence of these options is often a source of confusion for students. In particular, many have never been exposed to the specialist level degree. It represents an intermediate level of training that falls between the master's and doctoral levels.

Because the APA has always asserted that the doctoral degree must be earned for entry into any type of professional practice in the field, it only gives accreditation to school psychology programs offering a doctoral degree. The APA does not provide training standards or evaluate programs at the master's or specialist level. However, the National Association of School Psychologists (NASP) provides scenarios for entry into school psychology with either a doctoral or a specialist level degree. As a result, NASP accredits programs that grant both levels of degrees, but it does not accredit school psychology programs that only grant a master's degree.

To work in public school settings, school psychologists do not need to be licensed as a psychologist but must instead be certified by the states in which they work. Most states now only provide certification to school psychologists who have already earned national certification. National certification as a school psychologist is granted by the NASP and requires a minimum of the specialist level degree along with successful completion of the Praxis School Psychology Exam. This creates a situation in which working as a school psychologist in most states requires at least a specialist level degree.

As a result, students pursuing training in school psychology are increasingly viewing the specialist degree as the shortest path to their careers. Equal numbers of school psychologists are seeking specialist and doctoral level degrees, with a strong trend in recent years toward increased numbers seeking the specialist level degree (Curtis et al., 2002). As a result, some expect the number of school psychologists with a doctoral degree to continue to decline (Curtis, Hunley, et al., 2004).

As discussed in Chapters 9 and 10, careers that involve the applied practice of psychology in working with the public typically require a license. For this reason, any educational or school psychologist who seeks to establish a private practice or provide services to the general public that are psychological in nature must be licensed. Because most states only allow those individuals with a doctorate to be fully licensed as psychologists, the work of school psychologists who only completed training at the specialist level is typically restricted to the school setting. However, some states have created licenses for school psychologists that require a specialist level degree. Although educational and school psychologists can theoretically offer in private practice many of the same services they provide in educational settings, state laws prohibit such work unless the practitioner is licensed. As a result, few educational and school psychologists operate independent practices, and these numbers may shrink as more school psychologists choose the specialist degree option.

Variations in Graduate Programs

Doctoral programs in educational psychology and school psychology vary in their focus and the nature of training they offer. Therefore, they produce graduates with distinct areas of expertise. Programs in educational psychology even differ in their titles, using names such as learning and motivation, instructional psychology and technology, and evaluation and measurement. Doctoral programs in school psychology tend to adhere to either a scientist–practitioner or an applied professional training model (Jackson, 1997). These two approaches to training are similar to the training models in clinical psychology and counseling psychology programs. The scientist–practitioner programs emphasize a traditional, broad-based training with strong empirical/statistical components. The applied professional programs emphasize training in applied endeavors. In fact, school psychology still shares much in common with the clinical and counseling psychology subfields as all three are viewed as general practice specialties that often result in careers as health service providers. This means that these psychologists are trained specifically in applied techniques and interventions, often with enough breadth to allow them to work with a variety of different populations on a variety of different issues. The curricula and training standards across these three subfields are more similar than different (Cobb et al., 2004).

Training at the specialist level in school psychology presents additional types of variations in graduate programs. Many programs require a combined master's and specialist degree. Students typically must successfully complete the master's program before being admitted to the specialist program. Other graduate programs in school psychology offer the specialist degree by itself. Both program types are often similar in their overall requirements of coursework and practicum/internship experience. The combined master's and specialist programs sometimes require more coursework, practicum, or research experience.

Earning the Degree

As with most graduate degrees, doctoral and specialist degrees in the subfields of educational and school psychology involve various components of training. Formal coursework is a foundation of all programs. In addition, most doctoral programs in educational psychology, and some of those in school psychology, place emphasis on training in both research (e.g., methods, experimentation, statistical analysis) and applied intervention (e.g., assessment, evaluation, counseling). Other doctoral and specialist programs in school psychology will place most of the emphasis on applied endeavors. Advancing in all of these programs will result in less coursework and greater supervised experience and independent study. Students in programs with a heavier research emphasis can expect to spend time conducting research as well as gaining applied experience. Students in programs that emphasize applied training will spend much of their time outside of class engaged in closely supervised intervention activities in educational and school settings.

Preparing for Graduate Training as an Undergraduate

As an undergraduate student considering the possibility of pursuing graduate training in the educational or school psychology subfields, it is important to keep in mind that there are things you can and should be doing now to prepare. In particular, the coursework and activities you engage in now can affect graduate programs' interest in you in the future.

Coursework.   Given the variations we have discussed within programs in the educational and school psychology subfields, it is difficult to establish absolute recommendations for undergraduate coursework that will best prepare you for graduate level training. However, there are core courses in most undergraduate psychology curricula that are vital for students aspiring to enter educational and school psychology graduate programs. These courses, as well as relevant course areas outside of psychology, are listed in Box 11.3. Notice that although courses in development, research, and education are important, students also benefit from a solid background in psychological testing and diversity.

Activities. The nature of the career you desire should shape the graduate programs to which you apply. In turn, the nature of these programs should shape the types of activities you engage in to prepare yourself for this training and establish yourself as a worthy applicant. Programs with greater emphasis on research skills and training (e.g., doctoral programs in educational psychology, scientist–practitioner doctoral programs in school psychology) will value applicants who have strong research skills and experiences as undergraduates. Although research experience will not be a disadvantage for students applying to the more applied programs, these programs may also value direct experience with student populations in educational settings. Direct experience working with an educational or school psychologist can be difficult to come by, but general experience in school systems working with student populations is also helpful.

Box 11.3 *Recommended Undergraduate Coursework for Educational and School Psychology*

Course Areas Within Psychology	*Course Areas Outside of Psychology*
Developmental psychology	Statistics
Child/adolescent psychology	Education (instruction and
Family psychology	curriculum)
Research methods	Special education
Experimental psychology	
Principles of psychological testing	
Cross-cultural psychology	
Ethnic minority psychology	
Ethics	
Learning and behavior	

Working in Areas Related to Educational and School Psychology with a Bachelor's Degree

As discussed in earlier chapters, the bachelor's degree in psychology can be thought of as a liberal arts or preprofessional degree. It does not automatically qualify you to enter a particular career field, nor does it provide you with a defined set of skills that employers easily recognize. Instead, your ability to secure employment in an area related to educational or school psychology with only a bachelor's degree will in large part depend upon you gaining relevant experience as an undergraduate, identifying positions for which you qualify, and effectively conveying your knowledge and skills to potential employers. There are several career and employment opportunities that tap aspects of educational and school psychology. Many of these bachelor's level careers allow for working directly with students and instructors. The most common options include teaching and human services positions.

Human/Social Service Specialists

The careers of human/social service specialists are as varied as their job titles. Whether working in the capacity of a case manager, patient representative, or consultant, these individuals often serve as a liaison between their clients and an agency that can provide services to them. These positions typically exist in state and county governments as well as nonprofit organizations. Although the responsibilities vary greatly, many human/social service specialists deal directly with children, and often this includes emphasis on their education and access to educational resources. Other human/social service specialists work to ensure that the agencies and institutions that provide services to these individuals do so in accordance with laws and regulations. According to the US Department of Labor (2014), the median salary estimate was $29,230 for human service assistants and $40,050 for community and social service specialists.

Teachers

Psychology students who find the educational and school psychology subfields of interest but who will seek employment with a bachelor's degree might want to consider teaching. Teachers have the opportunity to work closely with students, parents, and other school staff to support the education and overall well-being of the students. Although teachers may not conduct research or articulate theory on educational processes, they are on the front lines of putting such research and theory into practice. Teachers who are well versed in educational research and its implications are involved daily in working to improve the learning of their students and the materials and techniques used to accomplish this goal. And although teachers do not provide counseling, intervention, or assessment services directly to students and families, they often play a vital role in the success of these services. In other words, the work of educational and school psychologists often depends heavily on the support and applied skills of teachers. Teaching positions thus provide an opportunity to be involved in this work and interact with students. Keep in mind that even though undergraduate psychology programs do not prepare students to earn a teaching certification, many school districts allow individuals to teach while they work to earn their certification. Most states maintain some version of this process known as an alternate or nontraditional route to earning teaching credentials. According to the US Department of Labor (2014), the median salary estimate was $53,590 for elementary school teachers.

An Insider's Perspective

The Science of People: A Career in School Psychology

William Pfohl, PsyD, NCSP
Western Kentucky University

Most who enter an applied area of psychology (e.g., school psychology, clinical psychology, industrial–organizational psychology) want to *make a difference*. They want a hands-on career with "real people" in real settings. School psychology is that profession. Making a difference is done in direct and indirect services. Working with a teacher who is having classroom discipline problems, working with a parent to help him or her understand the impact of autism on education and family, or developing a school safety program to prevent bullying are all within the activities and daily practice of a school psychologist.

School psychologists work in school settings with a wide range of ages, potentially birth to 22 years of age. They work with children, parents, administrators, educators, and outside agencies, all in an effort to address students' academic and emotional needs.

They help enhance students' learning environments, emotional well-being, and capacity to cope with life events. School psychologists' careers are varied, never boring. Many provide assessment and treatment of those with disabilities and handicapping conditions. Others counsel parents and students about personal and emotional issues. Others consult by providing an array of academic and mental health services or helping to prevent the emergence of problems. Others write grants and conduct program evaluations; many are currently emphasizing school safety issues and the prevention of school violence. Others train future school psychologists in university graduate programs.

I started college as a biochemistry major due to my love of science in high school. Quickly I discovered my passion was people, not labs and studying plants or animals. After visiting with a career counselor, I selected psychology as my major. I have never regretted it – studying the Science of People. School psychology as a career was nurtured by one of my professors since I had never heard of "school psychology." After completing my graduate training, I joined a statewide school psychology organization. An experienced school psychologist took me under her wing and introduced me to the world of professional school psychology organizations. While I worked as a practitioner in public schools, I became the newsletter editor and then president of the group. I re-entered graduate school 6 years later for my doctorate and then became a trainer of future school psychologists in a university setting. I still find the occupation rewarding and interesting to this day. Although you may go to work each day at the same site, the days are varied, fast paced, and at times stressful. The job is typically not routine. I have also maintained my professional leadership involvement in professional organizations including twice being elected as president of the National Association of School Psychologists. I also served as President of the International School Psychology Association. These positions allow me to make a difference for children *and* the profession in practice, policy, and training.

A career that makes a difference is what school psychology is, and I have the opportunity to apply daily what I know about the "Science of People."

Note: Dr. William Pfohl is a school psychologist and a professor of psychology at Western Kentucky University, where he previously served as coordinator of the school psychology program. Dr. Pfohl has twice served as president of the National Association of School Psychologists and is a former president of the International School Psychologists Association. In addition to teaching courses on assessment, psychopathology, and child behavior, Dr. Pfohl maintains a private practice specializing in child and family issues.

Professional Spotlight

Rebecca S. Martínez, PhD, NCSP

Education:

- Bachelor of Science (BS) in Psychology from the University of Florida, Gainesville (1993)
- Master of Science (MS) in Program Evaluation from the University of Texas at Austin (2001)
- Doctor of Philosophy (PhD) in Educational Psychology from the University of Texas at Austin (2002)

Position:

Associate Professor and Director of the Academic Well-Check Program (http://portal.education.indiana.edu/awcp/AWCP.aspx), Department of Counseling and Educational Psychology, School Psychology Program, Indiana University

Description of Position:

My job duties primarily focus on research but also emphasize excellence in teaching and service.

Most Significant Professional Accomplishment:

I received the Bloomington Chamber of Commerce *2008 Leading Light Award* at the Seventh Annual Franklin Initiative's Monroe County Educators of the Year Award Ceremony for my work in developing the Academic Well-Check Program (AWCP).

Favorite Publication:

Martinez, R. S. (2014). Best practices in instructional strategies for reading in general education. In A. Thomas & Harrison, P. (Eds.). *Best practices in school psychology* (6th ed.). Bethesda, MD: National Association of School Psychologists.

Areas of Research:

I investigate prevention and early intervention of reading and math difficulties, Response-to-Intervention (RTI), and ways to create school-wide supports for English language learners and students struggling academically.

Professional Memberships:

- National Association of School Psychologists (NASP)
- Indiana Association of School Psychologists (IASP)
- Council of Directors of School Psychology Programs (CDSPP)

Most Rewarding Aspect of Your Career:

The most rewarding aspect of my career is having a widespread positive influence on children's school experiences because I have the opportunity to teach and train future school psychologists who will directly impact thousands of children, teachers, and parents.

> **Words of Advice to the Student Who is Interested in Your Subfield:**
> First, learn all you can about school psychology by visiting the National Association of School Psychologists' website (www.nasponline.org). Next, find a local school psychologist and contact him or her about your interest in the field. Ask if you can shadow him or her for a day to see if school psychology is for you. Then, do well in your undergraduate courses so you will be competitive when you apply to school psychology graduate programs. Finally, if you decide to go into school psychology, know that you are embarking on a wonderfully challenging yet equally rewarding career path!

Suggested Exercises

1. Investigate graduate programs in either educational or school psychology. Once you find a program that fits your interests, identify a faculty member whose work appeals to you. Read a recent publication by this faculty member and generate questions about this work. Consider contacting this individual with your questions after having a trusted faculty member in your undergraduate program provide guidance and feedback on how best to initiate this conversation.

2. Contact a school psychologist within a school or school district that you previously attended as a student. Inquire about the possibility of interviewing him or her, either in person, by phone, or by email, to gain a better understanding of the nature of their work and their career choice. Interviewing a school psychologist in a setting that is familiar to you will allow your questions and their responses to be more meaningful as you seek to learn about the career.

3. Think of an aspect of your learning or functioning in a school setting that has been a source of difficulty (e.g., reading comprehension, social relationships, stress management, study habits). Conduct a literature search to find articles in education and school psychology journals that address this topic. As you read these articles, think both about how the authors are working with this subject as part of their careers and how their findings might be of benefit to you in your educational pursuits.

Suggested Readings by Topic Area

School Psychology

Merrell, K. W., Ervin, R. A., & Peacock, G. G. (2012). *School psychology for the 21st century: Foundations and practices* (2nd ed.). New York, NY: Guilford Press.

Gutkin, T. B., & Reynolds, C. R. (Eds.). (2009). *The handbook of school psychology* (4th ed.). Hoboken, NJ: Wiley.

Educational Psychology

O'Donnell, A. M., Reeve, J., & Smith, J. K. (2012). *Educational psychology: Reflection for action* (3rd ed.). Hoboken, NJ: Wiley.

Slavin, R. E. (2011). *Educational psychology: Theory and practice* (10th ed.). Boston, MA: Allyn and Bacon.

Resources

- Educational Psychology – Division 15 of APA
  - apadiv15.org
- School Psychology – Division 16 of APA
  - http://www.apadivisions.org/division-16
- National Association of School Psychologists
  - www.nasponline.org

References

American Psychological Association. (2011). *2009 doctorate employment survey*. Washington, DC: Author. Retrieved from http://www.apa.org/workforce/publications/09-doc-empl/index.aspx

American Psychological Association. (2014). *Graduate study in psychology 2014*. Washington, DC: Author.

Cobb, H. C., Reeve, R. E., Shealy, C. N., Norcross, J. C., Schare, M. L., Rodolfa, E. R.,... Allen, M. (2004). Overlap among clinical, counseling, and school psychology: Implications for the profession and combined-integrated training. *Journal of Clinical Psychology, 60*, 939–955. doi:10.1002/jclp.20028

Curtis, M. J., Grier, J. E. C., Abshier, D. W., Sutton, N. T., & Hunley, S. A. (2002). School psychology: Turning the corner into the twenty-first century. *Communiqué, 30*(8), 1–5.

Curtis, M. J., Grier, J. E. C., & Hunley, S. A. (2004). The changing face of school psychology: Trends in data and projections for the future. *School Psychology Review, 33*, 49–66.

Curtis, M. J., Hunley, S. A., & Grier, J. E. C. (2004). The status of school psychology: Implications of a major personnel shortage. *Psychology in the Schools, 41*, 431–442.

Fagan, T. K., & Wise, P. S. (2000). *School psychology: Past, present, and future*. Bethesda, MD: National Association of School Psychologists.

Finno, A. A., Michalski, D., Hart, B., Wicherski, M., & Kohout, J. L. (2010). *Salaries in psychology 2009: Report of the 2009 APA Salary Survey*. Washington, DC: American Psychological Association. Retrieved from http://www.apa.org/workforce/publications/09-salaries/index.aspx

Graves, S. L., Jr., & Wright, L. B. (2007). Comparison of individual factors in school psychology graduate students: Why do students pursue a degree in school psychology? *Psychology in the Schools, 44*, 865–872.

Jackson, K. A. (1997). School psychology. *Eye on Psi Chi, 1*, 26–27, 30.

Reschly, D. J. (2000). The present and future status of school psychology in the United States. *School Psychology Review, 29*, 507–522.

US Department of Labor. (2014). *May 2013 national occupational employment and wage estimates*. Retrieved from http://www.bls.gov/oes/2013/may/oes_nat.htm

Chapter Twelve
Careers in Exercise and Sport Psychology

Exercise and Sport Psychology Defined

Division 47 of the American Psychological Association (APA) is devoted to exercise and sport psychology (2014a; http://www.apadivisions.org/division-47). Division 47 (2014b) defines exercise and sport psychology as "the scientific study of the psychological factors that are associated with participation and performance in sport, exercise, and other types of physical activity" (http://www.apadivisions.org/division-47/about/resources/what-is.aspx). According to Division 47 (2014b), two broad themes run through the subfield of exercise and sport psychology. The first includes the use of psychological principles to help athletes "achieve optimal mental health and…improve performance (performance enhancement)" (http://www.apadivisions.org/division-47/about/resources/what-is.aspx). The second theme focuses on "understanding how participation in sport, exercise, and physical activity affects an individual's psychological development, health, and well-being throughout the life span" (http://www.apadivisions.org/division-47/about/resources/what-is.aspx). It is important to note here that the field of exercise and sport psychology is not exclusively applied to athletes. Rather, the field makes significant contributions to understanding and helping all individuals that engage in any form of physical activity.

Another major organization contributing to and helping define the field is the Association for Applied Sport Psychology (AASP; www.appliedsportpsych.org). In describing exercise and sport psychology, AASP (2013a) divides the

Majoring in Psychology: Achieving Your Educational and Career Goals, Second Edition.
Jeffrey L. Helms and Daniel T. Rogers.
© 2015 John Wiley & Sons, Ltd. Published 2015 by John Wiley & Sons, Ltd.

subfield into three interrelated areas: social psychology, performance enhancement/intervention, and health and exercise psychology.

- The *social psychology area* "focuses on individual and group processes in sport and exercise settings. This area applies social psychological principles in examining factors related to the sport participant, coach, team, and spectator" (http://www.appliedsportpsych.org/about).
- The *performance enhancement/intervention area* "focuses on research, theory, and practice intended to improve performance in exercise and sport. This area is also concerned with the effects of sport psychology interventions on the well-being of participants in exercise and sport" (http://www.appliedsportpsych.org/about).
- Whether it be in the professional, amateur, or leisure arena, the *health and exercise psychology area* "focuses on the application of psychological principles to the promotion and maintenance of health-enhancing behaviors over the lifespan, including play, leisure physical activity and structured exercise, and the psychological and emotional consequences of those behaviors. Researchers in this area also investigate the role of exercise in disease remediation, injury rehabilitation, and stress reduction" (http://www.appliedsportpsych.org/about).

The Work

Core Activities

As you can probably guess from the descriptions from Division 47 and the AASP, professionals in the exercise and sport psychology subfield contribute to psychology in a number of ways. These contributions can be categorized into the following three broad areas: research, practice, and teaching/training.

Research. Developing and testing new ideas is the foundation upon which exercise and sport psychology rests. It is not an overstatement to say that this subfield is founded on and grows as the result of rigorous empirical research. Given that these new developments successfully undergo review by peers in the field, the research findings can be published so that others in the field may benefit. The primary method of disseminating information on new developments in the subfield is through publication in scholarly, peer-reviewed journals. The growth in the subfield, as well as its interconnections with other disciplines outside of psychology, can be seen via some of the major publications in the field. Box 12.1 provides a list of some of the major

Box 12.1 *Journals that Publish Exercise and Sport Psychology Research*

- *Adapted Physical Activity Quarterly*
- *Health Psychology*
- *Human Movement Science*
- *International Journal of Sport and Exercise Psychology*
- *Journal of Aging and Physical Activity*
- *Journal of Applied Biomechanics*
- *Journal of Applied Sport Psychology*
- *Journal of Clinical Sport Psychology*
- *Journal of Experimental Psychology: Human Perception and Performance*
- *Journal of Sport and Exercise Psychology*
- *Motor Control*
- *Research Quarterly for Exercise and Sport*
- *The Sport Journal*
- *The Sport Psychologist*

publications in the area. Note that the titles do not always use the term *psychology*. For example, some of the journals use terms like *physical activity*, *biomechanics, movement science*, and *health science*. We will say more about terminology later in the chapter.

As can be seen in Box 12.1, the range of publication outlets is broad. However, research topic areas covered by the various journals may not be as readily apparent. As an illustration and to give you an idea of the research areas studied by exercise and sport psychology professionals, here are some topics recently covered by articles published in the journals listed in Box 12.1:

- gay, lesbian, bisexual, and transgender issues in sport;
- adapting exercise and physical activity for those persons with disabilities;
- psychological issues associated with officiating/refereeing;
- alcohol and drug use among student athletes;
- coping with competitive pressure and sport performance anxiety;
- disordered eating in dance professionals;
- gambling by student and professional athletes;
- working with athletes who dope;
- coaching and motivational behavior; and
- maintaining an exercise program.

For exercise and sport psychologists focused on research as their primary pursuit and those employed in an academic environment, activities will be similar to those discussed in Chapter 16 (i.e., teaching, research, and professional service). Interestingly, many exercise and sport psychologists often consult with their home universities' athletic and exercise programs, even when their positions are not housed in the athletic departments. In other words, the university's sports teams and exercise programs make good use of these professionals' expertise regardless of where they may happen to be on campus. Of course, those that consult with their schools' programs possess the education, training, and licensure necessary to provide those services (even when the services are provided for no charge). Training and preparation requirements necessary to do that type of work are covered later in the chapter.

Practice. The second domain in which exercise and sport psychology professionals contribute is the practice arena (i.e., provision of psychological services to individuals, groups, and organizations). In their original recognition of sport psychology as a proficiency area in 2003, APA (2014) identified populations and groups that would be served by sport psychologists. According to the proficiency designation, those served by the profession include:

- "Youth/junior sport participants and organizations
- High school athletes and athletic departments
- Intercollegiate athletes and athletic departments
- Professional athletes, teams, and leagues
- Masters/seniors sport participants and organizations
- Injured athletes
- Elite athletes and sports organizations (e.g., Olympic athletes and National Governing Bodies)
- Recreational athletes
- Athletes with permanent disabilities
- People who are involved with, but not directly participating in, sports (families, coaches, administrators, officials)." (APA; http://www.apadivisions. org/division-47/about/sport-proficiency/index.aspx)

As can be seen from this long list of beneficiaries, the populations served are quite extensive and are not limited to professional athletes.

The types of services provided by exercise and sport psychology practitioners, along with an example of each service, include:

- assessment: e.g., evaluating athletes for healthy coping strategies; assessing a potential player's emotional stability relative to the level of performance required (moving from the amateur to the professional level);

- treatment: e.g., treating children involved in dance/ballet for eating disorders; treating performance anxiety;
- consultation with teams and coaches: e.g., consulting with a coach on effective strategies for dealing with a problem player or the loss of a player due to a team trade;
- research (even for practitioners): e.g., evaluating the effectiveness of a stress reduction program for gymnasts;
- program development: e.g., developing an appropriate exercise program for individuals over the age of 65 who attend a senior community center; developing a program to address inappropriate parental involvement at children's sporting events; and
- policy development, analysis, and implementation: e.g., assisting high school athletic associations in developing policies on student–athlete gambling and doping.

Teaching and training. As is the case with all areas of psychology, one of the main areas in which exercise and sport psychologists contribute to the discipline is through teaching and training. A significant proportion of those who identify themselves as exercise and sport psychologists hold academic positions at colleges and universities. Additionally, exercise and sport psychologists often provide psychoeducation as part of their practices. This type of teaching/education is geared specifically toward impacting the psychological functioning of the audience (e.g., educating a group of people on ways to incorporate exercise into their daily lives).

Employment Settings and Salary Expectations

Employment settings for exercise and sport psychology professionals consist of academic positions at colleges/universities in psychology, exercise science, movement science, sport science, and kinesiology departments. However, McCullagh, Noble, and Portenga (2013) point out that academic positions for these individuals are predominantly in kinesiology departments. As a result, future opportunities within psychology departments (as opposed to opportunities in kinesiology departments) may be more limited. Regardless, providing services to the public (outside of academe) is still relegated to doctoral-level licensed psychologists and not the kinesiology-trained/ research-oriented professionals who are almost exclusively situated in the research environment.

As you might have guessed, another employment setting is within the private clinical and/or consulting practice area. In this setting, licensed psychologists provide a variety of applied services to a wide range of individuals. However, only a portion of their work is in the exercise and sport psychology domain. Practices fully devoted to exercise and sport psychology are extremely rare.

Private practice (where a portion of the work is related to exercise and sport psychology) and the academic setting are the most common employment settings. Other settings like working for the United States Olympic Committee and in sport rehabilitation facilities encompass very few positions. In fact, sport rehabilitation facilities will often refer clients/patients out for psychological services. Highlighting the rarity of positions in these particular settings is not meant to be discouraging but rather informative. Limited positions in these settings are another reason to make sure your training is broad. AASP and the North American Society for the Psychology of Sport and Physical Activity (NASPSPA) have listings of some of the current job openings in the field. AASP's listing may be found at http://www.appliedsportpsych.org/resource-center/employment-opportunities. NASPSPA's listings may be found at http://www.naspspa.org/employment-postings/employment-postings.

In terms of salary, income varies by work setting, reputation, and experience. Salaries for academic positions will be consistent with those noted in Chapter 16, and salaries for practitioners will be consistent with those noted in Chapter 10.

Training and Preparation

Earning a Degree

For research and applied positions, a doctorate is typically the entry-level degree. Given what you have read so far, this fact probably is not a surprise given that, by its very nature, exercise and sport psychology is an interdisciplinary field requiring significant depth and breadth of knowledge. As a result of its interdisciplinary nature, training may take place in sport science departments, kinesiology departments, health science departments, and psychology departments to name a few. Regardless of where your training takes place, Van Raalte and Williams (1994) recommend that you seek additional training and coursework in the areas not represented in your home department. Furthermore, given the increasing interest in the field, competition may squeeze out master's level practitioners in favor of doctoral level individuals. This becomes truer as states/jurisdictions move toward requiring licensure at the doctoral level in order to practice in the area.

Another issue that you will want to keep in mind when pursuing training in this area is the actual path of your training. Two distinct academic training paths prepare students for work in the broad subfield of exercise and sport psychology (McCullagh et al., 2013). These two paths are psychology and kinesiology (i.e., the study of movement, broadly defined). Choosing the kinesiology path will open additional opportunities in the research area (e.g., physiological and rehabilitation issues) but will close the doors associated with being a licensed psychologist (e.g., independent practice outside of an academic setting). Choosing the psychology path will open the doors associated with being able to practice more broadly because of the necessary licensure at the doctoral level. The broad training will allow the psychologist who has training in the mental health areas (as compared to the kinesiologist) to work with individuals, including athletes who have complicating mental health problems (e.g., anxiety, depression, eating disorders). The additional skills that come from being trained via the psychology path will benefit you too in terms of employment opportunities because you will not be limited to working with athletes only or to working in an academic/ research setting. Regardless of the path chosen, each has benefits and limitations. As a result, an understanding of *how* you want to work in the area will assist you greatly in the decision of which path to pursue.

In addition to the insight you gained via the self-assessment in Chapter 4, understanding the training and qualifications that the typical exercise and sport psychologist brings to the table will also help in your selection of which path best fits you and your goals. AASP (2013b) specifies the training needed to be eligible for their certification. Certification through AASP is the standard in the field. In addition to a doctoral degree in an exercise and sport psychology area, coursework and supervised practice must also be completed. The required coursework for AASP certification includes:

- "Three sport and exercise psychology courses (two at the graduate level);
- One course from each of the following categories:
  - professional ethics and standards,
  - biomechanical and/or physiological bases of sport,
  - historical, philosophical, social, or motor behavior bases,
  - psychopathology and its assessment,
  - counseling skills (a graduate course),
  - research design, statistics, or psychological assessment,
  - biological bases of behavior,
  - cognitive-affective bases of behavior, and
  - individual behavior; and
- Demonstrated competence within skills/techniques/analysis in sport or exercise and related experiences (e.g., coaching, clinics, participation in sport)." (http://www.appliedsportpsych.org/consultants/become-certified)

To a large extent and not surprisingly, the required graduate-level coursework parallels the coursework required of clinical psychology, school psychology, and counseling psychology doctoral programs that are APA-accredited. See the chapters devoted to these subfields for more information and associated accreditation issues.

Importantly, completion of certain coursework is not the only requirement. Supervised experience is also mandatory. The supervised experience required for certification by AASP (2013b) includes:

- "400 total hours of mentored experience in sport and exercise psychology;
- 100 of the total hours must be in direct contact with clients;
- 40 of the total hours must be mentorship received from an AASP-approved mentor; in addition, all of the 400 total hours must be verified by this mentor; and
- Only those hours actually spent in the preparation and delivery of sport and exercise psychology services are eligible for inclusion." (http://www.appliedsportpsych.org/consultants/become-certified)

Although master's level applicants are allowed to pursue certification by AASP, the requirements are more extensive for obvious reasons. Additionally, individuals with doctorates in kinesiology likely will take significantly longer to get certified because of the lack of background in psychology in their degree programs. In other words, those individuals would likely have to spend significant additional time in order simply to meet the extensive (yet minimal by psychology's standards) coursework requirements.

Licensure Issues

In terms of state licensure, it is not typically required for researchers, educators, and policy specialists. However, those who practice (i.e., provide treatment, assessment, and diagnosis) do require licensure by the respective state board of psychology. Please see Chapter 10 for discussion of the licensure process. In short, you will want to seek an APA-accredited doctoral program in clinical, school, or counseling psychology that emphasizes, provides a track in, or conducts significant research in exercise and sport psychology. Additionally and as noted earlier, this subfield also recognizes and strongly encourages certification through the AASP.

AASP-certified consultants agree to abide by the AASP *Code of Ethics*. Authored by James Whelan (AASP, 2013c), the code may be found at http://www.appliedsportpsych.org/about/ethics/ethics-code. As noted in the code, it draws heavily from APA's 1992 *Code of Ethics*, yet another overlap in their respective standards. (See http://www.apa.org/ethics for the current APA code.) Furthermore, although trained at the doctoral level, those who choose the kinesiology path mentioned earlier will be relegated mainly to academic careers given the limitations associated with not being licensed as a psychologist.

Training Programs

Sachs, Burke, and Schweighardt (2014) provide information on over 100 master's and doctoral programs in the United States as well as eight other countries. They cover the subfield of applied sport psychology as well as information on programs that have some sport psychology component. Interestingly, the majority of the programs are in sport science or kinesiology with a specialization in sport psychology and not specifically in exercise and sport psychology. Fewer programs exist in psychology with this emphasis. As a result, and given that the programs that exist are within larger counseling psychology and clinical psychology programs, admission is highly competitive. When reviewing any of the exercise and sport psychology programs, you are encouraged to be mindful of quality because this varies and changes over time. As a reminder, you will want to review the information relating to selecting graduate programs which can be found in Chapter 7.

Preparing for your Graduate Training

The first step to becoming an exercise and sport psychologist is to ensure a solid undergraduate education. This foundation will serve you well as you pursue graduate and postgraduate education in the field. In addition to your regular coursework in psychology (i.e., research methods, experimental psychology, physiological psychology, etc.), McCullagh et al. (2013) recommend that basic courses in the kinesiology area be included in your coursework. In fact, they go so far as to recommend a minor or a double major with kinesiology. Regardless, courses like exercise physiology, biomechanics, motor learning and control, and sport sociology will benefit students desiring to pursue this subfield. Note that prerequisite coursework may need to be completed in areas like biology, chemistry, mathematics, or other physical sciences prior to enrolling in these courses.

Galli (2013) offers three pieces of advice to undergraduate students who are interested in this subfield. First, he recommends double majoring in psychology and exercise science as well as including coursework in the related discipline areas, which is consistent with McCullagh et al.'s (2013) advice. Second, he recommends getting experience by assisting faculty who are involved in the field with their research. This recommendation is consistent with advice offered by us in the chapter devoted to preparing for graduate school. To reiterate, research experience should be the cornerstone of your undergraduate experience. As part of getting experience, Galli also suggests volunteering as a coach or assistant coach and working in a sport environment. Third, Galli suggests that you make connections with exercise and sport psychology professionals. These connections can be made through faculty at your home institution, graduate schools you are considering, and conferences in the field.

Working in Areas Related to Exercise and Sport Psychology with a Bachelor's Degree

As you can see from the information provided throughout this chapter, working as an exercise and sport psychologist clearly involves education and training at the doctoral and postdoctoral level (i.e., after receiving your doctoral degree). However, if you have an interest in exercise and sport psychology there are opportunities to work in environments that value individual and team sports as well as exercise. Some of these include:

- coaching youth sports in a school setting (e.g., a local middle school) or in a community setting (e.g., the Boys and Girls Clubs);
- physical education teacher with a double major in psychology (This would require a teaching certificate.);
- research assistant in a sport and exercise psychology lab;
- recreational worker (e.g., within the National Park Service and state park associations);
- recreational/activity therapist in a hospital setting where you would plan and implement recreational activities with patients;
- coaching assistant in a sport or exercise program; and
- health fitness instructor, exercise specialist, and personal trainer (To learn more about these professions and certification visit the American College of Sports Medicine at www.acsm.org.).

Bachelor's level salaries vary widely. For example, the median salary for a fitness instructor in 2012 was $31,720 (O*NET, 2012b), and the median salary for school teachers (which would include physical education teachers) in 2012 was $55,050 (O*NET, 2012a). As a result, we encourage you to visit the Occupational Information Network at www.onetonline.org to learn more about your particular interest area.

An Insider's Perspective

A Counseling Sport Psychologist's Journey: Reflections and Observations

Christopher M. Carr, PhD
St. Vincent Sports Performance Center – Indianapolis, IN

When I began my doctoral studies, I knew that I wanted to be a "sport" psychologist. More specifically, I wanted to be a counseling psychologist that had a developed competency in the practice of applied sport psychology. I did not believe that my background as a four-year collegiate football player or graduate assistant college football coach was sufficient in order to be competent. In fact, I found that my own athletic and coaching experience was unique to me and not necessarily transferable to any other athlete (even in football). What I have found is that my preparation in my counseling psychology doctoral program (which included a minor in sport/exercise psychology), in addition to my one-year clinical research assistantship in the Sport Psychology Department of the United States Olympic Training Center

in Colorado Springs (USOC), has led to my career growth, success, and professional satisfaction. In essence, I am doing exactly what I want to do for the rest of my career.

My first postdoctoral position was at Washington State University (WSU), where I was the full-time athletic department counseling sport psychologist. My role was to provide comprehensive psychological services for the athletes, coaches, and support staff at this PAC-10 athletics department. This position was a great "first" sport psychology position; the athletic department was competitive but lacked some of the external distractions of larger and more well-known programs. I learned here that the athletic director is the *most* important support system that a sport psychologist can have in this type of position. Without this support, coaches are more tentative to utilize the service, and there is often difficulty in program development opportunities (e.g., leadership seminars).

It was during my first year at WSU that I was contacted by USA Skiing and became the consulting sport psychologist for the US Men's Alpine Ski Team. This 10-year relationship was instrumental in my experiences and opportunities to grow in my development as a counseling sport psychologist. Attending on-hill camps, traveling to international competitions, coordinating sport psychology team/coaching programs, and consulting with individual athletes were all integral experiences that I believed I had prepared for well. I cannot imagine a psychologist with no sport psychology training (either academic or supervised experience) being able to optimize such a consultation with an elite Olympic-level team.

I spent 1 year at Arizona State University in a combined athletic department/university counseling center staff sport psychologist position before being hired at The Ohio State University (OSU) to become the full-time athletic department sport psychologist. My position was housed in the OSU Sports Medicine Department, and since that time (1995), I have built my practice either within or in consultation with sports medicine departments. During my five years at OSU, I was integrally involved with one of the largest NCAA Division I athletic departments, and within my first month of being there I realized that I would need help. Again, with the support of the OSU athletics director and the OSU administration, I was able to propose and create a postdoctoral fellowship in counseling and sport psychology. This position allowed me the opportunity (and privilege) of mentoring four postdoctoral fellows. These fellows were involved within the structure of the OSU Athletic Department and had their own individual case loads, team consultations, and involvement with sport psychology programs (e.g., coaching seminars). During my time at OSU, I found that my training as a counseling psychologist was most influential in creating my niche within the athletic department. Being able to navigate my roles as therapist, consultant, educator, group facilitator, and lecturer was necessary to impact the psychological

health of the over 800 student-athletes. I have found that the ability to serve and function optimally in multiple roles can greatly add to successful career growth.

My family and I returned to central Indiana in 2000 as I moved my practice into an orthopedic sports medicine clinic. In 2006 I was hired by St. Vincent Healthcare to develop and coordinate a sport and performance psychology program. This program, housed within St. Vincent Sports Performance (SVSP), provides comprehensive sport and performance psychology services. I coordinate psychological services for collegiate athletic departments and serve as the Consulting Sport Psychologist for the Purdue University Athletics Department, returning to the role I held from 2001–2007 in January of 2014; I also spent 2007–2013 as the Consulting Sport Psychologist with the Indiana University Athletics Department. Currently, Purdue contracts with SVSP for my services as their consulting psychologist for athletics, and I am on-campus 2 days per week and coordinate the other mental health providers on campus.

I believe that I will always be involved with collegiate athletics. The athletes' developmental challenges are unique and enjoyable to deal with from a psychological standpoint; I also very much enjoy the professionalism that most coaches and support staff demonstrate in their desire to be the best and provide the best care. It is a dynamic and energetic environment. However, the stigma toward psychology still exists. Regardless, I am optimistic and have seen (especially over the past 5–10 years) an increase in new hiring of sport psychologists within major

NCAA Division I athletic departments. In all of these hires, the sport psychologist was a licensed psychologist with a demonstrated competency in the field of sport psychology. I think this model best provides for the comprehensive care of the athlete client. In fact, I spent one month in Beijing, China in 2008 as the USA Olympic Diving Team Sport Psychologist (having consulted with them since 2004). It was clear that most of my consultations with athletes and coaches dealt with more "personal" dynamics that could have directly or indirectly impacted their performance.

As I view the next 10–15 years of my career (with 22 years of experience in sport psychology behind me), I am optimistic about the growth of our field. Although I am biased toward the hiring of licensed psychologists for sport psychologist positions within collegiate and professional sports, I do see a future where the academic (i.e., kinesiology and sport science) and applied (e.g., counseling psychology) fields collaborate in a scientist–practitioner model of enhancing the care we provide for athletes. This combination of research, education, and applied interventions/counseling must evolve through collaboration and dialogue. I am hopeful that this future will come to fruition.

Note. Dr. Christopher Carr earned his PhD in Counseling Psychology with a minor in Sport and Exercise Psychology from Ball State University. In addition to his work with collegiate, professional, and Olympic athletes and sports organizations, he was president of APA's Division 47 – Exercise and Sport Psychology. His publications include numerous book chapters and academic articles predominantly in the area of sports medicine and physical medicine in the area of sport and performance psychology.

Professional Spotlight

Kate F. Hays, PhD

Education:
- Bachelor of Arts in Psychology from University of New Hampshire
- Master of Arts in Psychology from Boston University
- PhD in Clinical Psychology from Boston University

Position:
Owner/Director of "The Performing Edge" in Toronto, Canada

Description of Position:
I provide individual and small group consultation, coaching, therapy, and

workshops to athletes, performing artists, and business people to optimize mental skills for performance, both at my own practice and as a consultant at a sports medicine clinic. I offer small group telephone conference calls to train and support practitioners aspiring to practice sport or performance psychology.

Most Significant Professional Accomplishment:

I was a visiting scholar at Geelong Grammar School (Australia) by invitation of Martin E. P. Seligman, extending positive psychology to mental skills in optimal performance (in sport, performance, academics) for students, faculty, and community members.

Favorite Publication:

Hays, K. F. (Ed.). (2009). *Performance psychology in action: A casebook for working with athletes, performing artists, business leaders, and professionals in high-risk occupations.* Washington, DC: American Psychological Association. doi:10.1037/11876-000

Areas of Research:

My current areas of research are the applications of sport psychology to the performing arts, the intersection of performance psychology and positive psychology, and the mental benefits of physical activity.

Areas of Practice:

My current areas of practice are sport and performance psychology and general outpatient clinical psychology.

Professional Memberships:

- American Psychological Association
  - o Fellow of Divisions 29, 42, and 47
  - o President, Division 47 (Exercise and Sport Psychology): 1999–2004
- Association for Applied Sport Psychology
- Ontario Psychological Association
- Canadian Psychological Association

Most Rewarding Aspect of Your Career:

The most rewarding aspects of my career are being able to make connections between disparate elements of the profession in order to help the profession grow, offering quality services to people otherwise unserved or underserved, and finding a profession (and a niche within the profession) that continues to engage my interest and skills after typical retirement age.

Words of Advice to the Student Who is Interested in Your Subfield:

I encourage those with an interest in sport psychology to develop knowledge of the whole person (soma as well as psyche), through coursework, supervised experience, and on-going education in both psychology and sport sciences. When you obtain formal education to the highest degree possible, you maximize your professional options over time – particularly in a multidisciplinary field such as exercise and sport psychology.

Web Address:

www.theperformingedge.com

Suggested Exercises

1. Using your college's course catalog, identify courses that are related to exercise and sport psychology. Answer the following questions for each course.
   a. What department offers the course?
   b. Is it an undergraduate or graduate level course?
   c. Is it part of a concentration, minor, or major program?
   d. Which professor usually teaches it?
2. Using the consultant finder on the AASP web site (http://www. appliedsportpsych.org/certified-consultants/find-a-consultant), find a certified consultant in your general geographic area. Answer the following questions based on the consultant's profile:
   a. Where is the person employed?
   b. What is the person's job title?
   c. What is the person's contact information?
   d. In what sports does the person consult?
   e. What age client does the person see?
   f. What subspecialties and specializations do the person list?
   g. Is the person a licensed psychologist?
3. Using an article from one of the exercise and sport psychology publications noted in the chapter, answer the following questions.
   a. What is the title of the article?
   b. Who are the authors?
   c. What are their affiliations?/Where do they work?
   d. In three or four sentences describe the article's findings.

Suggested Readings

Burton, D., & Raedeke, T. D. (2008). *Sport psychology for coaches*. Champaign, IL: Human Kinetics.

Murphy, S. M. (Ed.). (2004). *The sport psych handbook*. Champaign, IL: Human Kinetics.

Tenenbaum, G., & Eklund, R. C. (Eds.). (2007). *Handbook of sport psychology* (3rd ed.). New York, NY: Wiley.

Van Raalte, J. L., & Brewer, B. W. (Eds.). (2013). *Exploring sport and exercise psychology* (3rd ed.). Washington, DC: American Psychological Association.

Weinberg, R. S., & Gould, D. (2010). *Foundations of sport and exercise psychology* (5th ed.). Champaign, IL: Human Kinetics.

Williams, J. M. (Ed.). (2009). *Applied sport psychology: Personal growth to peak performance* (6th ed.). Boston, MA: McGraw-Hill.

Resources

Professional organizations fully or partially devoted to exercise and sport psychology (and related areas):

- American Alliance for Health, Physical Education, Recreation, and Dance (AAHPERD): www.aahperd.org

- American College of Sports Medicine: www.acsm.org
- American Psychological Association's Division 47 – Exercise and Sport Psychology: http://www.apadivisions.org/division-47
- Association for Applied Sport Psychology: www.appliedsportpsych.org
- British Association of Sport and Exercise Sciences: www.bases.org.uk
- Canadian Society for Psychomotor Learning and Sport Psychology: www.scapps2013.org
- International Society for Sport Psychology: issponline.org
- North American Society for the Psychology of Sport and Physical Activity: www.naspspa.org

Other Web Resources

- Human Kinetics: www.humankinetics.com
- SelfhelpMagazine.com (provides article synopses and brief articles on sport performance and sport psychology): http://www.selfhelpmagazine.com/articles

References

American Psychological Association. (2014). *APA sport psychology proficiency.* Retrieved from http://www.apadivisions.org/division-47/about/sport-proficiency/index.aspx

American Psychological Association – Division 47 – Exercise and Sport Psychology. (2014a). Retrieved from http://www.apadivisions.org/division-47

American Psychological Association – Division 47 – Exercise and Sport Psychology. (2014). *What is exercise psychology and sport psychology.* Retrieved from http://www.apadivisions.org/division-47/about/resources/what-is.aspx

Association for Applied Sport Psychology. (2013a). *About AASP.* Retrieved from http://appliedsportpsych.org/about

Association for Applied Sport Psychology. (2013b). *Become a certified consultant.* Retrieved from http://appliedsportpsych.org/consultants/become-certified

Association for Applied Sport Psychology. (2013c). *Ethics code: AASP ethical principles and standards.* Retrieved from http://www.appliedsportpsych.org/about/ethics/ethics-code

Galli, N. (2013). *Tips for undergraduate students interested in a career in sport and exercise psychology.* Retrieved from http://www.appliedsportpsych.org/resource-center/professional-resources-for-sport-and-exercise-psychology/tips-for-undergraduate-students

McCullagh, P., Noble, J. M., & Portenga, S. (2013). Education for becoming a sport psychologist. In J. L. Van Raalte & B. W. Brewer (Eds.), *Exploring sport and exercise psychology* (3rd ed., pp. 453–465). Washington, DC: American Psychological Association. doi:10.1037/14251-020

Occupational Information Network. (2012a). *Summary report for: 25-2031.00 – Secondary school teachers, except special and vocational education.* Retrieved from http://online.onetcenter.org/link/summary/25-2031.00

Occupational Information Network. (2012b). *Summary report for: 39-9031.00 – Fitness trainers and aerobics instructors.* Retrieved from http://online.onetcenter.org/link/summary/39-9031.00

Sachs, M. L., Burke, K. L., & Schweighardt, S. L. (Eds.). (2014). *Directory of graduate programs in applied sport psychology* (11th ed.). Indianapolis, IN: Association for Applied Sport Psychology.

Van Raalte, J. L., & Williams, J. M. (1994, June). *Graduate training and career possibilities in exercise and sport psychology*. Retrieved from http://www.apadivisions.org/division-47/about/resources/training.aspx

Chapter Thirteen
Careers in Health Psychology

Health Psychology Defined

Historically, the field of psychology debated about the impact of nature (i.e., genetics) and nurture (i.e., environmental factors) on development and a host of other areas. The conversations eventually led to the understanding that both nature and nurture impact all aspects of who we are, and in doing so they affect each other in complex ways. A similar debate also took place within the field of health psychology. The debate centered on the influence of biological, psychological, and sociocultural factors on health. Although researchers and practitioners may focus on one of these factors more than the other two factors, the impact of all three shapes the subfield of health psychology. In fact, the field of health psychology is guided by and rooted in a *biopsychosocial* framework. This framework ensures that all of the contributive factors to our health are considered. This is where health psychology shines as a subfield.

The American Psychological Association's (APA) Division 38 is devoted to the subfield of health psychology. APA Division 38 – Health Psychology (APA Division 38; 2014b) concentrates on:

- "Advancing contributions of the psychology discipline toward understanding health and illness through basic and clinical research and by encouraging the integration of biomedical information about health and illness with current psychological knowledge;

Majoring in Psychology: Achieving Your Educational and Career Goals, Second Edition.
Jeffrey L. Helms and Daniel T. Rogers.
© 2015 John Wiley & Sons, Ltd. Published 2015 by John Wiley & Sons, Ltd.

- Promoting education and services in the psychology of health and illness; and
- Informing the psychological and biomedical community, as well as the general public, on the results of current research and service activities in this area." (http://www.health-psych.org/AboutMission.cfm)

APA Division 38 (2014b) notes that their mission is reinforced by reports from the US Surgeon General's Office that state that mortality in the United States is significantly influenced by behavioral factors. They go on to note that "these reports recommend that behavioral risk factors (e.g., drug and alcohol use, high risk sexual behavior, smoking, diet, a sedentary lifestyle, stress) be the main focus of efforts in the area of health promotion and disease prevention" (http://www.health-psych.org/AboutMission.cfm). In short, health psychology is an interdisciplinary field devoted to promoting, improving, and maintaining healthy functioning as well as preventing and treating illness.

The Work

Core Activities

According to Gurung (2014), the health psychology subfield can be divided into three broad areas of study. These three areas are:

1. stress and coping;
2. health behaviors; and
3. issues in health care.

Within each of these broad areas health psychologists contribute via their research, practice, and teaching/training.

Research. As is the case with all subfields of psychology, research is the foundation upon which all of health psychology is built. As such, it is imperative that new insights, findings, and advancements in the field be available to others in the field. Prior to their dissemination, rigorous peer review must take place. Once the findings are reviewed, publication may then take place. Health psychology research is published in a variety of journals in the fields of psychology, medicine, and health sciences, just to name a few. For a sampling of journals that publish health psychology-related research, see Box 13.1.

Box 13.1 *Journals that Publish Health Psychology Research*

- *Annals of Behavioral Medicine*
- *Health Psychology*
- *International Journal of Behavioral Medicine*
- *Journal of Behavioral Medicine*
- *Journal of Clinical Psychology in Medical Settings*
- *Journal of Pediatric Psychology*
- *Pain*
- *Psychology and Health*
- *Psychosomatic Medicine*
- *The Health Psychologist* (newsletter)

The type of research pursued and eventually published in these outlets is as varied as the subfield itself. Some of the topics recently covered in these publications include:

- the impact of culture on health;
- eating, dieting, and exercise/physical activity;
- smoking, alcohol use, and drug use;
- (lack of) access to health care and health care policy;
- coping with chronic pain;
- chronic illness (e.g., diabetes, asthma);
- cardiovascular issues (e.g., hypertension and stroke);
- the impact of psychological and biological factors on the immune system (psychoneuroimmunology); and
- sexually transmitted infections (e.g., herpes, HIV, HPV).

For health psychologists primarily focused on research, including those employed in an academic environment, activities will be similar to those discussed in Chapter 16. Notably, the activities of these academic and research-oriented health psychologists often entail strong ties to local clinics and hospitals that can provide participants for their research studies. As a result, interdisciplinary collaboration with health care providers (as well as other researchers) is not strictly the purview of clinical health psychologists. It is also a necessary activity for the academic/experimental health psychologist. Establishing and maintaining these strong relationships with the medical community is very important to the viability of research programs.

Practice: Applying the research findings. Although the roots of the general research area of health psychology go back to the mid 1900s, the practice area of health psychology (i.e., clinical health psychology) was not recognized as a specialty by APA until 1997 (2014c). As part of the recognition, the practice area was defined, populations served were acknowledged, problems typically addressed were delineated, and common practice procedures were noted.

According to the specialty designation by APA (2014b), the *practice* of clinical health psychology:

> applies scientific knowledge of the interrelationships among behavioral, emotional, cognitive, social, and biological components in health and disease to the promotion and maintenance of health; the prevention, treatment, and rehabilitation of illness and disability; and the improvement of the health care system. The distinct focus of Clinical Health Psychology...is at the juncture of physical and emotional illness, understanding and treating the overlapping challenges. (http://www.apa.org/ed/graduate/specialize/health.aspx)

Clinical health psychologists serve populations across the lifespan, from prenatal issues of expectant mothers to geriatric issues. In addition to working with patients' families and other health care providers, clinical health psychologists work with a variety of individuals including but not limited to persons diagnosed with diabetes mellitus, pain, HIV/AIDS, alcohol/drug problems, cardiovascular diseases, cancers, stroke, eating disorders, weight problems/obesity, premenstrual syndrome, infertility and reproductive issues, sickle cell disease, dental disease, hypertension, and stress-related problems. Because of their keen awareness of the impact of the environment on health problems, health psychologists work not only with the patients and their immediate families but also with communities. In working with all of these various stakeholders, clinical health psychologists can address multifaceted health problems both at the prevention stages and at the treatment stages (APA Division 38, 2014b).

Like all psychologists that provide health care services to the public, health psychologists possess a broad range of skills. These include psychological assessment, intervention, and consultation skills. However, health psychologists build on these basic clinical skills. For example, health psychologists specialize their consultation skills so that they can provide services to other health care providers and staff. In fact, the level of interdisciplinary collaboration is high within the field (APA Division 38, 2007). Health-focused intervention strategies (e.g., biofeedback, hypnosis, relaxation training) and assessment instruments (e.g., tests assessing a person's behavioral health, readiness for transplant surgery, or experience of postoperative pain) are other examples of the specialization of their general clinical abilities. Importantly and because of their appreciation for environmental influences, health psychologists often utilize family therapy and interventions in their practices (APA Division 38, 2007).

For applied/practicing health psychologists, major figures in the subfield of health psychology convened in 2007 to consider, formulate, and endorse "the foundational and functional competencies expected of a well-trained, entry level clinical health psychologist" (APA Division 38, 2007, p. 6). The resulting document (referred to as the Tempe Summit Report) outlined six functional competencies that all health psychologists providing services to the public (i.e., individuals, families, groups, organizations) must possess. These six competencies are:

1. assessment (e.g., evaluating a person's psychological readiness for gastric bypass surgery);
2. intervention (e.g., helping an individual develop exercises that will decrease his experience of pain);
3. consultation (e.g., with other health care providers like physicians, rehabilitative specialists, dietitians);
4. research (even for practitioners);
5. supervision and training; and
6. management/administration – including:
   a. program development and evaluation of program effectiveness (e.g., healthy lifestyle programs, smoking cessation programs); and
   b. business management of a health psychology practice (e.g., recording keeping and hiring employees).

Teaching and training. As is the case with all areas of psychology, one of the main areas in which health psychologists contribute to the discipline is through teaching and training. As a result, a significant proportion of those who identify themselves as health psychologists hold academic positions at colleges and universities. Additionally, health psychologists often provide psychoeducational activities as part of their practices. These psychoeducational activities are geared specifically toward impacting the healthy functioning of the audience (e.g., educating a group of people at the local community center on ways to adjust their diet and lifestyles to reduce the risks of heart problems and diabetes in later life).

Focusing on the Future

It is important to highlight that none of these contributions exists in a stagnant field. In fact, the subfield of health psychology is very active as can be seen in the research areas noted previously. In addition, the subfield of health psychology is future driven. Health psychology envisions a very bright future that is full of positive contributions to our everyday lives. In looking toward the future with hope, Straub (2012) notes the following five challenges for the subfield:

1. increasing the healthy lifespan of all people;
2. reducing health discrepancies based on gender, culture, and socioeconomic status;
3. providing equal access to preventive health care services;
4. applying evidence-based approaches to healthy living; and
5. supporting and spearheading health care policy reform.

Employment Settings and Salary Expectations

For those health psychologists who focus their careers on conducting research, colleges and universities will be the primary setting for their work. Affiliations within a university may include appointments in the psychology department, health science department, and medical school. Research-oriented health psychologists also find employment in research institutes within universities as well as within government agencies (e.g., the National Institutes of Health and the Centers for Disease Control).

For those health psychologists who focus on providing direct health care services, clinical settings dominate. These settings include private practices and hospital settings. For those in private practices, most will perform activities both within and outside of the health psychology domain (i.e., practice both general clinical and health psychology). It is important to note that many individuals practicing in the clinical health psychology area do so in group practices. That is, they work alongside physicians, nurses, and other health care workers to provide the full spectrum of services patients need. This is akin to a one-stop shop for your health care needs.

Recent searches using PsycCareers – APA's Online Career Center (http://jobs.psyccareers.com) produced a myriad of advertisements based on a search of "health psychology." Both research-oriented and applied/clinical health psychologist positions were represented. Box 13.2 provides a sampling of those openings.

Salaries of health psychologists vary by work setting, reputation, and experience. Salaries for academic positions will be consistent with those

Box 13.2 *Recent Openings in the Health Psychology Subfield*

- Assistant or associate professor of health psychology
- Behavioral health psychologist
- Director of clinical training
- Director of psychosocial oncology and palliative care services
- Eating disorders clinic manager
- Health outcomes researcher
- Health psychologist for private practice specializing in geropsychology and rehabilitation
- HIV/AIDS community care and prevention advisor
- Manager of a chronic pain program
- Pain psychologist
- Psychologist at a medical center
- Public health and environment researcher
- Research associate
- Rehabilitation psychologist in a medical school

noted in Chapter 16. Academic positions within medical school settings will be somewhat higher paid than traditional university settings. Salaries for practitioners will be consistent with those noted in Chapter 10. In short, the median annual wage in 2012 for clinical, counseling, and school psychologists was $67,650 (Occupational Information Network [O*NET], 2012a).

Training and Preparation

Earning a Degree

Given the information presented about the breadth of this subfield, including the research and practice areas addressed in the preceding section, it should come as no surprise that a doctoral degree is typically the entry-level degree for both research and applied positions. This is due in no small part to the interdisciplinary nature of the field. Although specific to the applied area of clinical health psychology, APA's recognition of the specialty (2014c) highlights the advanced knowledge necessary and distinctive to the subfield. In particular it notes that "clinical health psychology requires a broad understanding of biology, pharmacology, anatomy, human physiology, pathophysiology, and psychoneuroimmunology" (http://www.apa.org/ed/

graduate/specialize/health.aspx). The extensive knowledge base also includes such topics as physician–patient relationships, health policy and care delivery, and diversity issues in health care.

Licensure Issues

It is important to note that those who deliver health care services must be licensed by the respective state board of psychology. However, state licensure is not typically required for researchers, educators, and policy specialists. Please see Chapter 10 for a discussion of the licensure process. In short, you will want to seek an APA-accredited doctoral program in clinical or counseling psychology that emphasizes, provides a track in, or conducts significant research in health psychology if you want to practice (i.e., do applied work) in this area. Additionally, this subfield also recognizes and encourages post-licensure board certification through the American Board of Clinical Health Psychology, which is a part of the American Board of Professional Psychology (www.abpp.org; n.d.).

Training Programs

Multiple resources provide information on graduate program offerings in health psychology. Updated annually, *Graduate Study in Psychology* (GSP; APA, 2014a) provides information on graduate programs offering an emphasis in health psychology. Another resource compiled by Norcross and Sayette (2014) lists programs that self-identify as having a concentration or track in health psychology/behavioral medicine. A list for clinical and a list for research-oriented graduate training programs are provided on APA Division 38's (2014a) website (http://www.health-psych.org/LandingEducation.cfm). Looking to the more distant future, the Association of Psychology Postdoctoral and Internship Centers (APPIC; n.d.) lists predoctoral internships with major and minor rotations in health psychology. For postdoctoral training (often required for licensure), APPIC also provides a list of sites with a health psychology emphasis.

In reporting these resources and information, it is important to note that much of the information provided in these databases and lists is based on self-reports by individual graduate programs. As such, and when reviewing any health psychology programs, you are encouraged to be mindful of quality because this varies and changes over time. In fact, we encourage you to review the information on selecting graduate programs that can be found in Chapter 7. In brief and to reiterate an earlier point, you will want to ensure that the graduate program is at a *minimum* APA-accredited if in the applied area and that those in the non-service delivery (i.e., research) area have strong track records for research and publication.

Preparing for Your Graduate Training

The first step to becoming a health psychologist is to ensure a solid undergraduate foundation in psychology. This foundation will serve you well as you pursue graduate and postgraduate education in the field. As described in APA's recognition of the specialty (2014b), coursework in the areas of biology, pharmacology, anatomy and physiology, and pathophysiology will be helpful. Note that many of these courses and areas of study may require prerequisite coursework (i.e., completion of lower level biology, chemistry, mathematics, or other physical sciences prior to enrollment). Keep this in mind as you plan your coursework. Additional coursework in statistics is also not a bad idea because most good graduate training programs in health psychology have a strong research foundation (including the applied clinical programs). Again though, this coursework is above and beyond that required by your psychology major (e.g., experimental psychology, physiological psychology, psychopharmacology).

Your undergraduate preparation should also include research experience. This suggestion is a reiteration of an earlier recommendation by us. In fact, we encourage you to revisit Chapter 6 as it would be redundant to provide that general information again here.

Working in Areas Related to Health Psychology with a Bachelor's Degree

As you can see from the information provided, a specialty in the subfield of health psychology clearly involves training at the doctoral and postdoctoral levels. However, if you have an interest in health psychology there are opportunities to work with a bachelor's degree in environments that value many of the same principles as those found in the subfield of health psychology. Some of these include occupational therapy assistant, research assistant in health settings, and medical–surgical hospital support staff/health educator.

- Occupational therapy assistant/aide: These individuals assist occupational therapists in the delivery of rehabilitative services to patients who have health impairments (e.g., post-stroke). They can assist patients in learning independent living skills so that they can return to the community or to lower levels of care. (O*NET, 2012d)
- Research assistant in health settings: These individuals assist with the protocols associated with drug trials, assist with data collection and analysis, and other supervised research activities. (O*NET, 2012b)

- Medical-surgical hospital support staff/health educator: These individuals assist in educational programs for the patients and public including providing families with information on support systems available in the community (e.g., diabetes support groups). (O*NET, 2012c)

Bachelor's level salaries vary based on the type of position. As a result, you are encouraged to take a look at the O*NET website (www.onetonline.org) for current salary information. Additionally, because students who are interested in health psychology are often similar to students who are interested in neuropsychology, you are encouraged to review Chapter 14.

An Insider's Perspective

Health Psychology and Culture: An Exciting Area of Study

Regan A. R. Gurung, PhD
University of Wisconsin – Green Bay

What is one of the hottest areas of research in the subfield of health psychology? The answer is "studying cultural differences." Culture is more important now than it has ever been. The United States is more culturally diverse now than it has ever been. World politics is rife with the clashing of cultural factions (e.g., Shias and Sunnis in the Middle East; caste and tribal genocide in Africa). Through this all, the disparities between different cultural groups – especially the rich and the poor – map onto significant health disparities. How does the culture that we come from and surround ourselves with influence our health and behaviors? Answering this question with a concerted look at sources of influence outside a person (i.e., not just his or her biology or psychology) is a distinctive feature of the approach taken by many health psychologists today. Most behaviors that influence health – whether healthy ones such as physical activity and eating nutritionally balanced diets or unhealthy ones such as smoking or drinking excessively – depend heavily on the culture in which we grew up.

We often ignore the importance of culture, partly because we rarely acknowledge its many dimensions. For example, what do your parents, your best friends, and your spiritual/religious beliefs have in common? Answer: They each constitute the major socialization forces of culture. Take parents for example. Whether we do something because they told us to (e.g., "Eat your greens!") or exactly because they told us *not to* (e.g., "Don't smoke!"), parents have a strong influence on us. In the same way, if our friends exercise, we are more likely to exercise also. As another example, consider religions, which have different prescriptions for what individuals should or should not do. Muslims cannot eat pork or drink alcohol. Hindus cannot eat beef. Unfortunately, discussions of culture are often limited to just race or ethnicity, when a broader discussion is required to understand fully the precedents of health and health behaviors. Culture is not just race or ethnicity; it also includes religion, age, gender, family values, the region of the country in which a person was raised, and many other features. Understanding the dynamic interplay of the cultural forces acting on us can greatly enhance how we face the world and how we optimize our way of life.

There are many examples of cultural health disparities: the infant death rate among African Americans is still more than double that of European Americans; heart disease death rates are more than 40% higher for African Americans than for European Americans. In general, health care and disease incidence (e.g., tuberculosis) rates vary significantly across ethnic groups. Individuals in Wisconsin are more likely to be heavy drinkers (sadly Wisconsin is the number one state in the US in regard to drinking rates). Individuals in California, Utah, and Hawaii are less likely to smoke. American Indians/Native Americans are more likely to die from diabetes and be obese than many other ethnic groups. Men are more likely to have

lung cancer than women. These are just some of the many cultural differences in health.

One of the most pressing needs for health psychology is to spend more time and energy on examining how cultural differences influence health and behavior. The plot thickens because culture can play multiple roles within an investigation. For example, a certain ethnic group may have a biological predisposition for a certain illness (a biological component), and they may also experience more stress from prejudice or discrimination (a psychological component), but they may also have stronger social networks (a social component). Consequently, the researcher has to balance multiple systems, variables, and levels. A number of health psychologists have drawn attention to this problem, but there is a lot more to be done and a great need for culturally educated health psychologists.

Note. Dr. Gurung is Ben J. & Joyce Rosenberg Professor of Psychology and Human Development at the University of Wisconsin – Green Bay. He is the author or editor of 13 books including the third edition of *Health Psychology: A Cultural Approach* (2014). In addition to his books, he has authored or co-authored over 100 peer-reviewed journal articles, book chapters, and invited journal articles. Dr. Gurung is a Fellow of the American Psychological Association, the Association for Psychological Science, and the Midwestern Psychological Association. He is actively involved in several divisions including Division 2 (Society for the Teaching of Psychology) and Division 38 (Health Psychology).

Professional Spotlight

Chris Dunkel Schetter, PhD

Education:

- Bachelor of Arts in Psychology from Connecticut College (1974)
- Master of Arts and Doctor of Philosophy (PhD) in Social Psychology from Northwestern University (1982)
- Postdoctoral Fellowship – National Science Foundation (1982–1983)
  - o University of California, Berkeley – Department of Psychology
  - o Sponsor: Richard Lazarus

Employer:

Department of Psychology, University of California, Los Angeles

Position:

Professor of Psychology, Director of UCLA's Health Psychology Program

Description of Position:

My job duties involve research, teaching, administration, and professional service. I teach and mentor the research of graduate and undergraduate students, and postdoctoral fellows.

Most Significant Professional Accomplishments:

My most significant professional accomplishments include the UCLA Distinguished Teaching Award and the American Psychological Association's Division 38 Senior Investigator Award for Outstanding Contributions to Health Psychology. I am also proud of the Strickland Daniels Mentoring Award from APA Division 35 – Psychology of Women.

Favorite Publication:

Dunkel Schetter, C. (2011). Psychological science on pregnancy: Stress processes, biopsychosocial models, and emerging research issues. *Annual Review of Psychology, 62*, 531–558. doi:10.1146/annurev.psych.031809.130727

Areas of Research:

My primary program of research is on stress processes in pregnancy. In this work, my students and I examine various aspects of prenatal maternal stress including exposure to and perceptions of stress, emotions, behaviors, and effects on preterm birth and low birth weight. We also study social relationships, race and ethnicity, and cultural factors as they modify or are associated with stress or outcomes. My current research is focused mainly on unique risk factors and mechanisms involving African American and Latina women, the role of social support and other resilience factors in pregnancy, and on preventive interventions. I am one of many Co-Principal

Investigators in the Community Child Health Network, which studies the effects of stress and resilience in parents following the birth of a child on maternal allostatic load and effects on the birth and development of children of a subsequent pregnancy.

Most Rewarding Aspect of Your Career:
Rewards come from teaching those who really want to learn and see the world differently by understanding science, and from conducting research; the process and outcomes of scientific discovery are still a big thrill for me after many years in this career. I love seeing and instilling this passion in my students and protégés. It is also rewarding to help build programs and organizations to do excellent training and research, and to use psychological science to address society's problems, especially in areas of health.

Words of Advice to the Student Who is Interested in Your Subfield:
Have a multifaceted approach to research, and explore as much as you can of all kinds of psychological science. Read with an open and inquiring mind!

Suggested Exercises

1. Using your college's course catalog, identify courses that are related to health psychology. Answer the following questions for each course.
   a. What department offers the course?
   b. Is it an undergraduate or graduate level course?
   c. Are there any prerequisites for the course?
   d. Is it part of a concentration, minor, or major program?
2. Using the online list of programs on Division 38's web page or *Graduate Study in Psychology* (APA, 2014a), locate a health psychology graduate program that interests you and answer the following questions.
   a. What is the name of the university?
   b. Who is the program director?
   c. What type of degree does it offer?
   d. Is the program accredited?
   e. What are the program's research and clinical focus areas?
3. Using an article from one of the health psychology publications noted in the chapter, answer the following questions.
   a. What is the title of the article?
   b. Who are the authors?
   c. What are their affiliations? Where do they work?
   d. In three or four sentences describe the article's findings.
4. Using PsycCareers – APA's Online Career Center (jobs.psyccareers.com), search for a health psychology-related position opening. Answer the following questions.
   a. What is the title of the position?
   b. Where is it located (hospital, research institute, university)?

c.   What are the job responsibilities?
d.   Does it specify a particular area of health psychology (e.g., pain management, smoking cessation, obesity)?
e.   What are the requirements for the position (e.g., doctorate, research experience, licensure)?
f.   How do you apply for the position?

Suggested Readings

Belar, C. D., & Deardorff, W. W. (2009). *Clinical health psychology in medical settings: A practitioner's guidebook* (2nd ed.). Washington, DC: American Psychological Association.

Miller, S. M., Bowen, D. J., Croyle, R. T., & Rowland, J. H. (Eds.). (2009). *Handbook of cancer control and behavioral science: A resource for researchers, practitioners, and policymakers*. Washington, DC: American Psychological Association.

Quick, J. C., & Tetrick, L. E. (Eds.). (2011). *Handbook of occupational health psychology* (2nd ed.). Washington, DC: American Psychological Association.

Spiers, M. W., Geller, P. A., & Kloss, J. D. (Eds.). (2013). *Women's health psychology*. Hoboken, NJ: Wiley.

Stroebe, W. (Ed.). (2009). *Dieting, overweight, and obesity: Self-regulation in a food-rich environment*. Washington, DC: American Psychological Association.

Taylor, S. E. (2012). *Health psychology* (8th ed.). Boston, MA: McGraw-Hill.

Wright, R. A., & Gendolla, G. H. E. (Eds.). (2012). *How motivation affects cardiovascular response: Mechanisms and applications*. Washington, DC: American Psychological Association.

Resources

Health Psychology and Related Professional Organizations:
- American Psychosomatic Society: www.psychosomatic.org
- British Psychological Society's Division of Health Psychology: www.health-psychology.org.uk
- European Health Psychology Society: www.ehps.net
- Health Psychology (American Psychological Association – Division 38): www.health-psych.org
- International Association for the Study of Pain: www.iasp-pain.org
- International Society of Behavioral Medicine: www.isbm.info
- Rehabilitation Psychology (American Psychological Association – Division 22): http://www.apadivisions.org/division-22
- Society of Behavioral Medicine: www.sbm.org

Other Internet Resources:

- Centers for Disease Control and Prevention: www.cdc.gov
- Health Psychology and Rehabilitation: www.healthpsych.com
- US Department of Health and Human Services – National Institutes of Health: www.nih.gov

- US Department of Health and Human Services: www.healthfinder.gov
- World Health Organization: http://www.who.int/en

References

American Board of Professional Psychology. (n.d.). *Clinical health psychology.* Retrieved from http://www.abpp.org/i4a/pages/index.cfm?pageid=3308

American Psychological Association. (2014a). *Graduate study in psychology: 2014.* Washington, DC: Author.

American Psychological Association. (2014b). *Public description of clinical health psychology.* Retrieved from http://www.apa.org/ed/graduate/specialize/health. aspx

American Psychological Association. (2014c). *Recognized specialties and proficiencies in professional psychology.* Retrieved from http://www.apa.org/ed/graduate/specialize/recognized.aspx

American Psychological Association – Division 38 – Health Psychology. (2007). *Tempe summit report: Application of the competency model to clinical health psychology.* Washington, DC: Author.

American Psychological Association – Division 38 – Health Psychology. (2014a). *Education and training resources.* Retrieved from http://www.health-psych.org/LandingEducation.cfm

American Psychological Association – Division 38 – Health Psychology. (2014b). *Our mission.* Retrieved from http://www.health-psych.org/AboutMission.cfm

Association of Psychology Postdoctoral and Internship Centers. (n.d.). *APPIC online directory.* Retrieved from https://membership.appic.org/directory/search

Gurung, R. A. R. (2014). *Health psychology: A cultural approach* (3rd ed.). Belmont, CA: Cengage.

Norcross, J. C., & Sayette, M. A. (2014). *Insider's guide to graduate programs in clinical and counseling psychology* (2014/2015 ed.). New York, NY: Guilford.

Occupational Information Network. (2012a). *Summary report for: 19-3031.02 – Clinical psychologists.* Retrieved from http://online.onetcenter.org/link/summary/19-3031.02

Occupational Information Network. (2012b). *Summary report for: 19-4061.00 – Social science research assistants.* Retrieved from http://online.onetcenter.org/link/summary/19-4061.00

Occupational Information Network. (2012c). *Summary report for: 21-1091.00 – Health educators.* Retrieved from http://online.onetcenter.org/link/summary/21-1091.00

Occupational Information Network. (2012d). *Summary report for: 31-2012.00 – Occupational therapist aides.* Retrieved from http://online.onetcenter.org/link/summary/31-2012.00

Straub, R. O. (2012). *Health psychology: A biopsychosocial approach* (3rd ed.). New York, NY: Worth.

Chapter Fourteen
Careers in Neuropsychology

Neuropsychology Defined

Although the subfield of neuropsychology has been around since at least the mid 1900s (Boake & Bieliauskas, 2007), the clinical/applied area of neuropsychology was not recognized by the American Psychological Association (APA) as a specialty area of practice until 1996 (APA, 2014c). According to APA's (2014b) recognition, the specialty area of clinical neuropsychology:

> applies principles of assessment and intervention based upon the scientific study of human behavior as it relates to normal and abnormal functioning of the central nervous system. The specialty is dedicated to enhancing the understanding of brain-behavior relationships and the application of such knowledge to human problems. (http://www.apa.org/ed/graduate/specialize/neuro.aspx)

In other words, experimental neuropsychology develops and clinical neuropsychology applies knowledge of brain–behavior relationships to human problems. It is important to note that although the bulk of the chapter focuses on the applied clinical area of neuropsychology, the experimental area of neuropsychology is just as important. Both complement each other. In fact, without the experimental area of neuropsychology, there would be no applied clinical area of neuropsychology.

Majoring in Psychology: Achieving Your Educational and Career Goals, Second Edition.
Jeffrey L. Helms and Daniel T. Rogers.
© 2015 John Wiley & Sons, Ltd. Published 2015 by John Wiley & Sons, Ltd.

The Work

Core Activities

As is the case with all subfields of psychology, neuropsychologists contribute to the discipline via their activities in the areas of research, practice, and teaching/training. Each of these activities is described here.

Research. As noted in the opening to the chapter, before clinical neuropsychologists can apply scientific knowledge to human problems (i.e., practice), there must first be research to support/develop the application. As a result, scientific research is the foundation on which both experimental neuropsychology and clinical neuropsychology are built. Given the intradisciplinary and interdisciplinary nature of the field, it is not surprising that, in addition to the field of neuropsychology, the fields of neuroscience, cognitive psychology, rehabilitative psychology, medicine, and gerontology, among others, produce excellent research on which neuropsychological practice relies. All of these fields, including applied (i.e., clinical) neuropsychology, are known for their research expertise and the production and dissemination of high quality neuropsychological research.

Once the research is complete, an article (i.e., paper) describing the research and results can be submitted for publication to one of the neuropsychological journals. Of course, prior to publication, the article must undergo review by peers in the field. After it clears the review process (which can take a long time and is not guaranteed), the research results may be published. A host of publications provide outlets for neuropsychological research. However, keep in mind that the neuropsychologist will be reading research from the closely related fields mentioned in the earlier paragraph in order to keep on top of the ever-changing field. Regardless, some of the publications in the field that you may find helpful as you explore this career are noted in Box 14.1. As noted throughout the book, journals are an excellent resource to explore current happenings in a field.

Although the journal titles noted in Box 14.1 give a small glimpse into the area, a sampling of topics studied (i.e., researched) by neuropsychologists may prove more useful. Here are some topics that recently appeared in some of the journals listed in the table:

- developing culturally sensitive neuropsychological tests;
- cognitive functioning in adults with autism;
- memory functioning in individuals diagnosed with schizophrenia;
- the impact of Alzheimer's disease on language;

> **Box 14.1** *Journals that Publish Neuropsychological Research*
>
> - *Aging, Neuropsychology, and Cognition: A Journal on Normal and Dysfunctional Development*
> - *Applied Neuropsychology*
> - *Archives of Clinical Neuropsychology*
> - *Child Neuropsychology*
> - *Cognitive Neuropsychology*
> - *Developmental Neuropsychology*
> - *Journal of Clinical and Experimental Neuropsychology*
> - *Memory*
> - *Neuropsychological Rehabilitation*
> - *Neuropsychology*
> - *The Clinical Neuropsychologist*

- the neuropsychological components of dyslexia;
- recovery from brain infections in persons diagnosed with HIV;
- long-term outcome for individuals who suffer a traumatic brain injury;
- effectiveness of educational programs that encourage use of helmets when cycling;
- stroke rehabilitation issues; and
- neuropsychological effects of toxin exposure in industrial and military settings.

For neuropsychologists primarily focused on research and those housed in an academic environment, activities will be similar to those discussed in Chapter 16. In addition, careers associated with experimental psychology, physiological psychology, and cognitive psychology are covered in Chapter 8. Given the obvious overlap neuropsychology has with these areas and to eliminate redundancy, we encourage you to visit or revisit those chapters.

Practice. As part of the recognition of the specialty by APA in 1996, the practice area was defined, populations served were acknowledged, problems typically addressed were delineated, and common practice procedures were noted. The specialty designation defined the practice domain in the following way:

> The practice of clinical neuropsychology encompasses roles that address psychological or behavioral manifestations of neurological, neuropathological, pathophysiological, and neurochemical changes in brain disease and the full range of aberrations in the central nervous system that may arise during development. (p. 149)

In general, clinical neuropsychologists serve all populations at all phases of the developmental life cycle. They serve both children and adults, including those in medical-surgical and rehabilitation contexts. In terms of services for children, pediatric neuropsychologists work with children who have learning disabilities and developmental disabilities. APA's specialty recognition (1996) notes that these pediatric neuropsychologists are increasingly receiving referrals from other pediatric care providers for such issues as drug abuse and dependence, HIV/AIDS, and toxin exposure.

Although overlap exists in treatment issues, the practice of neuropsychology with adults can be quite different from clinical practice with a pediatric population. Even though certain types of neuropsychological traumas are common in the two groups (e.g., accidents), APA's specialty recognition (1996) acknowledges that adult populations often present for services with quite different issues. Based on the specialty recognition description, these issues appear to fall into two broad categories:

1. Neurological problems: This category includes issues like dementias due to disease processes like Alzheimer's and Parkinson's diseases, cerebrovascular accidents, tumors, infectious diseases that affect the central nervous system, and degenerative and demyelinating diseases (e.g., multiple sclerosis).
2. Psychiatric problems: This category includes problems like differential diagnostic issues for dementia and depression, somatoform disorders that appear to have a neurological component, and psychotic symptoms related to neurological problems.

Because of the nature of their expertise, APA (1996) notes that clinical neuropsychologists also work with individuals who have general medical and surgical issues. These individuals may include:

- geriatric populations whose health status is complicated by dementia, making management more difficult;
- candidates for surgery (e.g., potential kidney and heart transplant recipients); and
- persons who have chronic pain subsequent to a neurological incident.

APA's specialty recognition notes that referrals from other health professionals often focus on requesting assistance in differential diagnosis (i.e., determining if a situation is due to one disorder or another or both) and the untangling of the psychological and medical components to a presenting problem. Neuropsychologists are also extremely helpful in establishing a baseline of functioning for patients. This baseline (i.e., where the patient started) can be used in the future to judge disease and recovery rates (i.e., how much the patient improved or did not improve). Neuropsychologists also get their fair share of referrals for behavioral and rehabilitative interventions geared toward addressing a patient's limitations due to impaired neurological functioning.

The 1996 specialty designation by APA noted common practice procedures, including: "neuropsychological assessment, cognitive remediation and intervention, agency and institutional consultation, education and counseling for individuals and families, and selected psychotherapies or behavior therapies as appropriate for neurologically involved individuals" (p. 150). These common practice procedures were described in more depth in the report from the Houston Conference on Specialty Education and Training in Clinical Neuropsychology (Houston Conference Report; Hannay et al., 1998). Consistent with the core domains articulated by APA's Commission for the Recognition of Specialties and Proficiencies in Professional Psychology (CRSPPP), the seven core professional activities of neuropsychologists (along with an example of each) include:

1. assessment: e.g., assessment of memory functioning in individuals diagnosed with dementias;
2. intervention: e.g., development of rehabilitative programs for individuals who have suffered a traumatic brain injury;
3. consultation: e.g., consultation with physicians and rehabilitative specialists when neuropsychological issues are suspected; helping other professionals differentiate between a dementing process and depression;
4. supervision and training: e.g., supervision of future neuropsychologists as well as assistants and aides; supervising trainees in the administration and interpretation of neuropsychological tests;
5. research and inquiry (even for practitioners): e.g., evaluating an intervention program that a practitioner developed for use with individuals adjusting to the aftermath of a stroke or to see if interventions to improve memory functioning have helped;
6. consumer protection: e.g., ensuring patients are receiving the care necessary to address all of their respective deficits, not just medical issues; and
7. professional development: e.g., continuing education to stay on top of a rapidly (almost daily) changing field, learning new assessment and intervention tools.

Teaching and training. As is the case with all areas of psychology, one of the main ways in which neuropsychologists contribute to the discipline is through teaching and training. As a result, many of those who identify themselves as neuropsychologists hold academic positions at colleges and universities, including medical schools. Additionally, neuropsychologists often provide psychoeducational activities as part of their practices. These psychoeducational (i.e., teaching) activities can include such things as educating caregivers on the neuropsychological problems associated with stroke, dementias, and traumatic brain injuries.

Employment Settings

Because of the strong scientific foundation of this area of psychology, many neuropsychologists contribute to the subfield in the college/university setting (i.e., academic positions). Within the college, university, or medical school setting, neuropsychologists are found in departments of psychology, health science, psychiatry, and neurology. Also as noted previously, the fields of neuroscience and gerontology (among others) contribute significantly to the subfield of neuropsychology and have significant scientific overlap. As a result of the overlap, neuropsychologists also return the favor in terms of contributions and as such are valued members in these academic disciplines as well. Due to the common characteristics shared with academe, we encourage you to review the information in Chapter 16.

Another setting where neuropsychologists contribute to the subfield is the applied setting (e.g., a clinical or consulting practice). As noted in APA's recognition of the specialty (1996):

> Clinical neuropsychologists function primarily on referral from health, education, and legal professionals; agencies and institutions; and in response to needs of other service systems (e.g., courts, schools, extended rehabilitation facilities and general care facilities, military installations, and chemical treatment facilities). Primary employment settings are estimated to be almost equally divided between hospital-medical centers, private practice, and a combination of (salaried) hospital or clinic-based employment, and private practice. (p. 150)

For those neuropsychologists even more aligned with the neurosciences, positions at research institutes also provide employment opportunities. Such positions can be found in government agencies like the National Institutes of Health (NIH; www.nih.gov). Some of the member institutes of the NIH that are of particular interest to those in the neuropsychological subfield include:

- National Institute on Aging: www.nia.nih.gov
- National Institute on Alcohol Abuse and Alcoholism: www.niaaa.nih.gov
- National Institute on Drug Abuse: www.nida.nih.gov
- National Institute of Mental Health: www.nimh.nih.gov
- National Institute of Neurological Disorders and Stroke: www.ninds.nih.gov

Salaries

Needless to say, salaries vary by work setting, reputation, and experience. Salaries for academic positions will be consistent with those noted in Chapter 16. Academic positions within medical school settings will pay somewhat better than traditional university settings (e.g., departments of psychology, neuroscience departments). Salaries for practitioners will be consistent with those noted in Chapter 10. In short, the median annual wage in 2007 for clinical, counseling, and school psychologists was $67,650 (Occupational Information Network [O*NET], 2012a). O*NET also reports that projected growth in these areas is likely to be about average over the next 10 years. However, a neuropsychology specialty, including board certification, is very likely to command salaries significantly higher than the median wages noted for all clinical, school, and counseling psychologists as lumped together in O*NET.

The projected growth estimated by O*NET is supported by a recent search using PsycCareers – APA's Online Career Center (http://jobs.psyccareers.com). That search produced 52 advertisements using the terms "neuropsychology" and "neuroscience." Some of the positions available included:

- assistant professor of neuroscience;
- chair of neuroimaging research;
- pediatric neuropsychologist at a medical school;
- licensed neuropsychologist at an adult rehabilitation hospital; and
- lead scientist – children's brain function lab.

Training and Preparation

Earning a Degree

Given the information presented about the breadth and depth of this subfield, including both the research and practice areas addressed, it should come as no surprise that a doctoral degree is typically the *base* entry-level degree for both research and applied positions. This fact is due in no small part to the interdisciplinary nature of the subfield that combines the disciplines of psychology, biology, chemistry, and health science, among others. Furthermore, the Houston Conference Report puts forth an expectation that postdoctoral education and training in clinical neuropsychology be equal to at least 2 full-time years (Hannay et al., 1998). In other words, the *general* clinical skills associated with basic neuropsychological training begin in the doctoral program with the neuropsychological component growing stronger during the predoctoral internship. However, and building upon these prior aspects of training, a *specialty* in clinical neuropsychology requires extensive *post*doctoral training. APA's (1996) recognition of the specialty supports this perspective on training and highlights the advanced knowledge necessary and distinctive to the field.

The Houston Conference Report (Hannay et al., 1998), supported by many in the field, offered specifics when it comes to the knowledge base required for specialization in clinical neuropsychology. The report noted that neuropsychologists possess knowledge in the general psychological area (e.g., statistics, biological bases of behavior, cognitive psychology, human development), the general clinical psychological area (e.g., tests and measures, interviewing and diagnostic techniques, ethics), the general brain–behavior area (e.g., neuroanatomy, neurological disorders, neuroimaging, neurochemistry), and the clinical neuropsychology area (e.g., neuropsychological assessment and interventions, ethics related to neuropsychology, neuropsychological research skills). As a result, a "short" doctoral program rarely has enough time to cover all of these necessary areas, leaving it to postdoctoral residency and continuing education to complete the *base-level* training.

Licensure Issues

It is important to note that although state licensure is not typically required for researchers and educators within academic environments (e.g., experimental neuropsychologists), licensure by the respective state board of psychology is required to practice in the applied neuropsychological area (i.e., those that provide treatment, assessment, and diagnosis). Please see Chapter 10 for a discussion of the licensure process. In short, you will want to seek an APA-accredited doctoral program in clinical, school, or counseling psychology that emphasizes, provides a track in, or conducts significant research in neuropsychology if you want to practice (i.e., do applied work) in this area. Additionally, this subfield also recognizes and encourages board certification through the American Board of Clinical Neuropsychology (www.theabcn.org), which is a part of the American Board of Professional Psychology (www.abpp.org).

Training Programs

The American Psychological Association's Division 40 (Clinical Neuropsychology, n.d.) has a website that provides a searchable database for graduate, internship, and postdoctoral training programs in clinical neuropsychology. It can be found at http://www.div40.org/training/index.html.

Another place to get information on training programs is *Graduate Study in Psychology* (GSP; APA, 2014a). GSP provides information on graduate programs offering an emphasis in clinical neuropsychology, neuropsychology, and neuroscience.

In highlighting these resources, it is important to note that GSP (2014) and Division 40's website databases are based on self-reports by individual graduate programs. As such and when reviewing any neuropsychology programs, you are encouraged to be mindful of quality since this varies and changes over time. Before starting your search, we encourage you to review the information in Chapter 7.

Preparing for Graduate Training

The first step to becoming a neuropsychologist is to ensure a solid undergraduate foundation in psychology. This foundation will serve you well as you pursue graduate and postgraduate education in the field. As alluded to in APA's recognition of the specialty and in the Houston Conference Report (Hannay et al., 1998), coursework in the areas of biology, pharmacology, anatomy and physiology, and pathophysiology will be helpful. Note that many of these courses and areas of study may require prerequisite coursework (i.e., prior completion of lower level biology, chemistry, mathematics, or other physical sciences courses). Keep this in mind as you plan your coursework. Additional coursework in statistics is also a good idea. Again though, this coursework is above and beyond that required by your psychology major. In fact, you are strongly encouraged to take and excel in experimental psychology, psychometrics, perception, cognitive psychology, physiological psychology, and psychopharmacology when these courses are available.

Your undergraduate preparation should also include research experience. This suggestion is a reiteration of one of the chief recommendations we give throughout the book. In fact, we encourage you to visit or revisit Chapter 6 as it would be redundant to provide that general information again here.

Working in Areas Related to Neuropsychology with a Bachelor's Degree

As you can see from the information provided, a specialty in the neuropsychology subfield clearly involves substantial training at the doctoral and postdoctoral levels, as well as licensure if professional practice is involved. However, if you have an interest in neuropsychology there are opportunities to work with a bachelor's degree in environments that value the same principles as those found in the subfield of neuropsychology. Some of these include social science research assistants, occupational therapist aides, rehabilitation counselors, and health educators.

Social Science Research Assistants

According to the O*NET (2012b), social science research assistants are supervised by social scientists (e.g., neuropsychologists, neuroscientists). Social science research assistants help with "laboratory, survey, and other social research [and] may perform publication activities, laboratory analysis, quality control, or data management" (http://online.onetcenter.org/link/summary/19-4061.00). This assistance is typically provided for activities that are "more routine" according to the O*NET. Duties can include communicating with supervisors and research participants and collecting, processing, and analyzing research data. O*NET reported that median wages in 2012 were approximately $37,140 and projected that growth in the field over the next 10 years would be faster than average.

Occupational Therapist Aides

Occupational therapist aides assist occupational therapists (OTs) in "planning, implementing, and administering therapy programs to restore, reinforce, and enhance performance" (O*NET, 2012e; http://online.onetcenter.org/link/summary/31-2012.00). OTs are used extensively with individuals recovering from neurological events like strokes and head injuries (e.g., from motor vehicle accidents). The O*NET reported that the 2012 median annual salary was $26,850 and that projected growth in the field would be much faster than average over the next 10 years.

Rehabilitation Counselors

According to O*NET (2012c), rehabilitation counselors "counsel individuals to maximize the independence and employability of persons coping with personal, social, and vocational difficulties that result from birth defects, illness, disease, accidents, or the stress of daily life" (http://online.onetcenter.org/link/summary/21-1015.00). When working in a rehabilitation hospital or center, these counselors help coordinate patients' activities as well as assist in evaluating patients' needs. They also may help execute rehabilitation programs developed by the patients' physicians and psychologists. According to the O*NET, the median annual salary for rehabilitation counselors in 2012 was $33,880. O*NET projects growth in this field to be faster than average over the next 10 years.

Health Educators

According to O*NET (2012d), health educators:

- "Promote, maintain, and improve individual and community health by assisting individuals and communities to adopt healthy behaviors;
- Collect and analyze data to identify community needs prior to planning, implementing, monitoring, and evaluating programs designed to encourage healthy lifestyles, policies, and environments; and
- May also serve as a resource to assist individuals, other professionals, or the community, and may administer fiscal resources for health education programs." (http://online.onetcenter.org/link/summary/21-1091.00)

More specific to the field of neuropsychology, these individuals may assist in educational programs for patients and the public (e.g., helmet safety and car seat safety programs) and provide families with information on support systems available in the community (e.g., Alzheimer's support groups). In terms of wages, the 2012 median annual salary was $48,790 (O*NET). The O*NET also projects a growth rate faster than average over the next 10 years.

An Insider's Perspective

Clinical Neuropsychology – Expanding our Borders

Maria T. Schultheis, PhD
Drexel University

By definition clinical neuropsychology is the study of the relationship between the brain and behavior. In this sense we often think of neuropsychologists as individuals who work with clinical populations that have cognitive impairment as a result of neurological (e.g., stroke, multiple sclerosis), psychiatric (e.g., dementia, schizophrenia) or other compromise (e.g., traumatic brain injury). In this role, neuropsychologists rely on assessment tools that evaluate cognition, and these tools are traditionally paper-and-pencil-based tasks. However, if we expand our thinking about the subfield of neuropsychology, new opportunities abound as a result of advancements in science, medicine, and technology.

First, consider the opportunity to advance our current assessment methodologies. Technologies, such as neuroimaging, have revolutionized our understanding of brain structure and functioning. As a result, it is reasonable that neuropsychologists will play a significant role in continuing to use this technology to improve our understanding of brain–behavior relationships. Other innovative technologies such as virtual reality simulation, wireless sensors, and smart technologies may also afford new creative techniques for evaluating human behavior. In particular these new methods may help address one of the biggest challenges faced by neuropsychologists, which is the evaluation of cognition in everyday tasks (e.g., driving, working, etc.) and increasing the ecological validity of neuropsychological measures. These technologies offer the opportunity to objectively capture brain–behavior observation in naturalistic settings that can better inform an individual's functioning.

Second, consider the new integrated approach to medicine. Although many clinical specialty areas functioned independently in the past, the new focus on interdisciplinary approaches and translational clinical research has encouraged the true integration of the science and practice of neuropsychology. For example, the application of new technologies offers future neuropsychologists an opportunity to work with a wide variety of experts (e.g., engineers, neuroscientists, clinicians) in the development of new techniques for understanding the brain–behavior relationships. Future neuropsychologists will also have the opportunity to study the human brain–behavior relationship across the spectrum, including incorporating the genetics of disorders, defining the natural course of the aging brain, defining the pharmacological needs of different disorders, and creating uniquely tailored clinical interventions for individuals. The growing knowledge base gained by the various sciences can only serve to expand the role and contributions that neuropsychologists can bring in the future.

Indeed, in addition to traditional roles of clinical assessment and treatment of cognitive disorders, neuropsychologists are now in the role of defining the application and integration of this growing knowledge. As experts in brain–behavior relationships, future neuropsychologists can serve to answer the new questions that will be raised, such as the appropriate development of new methodologies, the validation of these approaches, and the clinical application of the scientific findings. As such, opportunities for neuropsychologists expand well beyond the clinical setting and into work within laboratories, universities, businesses, and medicine. Natural collaborations with cognitive neuroscience, genetics, biomedical engineering, and neuropharmacokinetics all offer innovative environments for future neuropsychologists.

Finally, given the diverse options available in neuropsychology, one of the greatest advantages of this training is the opportunity to be involved and contribute in more than one area. That is, a career in neuropsychology can offer great variability in one's career, which can include clinical, research, industry, and academic work individually or in combination. As a result, stagnation can be minimized, and opportunities for innovation and creativity can be maximized. In sum, future neuropsychologists have a great opportunity to redefine the field and contribute to the larger goal of understanding brain–behavior relationships.

Note: Dr. Maria T. Schultheis earned her master's degree in biological science and her PhD in clinical psychology with a concentration in neuropsychology. She is currently an Associate Professor in the Department of Psychology and in the School of Biomedical Engineering, Science, and Health Systems at Drexel University in Philadelphia, PA. She is also the Director of Clinical Training for the graduate program in Clinical Psychology at Drexel. Her research centers on the application of technology to psychology, driving behavior after brain injury, and neurorehabilitation. Her research has been supported by grants from organizations like the National Multiple Sclerosis Society, the National Institutes of Health, and the National Institute for Disability and Rehabilitation Research. Her work has resulted in dozens of publications and presentations and was acknowledged by APA Division 40 – Clinical Neuropsychology with the Early Career Award in 2007 and Fellow status in 2011.

Professional Spotlight

Antonio E. Puente, PhD

Education:
- Bachelor's Degree in Psychology from University of Florida (1973)

- Master of Science Degree (MS) in Biopsychology and Clinical Psychology from University of Georgia (1978)
- Doctor of Philosophy (PhD) in Biopsychology from University of Georgia (1978)
- Postdoctoral Training at Northeast Florida State Hospital (1979–1981)
- Licensed Psychologist in North Carolina

Positions:
Professor of Psychology at the University of North Carolina, Wilmington

Founder and Co-director of Cape Fear Clinic (a bilingual mental health clinic for the poor and uninsured)

Clinical Neuropsychologist in Private Practice

Description of Positions:
My job duties include:

- teaching (from the undergraduate level to the post-doctoral level);
- research (primarily in neuropsychology);
- service (within the university and with various organizations outside the university);
- clinical service (neuropsychology practice); and
- public policy development (e.g., Medicare).

Most Significant Professional Accomplishment:
My most significant professional accomplishment actually relates to my family. I was fortunate enough to present colloquia at each of my three children's undergraduate and graduate schools (when they were students there). In fact, two of my children are in the field of psychology. My daughter attended the PsyD program at the Florida Institute of Technology, and my son attended the PhD program in Clinical Psychology at the University of Georgia.

Favorite Publications:
Puente, A. E., Matthews, J., & Brewer, C. (Eds.). (1992). *Teaching psychology in America: A history.* Washington, DC: American Psychological Association. doi:10.1037/10120-000

Puente, A. E., & McCaffrey, R. (Eds.). (1992). *Handbook of neuropsychological assessment: A biopsychosocial perspective.* New York, NY: Plenum Press.

Area of Research:
My primary area of research is the interface between culture and clinical neuropsychology.

Area of Practice:
My current area of practice is within the broad area of clinical neuropsychology. As part of my practice I conduct both clinical and forensic neuropsychological assessments as well as provide rehabilitation therapy.

Professional Memberships:
- American Psychological Association
  - o Member of Divisions 1, 2, 6, 26, 38, 40, 45, and 52
  - o Fellow of Divisions 1, 2, 6, 26, 40, and 52
  - o President of Division 40 (2002-2003)
- International Neuropsychological Society (member; 1995–present)
- Latin American Neuropsychological Society (member; 1991–present)
- National Academy of Neuropsychology
  - o Founding Member, Fellow, and Past President
- North Carolina Psychological Association
  - o Board of Directors (1985–1991) and Past President (1989–1990)
- Sociedad Interamericana de Psicología (1993–present)
- Hispanic Neuropsychological Society
  - o Founding Board Member and Past President

Most Rewarding Aspect of Your Career:	Words of Advice to the Student Who is Interested in Your Subfield:
The most rewarding aspect of my career is the evolution of balance between my family life and career. Within the profession itself, the most rewarding aspect is my ability to strike a balance among pedagogy, investigation, and service.	My advice to the undergraduate is to develop a vision, enact a trajectory, pursue it with diligence and perseverance while remaining flexible, enjoy the fruits of your success, share it with those seeking to understand and serve, and, above all, do not forget why you got involved with psychology.

Suggested Exercises

1. Using the online directory of training programs on Division 40's web page (www.div40.org) or a recent GSP publication, locate a neuropsychology or neuroscience program that interests you and answer the following questions.
    a. What is the name of the university?
    b. Who is the program director?
    c. What type of degree does it offer?
    d. Is the program accredited?
    e. What are the program's research and/or clinical focus areas?
2. Using an article from one of the neuropsychology publications noted in the chapter, answer the following questions.
    a. What is the title of the article?
    b. Who are the authors?
    c. What are their affiliations? Where do they work?
    d. In three or four sentences, describe the article's findings.
3. Using PsycCareers – APA's Online Career Center (jobs.psyccareers.com), search for a neuropsychology-related position opening. Answer the following questions.
    a. What is the title of the position?
    b. Where is it located (hospital, research institute, university)?
    c. What are the job responsibilities?
    d. Does it specify a particular area of neuropsychology (e.g., brain injury, geriatric, pediatric)?
    e. What are the requirements for the position (e.g., doctorate, research experience, licensure)?
    f. How do you apply for the position?

Suggested Readings

Attix, D. K., & Welsh-Bohmer, K. A. (Eds.). (2005). *Geriatric neuropsychology: Assessment and intervention*. New York, NY: Guilford.

Banich, M. T., & Compton, R. J. (2011). *Cognitive neuroscience* (3rd ed.). Boston, MA: Cengage.

D'Amato, R. C., Fletcher-Janzen, E., & Reynolds, C. R. (Eds.). (2005). *Handbook of school neuropsychology*. New York, NY: Wiley

Elias, L., & Saucier, D. (2005). *Neuropsychology: Clinical and experimental foundations*. Boston, MA: Allyn & Bacon.

Kolb, B., & Whishaw, I. Q. (2008). *Fundamentals of human neuropsychology* (6th ed.). New York, NY: Worth.

Lezak, M. D., Howieson, D. B., Bigler, E. D., & Tranel, D. (2012). *Neuropsychological assessment* (5th ed.). New York, NY: Oxford University Press.

Morgan, J. E., & Ricker, J. H. (Eds.). (2008). *Textbook of clinical neuropsychology: Studies on neuropsychology, neurology, and cognition*. London, England: Taylor and Francis.

Resources

Neuropsychology and Related Organizations

- American Academy of Clinical Neuropsychology: www.theaacn.org
- American Board of Clinical Neuropsychology: www.theabcn.org
- American Academy of Pediatric Neuropsychology: www.theaapn.org
- American Board of Professional Neuropsychology: abn-board.com
- American Psychological Association – Division 6 – Behavioral Neuroscience and Comparative Psychology: http://www.apa.org/divisions/div6
- American Psychological Association – Division 40 – Clinical Neuropsychology: www.div40.org
- American Psychological Association – Division 22 – Rehabilitation Psychology: http://www.apadivisions.org/division-22
- Association for Neuropsychology Students in Training: www.div40-anst.com
- British Psychological Society – Division of Neuropsychology: http://www.bps.org.uk/networks-and-communities/member-networks/division-neuropsychology
- International Neuropsychological Society: www.the-ins.org
- National Academy of Neuropsychology: www.nanonline.org

Other Neuropsychology Resources on the Web

- Neuropsychology Central: www.neuropsychologycentral.com
- Annenberg Media: www.learner.org
  - The Brain – An online series of 32 videos on such topics as memory, Alzheimer's disease, aggression/violence, and neurorehabiliation.
    - http://www.learner.org/resources/series142.html

References

American Psychological Association. (1996). *Archival description of clinical neuropsychology*. Retrieved from http://www.div40.org/pdf/Archival%20Description%20of%20Clinical%20Neuropsychology.pdf

American Psychological Association. (2014a).*Graduate study in psychology: 2014*. Washington, DC: Author.

American Psychological Association. (2014b). *Public description of clinical neuropsychology.* Retrieved from http://www.apa.org/ed/graduate/specialize/neuro.aspx

American Psychological Association. (2014c). *Recognized specialties and proficiencies in professional psychology.* Retrieved from http://www.apa.org/ed/graduate/specialize/recognized.aspx

American Psychological Association – Division 40 – Clinical Neuropsychology. (n.d.). *Listing of training programs in clinical neuropsychology.* Retrieved from http://www.div40.org/training/index.html

Boake, C., & Bieliauskas, L. A. (2007, Summer). Development of clinical neuropsychology as a psychological specialty: A timeline of major events. *The ABPP Specialist,* 42–43.

Hannay, H. J., Bieliauskas, L. A., Crosson, B. A., Hammeke, T. A., Hamsher, K. deS., & Koffler, S. P. (1998). Proceedings: The Houston Conference on Specialty Education and Training in Clinical Neuropsychology. *Archives of Clinical Neuropsychology, 13*(2).

Occupational Information Network. (2012a). *Summary report for: 19-3031.02 – Clinical psychologists.* Retrieved from http://online.onetcenter.org/link/summary/19-3031.02

Occupational Information Network. (2012b). *Summary report for: 19-4061.00 – Social science research assistants.* Retrieved from http://online.onetcenter.org/link/summary/19-4061.00

Occupational Information Network. (2012c). *Summary report for: 21-1015.00 – Rehabilitation counselors.* Retrieved from http://online.onetcenter.org/link/summary/21-1015.00

Occupational Information Network. (2012d). *Summary report for: 21-1091.00 – Health educators.* Retrieved from http://online.onetcenter.org/link/summary/21-1091.00

Occupational Information Network. (2012e). *Summary report for: 31-2012.00 – Occupational therapist aides.* Retrieved from http://online.onetcenter.org/link/summary/31-2012.00

Chapter Fifteen
Careers in Forensic Psychology

Forensic Psychology Defined

The field of forensic psychology is a much broader area than most people think. In recording the history of the field, Bartol and Bartol (1999) defined forensic psychology as:

> both (a) the research endeavor that examines aspects of human behavior directly related to the legal process...and (b) the professional practice of psychology within, or in consultation with, a legal system that encompasses both criminal and civil law and the numerous areas where they interact. Therefore, forensic psychology refers broadly to the *production* and *application* of psychological knowledge to the civil and criminal justice systems. (p. 3, italics in original)

On the application side, forensic psychology is one of the newest subfields officially recognized by the American Psychological Association's (APA) Commission for the Recognition of Specialties and Proficiencies in Professional Psychology (APA, 2014b). The initial recognition came in 2001. As part of the recognition, APA defined the applied side of forensic psychology as:

> the professional practice by psychologists within the areas of clinical psychology, counseling psychology, school psychology or another specialty recognized by the American Psychological Association, when they are engaged as experts and represent themselves as such, in an activity primarily intended to provide professional psychological expertise to the judicial system. (http://www.apa.org/ed/graduate/specialize/forensic.aspx)

Majoring in Psychology: Achieving Your Educational and Career Goals, Second Edition.
Jeffrey L. Helms and Daniel T. Rogers.
© 2015 John Wiley & Sons, Ltd. Published 2015 by John Wiley & Sons, Ltd.

However, as Bartol and Bartol (1999) noted, application is only one of the two broad aspects of forensic psychology, with the other being production (i.e., research). Because of these different aspects and areas within forensic psychology, this subfield of psychology is often referred to by different names. These names include: legal psychology, criminal psychology, psychology and law, police psychology, correctional psychology, and investigative psychology. For reading ease, we will use the term forensic psychology when referring to any and all of these areas.

Additionally, and by the very nature of the field and its relationship to the legal system, forensic psychology is often broken down further. The breakdown mirrors that of the American judicial system. The two broad divisions within forensic psychology are criminal forensic psychology and civil forensic psychology. Criminal forensic psychology interacts with the criminal legal system. In short, forensic psychology brings its skills to bear on processes involved in how criminal law is established, how suspects are investigated and adjudicated, and how offenders are punished. Civil forensic psychology interacts with the civil legal system (e.g., family and administrative courts). Criminal law focuses its energies on punishment; civil law focuses its energies on redress of wrongs. Redress typically occurs via compensation or restitution (e.g., malpractice claims, personal injury claims). These two divisions will become clearer when activities in the respective areas are discussed.

As might be guessed based on the description of the field, tension exists in the relationship between psychology and the legal system. The tension highlights the challenges inherent in the subfield of forensic psychology. Although the legal system deals in absolutes (e.g., guilt vs. innocence; legal vs. illegal), psychology is based on research, and the opinions psychologists offer are informed by this research (e.g., statistical analyses of group data). As a result, the dichotomous field of law sometimes clashes with the statistically rooted field of psychology. This does not mean that value is not derived from psychology's involvement with the legal system. It is actually the exact opposite. High value is placed on psychologists' involvement because they consider all the variables and circumstances that impact a situation and offer expert opinions, reports, treatment, etc., based on research findings as opposed to nonscientific personal opinions or beliefs.

Contributions to the Discipline of Psychology

As might be guessed from the description of the breadth of this subfield, forensic psychologists contribute to the discipline in a number of ways. The four main ways are research, public policy development and analysis,

Box 15.1 *Top Journals That Publish Forensic Psychology Research*

1. *Law and Human Behavior*
2. *Psychology, Public Policy, and Law*
3. *Behavioral Sciences and the Law*
4. *Criminal Justice and Behavior*
5. *Applied Cognitive Psychology*

Note. Information comes from Helms (2009).

education, and clinical practice. In terms of research, some of the topics studied include jury selection, domestic violence, eyewitness testimony, police lineup procedures, confession, stalking, child abuse, guardianship, and child custody. For readers curious about what topics are currently being researched and published, you are encouraged to obtain a copy of one of the top journals in the field and peruse the table of contents. See Box 15.1 for a list of the top five journals that publish forensic psychology research.

Forensic psychologists also assist in the development of policy including analyzing a policy's effects. For example, a forensic psychologist may evaluate the impact of a new policy that diverts people from prison to drug treatment when warranted. This information can then be used by policy makers (e.g., legislators) to remedy any issues with the new policy.

In terms of education, forensic psychologists teach, train, and mentor the next generation of forensic psychologists. Contributions are made to the field via teaching specialized courses in forensic psychology in an undergraduate or graduate program, supervising student-trainees on practica and internship, and collaborating with colleagues newly interested in the field.

Last but not least are the contributions made in the clinical practice domain. The forensic psychologist that works in the clinical practice area provides assessments/evaluations, treatment, and consultation to and for the courts, attorneys, and other legally involved parties (e.g., defendants). Because clinical practice is arguably the largest area within forensic psychology, an upcoming section provides more information.

Although clinical practice is the largest area, significant contributions are made to forensic psychology from a host of other subfields of psychology.

Here are some examples of topics in the respective psychology subfields that are forensically related:

- Developmental psychology:
  - Effects of divorce and custody arrangements on children
  - Elder maltreatment and abuse
  - Social psychology
  - Racial profiling
  - Jury decision making research
- Cognitive psychology:
  - Eyewitness evidence
  - False memories and recovered memories
- Neuropsychology:
  - Malingering and feigning memory problems
  - The effect of brain development on juvenile delinquency
- Industrial–organizational psychology:
  - Workplace harassment
  - Workplace violence
- School psychology:
  - Bullying
  - School violence

Core Activities of the Forensic Psychologist

For forensic psychologists focused on research and those housed in an academic environment, activities are similar to those discussed in Chapter 16. As a result, the focus of this section is predominantly on the applied areas of forensic psychology. For practitioners that provide services to the public (i.e., individuals, attorneys, courts), activities include the major components discussed below.

Assessment

As noted in Chapter 10, assessment is one of the main distinctions between psychology and the other mental health professions. This distinction, based in part on psychologists' abilities to develop reliable and valid tests and testing procedures, carries over to the forensic psychology subfield as well. Forensic psychologists use psychological tests, interviews, observations, and review of records to provide these assessments. The assessments can be requested by the court, an individual, an organization, or an attorney. Because of the number of potential referral sources and the value placed on the forensic psychologist's work, hundreds of thousands of forensic psychological assessments are provided each year. The assessments that forensic psychologists provide are divided into the two broad areas noted earlier, civil and criminal forensic psychology areas. Here are some common types of assessments in the two areas:

- Civil forensic psychological assessment:
  - *Child custody:* These assessments assist the court in determining the best living arrangements for a child.
  - *Guardianship:* These assessments assist the court in determining if a person can care for himself/herself or if the person needs someone to help with providing the care.
  - *Competency to make treatment decisions:* These assessments help the court determine if a person is capable of making sound treatment decisions (e.g., accepting/refusing psychoactive medications).
  - *Personal injury evaluations:* These evaluations help determine if an injury (e.g., depression, brain injury) is due to another's negligence (e.g., auto accident) or if it is pre-existing.
- Criminal forensic psychological assessment:
  - *Competency to stand trial/competency to be adjudicated:* These assessments help the court determine if a defendant is able to understand the charges, understand the legal issues and procedures in the case, understand the dispositions and penalties possible, etc. (*Dusky v. United States*, 1960).
  - *Competency to waive* Miranda *rights:* These evaluations help the court determine if a person knowingly, intelligently, and voluntarily waived the right to silence and assistance of an attorney (*Miranda v. Arizona*, 1966).
  - *Transfer evaluations:* These evaluations assist the court in determining if a juvenile should remain in the juvenile court system for treatment and rehabilitation or if he/she should be transferred to the adult court system.
  - *Competency to be sentenced and executed:* These assist the court in determining if a person understands what is being done to them and why.
  - *Violence risk assessment:* These assessments assist the court, parole boards, schools, and other entities in determining the risk of violence of an individual given certain circumstances and contexts (e.g., inpatient vs. outpatient; community placement vs. incarcerated).

Treatment

Another common activity of forensic psychologists is treatment. Treatment can be defined as the provision of psychological, therapeutic techniques to change behavior, thoughts, and emotions. Forensically relevant treatment can be self-initiated or court ordered. As is the case with assessment, treatment in the forensic area is divided into civil and criminal domains. The following is a list of some common treatment circumstances seen by forensic psychologists.

- Civil forensic psychological treatment:
  - *Victim treatment:* This treatment includes child and adult victims as well as victims of domestic and stranger violence. Treatment of those individuals that have been victimized is one of the larger areas of practice for some forensic psychologists.
  - *Treatment of law enforcement professionals:* This type of treatment assists law enforcement professionals in coping with the stressors associated with their jobs (e.g., working in a prison setting, killing someone in the line of duty, witnessing violence).
  - *Divorce mediation/dispute resolution:* This type of treatment (or intervention) assists families and parties in resolving conflict due to differing goals and needs.
- Criminal forensic psychological treatment:
  - *Sex offender treatment:* This type of treatment works with individuals who have been adjudicated (i.e., convicted) of a sex offense and has the goal of eliminating or reducing recidivism.
  - *Drug dependence treatment:* This type of treatment focuses on individuals (usually referred by the court) with drug dependence problems. Psychological treatments have been shown to be significantly more effective than incarceration in reducing recidivism for individuals with these difficulties.
  - *Multisystemic therapy:* This is an empirically validated community-based treatment program used with juveniles who have histories significant for delinquency, including violent offenses and drug use (Henggeler et al., 1999).

Consultation with Attorneys, Courts, and Insurance Companies

Because of forensic psychologists' expertise in human behavior, they are often sought out by attorneys, courts, and insurance companies for their perspectives. Although these consultations may lead to a referral for an assessment or treatment, they are often used to clarify issues in a particular case. Here are some circumstances when a consultation may be sought:

- an insurance company consults with a forensic psychologist regarding an insurance claim that may involve fraud (e.g., individual malingering pain in an effort to increase insurance payment/settlement);
- an attorney seeks out a forensic psychologist for a consultation on what treatments are available in the community for a particular problem that the attorney's client has; and
- an attorney hires a forensic psychologist to review a client's medical and treatment records prior to filing a malpractice lawsuit.

Trial Consultation

Due to the adversarial nature of the US justice system, there is, by definition, a winner and a loser when all is finished. Depending on the circumstances, the "loser" can potentially lose his/her freedom (in criminal court) or large sums of money (in civil court). As a result of the high stakes nature of the legal process, both parties involved sometimes use trial consultants. Trial consultants can help with jury selection as well as case theme development and strategies. For example, trial consultants can conduct a survey of the community (i.e., potential jurors) to learn what type of juror is likely to be more favorable to their side (e.g., more or less likely to convict). Based on the results of the survey, attorneys can make decisions about who they would like to have as jurors during the *voir dire* process (i.e., the examination to determine the suitability of a potential juror). Due to the nature of this work, trial consultants are methodologically sophisticated (i.e., they have excellent skills in research methods and applied statistics).

Testimony

Due to the nature of the work, forensic psychologists are often called to testify in court or give a deposition to attorneys. Sometimes, forensic psychologists are specifically hired as experts to provide this testimony. For example, a forensic psychologist may have a specialty in the treatment of posttraumatic stress disorder (PTSD) in battered women. An attorney that knows of this expertise may retain (i.e., hire) the psychologist to provide testimony regarding PTSD. Other times forensic psychologists provide testimony regarding the findings in their psychological assessments or during the course of treatment. Regardless of the circumstances or who retained the expert (the court, the prosecution/plaintiff, or the defense) and given the adversarial nature of the process, testifying in court is stressful.

Program Development and Administration

Another area of practice for the forensic psychologist is program development and administration. Due to the breadth and depth of training and knowledge in human behavior, forensic psychologists are equipped to develop effective programs that address particular problems encountered by individuals entangled in the justice system. These programs are in such areas as treatment for battered women, abused children, sex offenders, and at-risk youth. Once developed, forensic psychologists often are hired specifically to administer the program. The activities involved in administering (i.e., running) a program include hiring qualified staff, supervising staff, evaluating the effectiveness of the program, and changing the program to meet the needs of those it serves.

A Note about Criminal Profiling

Criminal profiling is the development of a description of the likely perpetrator of a crime who has yet to be apprehended. A profile may include information on the personality and psychological characteristics of the offender as well as physical attributes (e.g., sex, race/ethnicity, height, weight) and behavior relevant to the crime. The primary purpose of the profile is to narrow the investigation and shorten the time to apprehension of the offender. Profiling is an art and not a science. As such, psychology, and in particular forensic psychology, steers clear of this area for the most part. In addition to being an art and not a science, other reasons that criminal profiling is routinely not included in the forensic psychology domain are:

- Training in profiling has typically fallen under the domain of law enforcement agencies, particularly the Federal Bureau of Investigation (FBI). As such, it is rarely available to those outside the FBI. Forensic psychology programs do *not* train students in criminal profiling.
- The job market for criminal profilers is almost nonexistent. There is little need for these types of jobs beyond existing law enforcement personnel who might engage in it as needed.
- Criminal profiling often utilizes stereotypes about populations to derive the profile. The use of stereotypes by law enforcement officials has contributed to disproportionate representation of minorities in the justice system in this country, and it has contributed to inaccurate profiles.

Training Required to be a Forensic Psychologist

For research and academic positions, a doctorate is typically the entry level degree, although some master's level research positions are available in large agencies (e.g., the Department of Justice, the Office of Juvenile Justice and Delinquency Prevention). As noted earlier, forensically oriented topics are addressed by many of the subfields of psychology including experimental, social, developmental, and cognitive psychology. As such, students interested in the forensic topics typically addressed by these sub-fields of psychology are encouraged to identify particular researchers in these fields, the university programs where the researchers work, and information regarding application and admission to graduate training in those programs. For more information on graduate school application procedures, please see Chapter 7.

For applied positions, a master's degree is likely sufficient for many treatment provider positions inside of correctional facilities. According to a survey of master's level psychology practitioners, approximately 31% worked within a state's department of corrections (MacKain, Tedeschi, Durham, & Goldman, 2002). DiCataldo et al. (2008) reported that the main activity of the master's level practitioner is the provision of treatment. In fact, the study indicated that almost half (46.3%) of the master's level practitioner's work week is spent providing therapy.

However, the Forensic Specialty Council (2007), the group responsible for developing and submitting to APA the education and training guidelines used to establish the specialty, recommends a different path to forensic specialization and training. Specifically, the Forensic Specialty Council clearly states that to function as an applied forensic psychologist, postdoctoral training is required. The Council and others suggest a progression from:

- general training at the doctoral level in clinical, counseling, or school psychology including supervised practica;
- postdoctoral training in a forensically oriented environment under a forensic psychologist;
- licensure as a psychologist in the respective jurisdiction; to
- board certification by the American Board of Forensic Psychology (this aspect is preferred but not required).

It is important to note that state licensure is not typically required for researchers, educators, and policy specialists, including those researchers, educators, and policy specialists who give expert testimony. However, those who provide treatment, assessment, and diagnosis do require licensure.

(Please see Chapter 10 for discussion of the licensure process.) This requirement, along with laws and statutes excluding the involvement of nondoctoral-level practitioners in some areas of forensic practice (e.g., assessment, some expert roles), makes it imperative that students understand the limitations associated with different degree levels.

Additionally, one question that students routinely ask is whether or not a law degree is needed to practice in the forensic psychology subfield, especially given the overlapping nature of the areas and the knowledge required to practice effectively. It is true that some psychologists chose to attend law school (JD degree) or attain a Masters of Legal Studies degree (MLS). As a matter of fact, several joint degree programs exist. These joint degree programs allow the student to simultaneously pursue a graduate psychology degree and the law degree (e.g., JD/PhD programs). Although excellent training, these are not necessary to be a forensic psychologist. What is necessary is an understanding of and familiarity with the law as it applies to your particular area of practice whether it is research endeavors, assessment, or treatment.

Forensic Psychology Training Programs

There are a number of graduate programs that train individuals in forensic psychology or have an emphasis or track in forensic psychology. Three resources that list or have a directory of programs are:

- American Psychology-Law Society (APLS): http://www.apadivisions. org/division-41/education/programs/index.aspx
- *Graduate Study in Psychology* (APA, 2014a)
- Helms and Mayhew's (2006) *Undergraduate Preparation for Graduate Training in Forensic Psychology*: http://teachpsych.org/resources/ Documents/otrp/resources/helms06.pdf

Although these resources provide excellent starting points, the interested student is cautioned because program quality varies widely, especially over time. Because of the wide disparity between programs, this book's first author (Helms) initiated a program rankings study that was presented at the 2008 APLS conference. The survey was emailed to those individuals who were actively involved in the field of forensic psychology. The top-ranked clinically oriented and research-oriented doctoral programs are listed in Box 15.2. This information will hopefully provide additional perspectives on the programs available to pursue for graduate study in this subfield.

Box 15.2   *Top Programs in Forensic Psychology*

Top Clinically Oriented Forensic Programs
1.   Simon Fraser University
2.   University of Nebraska – Lincoln
3.   University of Alabama
4.*   John Jay College of Criminal Justice
4.*   Sam Houston State University

*Denotes a tie

Top Research-Oriented Forensic Programs
1.   University of Nebraska – Lincoln
2.   John Jay College of Criminal Justice
3.   Simon Fraser University
4.   Florida International University
5.   University of Arizona

Note. Information comes from Helms (2008).

Preparing for Graduate Training in Forensic Psychology

For those students interested in increasing their chances of getting accepted into a graduate program that emphasizes forensic psychology, a study by this book's first author and a colleague (Helms & Mayhew, 2006) can provide some help toward selecting undergraduate courses. For the study, Helms and Mayhew surveyed individuals involved in selecting students for graduate study in forensic psychology and complemented these findings with information provided by forensic psychology graduate programs. Based on a three-point scale where 1 was *optional*, 2 was *recommend*, and 3 was *require*, mean ratings placed six undergraduate courses in the *recommend* to *require* range. They were:

Course	Mean (SD)
Research Methods	2.98 (.14)
Statistics	2.96 (.20)
Abnormal Psychology	2.44 (.71)
Experimental Psychology	2.29 (.71)
Introduction to Forensic Psychology	2.24 (.69)
Social Psychology	2.18 (.70)

Table 15.1 Activities Rating Means and Percentages for People Involved in Forensic Psychology Graduate Student Selection

Activity	M (SD)	High	Medium	Low
Previous research activity	2.94 (.24)	93.9	6.1	0.0
Letters of recommendation	2.82 (.44)	84.0	14.0	2.0
Statement of goals and objectives	2.70 (.46)	70.0	30.0	0.0
Interview	2.38 (.67)	48.0	42.0	10.0
Work experience	1.96 (.64)	18.0	60.0	22.0
Clinically related public service	1.84 (.59)	10.2	63.3	26.5
Extracurricular activity	1.36 (.56)	4.0	28.0	68.0

Note. Means based on *High* = 3, *Medium* = 2, and *Low* = 1. Information comes from Helms and Mayhew (2006).

As can be seen from the mean ratings, it is clear that high value is placed on the scientific basis of psychology. As a result, those students interested in pursuing graduate training with an emphasis in forensic psychology are strongly encouraged to take and excel in the more research-oriented coursework in the undergraduate curriculum.

As noted in the first part of the book, there is more to getting accepted to graduate school than good grades. As a result, Helms and Mayhew (2006) also asked people involved in the selection of graduate students for forensic psychology programs to rate the importance of some common activities. Table 15.1 presents the results. It is clear from the results that research activity is highly valued (and complements the ratings of undergraduate coursework noted earlier). Additionally, letters of recommendation, the applicant's statement of goals and objectives, and an interview received mean ratings in the "medium" to "high" ranges. It is also important to mention those activities that were not rated as high. Work experience, clinically related public service, and extracurricular activity received mean ratings in the "low" to "medium" range. Although this does not mean they are not valued, it does mean that other activities are valued more. Given that most students have limited time, this information can assist students in making the most of the time that is available, especially if the goal is gaining admission to a graduate program with an emphasis in forensic psychology.

Employment in the Forensic Psychology Subfield

Settings

As you probably guessed based on the variety of activities, there are a range of employment opportunities in the subfield of forensic psychology. Box 15.3 provides some examples of recent position openings in forensic psychology. In terms of research-oriented positions, opportunities in research institutes and government agencies like the Department of Justice and the Office of Juvenile Justice and Delinquency Prevention are possible. Of course, the main employment setting for those interested in research is academe. As such, colleges and universities that have a commitment to research are likely places of employment, and most academic environments encourage (or even require) the expansion of knowledge in a person's field

---

Box 15.3 *Recent Forensic Psychology Position Openings*

Forensic Psychologist at a Secure Medical Facility (Alabama)
- Forensic evaluation and treatment of criminally committed patients.

Forensic Psychologist at a Forensic Hospital (Nova Scotia)
- Assessment, treatment, and consultation as well as active involvement in program planning and evaluation, ongoing research, clinical supervision, and various administration and operational activities.

Forensic Psychologist at a Sex Offender Treatment Center (Minnesota)
- Provide services to patients civilly committed as mentally ill and dangerous or sexually dangerous persons, and individuals with cognitive disabilities who have sexually offended.

Forensic Psychologist at a State Hospital (California)
- Provide substance abuse treatment, treat seriously mentally ill individuals, design behavior plans, provide behavior therapy.

Master's Level Practitioner at State Youth Commission School (Texas)
- Provide group, family, and individual therapy; administration and interpretation of psychological evaluations of youth at-risk of suicide or in need of special treatment services.

Note. Information comes from job advertisements posted on the APLS and APA websites.

of expertise via research and publication. For those interested in more of the training side of education, professional schools and medical schools provide opportunities.

As noted in the study by MacKain et al. (2001), many master's level practitioners work in correctional settings, especially at the local and state level. When it comes to the federal level, most openings are for those at the doctoral level because licensure to practice independently is often required. Prisons at both the state and federal level also typically provide training opportunities for those in need of supervised experience prior to licensure. Additionally, the pay tends to be quite good, and positions tend to be plentiful. Unfortunately, the reasons for the good pay and plentiful positions tend to correlate with retention issues. Stress is a big factor in these settings and often leads to individuals seeking different employment opportunities. Regardless, most agree that the training and learning opportunities in these environments are excellent for the forensic psychologist.

If the correctional setting (i.e., jails and prisons) is not a good fit or interesting to you, opportunities inside law enforcement agencies may be a better fit. Opportunities with probation and parole departments are available to those with forensic psychology expertise. For example, a recent advertisement recruiting doctoral-level, licensed, forensic psychologists for the California Board of Parole Hearings indicated multiple openings in the state. Individuals in these settings provide assessments of individuals coming up for parole for the parole boards. Police departments also hire forensic psychologists. Although most outsource their forensic psychological needs (i.e., hire consultants on an "as needed" basis), some police agencies hire forensic psychologists to treat stress reactions in officers, evaluate officers for fitness for duty after a traumatic incident, and evaluate potential police recruits for jobs.

Another setting for forensic psychologists is court clinics. In order to avoid or limit delays in the judicial process, some court systems hire forensic psychologists to evaluate defendants on-site instead of transporting them to the local state hospital for the evaluation. Keeping defendants on-site saves both time and money. However, the services are not limited to evaluation, although it is the main function. Forensic psychologists in the court clinic have the opportunity routinely to consult with judges and attorneys as well as to provide brief therapy and crisis intervention services.

Other settings that employ forensic psychologists include hospitals (especially state psychiatric hospitals). When an individual is found not guilty by reason of insanity or an individual is found to be a danger to himself/herself or to another person, that individual is most often hospitalized at a state psychiatric facility. In order to remain hospitalized, the person must continue to meet certain legal criteria. These criteria include having a mental illness, being a danger to self or others, benefitting from treatment, and the hospital being the least restrictive environment necessary to accomplish the treatment. Forensic psychologists via assessment and testimony help the courts determine whether or not a person should remain in the hospital. Some state hospitals also house individuals who are found incompetent to stand trial. Depending on the state, these hospitals provide competency restoration programs (i.e., programs designed to help an individual become competent so that she/he can go to trial or resolve the legal issues at hand). Forensic psychologists often develop and administer these programs.

Last but not least, some forensic psychologists are self-employed. In other words, they have their own private forensic psychology practices. Because forensic psychologists in this environment are generally free to pick and choose the types of cases they accept, the work they do is quite broad sometimes. For example, although a forensic psychologist in private practice may specialize in custody evaluations while another forensic psychologist specializes in trial consultation and jury selection, both forensic psychologists will likely work on cases in other forensic areas as well. Along these same lines, it is important to note that most private practitioners incorporate nonforensic areas into the practice. This is done in part to limit the stress involved as well as continue to keep their skills fresh in other areas (e.g., general clinical skills like psychotherapy).

Salaries

Salaries for academic positions will be consistent with those noted in Chapter 16. Salaries for practitioners will be consistent with those noted in Chapter 10. In short, the median annual wage for clinical, counseling, and school psychologists was $67,650 (Occupational Information Network [O*NET], 2012). However, salaries for practitioners are dependent on the area of the country, the work setting, and the forensic psychologist's reputation and experience. For example, high stress positions in high security forensic hospitals and prison settings will likely command much higher salaries. Additionally, a forensic psychologist with more experience and who is well known in his/her practicing community will likely command higher pay than someone who is just getting licensed.

Special Employment Issues

Although each employment area has idiosyncrasies related to hiring procedures, there are several issues specific to employment in the field of forensic psychology that warrant mentioning. First, background checks (along with fingerprinting) are routine. The thoroughness of the check varies (with federal positions requiring significantly more, including interviews of current and past associates, family, etc.). Regardless, all background checks will certainly reveal arrests as well as convictions including misdemeanors (e.g., public intoxication). Traffic violations also can cause problems since they can be interpreted as risk-taking behavior. Second, drug screening preemployment (and postemployment) is also routinely done. With regard to this issue, it is important to emphasize that agents and detectives who interview friends, former friends, family, teachers, roommates, ex-boyfriends/girlfriends/wives/husbands/partners, etc., will ask about current and past drug use. Any drug use can prevent employment in many federal positions (e.g., federal prisons). These issues are not meant to scare but to inform and prepare the person interested in working in settings that require security clearance (e.g., prisons).

Working in Areas Related to Forensic Psychology with a Bachelor's Degree

As noted earlier, opportunities to practice forensic psychology are generally limited to those individuals with advanced graduate training, likely at the doctoral level. After reading the chapter, it makes sense that the knowledge required to practice adequately in this area would require such training, hence why many state and federal statutes require that doctoral level psychologists perform many of the tasks and activities noted. For example, would you want someone with a bachelor's degree consulting on jury selection with your attorney if you were on trial for murder? We wouldn't!

Although many activities are outside the skill set of a bachelor's level person, there are many that are not. As a matter of fact, there are quite a few opportunities for individuals who have a bachelor's degree, including those who are stopping at that educational level and those who are taking some time off prior to applying for graduate school (e.g., trying the field out to see if it might be a good fit). Some of the more common ways to get involved in the forensic psychology subfield with a bachelor's degree include the following.

Police or Law Enforcement Officer

Although this career does not always require a bachelor's degree, the degree will put an applicant significantly ahead of those without one. Even with a bachelor's degree, officer training is required in order to learn law enforcement procedures, gun use, vehicle use, etc. Regardless, this type of position will allow intimate involvement with the justice system from arrest through to incarceration. One of the benefits for an individual who may be considering this as an interim position prior to applying to graduate school is that the duties of a police officer, including court appearances, will increase comfort with the judicial process and judicial players (e.g., judges, clerks, and attorneys). As a result, anxieties related to being in the adversarial climate will likely diminish, thereby making you a better witness in the future. According to the US Department of Labor, Bureau of Labor Statistics' Occupational Outlook Handbook (OOH; 2014–2015b), median salary for these positions was approximately $56,980.

Correctional Officers

According to the OOH (2014–2015a), "correctional officers are responsible for overseeing individuals who have been arrested and are awaiting trial or who have been sentenced to serve time in a jail or prison." The OOH goes on to describe some of the duties that are involved in the job. These include:

- "Enforce rules and keep order within jails or prisons;
- Supervise activities of inmates;
- Aid in rehabilitation and counseling of offenders;
- Inspect facilities to ensure that they meet standards;
- Search inmates for contraband items; and
- Report on inmate conduct."(http://www.bls.gov/ooh/protective-service/correctional-officers.htm#tab-2)

The median salary for correctional officers in 2012 was approximately $38,970. Like police officers, these positions also will allow the person interested in the forensic psychology subfield to acclimate to the correctional and justice system environment.

Probation Officers and Correctional Treatment Specialists

According to the OOH (2015–2015c), "probation officers and correctional treatment specialists work with and monitor offenders to prevent them from committing new crimes" (http://www.bls.gov/ooh/community-and-social-service/probation-officers-and-correctional-treatment-specialists.htm). Some of the duties associated with this occupation include:

- "Evaluate offenders to determine the best course of rehabilitation;
- Provide offenders with resources, such as job training;
- Test offenders for drugs and offer substance-abuse counseling;
- Monitor offenders and help with their progress;
- Conduct meetings with offenders and their family and friends; and
- Write reports on the progress of offenders." (http://www.bls.gov/ooh/community-and-social-service/probation-officers-and-correctional-treatment-specialists.htm#tab-2)

In terms of pay, the OOH reports a median salary for professionals in this area was approximately $48,190 in 2012.

Other Positions

Some other positions that are available to applicants with a bachelor's degree in psychology include caseworker/case manager, program assistant, and mental health technician. Prior to and after being released on parole or released from the hospital, individuals can benefit from the additional support provided by a caseworker or case manager. In fact, it can be instrumental in the person remaining out of the facility. Such support can include assistance in identifying mental health services, employment, medication assistance, and housing.

Another possible position at the bachelor's level is program assistant. Program assistants provide support to professional staff at shelters, domestic violence prevention programs, at-risk youth programs, etc. Regardless of the type of program, the program assistant is on the front line in serving the program's clients. This is also true of mental health technicians in the forensic hospital setting. Due to other duties and responsibilities, nurses, psychologists, and psychiatrists cannot provide most of the moment-to-moment care of patients in these settings throughout the course of the day. These professionals rely heavily on mental health technicians to carry out specific activities and programs as well as provide front line and back up support to the medical staff.

An Insider's Perpective

Why Become a Forensic Psychologist?

Matthew T. Huss
Creighton University

Forensic psychology is one of the fastest-growing fields in psychology, and much of this growth is fueled by increasing media attention. Books, movies, and television shows are making it more and more interesting to become a forensic psychologist. Although the media sometimes focuses on the more sensational and less than realistic aspects of the field, there are many genuine reasons for students interested in the area to pursue it as a career. Here are three of them.

First, one of the most interesting aspects of forensic psychology is that it is the intersection of two very different disciplines, the law and psychology. The two disciplines are interdependent but hold very different viewpoints, often making the intersection somewhat messy. Although forensic psychologists do not have to be psychologists *and* attorneys, you do have to be well versed in both the law and psychology. Becoming an expert in one field is difficult enough, but the additional challenge of integrating the law into psychology is very attractive to many people.

Second, forensic psychology offers a diversity of job opportunities. Depending on the person's training, there are many settings in which a forensic psychologist can work, including law enforcement agencies, hospitals, juvenile detention facilities, government agencies, and mental health centers. A forensic psychologist can even open his or her own private practice or teach and conduct research at a college or university. This variety allows for a person to pursue many different paths either simultaneously or consecutively during a career.

Last but not least, there is no denying the sensational aspects that attract many people to forensic psychology. These aspects are even interesting to forensic psychologists who are around them on a regular basis. Simply put, forensic psychology is *sexy*. Forensic psychologists get to meet and evaluate some of the most notorious offenders of our time such as Ted Kaczynski, Charles Manson, and Jeffrey Dahmer. Through the use of jury selection techniques, they assist attorneys in influencing the outcome of famous trials such as O. J. Simpson's criminal trial for murder and Oprah Winfrey's civil trial for defamation of the beef industry in Texas. However, even the less public cases are inherently interesting to almost anyone.

In summary, these three potential reasons to become a forensic psychologist barely scratch the surface of possibilities within the profession. However, it should excite anyone with an interest in the field and encourage them to pursue more information.

Note. Currently a professor of psychology at Creighton University, Dr. Matthew Huss received his doctorate in clinical psychology and a master's in legal studies from the University of Nebraska – Lincoln. He has published dozens of journal articles and book chapters. One of his most recent publications is the second edition of his textbook titled *Forensic Psychology: Research, Clinical Practice, and Applications* (2014). He was named a state professor of the year by the Carnegie Foundation for the Advancement of Teaching and the Council for Advancement and Support of Education (CASE) in 2013. Dr. Huss's primary research interests focus on prediction of violence, domestic violence, and sex offenders.

Professional Spotlight

Gina M. Vincent, PhD

Education:
- Bachelor of Arts (BA) in Psychology from the University of Alaska – Anchorage
- Master of Arts (MA) in Law and Psychology from Simon Fraser University
- Doctor of Philosophy (PhD) in Experimental Psychology, Law and Psychology Specialization from Simon Fraser University

Employer:
University of Massachusetts Medical School – Law & Psychiatry Program, Department of Psychiatry

Position:
Research Associate Professor of Psychiatry

Description of Position:
My academic position is funded entirely by grants and contracts. As a

result, the duties involve writing and submitting grants, publishing, conducting research, mentoring some research associates, and engaging in some administrative and service work. Much of my grant funded work for the past five years has involved providing hands-on technical assistance to juvenile justice agencies and personnel for selecting, implementing, and occasionally creating risk assessment tools in their systems.

Most Significant Professional Accomplishment:

My most significant professional accomplishments were (1) receiving a five-year mentored K01 award from the National Institute of Drug Abuse to learn neuroimaging, and (2) developing and publishing guidelines for implementing risk assessment instruments in juvenile justice systems, which in some cases have demonstrated a 50% reduction in institutionalization.

Favorite Publication:

Vincent, G. M., Guy, L. S., & Grisso, T. (2012). *Risk assessment in juvenile justice: A guidebook for implementation.* Chicago, IL: John D. & Catherine T. MacArthur Foundation.

Areas of Research:

The common thread in my research is delinquency and juvenile justice. There are two primary areas: (1) the impact of implementing risk for reoffending assessments in juvenile justice settings and methods for maximizing its effectiveness, and (2) the underlying functionalities of substance abuse in callous-unemotional youth.

Professional Memberships:

- American Psychology-Law Society
  o Professional Development of Women's Committee Chair
  o APLS Conference Co-chair (2009)
- International Association of Forensic Mental Health Services
- Society for the Scientific Study of Psychopathy (SSSP)

Most Rewarding Aspect of Your Career:

The most rewarding aspect of my career is working with juvenile justice agencies to put research findings into practice and change juvenile justice policy in a manner that is conducive to adolescent development.

Words of Advice to the Student Who is Interested in Your Subfield:

If you are interested in the forensic psychology subfield, I recommend going to a graduate university that has a specialized PhD program in this area. If you do not pursue a clinical degree, most likely you will end up in academia or in a policy-related position. Given where these fields are headed, I strongly recommend getting grant writing experience as early in your training as possible. Within this field, try not to specialize too much. Keep your options open and be aware of opportunities that come your way.

Suggested Exercises

1. The APLS website (http://www.apadivisions.org/division-41) has a "Job Listings" page that gives information on academic and professional positions. Choose one position opening from each category and answer the following questions.
    *   What type of position is it (academic or professional)?
    *   Where is the position?
    *   How does an applicant apply?
    *   What does a person include in his/her application?
    *   What training is required for the position?
2. Locate an issue of one of the top journals listed in this chapter. Answer the following questions.
    *   What are some of the topics studied?
    *   Where do the authors work?
    *   Were any of the authors students?
3. For one of the authors cited in this chapter or on the APLS web page, do a web search for information on him or her. Answer the following questions.
    *   Where does the person work?
    *   What is the person's job (e.g., professor, student, clinician)?
    *   What other publications/presentations does the person have?
    *   If the person is a professor, what courses do they teach?
    *   What are some of the topics they study?
4. Research one of the forensically oriented graduate programs listed in one of the resources noted in this chapter. Answer the following questions.
    *   What is the name of the program?
    *   What degrees does the program offer?
    *   What are the application procedures?
    *   When is the application deadline?
    *   Do they require entrance exams (e.g., the GRE)? If so, what are the minimum scores? More importantly, what are the average scores of recent students?
    *   What other requirements do they have for admission?
    *   What, if any, financial support do they provide their students?
    *   What do their students end up doing when they graduate?
    *   What is their acceptance rate? How many people apply? How many people do they accept? How many people actually come to the program?

Suggested Readings

Case Examples in Forensic Psychology

Ewing, C. P. (2008). *Trials of a forensic psychologist: A casebook.* New York, NY: John Wiley & Sons.
Meyer, R. G., & Weaver, C. M. (2006). *Law and mental health: A case-based approach.* New York, NY: Guilford Press.

General Forensic Psychology

Goldstein, A. M. (Ed.). (2006). *Forensic psychology: Emerging topics and expanding roles.* New York, NY: John Wiley & Sons.

Huss, M. T. (2014). *Forensic psychology* (2nd ed.). New York, NY: John Wiley & Sons.

Resources

- American Psychology Law Society – Division 41 of the American Psychological Association
  - http://www.apadivisions.org/division-41
- American Psychology – Law Society's YouTube Channel
  - https://www.youtube.com/user/LawandPsychology
  - A series of videos of prominent figures in the field discussing their research and general topics in the field of forensic psychology (e.g., risk reduction, juvenile forensic psychology, testifying as an expert witness, and applying for graduate school in forensic psychology)
- American Board of Forensic Psychology
  - www.abfp.com

References

American Psychological Association. (2014a).*Graduate study in psychology: 2014.* Washington, DC: Author.

American Psychological Association. (2014b). *Public description of forensic psychology.* Retrieved from http://www.apa.org/ed/graduate/specialize/forensic.aspx

Bartol, C. R., & Bartol, A. M. (1999). History of forensic psychology. In A. K. Hess & I. B. Weiner (Eds.), *Handbook of forensic psychology* (2nd ed., pp. 3–23). New York, NY: John Wiley & Sons.

DiCataldo, F., Whitworth, D., Russo, R., Hanigan, B., MacHardy, M., Berman, G., . . . Zaitchik, M. (2008, March). *A survey of forensic mental health directors on the clinical role and duties of master's-level forensic psychology professionals.* Paper presented at the American Psychology – Law Society annual conference, Jacksonville, FL.

Dusky v. United States, 362 US 402 (1960).

Forensic Specialty Council. (2007). *Education and training guidelines for forensic psychology.* Retrieved from http://www.umassmed.edu/uploadedFiles/ET%20Guidelines%20final.doc

Helms, J. L. (2008, March). *Forensic psychology program rankings.* Poster session presented at the American Psychology – Law Society annual conference, Jacksonville, FL.

Helms, J. L. (2009, March). *Forensic psychology journal rankings.* Poster session presented at the American Psychology – Law Society annual conference, San Antonio, TX.

Helms, J. L., & Mayhew, L. L. (2006). *Undergraduate preparation for graduate training in forensic psychology.* APA Division 2 – Society for the Teaching of Psychology's Office of Teaching Resources in Psychology. Retrieved from http://teachpsych.org/resources/Documents/otrp/resources/helms06.pdf

Henggeler, S. W., Rowland, M. D., Randall, J., Ward, D. M., Pickrel, S. G., Cunningham, P. B., . . . Santos, A. B. (1999). Home-based multisystemic therapy as an alternative to the hospitalization of youth in psychiatric crisis: Clinical outcomes. *Journal of the American Academy of Child & Adolescent Psychiatry,* *38,* 1331–1339. doi:10.1097/00004583-199911000-00006

MacKain, S. J., Tedeschi, R. G., Durham, T. W., & Goldman, V. J. (2002). So what are master's-level psychology practitioners doing? Surveys of employers and recent graduates in North Carolina. *Professional Psychology: Research and Practice,* *33,* 408–412. doi:10.1037/0735-7028.33.4.408

Miranda v. Arizona, 384 US 436 (1966).

Occupational Information Network. (2012). *Summary report for: 19-3031.02 – Clinical psychologists.* Retrieved from http://online.onetcenter.org/link/summary/19-3031.02

US Department of Labor, Bureau of Labor Statistics. (2014–2015a). *Occupational outlook handbook: Correctional officers.* Retrieved from http://www.bls.gov/ooh/protective-service/correctional-officers.htm

US Department of Labor, Bureau of Labor Statistics. (2014–2015b). *Occupational outlook handbook: Police and detectives.* Retrieved from http://www.bls.gov/ooh/protective-service/police-and-detectives.htm

US Department of Labor, Bureau of Labor Statistics. (2014–2015c). *Occupational outlook handbook: Probation officers and correctional treatment specialists.* Retrieved from http://www.bls.gov/ooh/community-and-social-service/probation-officers-and-correctional-treatment-specialists.htm

Chapter Sixteen
Careers in Academe

Academe Defined

Academe refers to the academic (i.e., higher education) community and environment. Careers in this area include not only the traditional profession of university professor but also administrative positions like institute directors, department chairs, deans, and university presidents. According to the US Department of Labor, Bureau of Labor Statistics' Occupational Employment Statistics (OES; 2014), there were approximately 40,380 postsecondary (i.e., college/university) psychology teaching jobs in 2013. This is not surprising given that one of the leading employment settings for those with a doctorate in psychology is a college or university (Michalski, Kohout, Wicherski, & Hart, 2011). In fact, the majority of recipients of doctoral degrees in the nonhealth service provider areas of psychology (e.g., cognitive psychology, social psychology, experimental psychology) pursue academic-related employment upon graduation (Michalski et al., 2011). Additionally, the Occupational Information Network (O*NET; 2012) indicates that the outlook for employment of postsecondary teachers is positive. As such this is an excellent career to consider pursuing.

Employment Settings

Types of Settings

Although the types of settings for academic employment vary, many are already familiar to you. The main settings for psychologists in academe

Majoring in Psychology: Achieving Your Educational and Career Goals, Second Edition.
Jeffrey L. Helms and Daniel T. Rogers.
© 2015 John Wiley & Sons, Ltd. Published 2015 by John Wiley & Sons, Ltd.

are technical schools, community/junior colleges, 4-year colleges, universities, professional psychology schools, and medical schools (Michalski et al., 2011).

Technical schools typically have a very limited psychology curriculum, oftentimes only offering courses such as Introductory Psychology and Developmental Psychology. This limited curriculum makes sense given that the major areas of study in this setting will be more in line with employment-related skill areas like practical nursing, culinary arts, respiratory therapy, information technology, and automotive repair. Programs offered in technical schools are often geared toward certification in a particular skill area (e.g., computer programming) and are time-limited (i.e., 2 years or less).

Community colleges (sometimes called junior colleges) are similar to the technical schools in that they offer many of the same vocational training programs. However, community colleges also offer 2-year programs of study that often result in an associate's degree. These 2-year degrees almost always focus on general education requirements (e.g., English, math, and science). As a result, the psychology curriculum is also usually very limited. The focus is on foundational, or general educational, courses associated with the first 2 years of college.

Four-year colleges confer bachelor's degrees, including psychology degrees. These colleges rarely have graduate programs but instead focus their energies and resources on undergraduate education. Most 4-year colleges have a psychology program, including a full curriculum.

Universities are similar to 4-year colleges in that they also have a wide variety of undergraduate degree programs, including psychology. However, in addition to the undergraduate programs, universities have extensive graduate program offerings, sometimes including psychology.

Professional psychology schools can be within a university setting or freestanding (i.e., not affiliated with a university). These programs focus exclusively on graduate training in applied areas of psychology and are usually private (i.e., not state/government funded). Faculty at professional psychology schools focus almost exclusively on teaching required coursework and training activities (e.g., supervising students learning psychological tests).

Medical schools are similar to professional schools in that psychology faculty in this setting are predominantly involved in training activities. Additionally, faculty may be conducting research in hospital clinics, training predoctoral interns, or supervising postdoctoral residents. Regardless, their function is predominantly applied.

Setting Matters

Although the actual activities are described in the Professorial Activities section later in the chapter, it deserves mentioning here that setting does matter. Relative emphasis on the major activities (i.e., teaching, professional service, and research) varies significantly by setting. In technical schools, community colleges, and professional psychology schools, the emphasis is heavily weighted toward teaching. As a result, there is limited and sometimes no expectation to contribute to the discipline in other ways (e.g., research). At 4-year colleges and universities emphasis on teaching relative to research varies. At research-intensive universities there are high expectations regarding research productivity (i.e., publishing research and garnering grant money) and lower expectations regarding teaching. Approximately 25% of academic positions are in this type of setting (Berger, Kirshstein, & Rowe, 2001). Less emphasis on research productivity is seen at 4-year colleges and more teaching-focused universities. However, keep in mind that the term "less" does not mean "none." In fact, most 4-year colleges and almost all universities expect that a portion of a professor's time will be devoted to research activities and publishing.

Because of the emphasis on research, universities typically require less teaching. It is not unusual at very research-intensive universities for faculty to teach only two or three courses during an academic year, sometimes less. At 4-year colleges and less research-intensive universities, the teaching load can hover at around six to eight courses per year. At community colleges and technical schools where research expectations generally do not exist, teaching loads can be around 10 to 12 courses per year.

Professorial Activities

Professorial activities fall into three major domains. These domains are teaching, supervision, and mentoring; research; and professional service. In addition to addressing each of these domains separately, Box 16.1 provides a list of the top tasks associated with being a psychology professor.

Teaching, Supervision, and Mentoring

As the name suggests, the major activities in this domain center on direct interaction with students. These activities are typically the ones that students and outside observers use to describe a career in academe.

Box 16.1 *Top Tasks Associated with Being a Psychology Professor*

1. Develop and give lectures to students
2. Evaluate and grade students' work (laboratory work, assignments, term papers)
3. Initiate, facilitate, and moderate class discussions
4. Develop, administer, and grade examinations
5. Keep up to date on developments in the respective field (e.g., reading the current literature, attending professional conferences)
6. Prepare course materials (e.g., assignments, syllabi)
7. Revise curriculum, course content, and course materials
8. Maintain student records (e.g., grades)
9. Supervise students' laboratory work
10. Supervise students' field and research work
11. Maintain office hours for student advising
12. Conduct and publish research in the field of expertise
13. Provide career and academic advisement to students
14. Select and obtain materials (e.g., textbooks)
15. Work with colleagues to address problems that arise in teaching and research
16. Serve on departmental and university committees
17. Perform administrative duties (e.g., serving as department chair)
18. Develop materials for reading assignments
19. Participate in new student recruitment and orientation activities
20. Advise student organizations
21. Write grants to secure external funding for research activities
22. Participate in campus and community events
23. Consult with government and businesses

Note. Information comes from O*NET (2012).

Interestingly, being inside the classroom and having direct contact with students are relatively small parts of the work week for a faculty member. However, the activities that lead up to and follow being in the classroom and meeting with students devour a large portion of the faculty member's time. One of these activities is course preparation. Although some material changes little from year to year at the undergraduate level (e.g., elementary statistics), other material changes considerably. Developments in the respective subfields of psychology occur almost daily. As a result, the professor must keep up with the recent research in the field as well as new texts that become available. Once the professor is up to date in the respective area, the materials used in the course must be updated. Depending on the developments, these updates can take weeks of preparation prior to the semester starting along with significant amounts of time during the semester. This preparation is done with the specific intent of making time in front of the class as enriching as possible. In short, the syllabus, lectures, presentation slides, movie clips, handouts, activities, etc. are the culmination of significant effort by the professor, effort that is rarely seen by the students and outside observers.

In addition to course preparation activities, the professor also has evaluative responsibilities. Making and grading tests, essays, homework assignments, activities, and term papers take significant chunks of a professor's time. Once you "do the math" it becomes quite clear. Let's take an abnormal psychology term paper. If a professor spends 30 minutes reading/grading/giving feedback on each student's term paper, then grading papers for a class of 30 students would take 15 hours to complete. Because most professors would be teaching a couple of other courses alongside this one, a completion time of 45 hours would not be unrealistic. Remember, this estimate is for only one assignment. Of course, we know what the student is thinking. "Don't assign term papers!" As noted in Chapter 10, one of the skills that set us apart from other professions is our assessment skills (i.e., our ability to develop reliable and valid tests and measures). As such we know that measuring student learning in more than one way is better than giving only one opportunity or one type of measure. As a result, students will often have term papers, exams that have different types of questions (e.g., multiple choice, short answer, and essay), participation points, group activity grades, and homework assignments as part of a course. Rest assured; for most of us professors, grading is our least favorite activity. But it is essential to assessing student learning.

Professors also spend time supervising and mentoring. Supervision includes activities like observing a graduate student administering a psychological test or working for the first time with a patient who is depressed. Supervision also occurs with undergraduate students engaged in hands-on activities such as research projects, internships, and service learning projects. Mentoring of students often occurs informally but can also have more formal aspects. The more formal aspects include meeting with advisees and guiding students' directed or independent studies. Interestingly, for some professors, supervision and mentoring activities often involve other faculty members as the supervisee or mentee. For faculty members just beginning their careers it is important that colleagues be there to support the transition from graduate student to faculty member.

Research

Although different words can be used to describe the activities in this area (e.g., scholarship, creative activities), the bottom line is that careers in academe generally require research activity. Research activities include reviewing existing research literature, developing research protocols and procedures, gathering data, entering data, statistically analyzing data, interpreting the results, and presenting the results to the broader community. Even though more time will be spent in the process leading up to this presentation, making the findings available to a wider audience is often the defining aspect of this professorial activity. As a result, significant quantities of time are spent writing. Once the writing is complete, the manuscript can be submitted to professional conferences for possible inclusion in the presentation schedules. The manuscript is also often submitted for publication in a peer-reviewed journal, keeping in mind that most articles submitted for publication are rejected.

An additional aspect of research activities is the cost involved in some faculty members' research activities. Although some faculty members are fully financially supported by the university (an extremely rare circumstance) and some faculty do not require significant financial support for her or his particular research activities, many faculty require financial support to accomplish the research that is required for their academic position. As such, faculty often seek funding from external sources (i.e., grants). Grants can come from federal, state, and local governments as well as private philanthropic organizations or foundations. Regardless of the grant's origin, they are extremely competitive. Although the bulk of grant funding typically supports conducting a research project (e.g., acquiring materials, space, participants, and staff), it may provide for a faculty member's salary over the summer months when not under contract or being paid. It may also pay for trips to professional conferences to present research findings.

Professional Service

Last but not least, professional service is the third major domain of professional activities for those with a career in academe. Professional service can be broken down into two broad areas, university-based and community-based. University-based professional service includes activities in the faculty member's own department and outside the department. These activities commonly include serving on committees, fulfilling leadership roles, and advising student organizations. Academic settings typically require committees that are responsible for such things as revising the curriculum, assessing student learning, selecting applicants to interview for position openings, and addressing student academic concerns (e.g., plagiarism and cheating, grade appeals). This type of service ensures the smooth operation of the faculty member's department and the university as a whole.

Community-based professional service includes activities that center on the larger profession as well as the community outside the university (local, state, and beyond). Professional service to the larger profession may include such activities as serving as editor of a professional journal as well as serving as an officer of a professional association (e.g., one of the divisions of the American Psychological Association, APA; http://www.apa.org/about/division.html). Professional service also may include providing expertise to the community. This service can include having a small private practice, serving on the board of directors of an organization, helping a nonprofit agency evaluate their services, etc. Regardless of the setting, the intent of the service is to help move that person, group, or organization closer to a defined goal (e.g., reaching more people in need of services). The service itself is initiated based on the expertise the faculty member has relative to her/his educational background and training. It is important to note that professional service activities also require a large portion of the faculty member's time.

Relative Emphasis

Relative emphasis of each of the three domains of activities varies significantly by setting. As noted in the previous section, research-intensive universities value research productivity and garnering external funding (i.e., grants) the most. As a result, significantly less emphasis is given to activities in the teaching and service areas. However, this does not equate to *no* emphasis. In more teaching-focused academic settings, teaching comes first, meaning that the bulk of a professor's time and energy is spent in teaching, supervision, and mentoring activities. However, this does not mean that research and professional service are not valued or expected. That interpretation is not correct. It is all relative.

Working Conditions

Although the term "working conditions" typically refers to the actual work space (e.g., lighting, air quality), it is used here to describe the environmental, intangible, and relationship components of the academic profession that are not as easily quantified as salary and benefit packages. Although not easily quantifiable, these conditions significantly contribute to a person's quality of life. Box 16.2 lists some of these factors.

> **Box 16.2**   *Top 10 Physical and Social Factors that Influence the Nature of the Work for Psychology Professors*
>
> 1. Involves significant use of electronic mail
> 2. Allows freedom to make decisions
> 3. Involves public speaking
> 4. Involves significant amounts of interaction with others
> 5. Significantly more unstructured than structured
> 6. Involves working indoors
> 7. Involves telephone conversations
> 8. Involves face-to-face discussions
> 9. Long work week
> 10. Being exact and accurate is important
>
> *Note.* Information comes from O*NET (2014).

As emphasis on particular activities varies from one academic setting to another, so too do working conditions. Some of the variability can be due to collegiality issues (i.e., how well the coworkers get along with one another). Collegiality is difficult to determine as an outsider. That is, by the time a person finds out there is little collegiality in a particular environment it is often too late and the person has already accepted the position and started working. However, there are working conditions that can be explored prior to employment.

Academic Freedom

One of the cornerstones to academe is the concept of academic freedom. In defining academic freedom, the American Association of University Professors (AAUP; 1940/1970) states that "Teachers are entitled to full freedom in research and in the publication of the results.... Teachers are entitled to freedom in the classroom in discussing their subject" (http:// www.aaup.org/AAUP/pubsres/policydocs/contents/1940statement.htm). Without an environment that embraces this freedom, advances in the respective fields are potentially prevented. As a result, more than 200 education and scientific groups endorse the statement and principles underlying it. These organizations include APA's endorsement in 1961 and the Association for Psychological Science's endorsement in 1989. For a list of those colleges and universities that are currently censured (i.e., "unsatisfactory conditions of academic freedom and tenure have been found to prevail at these institutions") by the AAUP, please see their website at http://www.aaup.org/our-programs/academic-freedom/censure-list.

Facilities and Support

Facilities and support are additional pieces that contribute to the working conditions in academe. Typically, full-time professors get their own offices, computer equipment, phone, and furniture. Office supplies and some office support (i.e., secretarial/administrative help) are also common. However, updates to existing equipment and office space are typically much less frequent than in other work environments. Student computer labs, university resources (e.g., libraries, dining facilties, gyms), and laboratory space varies considerably in amount and quality. In short, facilities differ from institution to institution. For those of you who have transferred colleges, we guess that there are some significant differences in facilities between your current and previous schools.

Work Schedule

One of the most attractive parts of a career in academe is the flexibility in the work schedule. Although there are limits to the flexibility, as long as a faculty member "gets the job done," that member is often free to set her or his own office hours and also can have a voice in choosing the times of course offerings (e.g., days, evenings, online). The reason that the flexibility works relatively well is that faculty members typically work long hours and take work home with them, including over holiday/semester breaks. For example, as I (Helms) am writing this section it is 12:30 on a Saturday afternoon in June. The important piece to take away from the flexibility is that in order to be successful in a career in academe, a person has to be a self-starter and self-motivated. There is not a lot of supervision (i.e., someone looking over your shoulder). Instead, there is the expectation that a faculty member will seek out opportunities and direction as needed. On this same note, it is important to point out that the career in academe is not really a job or a career but rather a lifestyle. By lifestyle it is meant that the boundaries between work and home are often blurred, which may not fit for some people. Boundaries are blurred in the sense that not only do almost all faculty take work home with them in the evenings or on weekends/holidays but also many of their outside work activities involve fellow faculty members and their families. In other words, faculty members often spend social time together outside of work, not out of obligation but out of a genuine desire and interest to do so.

Educational Degree and Training Needed

Although a master's degree is sufficient for many community and technical colleges, competition is increasing. As a result, a doctoral degree will put you in a better place as an applicant. However, for colleges and universities the entry-level degree is the doctorate. More specifically, the doctor of philosophy degree (PhD) in psychology is the degree of choice. The particular area within psychology is less of an issue in that it depends on a hiring department's needs. For example, a recent advertisement for a job opening at our university did not indicate a specific area within psychology. Instead, the advertisement indicated the need for a person with experience in teaching courses in the areas of research methods and experimental psychology. This specified need of our department left the field open. As a result, we received applications from every subfield of psychology including social psychology, clinical psychology, experimental psychology, cognitive psychology, and health psychology.

There is an important note to be made regarding the emphasis on the PhD degree relative to other doctoral degrees, specifically the doctor of psychology degree (PsyD). Discrimination is still rampant in the academic community relative to the PsyD degree. Consequently, it is more difficult to get an academic position with the PsyD degree relative to the PhD degree. The discrimination is based on the inaccurate belief that individuals with PsyD degrees are incapable of doing the quality or quantity of research necessary for the position. Of course, this is a stereotype. As with most stereotypes, examples are available to bolster the argument for discrimination. Additionally, self-selection into a PsyD program usually means a desire to practice in a clinical setting, not teach and do research, meaning that few with the PsyD degree will pursue careers in academe.

Interestingly, the majority of doctoral programs provide no formal training in teaching skills. In fact, most "training" occurs on the job. That is, graduate students are assigned a course to teach as part of a teaching assistantship. The belief is that because a student has been a student for most of her or his life the student will naturally know what to do when confronted with the tasks involved. Of course, the same is not said for the research activities required in the position where graduate students spend most of their graduate training learning how to do good research. Regardless, some graduate programs are beginning to incorporate courses on teaching. In fact, a program, Preparing Future Faculty, was developed in 1993 that begins to address the inadequacies for preparing future faculty members.

The Preparing Future Faculty (PFF) program is a national movement to transform the way aspiring faculty members are prepared for their careers. PFF programs provide doctoral students, as well as some master's and postdoctoral students, with opportunities to observe and experience faculty responsibilities at a variety of academic institutions with varying missions, diverse student bodies, and different expectations for faculty. (www.preparing-faculty.org)

As part of the PFF program, a graduate student will have the opportunity to learn strategies to increase success as a future faculty member in the three main domains described earlier (i.e., teaching, supervision, and mentoring; research; and professional service). Given the traditional emphasis on research mentoring in graduate school (and assuming the students are already receiving sufficient mentoring in that area), many of the university programs participating in the PFF program and similar programs spend relatively more time mentoring future faculty in the domain of teaching compared to universities that do not participate. Some of the universities that have participated in the PFF program or have similar types of programs include Miami University (OH), University of Colorado-Boulder, University of Georgia, and University of New Hampshire. Sponsored by the Society for the Teaching of Psychology (Division 2 of the APA), Beers, Hill, and Thompson (2012) developed a resource guide to graduate student training in the teaching of psychology. The guide lists 51 graduate programs in psychology in 27 states that provide students with the opportunity to receive training in the domain of teaching.

Rank

As is the case with many careers, there are designated ranks associated with faculty positions. Here are some of the most common position rank/status designations.

Part-time/Adjunct Faculty

Part-time/adjunct faculty are contracted to teach typically only one or two courses for a particular semester. Because of their part-time status, they do not receive benefits. There are also no expectations to provide professional service or engage in research activities. In addition, there is no expectation that an adjunct faculty member will teach the following semester or year.

Visiting Faculty

Visiting faculty are also contracted for a specified length of time, typically 1 or 2 years. Although duties vary, visiting faculty usually teach heavy loads. There are usually low or no expectations regarding professional service and research productivity. Due to the full-time status of the position, visiting faculty receive benefits. However, once the contract is finished there is no opportunity to continue in the position.

Research and Clinical Faculty

Research and clinical faculty members' duties focus on the respective role. For research faculty, they were hired specifically to conduct research or supervise student research. For clinical faculty, they were hired specifically to train students in applied skills and supervise their work with patients. As such, research and clinical faculty typically do not "teach" in the traditional sense but rather supervise. Depending on the nature of their duties, research and clinical faculty can be full-time or part-time. Additionally, their positions may be time-limited (i.e., only for a specific length of time) or continuing (i.e., ongoing with no definite stop date to the contract).

Full-time Faculty

These faculty are traditionally the ones most often encountered by students. Full-time faculty include instructors, assistant professors, associate professors, and full professors. Instructors typically hold only the master's degree. As such, depending on the institution, they are not eligible for promotion to the professorial ranks. Instructors typically are utilized in lower-level courses like Introductory Psychology. The typical entry point to a career in academe is the assistant professor level. Promotion to the ranks of associate professor and full professor are not automatic. This process is described later in the chapter. Regardless, the typical progress when promotion occurs is from assistant professor to associate professor to full professor.

Due to the full-time nature of the position, all full-time faculty enjoy benefit packages (e.g., retirement and insurance). However, until obtaining tenure, full-time faculty still operate under a contractual system that typically runs 1 year at a time. Because of the uncertainty this creates, tenure is briefly described later in the chapter.

Salaries

The median salary for all postsecondary psychology teachers in 2013 was $68,980 (US Department of Labor, Bureau of Labor Statistics, 2013). This median includes all ranks. As a result, it may be more illustrative to look at the entry-level rank of the assistant professor. Table 16.1 lists the mean salaries of assistant professors based on setting.

It is important to remember that salaries vary based in part on location. For example, the median salary in 2012 for a psychology professor (all ranks) was $78,500 in Massachusetts and $55,500 in Louisiana (O*NET, 2012). The reason that the starting point is so important is that salaries in academe are very slow to rise. Given that there are typically only two promotions in a professor's lifetime (i.e., from assistant to associate and from associate to full professor) and neither are guaranteed, starting salary becomes even more important. Some people suggest that the lower salary and sparse raises are offset by the fact that most faculty contracts are for 9–10 months (i.e., faculty have their summers "off"). Although faculty do not get paid during the summer (unless they teach summer school, which is not always available or guaranteed and is not paid at the same rate as salary), faculty generally are in their offices catching up on research and preparing for the following semester, activities they are not able to complete during their contract due to other pressures on their time. Although faculty can sometimes supplement their salaries with consulting work and grants at some schools (not all schools allow outside consulting), as is the case with most careers, the "best" way to increase salary is to leave for a better/higher paying position. Unlike other jobs, finding employment is not easy, and

Table 16.1 Mean Salaries of Assistant Professors Based on Setting

Setting	Mean Salary
University psychology department	59,196
University education department	66,063
University business school	107,709
Four-year college – psychology department	50,836
Four-year college – education department	52,462
Two-year college	50,773
Medical school – psychiatry department	65,927
University-affiliated professional school of psychology	56,288
Independent professional school of psychology	51,544

Note. Information comes from APA's salary survey (Finno, Michalski, Hart, Wicherski, & Kohout, 2010).

when employment is found, it almost always requires moving to another state. This fact, obviously, is a significant disincentive to moving, especially once "roots are planted."

Finding Employment

Finding employment in academe can be tough. As noted in the previous section, the job seeker should be prepared to move. It is a rarity when a person does not have to make several significant moves to accomplish the goal of becoming a psychology professor and working in academe. Although there are lots of positions available, they are not typically next door, across town, or at the local university. As a matter of fact, most universities will not hire their own graduates for positions. Universities often want to bring in people with different backgrounds, training, and perspectives. As a result, the job search is typically at least regional if not national/international.

In terms of obtaining employment, APA's doctoral employment survey (Michalski et al., 2011) indicates that the most often used job search strategies included informal strategies (68.7%), use of electronic resources (32.8%), faculty advisors (29.4%), advertisements in APA's *Monitor on Psychology* (24.8%) and *Chronicle of Higher Education*, or other professional newsletter advertisements (18.1%). This same survey found that the most successful method was informal channels (i.e., friends, colleagues, and professors). Box 16.3 provides a list of websites that post academic position openings in psychology.

As noted previously, careers in academe are more consistent with a lifestyle than a 9-to-5 job. As such, the interview process for a faculty position is often quite different from interviews for other careers. Interviews tend to

---

Box 16.3   *Websites that Post Academic Position Openings in Psychology*

American Psychological Association
- http://www.apa.org/careers

Association for Psychological Science
- http://www.psychologicalscience.org/jobs

Chronicle of Higher Education
- chronicle.com

HigherEdJobs.com
- www.higheredjobs.com

be significantly longer, up to three days in some situations. This makes sense given that most interviewees will not be local. In addition to the process being longer due to travel requirements, the process is also longer due to the incorporation of one or two required presentations. One presentation is typically a lecture on a course topic, and the other presentation is on the applicant's research program. In addition to interviews with those in administration (e.g., the department chair, dean, vice president, provost), interviews with the current faculty also occur. These interviews occur both formally and informally. The informal interviews take place on the ride to and from the airport and hotel and during discussions over meals. During the process, the department may also set up time for an applicant to meet with a realtor in order to learn about housing, schools, etc. In all, it is a long and generally intense process.

Many applicants do not even get interviews. In the broad search we mentioned that our department recently completed, we received over 170 applications for one position. Obviously, some positions at some schools receive far fewer applications. Additionally, and unlike other careers, academic positions almost always start in the fall semester (i.e., August/September). As such, the interview season starts with application for positions in the fall and then continues with interviews for positions in the spring, acceptance of a position/offer in February/March/April, relocation in the summer, and initiation of the faculty position in the fall. In other words, it is a very long process.

You Don't Just Get to Stay!

Given the length of training, the accompanying educational background, and a grueling interview process, it would seem that a deep sigh of relief could be released upon securing that faculty position. The reality is that the work then begins because you don't just get to stay. A faculty member must demonstrate effectiveness in each of the three major domains noted earlier. The demonstration via an evaluation by the department chair typically takes place annually. A 3rd-year review also takes place typically and incorporates feedback on a faculty member's work since her or his arrival. This feedback is provided not only by the department chair but also by peers/colleagues. At some point usually between the 5th and 6th year of employment, the faculty member must apply for tenure. The application includes evidence of effectiveness in each of the three major domains and is typically submitted in the form of portfolios. Promotion to the associate professor level is usually addressed at this time as well. The tenure decision is made by the department chair, tenured department faculty, the college dean, the vice president of academic affairs or the provost, and the president of the university. Generally, all levels of review must be favorable for a faculty member to receive tenure and promotion. If it is not a favorable review, the faculty member is given a year to find another position (i.e., enough time to go through one academic job search cycle). Prior to tenure, there is no guarantee of another year of employment (i.e., a contract renewal). This is why the annual reviews and demonstrating effectiveness are so important. Tenure guarantees a contract renewal (except in the most unusual and extreme circumstances).

After tenure, post-tenure review is typically carried out every 5 years. This process is less strenuous but gives an opportunity for the faculty member to receive evaluative feedback on his or her work. Annual reviews continue for all faculty members typically. Eligibility for promotion from associate to full professor typically requires 5 years in the associate professor rank prior to application for promotion. It is important to note that many technical and community colleges and professional psychology schools (especially the private freestanding ones) do not have a tenure process. As such, employment is most often in the form of a contract, resulting in significantly less stable employment over the course of time.

Working in the Teaching Area with a Bachelor's Degree

As mentioned previously, teaching at the college level requires a minimum of a master's degree due in part to accreditation standards. However, a doctorate is really the entry-level degree. As a result, for someone interested in the teaching domain who does not want to pursue a graduate degree, teaching psychology at the high school level is the best alternative. In general, teaching at the high school level requires training in education and a specific content area (e.g., math, history, English), as well as a teaching certificate from the respective state's board of education. In most states, there are no clear requirements for teaching psychology in high school. However, APA (2012) has developed a set of guidelines that even if not adopted by a state may guide students in preparing themselves to effectively teach psychology at the high school level. Students interested in this route are encouraged to seek guidance from their university's education department. In fact, many students choose to double major in education and psychology, typically adding only one semester to their bachelor's degree program.

For those farther into their undergraduate education or those nearing graduation, most states offer a program for people interested in teaching who have degrees outside of education. Similar programs also exist at the national level (e.g., Teach for America). These programs allow a person to complete the training necessary to get a teaching certificate, usually in a relatively brief period of time (e.g., 12 months). Additionally, some states will allow you to teach while completing this training on an "emergency" or temporary certification (particularly in underserved areas). Again, students interested in this option are encouraged to contact an advisor in their institution's education department.

Teaching psychology courses at the high school level is competitive because it is often viewed as an elective (and fun!). However, most high schools do offer an introductory psychology course. Some even have Advanced Placement courses, meaning if a student passes an exam the student will get college credit for it. As a result, these courses are usually very rigorous. As a matter of fact, there is an entire organization within the APA devoted to teaching psychology in high school. Information can be found at http://www.apa.org/ed/topss/homepage.html

An Insider's Perspective

Being an Academic Psychologist: A Great Career Choice

Randolph A. Smith, PhD
Moravian College

In many ways, being an academic psychologist is like an extension of being a student. If you really enjoy the student role and lifestyle, then academe may be a good career choice for you. Here are three questions to consider.

1. *Do you enjoy learning?* Academic psychologists are constantly learning. The negative stereotype of a professor involves someone who pulls out old, yellowed lecture notes and goes to class teaching the same thing year after year. Nothing could be farther from the truth! In 30+ years of teaching, many "facts" that I used to teach are no longer factual. My experience illustrates why it is so important to never stop learning and why academic psychologists value life-long learning so highly. It is our job to keep up on the latest research and discoveries in our

field so that we can share it with students like you.

2. *Do you enjoy research?* As the book's authors point out, staying active in research is also part of the job for professors. Professors have the job not only of spreading knowledge through teaching but also of creating new knowledge through research activity. The majority of research produced in psychology comes not from psychologists who are full-time researchers but from the labs of academic psychologists. Although they may not have a laboratory full of rats, they do have classrooms full of waiting psychology students, who are most often the participants in psychology experiments – you may even have had that opportunity. Academic psychologists conduct research on virtually every topic represented in your introductory psychology class, so teaching is not a barrier for any research specialization a faculty member may want to pursue.

3. *Do you enjoy working with people?* Psychology professors have the opportunity (and responsibility) to work with a variety of different people including students, other faculty, administrators, and the public. Although it may be obvious that professors teach students, they may also serve as mentors to students. Faculty work with other faculty a great deal – often on committees at the department, college, or university level (some of the service the book's authors mentioned). Professors

also interact with administrators (e.g., deans, directors, vice presidents) to varying degrees. These interactions are important because the faculty member is representing the department to the higher administration. Being able to get along with, work well with, and enjoy working with a variety of people is an important trait for psychology professors.

If you answered these questions positively, take the next step. Find a mentor – a faculty member who will take a special interest in you, your education, and career goals. Often, someone who supervises you in a research project is a good candidate for a mentor. Perhaps your department has a shadowing program in which you spend a day (or longer) with a faculty member, learning what they do in their job. Perhaps your department has an undergraduate assistantship program in which you could serve as a teaching or research assistant to a faculty member. If none of these situations fit you, choose a faculty member to approach and ask if you can work in his or her research lab. Securing a mentor *and* obtaining research experience is a double bonus! If you ask most faculty, I believe that they will be able to mention a faculty member who was instrumental in helping them get on track or inspiring them as an undergraduate. Best wishes as you pursue your dream!

Note. Dr. Smith recently retired after serving as chair of and professor of psychology in the Department of Psychology at Lamar University for 6 years, at Kennesaw State University for 4 years, and at Ouachita Baptist University for 26 years. He is now teaching part-time in the Moravian College (Bethlehem, PA) Psychology Department. Dr. Smith has over 60 publications and nearly 100 professional presentations, many centering on teaching issues. He spent 12 years as editor of the premier scholarly teaching journal, *Teaching of Psychology*. Dr. Smith is a Fellow of both APA Division One (General Psychology) and Division Two (Society for the Teaching of Psychology). His significant contributions to the field were recognized in 2006 when he was awarded the highest teaching award in the profession of psychology, the American Psychological Foundation's Charles L. Brewer Distinguished Teaching of Psychology Award.

Professional Spotlight

Janie H. Wilson, PhD

Education:

- Bachelor of Science (BS) in Psychology from the College of Charleston
- Instead of a master's degree, I completed a qualifying project (much like a master's thesis) to move forward in the PhD program.
- Doctor of Philosophy (PhD) in Experimental Psychology from the University of South Carolina

Employer:
Georgia Southern University (Statesboro, GA)

Position:
Professor of psychology and coordinator of the MS program in psychology

Description of Position:
I teach both graduates and undergraduates in psychology. I also conduct research in rapport in teaching and ego depletion. My service includes coordinating the MS in psychology as well as directing the Disparities Elimination Summer Research Experience (DESRE) held on the Georgia Southern University campus.

Most Significant Professional Accomplishment:
It is a tie between the Georgia Southern University Award for Excellence in

Contributions to Instruction and a grant from the National Institute of Mental Health.

Favorite Publications:

Wilson, J. H., & Ryan, R. G. (2013). Student-teacher rapport scale: Six items predict student outcomes. *Teaching of Psychology*, 40, 130–133. doi:10.1177/0098628312475033

Legg, A. M., & Wilson, J. H. (2013). Instructor touch enhanced college students' evaluations. *Social Psychology of Education*, 16(2), 317–327. doi:10.1007/s11218-012-9207-1

Ryan, R. G., Wilson, J. H., & Pugh, J. L. (2011). Psychometric characteristics of the professor-student rapport scale. *Teaching of Psychology*, 38, 135–141. doi:10.1177/0098628311411894

Wilson, J. H., Ryan, R. G., & Pugh, J. L. (2010). Professor-student rapport scale predicts student outcomes. *Teaching of Psychology*, 37, 246–251. doi:10.1080/00986283.2010.510976

Areas of Research:

For the first decade of my academic career, I studied physiological responses of rats to stress, with an emphasis on social buffering. Many years ago I turned to the scholarship of teaching and learning as my primary research agenda. I conduct research on rapport as well as additional aspects of teaching and learning, such as student evaluations and ethical teaching. In the past few years, I have also begun a program of research on ego depletion, focusing on buffering against depletion.

Professional Memberships/Activities:

- Society for the Teaching of Psychology, Vice President for Programming, 2012–2014
- Fellow of the American Psychological Association, status awarded 2010
- Southeastern Psychological Association
- College faculty representative to the APA Teachers of Psychology in Secondary Schools (TOPPS), 2012–2014

Most Rewarding Aspect of Your Career:

My favorite activity is teaching, including teaching in the classroom and research on teaching.

Words of Advice to the Student Who is Interested in Your Subfield:

Since my training is in experimental psychology, I would tell students that they should get involved in research. Research of any kind will teach so much. After gaining some experience, focus on conducting research in an area of personal interest. Along the way, talk with your professor about presenting your work at conferences so you can become part of the professional community.

Suggested Exercises

1. Find an advertisement for a faculty position from one of the resources listed in the chapter. Answer the following questions.
   - Where is the position?
   - What rank is the position (visiting, instructor, assistant, associate, full)?

- Is it tenure-track, tenured, or another designation?
- What are the responsibilities of the position?
- Does the position seem more focused on teaching, research, or administration?
- What must a person do to apply?
- When is the deadline?

2. Research one of the faculty members in your department.
   - Does the person have a web page?
   - Does the person have a vita posted?
   - What research interests does the faculty member have?
   - What publications does the faculty member have? (Do a literature search.)
   - List one of the faculty's publications in APA style.
   - Where did the faculty member get his/her education? What field?
   - What courses does he/she teach?
   - What committees does the person serve on?
   - Did the faculty member teach elsewhere before coming to your school?
   - Is the faculty member a member of a professional organization? If so, which one(s)?

Suggested Readings

Buskist, W., Beins, B. C., & Hevern, V. W. (Eds.). (2004). *Preparing the new psychology professoriate: Helping graduate students become competent teachers.* Retrieved from http://teachpsych.org/Resources/Documents/ebooks/pnpp2004.pdf

Darley, J. M., Zanna, M. P., & Roediger, H. L., III. (Eds.). (2003). *The compleat academic: A career guide* (2nd ed.). Washington, DC: American Psychological Association.

Davis, S. F., & Buskist, W. (Eds.). (2002). *The teaching of psychology: Essays in honor of Wilbert J. McKeachie and Charles L. Brewer.* Mahwah, NJ: Lawrence Erlbaum Associates.

Forsyth, D. R. (2003). *The professor's guide to teaching: Psychological principles and practices.* Washington, DC: American Psychological Association.

Gaff, J. G., Pruitt-Logan, A. S., Sims, L. B., & Denecke, D. D. (2003). *Preparing future faculty in the humanities and social sciences: A guide for change.* Washington, DC: Association of American Colleges and Universities. Retrieved from http://www.preparing-faculty.org/PFFWeb.PFF4Manual.pdf

McKeachie, W. J., & Svinicki, M. (2013). *McKeachie's teaching tips: Strategies, research, and theory for college and university teachers* (14th ed.). Belmont, CA: Cengage.

Resources

- Preparing Future Faculty
  - www.preparing-faculty.org
- Teachers of Psychology in Secondary Schools (TOPSS)
  - http://www.apa.org/ed/topss/homepage.html
  - Contains information for those interested in and those already teaching high school
- Society for the Teaching of Psychology (STP)
  - Division 2 of the American Psychological Association
  - teachpsych.org

References

American Association of University Professors. (1940/1970). *1940 statement of principles on academic freedom and tenure with 1970 interpretive comments.* Retrieved from http://www.aaup.org/AAUP/pubsres/policydocs/contents/1940statement.htm

American Psychological Association. (2012). *Guidelines for preparing high school psychology teachers: Course-based and standards-based approaches.* Washington, DC: Author. Retrieved from http://www.apa.org/education/k12/teaching-guidelines.aspx

Beers, M. J., Hill, J. C., & Thompson, C. A. (2012, December). *The STP guide to graduate training in the teaching of psychology.* Retrieved from http://teachpsych.org/Resources/Documents/ebooks/gst2012.pdf

Berger, A., Kirshstein, R., & Rowe, E. (2001). *Institutional policies and practices: Results from the 1999 National Study of Postsecondary Faculty, Institution Survey.* Washington, DC: US Department of Education, National Center for Education Statistics (NCES).

Finno, A. A., Michalski, D., Hart, B., Wicherski, M., & Kohout, J. L. (2010, April). *Salaries in psychology 2009: Report of the 2009 APA salary survey.* Washington, DC: American Psychological Association. Retrieved from http://www.apa.org/workforce/publications/09-salaries/report.pdf

Michalski, D., Kohout, J., Wicherski, M., & Hart, B. (2011, May). *2009 doctorate employment suvey.* Washington, DC: American Psychological Association's Center for Psychology Workforce Analysis and Research. Retrieved from http://www.apa.org/workforce/publications/09-doc-empl/report.pdf

Occupational Information Network. (2012). *Details report for 25-1066.00 – Psychology teachers, postsecondary.* Retrieved from http://online.onetcenter.org/link/details/25-1066.00

Preparing Future Faculty. (n.d.). *The preparing future faculty program.* Retrieved from www.preparing-faculty.org

US Department of Labor, Bureau of Labor Statistics. (2014). *Occupational employment and wages, May 2013: 25-1066 psychology teachers, postsecondary.* Retrieved from http://www.bls.gov/oes/current/oes251066.htm

Chapter Seventeen
Assessing the Career Outlook for the Psychology Major

Introduction

As a student of psychology, you have a vested interest in the future of the field. The various directions the field takes could have a substantial impact on your professional career. To an extent, the successes and failures of psychology as a discipline will in part be your successes and failures. Thinking of the field's future in this way likely brings several questions to mind regarding your career goals. Will you be able to access the education and training you need? Will you be able to have the career you want, and in that career will you be able to engage in the work you want to do? Will you be financially secure in your career? What will your sense of professional identity be? How will society view your profession and accomplishments? In the coming years, forces at work within and outside of the field will play a large role in determining the answers to these questions. As we have seen throughout this book, being knowledgeable about these forces and their potential impact on you is the first step in ensuring that you succeed in achieving your career goals.

Predicting the future of a career in a field is never easy. It becomes even more complicated if you are still weighing multiple options in the field. However, you can gain an overall sense of the career outlook for psychology majors by assessing factors likely to guide the field as a whole in coming years. In this chapter, we provide a brief assessment of several of these factors that are already impacting psychology careers. Our discussion is organized into considerations of psychology's strengths, weaknesses, threats,

Majoring in Psychology: Achieving Your Educational and Career Goals, Second Edition.
Jeffrey L. Helms and Daniel T. Rogers.
© 2015 John Wiley & Sons, Ltd. Published 2015 by John Wiley & Sons, Ltd.

and opportunities, as well as what these factors might mean for bachelor's and graduate level students in the field.

Psychology's Strengths

Psychology has numerous strengths that establish a strong foundation for the field. Although change is certain to occur as the various subfields evolve, these strengths are unlikely to transform significantly in a short period of time. Among psychology's strengths, its scientific basis, ethical rigor, and recent growth are noteworthy for their likely influence on a variety of psychology careers.

Beginning with the early work of figures like Wilhelm Wundt, G. Stanley Hall, and William James, psychology has established itself to be a scientific discipline. In addition, psychology is one of the few hub sciences, meaning its focus and findings have clear connections to an array of related disciplines (Cacioppo, 2013). Today the field addresses a staggering array of topics that fall under the broad definition of behavior and mental processes. This is evidenced by the numerous subfields that have emerged in recent decades. Yet despite the enormous diversity among psychologists in terms of their subject matter and professional activities, their work remains rooted in science. They understand and appreciate the role played by theory, research methodology, experimentation, data collection, data analysis, and the dissemination of findings. Although some careers in the field may not engage in the active production of scientific knowledge, these psychologists will continue to be trained to understand scientific approaches and to apply research findings in their careers.

Psychologists in all subfields conduct their work with ethical rigor. They emphasize ethics in all of their activities for two reasons. First, ethical behavior forms a cornerstone of all psychologists' education and training. This is because they work directly with human and nonhuman animals as participants, subjects, patients, clients, and students. Many facets of this work, whether research, practice, teaching, or consultation, have a direct bearing on the well-being of others. Second, ethical standards and responsibilities are embedded in the professional activities of all psychologists. Although the American Psychological Association's (APA) "Ethical Principles of Psychologists and Code of Conduct" often serves as the ethical guide for psychologists, it also provides an excellent model for how psychologists view ethics. In this code, ethics are conceptualized both as rules, or guidelines, that are to be followed and as aspirational, general principles that all psychologists strive to uphold throughout their professional work. In other words, psychologists both adhere to clear ethical standards and uphold guiding values in their work in order to ensure that their actions promote well-being and do not cause harm.

Psychology has experienced substantial growth over recent decades. Data from the US Department of Education's National Center for Education Statistics (US NCES) provides some insight into this trend. The number of psychology bachelor's degrees granted in the US increased by over 70% between 1990 and 2010 (US NCES, 2013b). During that time frame, the average yearly growth in psychology bachelor's degrees granted outpaced the average yearly growth across all bachelor's degrees. This growth has resulted in psychology being consistently among the top undergraduate majors in US colleges and universities. During the same time period, the number of psychology master's degrees granted rose 121% (US NCES, 2013d). Much of this growth likely stems from increases in the number, diversity, and size of master's level programs. The number of psychology doctoral degrees granted during this time period has also increased, but at a lower rate of 49% (US NCES, 2013f). These figures indicate that much of the expansion in career areas in the field has been at master's and bachelor's levels.

Psychology's strengths have several implications for your career outlook. At the bachelor's level, expect your coursework to emphasize both the scientific and ethical principles of psychology. Recognize that these strengths in your education will become part of the expertise and skills you will possess. Familiarity with research methods, experimentation, statistical analysis, and scientific writing, as well as sensitivity to ethical issues in specific career settings, are core components of what psychology majors can offer potential employers. The increasing popularity of the psychology major means increased competition for employment at the bachelor's level. As a result, you should strive to identify your career goals and then work to distinguish yourself in your undergraduate education and experiences. At the graduate level, you should expect to witness increasing emphasis on scientific training and research productivity, especially at the doctoral level. The ethical principles of psychologists will continue to play a significant role in the education and training of graduate students as the field evolves. You should prepare yourself to conduct your graduate training and career in ways that conform to these principles. The growth occurring in the field at the master's level has not been as significant at the doctoral level. Some subfields have witnessed substantial growth while others have declined. To ensure your career success, remain cognizant of these trends and how they might be affecting graduate admissions, training, and career opportunities.

Psychology's Weaknesses

Although typically outshone by its strengths, there are several areas of weakness within the field of psychology that have been identified and discussed in recent years. Despite efforts to address these issues, each continues to affect the standing of the field and is likely to play an ongoing role in its career outlook. The viability of some careers may hinge on your ability to address the impact of these weaknesses.

As indicated in the previous chapters on careers in the field, psychology is an incredibly broad discipline. In fact, many large universities in the US have multiple psychology degree programs housed in separate academic divisions (e.g., clinical psychology in arts and sciences, school psychology in education, industrial–organizational psychology in business). In addition to having two large professional organizations in the US, psychologists within these organizations have further divided themselves into dozens of divisions based on their specific interests. Remarkably, many of these divisions are divided even further into smaller sections. This breadth is a testament to the far-reaching applications of psychological science, yet it also poses several problems. First, such diversity can at times contribute to a lack of cohesion. Psychologists sometimes struggle to communicate with each other when their expertise and interests differ. Schisms have at times emerged within the field along theoretical lines (e.g., behaviorism versus cognitivism) or between those who engage in varied professional careers (e.g., practitioners vs. academics). Second, those outside the field may at times struggle to understand who psychologists are and what exactly they contribute. A student taking a first psychology course, a patient seeking mental health care, and an organization looking to grant research funding, may all struggle to identify what psychology is.

As a field and area of study, psychology has had mixed experiences with promoting the diversity of its members. In terms of gender, the field has experienced a strong trend toward higher numbers of female students over the past two decades. In the 2011–2012 academic year, women were the recipients of 77% of the bachelor's, 80% of the master's, and 74% of the doctoral degrees granted in psychology (US NCES, 2013a). In fact at the graduate level, women earned more degrees than men in each of the subfields of psychology. In terms of racial composition, psychology has historically experienced an underrepresentation of minority students at the undergraduate level and graduate levels (Maton, Kohout, Wicherski, Leary, & Vinokurov, 2006). However, recent data suggest this pattern may be shifting. In the 2011–2012 academic year, minorities accounted for 37% of the US population and earned 36% of the bachelor's degrees (US NCES, 2013c), 33% of the master's degrees (US NCES, 2013e), and 27% of the doctoral degrees in psychology

(US NCES, 2013g). These percentages for bachelor's and master's degrees reflect steady increases in minority students since the late 1980s. The percentages for doctoral degrees reflect slower growth since the late 1990s.

Psychology has often failed to demonstrate the real-world applications of its theoretical and research developments. Despite the fact that some subfields concentrate on researching and providing direct applications to society, there remains a general sense in the field that we do not do enough to communicate the benefits of progress in psychological science. In particular, concerns have been voiced that the general public has limited understanding of what psychologists do and how psychologists' work impacts their daily lives. Such understanding on the part of the average citizen is critical. Individuals are more inclined to seek the beneficial services of applied psychologists when they are familiar with their expertise and offerings. In addition, individuals are more inclined to be supportive of funding for psychological research when they have an appreciation for how this science contributes to their well-being. Finally, information gleaned from psychological science can have an immediate positive impact on the lives of these individuals if it is properly explained and contextualized.

Psychology's weaknesses have several implications for your career outlook. At the bachelor's level, you might sometimes feel overwhelmed at the number of subfields and career options available. This can lead to uncertainty about career goals given that the bachelor's degree does not offer highly specialized knowledge and skills in an easily defined area. If you pursue training at the graduate level, you may find yourself having to select a subfield of focus before you feel ready given the need to apply to specialized programs of study. You should also be aware of how your gender and race may play a role in your education and training. At the bachelor's and master's levels, minority students are likely to find many opportunities and a level of diversity that is beginning to closely approximate the population. At the doctoral level, underrepresentation of minority students will be evident. At all levels, students are likely to notice the overrepresentation of women in each subfield. Although you may not directly feel the effects of psychology's struggle to educate the general public about our field, the viability of the field is in part dependent upon the perception of psychology as a useful contributor to society and the well-being of its members.

Psychology's Threats

Threats to the field of psychology come in varied forms. By threats we do not mean to invoke images of other disciplines plotting to bring down the field. Instead, we wish to convey that certain issues in society, such as higher education, health care, and legislation, have the potential to negatively impact the field. Often such issues are shaped by invariable shifts in the economy, public interest, and government, so they can be difficult to predict. Yet they can have far-reaching implications for the career outlook of many psychologists.

As described earlier, psychology has experienced substantial growth, particularly at the undergraduate and master's level, over the past few decades. Unfortunately, funding of psychology programs, and higher education in general, has lagged behind. As a result, many psychology departments have struggled to hire faculty, offer courses, and provide student resources to meet new demands. At the graduate level, psychology programs have expanded relatively little over this period of time with the exception of a few emerging subfields with strong research funding. In fact, much of the growth in graduate education has been concentrated in psychology professional school programs and in master's degrees in other mental health fields. Because these professional schools and master's level programs often generate their funding largely through student tuition, they are less susceptible to shifts in government funding for education and research. Therefore, this trend is not without consequences. For example, individuals who recently completed a doctorate in psychology reported a median debt of $50,000 when earning the PhD in contrast to $120,000 when earning the PsyD (APA, 2011). In addition, sharp increases in the number of master's level mental health practitioners in nonpsychology fields have led to increased competition for outpatient mental health careers and patients.

As previously discussed in Chapter 10, developments in insurance and managed care pose a specific threat to practitioners in these subfields. The most substantial threats have been to patients' ability to access affordable, quality mental health care, and to psychologists' ability to receive adequate compensation for providing these services. Although the picture has become increasingly bleak of late, legislative developments in recent years have brought renewed hope to patients and psychologists. The passage of two laws, the Paul Wellstone and Pete Dominici Mental Health and Addiction Equity Act and the Patient Protection and Affordable Care Act, opened the door to the possibility that insurance and managed care organizations will begin to cover medical and mental health care on equal terms and that such coverage may be more widely available. The regulatory success of such complex laws will certainly face many hurdles, including legal challenges, but there is optimism that the restrictions some insurers have previously placed on mental health coverage may begin to lessen and that access to such insurance may increase.

Another potential threat to the field is reduced funding for psychological research. The majority of funding for behavioral and social sciences research comes from government agencies, particularly the National Science Foundation (NSF) and National Institutes of Health (NIH). Although funding for behavioral and social science research typically falls well below that for other fields, flat budgets in recent years for NSF and NIH have only amplified this problem (Silver, Sharpe, Kelly, Kobor, & Sroufe, 2008). NSF has increased its emphasis on engineering and physical sciences, and NIH budgets for behavioral and social sciences have experienced limited growth. Although some gains have been made in funding for health and neuropsychological research, much promising research still remains unfunded.

In terms of career outlook, the threats to psychology pose several implications for you at the bachelor's and graduate levels. The increasing popularity of the undergraduate psychology major, coupled with slower growth in funding for higher education and research, creates a situation in which resources may be insufficient to ensure adequate education and training. Be mindful of how this situation might be affecting the psychology department at your institution and any others that you are considering attending. At the graduate level, if you decide to pursue a degree in a research-focused subfield, be aware of how the state of research funding might impact your graduate training and early career efforts. In addition, if you are considering academic careers or careers in the clinical or counseling psychology subfields, you must be mindful of how changes in insurance, higher education, and research funding might impact the availability of jobs and earning potentials.

Psychology's Opportunities

As you continue to formulate your career goals and progress through your education, it is vital to recognize some of the opportunities that psychology is poised to capitalize on. The US Bureau of Labor Statistics (2008) has projected varied growth for subfields of psychology between 2012 and 2022. Industrial–organizational (I/O) psychology is projected to grow at 53%, clinical/counseling/school psychology at 11%, and all other subfields combined at 11%. New psychologists will play a key role in shaping and guiding the growing and emerging areas. In addition, these are the most likely areas to generate new career opportunities.

The potential for growth within I/O psychology stems from two factors. First, this area is relatively new in the field, particularly in its efforts to provide increasing types and levels of direct services to businesses. Second, as businesses rapidly change in response to shifts in technology, the workforce, and increased globalization, the need for services from I/O psychologists is continually being renewed. For additional information on this subfield, refer to Chapter 9.

As already discussed in earlier chapters, health psychology and neuropsychology are among the fastest growing subfields. Their growth is in part due to their newness and need for expansion, but other factors have contributed as well. Health psychology and neuropsychology have both research and applied emphases. On the research side, improvements in imaging technology and assessment techniques have expanded the types of information these psychologists can gather. In addition, funding for this research has often exceeded that of other subfields in psychology as government and private organizations develop an increased interest in how behavior intersects with physical health. On the applied side, neuropsychologists and health psychologists are involved in work that has a direct impact on the lives of patients. Often they are working to address issues that are of major concern to individuals and society at large such as obesity, brain injury, smoking cessation, attention-deficit/hyperactivity disorder, and dementia. Increasingly psychologists with this type of expertise are becoming part of a shift toward integrated health care.

Other growth areas cross multiple subfields. For example, psychologists with expertise in cross-cultural and ethnic minority issues have become increasingly in demand as global and societal changes necessitate increasing knowledge about these issues and competence for them in research and practice. Psychologists with expertise in teaching and learning have the ability to apply this knowledge to the convergence on increasing demand for and increased use of technology in education. For psychologists with careers involving applied work, proficiency in multiple languages will likely continue to be a substantial asset. Most of the growth areas focus on issues that are by their nature interdisciplinary. For example, a movement in recent years known as positive psychology has investigated how individuals and groups flourish and lead fulfilling existences. Although psychologists have been heavily involved in this new way of thinking about behavior and mental processes, other disciplines have contributed substantially. Psychologists engaged in this and similar endeavors are capitalizing on the growing trend to share knowledge and expertise across disciplines in order to answer research questions and solve applied problems. The subfields of psychology that succeed as cultivating and capitalizing on these and other interdisciplinary collaborations stand the best chance of sustaining growth.

Psychology's opportunities have several implications for your training as well as your career outlook. At the bachelor's level, you should seek to be as informed as possible about emerging and growing areas in the field. Take coursework and secure research opportunities in these areas when they are available. This will provide excellent experience and assist you in deciding if these subfields fit your interests. At the graduate level, be aware of what career fields are poised for the greatest growth and consider how changes in funding might affect the availability and viability of graduate programs in these areas.

Conclusion

Psychology remains a fascinating and vibrant field of study that offers a diverse array of career options and experiences. Learning about the process of obtaining an education in the field and pursuing career goals can at times be daunting. At points you may feel that keeping up with your current academic responsibilities allows little time for implementing new study skills, assessing your career goals, or preparing for employment or graduate school. It is our intention that the information contained in this book be empowering and inspiring rather than overwhelming or intimidating. Knowledge about both the opportunities and challenges is essential. In particular, understanding the array of career options available to you and the various steps required to obtain these careers is vital. We hope that by formulating your career goals, and making educational and occupational decisions that will support these goals, you will place yourself on the surest path to success.

References

American Psychological Association. (2011). *2009 doctorate employment survey.* Washington, DC: Author. Retrieved from http://www.apa.org/workforce/publications/09-doc-empl/index.aspx

Cacioppo, J. T. (2013). Psychological science in the 21st century. *Teaching of Psychology, 40,* 304–309. doi:10.1177/0098628313501041

Maton, K. I., Kohout, J. L., Wicherski, M., Leary, G. E., & Vinokurov, A. (2006). Minority students of color and the psychology graduate pipeline: Disquieting and encouraging trends, 1989–2003. *American Psychologist, 61,* 117–131. doi:10.1037/0003-066X.61.2.117

Silver, H. J., Sharpe, A. L., Kelly, H., Kobor, P., & Sroufe, G. (2008). Behavioral and social science research in the administration's FY 2009 budget. In Intersociety Working Group, *AAAS report XXXIII: Research and development FY 2009* (pp. 195–202). Washington, DC: American Association for the Advancement of Science.

US Department of Education, National Center for Education Statistics. (2013a). *Table 318.30: Bachelor's, master's, and doctor's degrees conferred by postsecondary institutions, by sex of student and discipline division: 2011-12.* Retrieved from https://nces.ed.gov/programs/digest/d13/tables/dt13_318.30.asp

US Department of Education, National Center for Education Statistics. (2013b). _Table 322.10: Bachelor's degrees conferred by postsecondary institutions, by field of study: Selected years, 1970-71 through 2011-12_. Retrieved from https://nces.ed.gov/programs/digest/d13/tables/dt13_322.10.asp

US Department of Education, National Center for Education Statistics. (2013c). _Table 322.30: Bachelor's degrees conferred by postsecondary institutions, by race/ethnicity and field of study: 2010-11 and 2011-12_. Retrieved from https://nces.ed.gov/programs/digest/d13/tables/dt13_322.30.asp

US Department of Education, National Center for Education Statistics. (2013d). _Table 323.10: Master's degrees conferred by postsecondary institutions, by field of study: Selected years, 1970-71 through 2011-12_. Retrieved from https://nces.ed.gov/programs/digest/d13/tables/dt13_323.10.asp

US Department of Education, National Center for Education Statistics. (2013e). _Table 323.30: Master's degrees conferred by postsecondary institutions, by race/ethnicity and field of study: 2010-11 and 2011-12_. Retrieved from https://nces.ed.gov/programs/digest/d13/tables/dt13_323.30.asp

US Department of Education, National Center for Education Statistics. (2013f). _Table 324.10: Doctor's degrees conferred by postsecondary institutions, by field of study: Selected years, 1970-71 through 2011-12_. Retrieved from https://nces.ed.gov/programs/digest/d13/tables/dt13_324.10.asp

US Department of Education, National Center for Education Statistics. (2013g). _Table 324.25: Doctor's degrees conferred by postsecondary institutions, by race/ethnicity and field of study: 2010-11 and 2011-12_. Retrieved from https://nces.ed.gov/programs/digest/d13/tables/dt13_324.25.asp

US Bureau of Labor Statistics. (2013). _Employment projections: 2012-22_. Washington, DC: Author. Retrieved from http://www.bls.gov/emp/#data

Index

Note: Page numbers in *italic* refer to illustrations, those in **bold** to tables.
The letter b after a page number indicates a display box.

Majoring in Psychology: Achieving Your Educational and Career Goals, Second Edition.
Jeffrey L. Helms and Daniel T. Rogers.
© 2015 John Wiley & Sons, Ltd. Published 2015 by John Wiley & Sons, Ltd.